Handbook of Online Learning

Handbook of Online Learning

Innovations in Higher Education and Corporate Training

Editors

Kjell Erik Rudestam
The Fielding Graduate Institute

Judith Schoenholtz-Read
The Fielding Graduate Institute

Sage Publications
International Educational and Professional Publisher
Thousand Oaks ▪ London ▪ New Delhi

For information:

Sage Publications, Inc.
2455 Teller Road
Thousand Oaks, California 91320
E-mail: order@sagepub.com

Sage Publications Ltd.
6 Bonhill Street
London EC2A 4PU
United Kingdom

Sage Publications India Pvt. Ltd.
M-32 Market
Greater Kailash I
New Delhi 110 048 India

Printed in the United States of America

Library of Congress Cataloging-in-Publication Data

Rudestam, Kjell Erik.
    Handbook of online learning: Innovations in higher education and corporate training / Kjell Erik Rudestam, Judith Schoenholtz-Read.
        p. cm.
    Includes bibliographical references and index.
    ISBN 0-7619-2402-7 (c) — ISBN 0-7619-2403-5 (p)
    1. Education, Higher—Computer-assisted instruction—Handbooks, manuals, etc. 2. Internet in education—Handbooks, manuals, etc. 3. Employees—Training of—Computer-assisted instruction—Handbooks, manuals, etc. I. Schoenholtz-Read, Judith. II. Title.
LB2395.7 .R83 2002
378.1'734—dc21
                                        2001005395

05 06 07 7 6 5 4

Acquisitions Editor:	Jim Brace-Thompson
Editorial Assistant:	Karen Ehrmann
Production Editor:	Diane S. Foster
Copy Editor:	D. J. Peck
Typesetter/Designer:	Tina Hill
Proofreader:	Scott Oney
Indexer:	Molly Hall
Cover Designer:	Jane Quaney

Contents

Part II: IMPLEMENTING ONLINE LEARNING

C. Courses   353

Preface

For more than 30 years, we have devoted much of our professional lives to the education and training of graduate students and professionals. More than half of this time has been spent at the Fielding Graduate Institute, where we have been privileged to work alongside faculty and students who emphasize the interpersonal context of learning as much as the quality of educational outcomes. When Fielding first began to incorporate computer-mediated communication technology into the teaching and learning process, many students, faculty, and administrators were apprehensive that we would lose what we treasured most: the learning community itself. We have come to believe that this is not an idle threat, indeed, that it takes care and creativity to draw on and deploy technology in the form of online classrooms while maintaining scholarly rigor and interpersonal sensitivity.

We began our own faculty adventures in virtual space fairly blind to the possibilities and risks, supported only by significant experience in reaching out to a student body of geographically dispersed adult students and committed to fostering academic and personal growth and maintaining a vibrant scholarly community. The networked world can appear like an uncharted wilderness, and we have found—sometimes the hard way—that appropriate navigational tools are required to traverse it successfully. This handbook is derived from our experiences over the past several years of experimentation and concerted effort to be at the forefront of applying technological innovation to teaching students at a distance while maintaining the human component in our educational transactions. We hope that our readers may benefit from these experiences.

A primary purpose of this handbook is to explore the conceptual and pedagogical issues concerned with teaching over electronic networks. Second, we intend the book to serve as an immensely practical guide for educators and trainers who have the responsibility or opportunity to venture online to teach university students or corporate employees.

We are deeply appreciative of the authors of the chapters in this handbook. They practice what they preach. They are as creative and compassionate online as they are in person in their interactions with students and colleagues. Much of what we know, we have learned from them. We have learned even more from our students. They are the hidden assets that form the foundation of the book. We consider ourselves fortunate to have had the opportunity to spend time with them in the virtual classroom environment.

At a more personal level, we acknowledge our love and appreciation to our life partners, Janice Rudestam and David Read, who have sustained and tolerated us through the lengthy ordeal of putting this handbook together. Further appreciation goes to our friends and colleagues at Fielding, who continue to inform and inspire us, with special thanks going to Vicki Stevenson, who expertly formatted and edited several drafts of many of these chapters.

Finally, we are grateful to the professional and humane staff at Sage Publications, including our acquisitions editor, James Brace-Thompson; his assistant, Karen Ehrmann; our production editor, Diane Foster, and the rest of the Sage team.

Part **1**

CHANGING PHILOSOPHIES AND THEORIES OF LEARNING

Chapter 1

Overview

The Coming of Age of Adult Online Education

Kjell Erik Rudestam and Judith Schoenholtz-Read

From stepchild to wunderkind, technology that spawned the Internet has moved distance learning to the forefront of educational innovation in the 21st century. Sensing an opportunity to reach more students and supplement flagging tuition revenues, major educational institutions have proceeded to expand their mission to include activities in online education. In so doing, Robert Kegan's words take on special relevance: "It is one thing to let new people into an ongoing party; the newcomer is the one who must struggle to fit in. It is another thing to change the party; now it is the educator and the institution that must struggle to fit in" (Kegan, 1994, p. 273). Or, as Diane Halpern, winner of an award for Distinguished Career Contributions to Education and Training in Psychology, notes, "Changing the university is like changing a cemetery. You don't get help from the inhabitants" (Halpern, 1998). Nonetheless, with or without the sanction and blessing of faculty and students, technology-mediated instruction has taken the university and the corporate sector by storm.

The Internet and related technologies have demolished traditional institutional boundaries to expertise and knowledge. Access to knowledge of all kinds is now available to everyone. As Drucker (1999) notes, much like knowledge revolutions of the past—the discovery of paper and the printing press come to mind—the Internet gives everyone who seeks information access to resources once held within the ivory tower. Students can talk with experts from elite institutions by accessing their Web sites. Students can enter libraries, dialogue with professors worldwide, and enter chat rooms with knowledgeable individuals on almost any topic. These challenges to traditional systems of learning have given us the opportunity to rethink how knowledge is acquired and how to design online educational processes for the adult learner.

The primary purpose of this handbook is to clarify the conceptual issues that underlie effective online teaching and to offer practical guidance to educators and trainers who plan to teach in a virtual environment (VE). The chapters in the book were written by relative pioneers in the virtual classroom who share their experiences and suggestions for working effectively in this medium. If there is one central tenet to this handbook, it is this: The adoption of computer networks as the teaching vehicle of the future in higher education and corporate training demands a reexamination of our core beliefs about pedagogy and how students learn. The transfer of a classroom curriculum into cyberspace is deceptively simple, but doing so without an appreciation for the nuances and implications of learning online ignores not only the potential of this medium but also the inevitable realities of entering it. Before we tackle a discussion of the pedagogy itself, however, we need to provide a context for this educational revolution.

A Brief History of Computer-Assisted Instruction

The history of computer-assisted instruction, first attempted using time-sharing computers during the 1960s, is clearly described by Harasim and her colleagues (Harasim, Hiltz, Teles, & Turoff, 1995). Communication took place over dumb terminals connected to mainframe computers or dial-up telephone lines. In 1969, the U.S. government experimented with dedicated telephone lines for data exchange by constructing the ARPANET (Advanced Research Projects Agency Network) to connect researchers with remote computer centers to share resources. It was not long before these researchers wanted to exchange messages with one another about their projects. The electronic mail (e-mail) function was born and became immensely popular. Other communication networks (e.g., USENET, BITNET, CSNET) followed, still predominantly connecting researchers and scientists. Eventually, the Internet, a global network of networks, supplanted these individual efforts.

Murray Turoff is given credit for designing the first computer conferencing system in 1970 (Hiltz & Turoff, 1993). Today there are many conferencing systems available that support not only the discussion feature but also other more sophisticated features including personal messaging and audio and video capability. Bulletin boards, a common space for posting messages over the computer, were developed during the late 1970s (Sterling, 1992) but did not proliferate until a decade later. Both of these functions are at the heart of the implementation of computer networks for training and education. Computer conferencing systems were applied to course activity in higher education during the 1980s and remain a prominent feature of online education today. All of these variants have found their way into higher education in the public and private sectors.

Distance Education

Some educational institutions have conceived their mandate as training students who are geographically dispersed from one another and from the institutions themselves. They represent what has historically been known as "distance education." According to the U.S. Congress for Technology Assessment, distance education refers to "linking of a teacher and students in several geographic locations via technology that allows for interaction" (Daniel & Stevens, 1998, p. 162). However, many distance learning institutions that have come to adopt a strong online presence were functioning prior to the Internet by relying on individually directed study, mail, the telephone, and/or infrequent residential sessions for contact between students and instructors. One example is the United Kingdom's Open University, which initiated use of computer conferencing as a small adjunct to a large multimedia course (Harasim et al., 1995). Course tutors held discussion groups in closed conferences with relatively small numbers of students. Interestingly, the computer conferencing forum that was open to all students and tutors purely for socializing purposes generated the most traffic and became the most productive workspace. This unanticipated outcome, as we shall see, has significant implications for practitioners of online education. Another example, with which we are more personally acquainted and which serves as the source of much of our experience with online teaching, is the Fielding Graduate Institute based in Santa Barbara, California. Fielding, as is true for a few other academic institutions such as the Union Graduate School, Empire State College, and the University Without Walls, established a distance education model many years ago to provide an educational opportunity for a group of geographically dispersed, adult, mid-career professionals who could not easily give up their family and work responsibilities to move to a campus-based institution for a lengthy period of time. Today, Fielding offers graduate degree programs in clinical psychology, human and organizational behavior, educational leadership, organizational management, and organization development. Each program has its own unique blend of online and face-to-face seminars and tutorial experiences. In many cases, students have the option (or requirement) of taking courses as asynchronous online seminars. Several of the chapters in this handbook illustrate the ways in which these online courses are structured and taught.

It is important to clarify that there is a difference between distance education and computer-networked education. Adherence to a distributed model of training does not necessarily imply the adoption of an online teaching environment. Distance education flourished long before the advent of the personal computer (Maehl, 2000). Because the term distance education has traditionally implied delivery of instruction or course materials over a distance, educators who support a model of education that emphasizes student-initiated access to learning resources have recommended the use of the term distributed learning or flexible learning rather than distance learning to refer to new forms of online learning (Carr-Chellman & Duchastel, 2000). They liken it to what is called just-in-time learning in corporate America. Distance education institutions have not necessarily embraced online learning, but when they have done so the transition to a communication-based technology has often gone more smoothly because of the overlap of values and skills required to succeed in the virtual setting.

The Adult Learner

Educational institutions are reaching out as never before to adult learners. Most current online students are adult professionals looking for additional training (Green, 2000). In fact, the growth in adults entering school is staggering. From 1991 to 1999, attendance increased dramatically. According to a 1999 survey by the National Center for Education Statistics, just over 50% of 45- to 54-year-olds, 37% of 55- to 65-year-olds, and 20% of adults age 65 years or over are taking classes ("Distance Learning," 2000). Continuing education is the fastest growth area within the educational marketplace. The term lifelong learning has become a catchphrase to indicate the need, and wish, for ongoing personal growth and academic learning. The surge in continuing education throughout the life span is a function not only of increasing longevity and vitality but also of the explosion of knowledge and the accelerating need for new and increased professional skills during times of rapid and turbulent change. This suggests, of course, that formal education is no longer solely the province of the young, a means of prolonging adolescence until the responsibilities of adulthood take command. Higher education is increasingly adult-centered and, to be successful, must incorporate an understanding of adult development.

Work by Brookfield (1986) and Merriam and Caffarella (1999) suggests that learning is affected by stages of human development. Adult participation in learning is usually voluntary and is often stimulated by life transitions and changes where education can offer a resolution. Moreover, adults have complex lives with multiple demands on their time and energy; they appreciate flexibility and individualization in their learning experiences. According to Maehl (2000), these characteristics of adult learners invite the following recommendations for those charged with establishing formal educational programs for adults:

1. Incorporate problem-centered learning and directly address the life experiences of adult learners.

2. Provide an opportunity for adults to play a role in the design, direction, and implementation of the learning experience.

3. Offer flexibility in time, place, mode, and pacing to accommodate changing circumstances.

4. Recognize that the relationship between learner and teacher must be filled with mutual respect, emphasizing cooperation rather than control.

5. Provide a positive learning environment including regular and constructive feedback.

In our experience, teaching adults involves a respect for their situations in life. Most adults have multiple commitments—to family, work, and friends. This means that the opportunity to complete courses and training over the Internet can be a godsend, enabling them to retain those commitments and work around the built-in flexibility of the electronic environment. Second, the traditional model of the expert authoritative (if not authoritarian) professor and the passive naive student does not apply well to the average adult student, who may be academically uninformed but worldly wise and who brings a mature perspective into the (virtual) classroom informed by work experiences, family experiences, and life experiences. Adult students seek to be collaborative partners in the learning process and seem to thrive in academic settings that offer a facilitative and supportive milieu. To quote Nobel Prize winner Rabindrath Tagore about his music teacher: "He determined to teach me music, and consequently no learning took place" (cited in Brown & Duguid, 2000, p. 136). The qualities of education that seem to accommodate the developmental needs of adult students may be well captured by the online learning environment.

Market Issues and Demographics

Hanna & Associates (2000) cite consumer demand as the key factor that will create new forms of distance learning during the digital age. The demand comes from the need for lifelong learning and the need to continue professional and work-related training. Drucker (1999) highlights the need for knowledge workers of the future to have the ability to update their skills quickly and to take responsibility for their learning needs. In part due to changing demographics, specifically globalization and the aging and increasing professionalization of the population, adult students with diverse learning styles are returning to school in droves, driven by their own developmental interests and by the needs of their employers. The pressure to respond to these needs for just-in-time learning is a powerful force for change. Some institutions will be more capable of responding than will others, and new approaches to learning will continue to emerge to fill the vacuum.

The Institute for Higher Education Policy (2000) reports that distance education programs increased 72% from 1994-1995 to 1997-1998 and will expand by another 20% within 3 years. Distance courses have an enrollment of 1.6 million students. Online education is the most rapidly expanding segment of the distance learning market, valued at $2.6 billion or 1% of the higher education market in 2000 (Traub, 2000). The pace is accelerating. The virtual education market is predicted to be $10 billion by 2003, and the corporate learning market is predicted to be about $11 billion by the same time (Svetcov, 2000). Online courses enrolled about 700,000 students in 2000, and this number is expected to triple by 2002 (Green, 2000). At present, three quarters of 2- and 4-year colleges have online courses. This number is expected to reach 90% by 2004.

The potential of this vast educational market has attracted elite universities as well as community colleges, generated new online universities and learning companies, and stimulated corporate partnerships. "Corporate universities" are blossoming and are expected to increase in number from 480 to 1,600 over a few years. Most offer technical training, and some may begin to offer undergraduate degrees (Traub, 2000). As well, the armed forces are entering the online education marketplace. In a pilot effort, the U.S. Army has formed a partnership with Pricewaterhouse Cooper to operate a 5-year contract worth $435 million to develop the Army University Access Online Program. Pricewaterhouse will collaborate with a group of 29 higher education institutions—including historically Black colleges, community colleges, and e-learning companies—to develop a program that is expected to serve 12,000 students in the first year and eventually expand to enroll 80,000 students (Roach, 2001).

Higher Education and Online Technology

Not every educator is on the Internet bandwagon. Resistance to online teaching has been attributed to psychological variables such as faculty lack of confidence, feelings of loss, and lack of awareness and training in new approaches (Panitz & Panitz, 1998). Others fear for the demise of the university as we know it. Talbott (1998) cites the apprehension of faculty who are currently at the center of traditional teaching and learning models and anticipate losing status and power. Noble (1999) argues that higher education is being commercialized and that teaching is becoming a commodity that steals the faculty's control, knowledge, skill, and livelihood.

In addition to fears about the impact of online teaching on the educational enterprise itself are the paradoxical responses of consumers—both faculty and students—to the use of new technology in their lives (Mick & Fournier, 1998). Successful operation of new technology can lead to a greater sense of intelligence and efficacy, but failure can evoke feelings of stupidity and ineptitude. In addition to concerns about competency, there are built-in paradoxes to the technology itself. What seems radically new and innovative one day becomes old and obsolete the next day. What provides remarkable savings in efficiency and cost-effective service can inefficiently consume huge amounts of time and attention. What is experienced as fulfilling can easily become a craving for more and better technology. What has the potential for assimilating and joining people together on any number of topics and experiences can easily lead to a feeling of loneliness and isolation.

The available data suggest that, in spite of both substantive and specious concerns about the pervasive ongoing role of computers in our lives, the Internet is well infused in higher education at the present time and portends to continue to flow into all crevices of the educational fabric. Nearly every institution of higher learning has incorporated or intends to incorporate some aspects of online technology into its curriculum delivery system. The way in which online technology becomes operationalized, however, differs significantly among institutions. At this time, there appear to be three levels of application of computer conferencing technology in education: (a) as the primary teaching mechanism for one or more courses, (b) as an enhancement to traditional face-to-face courses, and (c) as a forum for discussions and information exchange with peers and experts and a means of accessing online resources (Harasim, 1998). Each of these options can be seen in traditional educational institutions and more recent entrants into the field of higher education that rely either exclusively or significantly on offering courses online. Most universities and training institutions use computer networks as an adjunct to more traditional classroom experiences. Some assignments or the occasional course might be offered online to take advantage of the medium's flexibility regarding time and place. In other schools, the online environment is fully integrated into the curriculum and plays a major role in the delivery of education.

The Players: Current Online Learning Environments

Online learning takes place within a variety of educational learning environments, from the traditional distance learning universities to e-learning for profit. What follows is our categorization of the dominant players in the online teaching profession today.

Nonprofit traditional distance learning universities. Traditional distance learning schools have ventured into the online environment and brought with them the values and educational philosophies of their traditional distance environments. Some have attempted to replicate their models in other countries. The United Kingdom's Open University has entered the U.S. market with an M.B.A. program for students without B.A. degrees (www.open.ac.uk). Athabasca University began as a correspondence program in Canada in 1972 and now offers several online graduate degree programs (www.athabasca.ca).

Other efforts represent the expansion of distance learning institutions directly into the online market. For example, the previously mentioned Fielding Graduate Institute, which began in 1974, offers programs that combine face-to-face and distance modalities as well as programs that are entirely online. The school is accredited by the Western Association of Universities and Colleges, and its doctoral program in clinical psychology is the only dispersed program to be accredited by the Committee on Accreditation of the American Psychological Association (www.fielding.edu).

Traditional university and e-learning partnerships. Traditional university and e-learning partnerships are rapidly expanding and include Stanford University's online master's program in electrical engineering and Duke University's online M.B.A. program. Other elite universities, including Columbia and Northwestern, have developed for-profit companies by partnering with online learning companies to offer courses on the Web. For example, UNext.com is working with Stanford, Columbia, and the University of Chicago to develop online courses (Green, 2000). UNext's Cardean University describes itself as a "learning community that serves individual students and Fortune 500 companies around the world" (www.unext.com). UNext is part of Knowledge Universe, a conglomeration of more than 40 e-learning companies and the brainchild of Michael Milken (Svetcov, 2000). With a plan to offer education to large corporations, one of its first alliances is with General Motors and intends to provide business and M.B.A. courses online to 88,000 employees. Other examples of e-business and university collaborations include the University of Colorado, which has formed a partnership with RealEducation to establish an Internet-based asynchronous study system (Beller & Or, 1998).

Organizations representing e-learning for profit. The Global Education Network (GEN) is a private for-profit company that plans to sell courses over the Internet. This venture has committed $20 million to attract notable university professors to develop CD-ROM materials for classes of about 30 students and one teaching assistant (Traub, 2000). The founders of GEN are eager to open academia to the "masses" by bringing known experts to anyone who wants access (p. 91). This approach raises significant ethical concerns regarding the ownership of intellectual property (Duderstadt, 1999), exemplified by legal action against a Harvard University law professor for his intention to sell his videotaped university lectures to GEN for online redistribution to other students (Traub, 2000).

New for-profit universities. The University of Phoenix is the largest and most financially successful new university that has both campus-based and online programs. University of Phoenix Online offers B.A. and M.A. programs as well as corporate certificate programs. It uses Microsoft Outlook Express to provide electronic classes that typically last between 5 and 6 weeks (www.uophx.com).

Jones International, founded in 1995, is an exclusively online university with students located in 57 countries. The school is accredited by the North Central Association of Colleges and Schools and offers undergraduate and graduate degrees. Other for-profit schools that offer graduate degrees online include Strayer University Online, De Vry's Keller School of Management, Capella University, Argosy University, and Walden University.

For-profit e-learning organizations. Beginning in 1998, Kaplan, in conjunction with the *Washington Post,* has developed online schools that are accredited by the North Central Association of Colleges and Schools. They include the Concord Law School, Kaplan College of Information Technology, and Kaplan College School of Business. The programs use video lecture, chat, and asynchronous formats. Another large for-profit company, Sylvan Learning Systems, has acquired part ownership of two South American universities and, in a separate venture, invested in ilearning.com to develop a platform for professional training career courses. Kaplan and Sylvan are examples of the expansion of commercial learning companies into the distance and online markets (Phillips, 2001).

Corporate online universities. Many major corporations have developed corporate universities with online components. The Corporate University Xchange (www.corpu.com) provides information for corporate university organizers that includes a newsletter, e-news, and an annual conference. Examples of corporate universities include Motorola University, Daimler Chrysler University Online, McDonald's Hamburger University, EMC University, General Motors University, NCR University, Shell Open University, and Vanguard University.

Nonprofit online learning efforts. An interesting and well-developed effort to enter the online learning environment is the Sloane Foundation's Asynchronous Learning Network (ALN), which has promoted asynchronous (anytime and anywhere) learning since 1994, holds an annual conference, and has a Web site (www.aln.org) containing various educational resources. Another nonprofit online learning venture is geteducated.com, which offers a catalog of courses for training teachers in online methods, provides lists of online degree programs, and offers the Virtual University Business Digest (www.geteducated.com).

Along with the enormous growth of online ventures, we have already witnessed the demise of some online learning schools in this competitive atmosphere, a trend that will no doubt continue. The California Virtual University never got off the ground in its effort to develop a consortium of online courses that could be accessed by students who live in California. Dow Jones University closed a virtual campus that had offered low-cost continuing education courses taught by high-profile business leaders. The courses suffered from low attendance and poor use of the chat rooms. Costs ran higher than expected, and the founders concluded that consumers are less interested in taking courses that do not lead to a degree (Phillips, 2001).

For many new players, the goal of collaboration between private enterprise and the university in the online market is profit sharing. However, the costs of marketing these programs, as well as the demands on faculty time for preparation and teaching, have been greatly underestimated.

Research on Online Education

This chapter cannot do justice to the increasing volume of studies that are intended to assess empirically the outcomes and processes of online teaching. Well-designed outcome research on online coursework is still sparse. Much of the research has used anecdotal reports, surveys, interviews, and self-report instruments with relatively small samples. The research that has been done has generally supported the finding that there are few differences in satisfaction and in quality of the learning experience, as measured by exam scores and student feedback, when Web-based courses are compared to traditional university classes (e.g., Hiltz, 1994; Hiltz & Turoff, 1993; Maki, Maki, Patterson, & Whittaker, 2000; Rudestam, Giannetti, & Stamm, in press; Smith, 2000; Tolmie & Boyle, 2000). Online courses are generally popular with students (e.g., Fleetwood et al., 2000; Schultz, 1998), and even in cases where students express a preference for the presence of a face-to-face instructor, objective testing reveals at least comparable learning outcomes in the virtual environment (VE) (Johnson, Aragon, Shaik, & Palma-Rivas, 2000).

Even though the available research supports the expansion of computer-mediated learning (CML), public concerns about online education have been expressed by many, including Nick Smith, a Republican representative from Michigan, who opined that students who take courses online rather than traditional courses interact less with other students and do not learn to think for themselves (Carnevale, 2000b). This criticism fails to appreciate the potential of online learning and related developments in pedagogy. Two frequently voiced concerns do not seem to be supported by the literature. One concern is that students do not develop critical thinking skills but rather learn only rote facts. However, meta-skills such as higher order thinking and taking the perspective of others seem to be well suited to the interactive online environ-ment (Lapadat, 2000). Students learn how to communicate in writing, how to give and receive feedback sensitively and effectively, and how to manage time and collaborate effectively.

The second concern is about the relative lack of interpersonal contact in the VE. However, this will depend on how the online course is structured. As Hiltz and Wellman (1997) put it,

> Despite earlier fears to the contrary by those who worry about the possible dehumanizing effects of computers, online communities provide emotional support and sociability as well as information and instrumental aid related to shared tasks. Online virtual classrooms combine characteristics of online communities and computer-supported workgroups. New software tools and systems for coordinating interaction may alleviate some of the problems of interacting online, like information overload and normless behavior. (p. 45)

The quality of interaction has been a major focus of research on success in the online learning environment. For example, Gundawardena, Lowe, and Carabajal (2000) examined process variables such as proficiency in computer skills, learner support, and social presence to identify the factors that predict graduate student satisfaction within a computer-mediated environment. Of eight process variables, the most significant predictors of satisfaction were computer competency and social presence (the degree to which a person is perceived as real by others).

Other efforts to study online interaction and learning outcomes have used qualitative methodologies. Through text analysis of course interactions (not available for studying the traditional classroom), the quality of the learn-ing experience can be assessed. Powers and Mitchell (1997) analyzed the con-tent of a graduate course on new technology and found that even though the course met for only a brief time, a community of learners emerged; stu-dents gave each other considerable support, the faculty role seemed less prominent, and students found the course to be time-consuming. In an ethnographic study that included text analysis, focus groups, and phone interviews of an online conference, Cox (1999) notes that students identified the "importance of pace and flow in online discourse as well as a sense of immersive presence. Sustained online discourse was found to be crucial in observing participatory thought and creating a supportive structure for col-laborative learning" (p. 1).

Ragan's (1998) studies of distance learning faculty from three universi-ties found that frequent and meaningful interaction between the learner and the instructor, the course materials, and other students was particularly important. The role of the teacher as moderator has been identified by Hiltz (1994) and Beaudin (1999) as critical to quality interaction and learning, whereas social bonds and peer support have been established as other inter-personal predictors of success in the online environment (Carnevale, 2000a).

At the same time, attrition seems to be the one area where students are more vulnerable in online courses, although this may be more of a reflection of the phenomenon of distance education, or even of graduate study in general (Lovitts, 2001), than of online learning per se. Hiltz (1994) found that dropouts and students who took incompletes were higher in asynchronous courses than in traditional classes even though grade distributions were not different. Tinto's (1975) research on retention in traditional education helps to guide us. Tinto discovered that the social integration of students is a key factor in retention. His findings stress the need to study the quality of inter-action and the ability of the community to build human connections. A collaborative study of adult distance learners (Dixon, 2001; Schoenholtz-Read, 2000) also points to the importance of social connections, specifically the students' connections with the faculty, as a factor in retention. The faculty's timely feedback is vital to the students' sense of self and can either help students to maintain their academic self-worth or diminish their confidence, making them vulnerable to withdrawing from courses and the program.

As universities and training institutions scramble to keep up with the onslaught of Internet-based distance education, there are scant data available to offer guidance to what works and what does not work. A recent report produced by the Institute for Higher Education Policy (2000), funded by the National Education Association, offers benchmarks for success. The following ingredients are distilled from those that were determined to be essential for quality education over the Internet:

- A reliable, optimally fail-safe technology delivery system with a well-supported and -maintained centralized infrastructure

- Clear guidelines and faculty-student agreement regarding times for completion of assignments and faculty response including timely constructive feedback to students

- The development, design, and delivery of courses based on clear guidelines regarding minimal standards, with the selection of technology used to deliver the course content determined by desired learning outcomes

- Courses designed to require students to demonstrate the skills of analysis, synthesis, and evaluation as well as the methods of effective research

- Facilitated interaction among students and between students and faculty

- Students prepared to participate on the basis of self-motivation, commitment, and access to the technology requirements

- Student access to electronic libraries on the Internet and training to obtain the necessary information
- Student and faculty access to adequate technical assistance and training prior to and during the courses

Online Teaching and Changes in Pedagogy

This brings us to a key proposition. We argue that optimal use of the electronic environment for teaching classes necessitates a shift in pedagogy and, moreover, that the use of the Internet as a medium for teaching and learning elicits epistemological changes in the individual that are worthy of consideration.

Electronic teaching developed from advances in communication technology, not from innovative changes in pedagogy. This fact has profound implications for identifying a suitable place for technology in training and education. Generally speaking, educational institutions that introduce computer-mediated communication (CMC) technology into their training programs do so within the context of their dominant pedagogical principles and historical attitudes toward education. When that pedagogy relies on the authoritative expertise of the instructor, who disseminates knowledge and information to relatively passive students using lectures supported by audio-visual aids, that same pedagogy is transposed to the electronic environment. In that context, instructional materials are presented to the students online in the form of lecturettes (either in real time or in archived video form), which the students download and provide evidence of absorbing through the completion of exams or written assignments. These measures of competence might take the form of responding to a set of exam questions on a Web site or writing a term paper and submitting it to the professor by e-mail. The professor evaluates the material and perhaps provides some feedback, and the student receives a grade in the course. Thus, reliance on a prevailing educational paradigm in the guise of computer-mediated coursework means that face-to-face instructional practices (and distance learning by correspondence) are now being replicated in a new medium. However, this might not be the best and most effective use of the online environment.

We would argue that taking full advantage of the opportunities of communication technology implies significant shifts in thinking about educational pedagogy. Schrage (1990) suggests that we need to shift our thinking from viewing technology as a means of managing information to regarding technology as a medium of relationships. As Schrage puts it, "Technology is really a medium for creating productive environments" (p. 67). Technologies can be effective if they are designed to empower students' engagement with the learning process and collaboration. Turkle (1995), among the most visionary thinkers regarding the impact of technology on the psyche, notes that a single person working alone on the computer can work through identity issues regarding control and mastery; once the computer is used as a communication medium, the control offered by the computer can be transformed into generating collaboration and intimacy.

Good education is "demand driven." It meets the individual needs of learners and is what in networking terminology is called "pull" technology rather than "push" technology. With push technology, there is often information overload because senders are responsible for sending messages; with pull technology, the recipient requests what he or she wants to receive. With a pull type of communication, it is like going from "drinking from a fire hose . . . to directing a fine water fountain stream" (Doucette, 1998, p. 26). The implication is that technology allows educational content to be highly individualized and "just in time," in the sense of being available when needed and at the appropriate level of difficulty (Romiszowski, 1998). By contrast, with traditional models of higher education and corporate training, resource materials frequently become outdated and might not be relevant to individual work environments and student needs. Unfortunately, only a very small number of companies fully integrate their organizational learning efforts with training and development programs (Paul, 1999). Similarly, many traditional schools have entered the online market by posting lecture materials on the Web.

Gergen (1995) eloquently describes how recent communication technologies, ranging from the personal computer to communication networks, expose us to a huge variety of opinions, values, personalities, and conventions from an ever-increasing number of people from diverse backgrounds and affiliations. A by-product of this technology revolution is the constructivist challenge to the authority of a particular grounded, rationally justified matrix of knowledge. Educators have written persuasively about the "drift toward a social conception of knowledge" (p. 3). This shift challenges the traditional view that education serves to transform the individual's mental world by emphasizing the notion of knowledge as the private possession of the person. Meaning shifts from the locus of the individual mind to communal participation. Thus, our knowledge of the world and the self occurs within the context of relationships, where meaning is defined through languaging (Wittgenstein, 1953) and is determined through the active engagement of two or more persons who share a culturally located context. Lectures and books, the traditional accoutrements of higher education, no longer carry prescriptive meaning; they just open up possible alternative interpretations that students differentially select.

The constructivist view conforms well to developmental possibilities provided by CMC in graduate education and training. Cyberspace becomes a medium in which the self is readily constructed in diverse ways and in which students readily form different opinions and interpretations regarding the same reading material and commentaries. This perspective stands at odds with the traditional model of education, dubbed by Freire (1985) the "nutritionist" model (and by Dabbagh, 2000, as the "instructivist" approach), which arranges its participants hierarchically dependent on their status as authors of knowledge. The hierarchy starts with the authority of the knowledge creators in a field (esteemed scientists and scholars who hold the truth that students need to discover and assimilate), moves to those who design curricula for students to master, and ends with teachers who dispense the goodies to hungry students who are expected to consume them. According to Gergen (1995), the nutritionist perspective does not fit well with how knowledge is actually generated. Education, he suggests, must abandon the task of discovering universal authoritative knowledge and move to giving teachers more authority about what to teach. And education must proceed within a dialogic relationship between students and teachers.

The Future of Networked Learning

The challenges to traditional systems of learning have given us the opportunity to rethink how knowledge is acquired. Distance learning provides the framework to reconstruct state, national, and global learning systems. The technological revolution gives traditional institutions pause to reconsider old pedagogies. It gives new distributed learning systems vast opportunity and has spawned an entrepreneurial culture that threatens the collegial culture of traditional academia (Bergquist, 1992). However, these challenges to traditional learning systems present less of a threat to corporate programs, where the emphasis is on time and cost efficiencies rather than on maintaining established training methods (Eisinger, 2000).

Looking toward the future, it appears that networked learning needs to be part of a larger strategy to reconceptualize education and to build learning organizations and a knowledge society (Senge, 2000). In a very real sense, globalization in the research and education sector is threatening the structure and function of the university and is turning all learning institutions into universities without walls (Jerome et al., 2000). Some of the acknowledged functions of the university—creating, preserving, and transmitting knowledge—are being appropriated by the Internet. It remains to be seen how other primary functions of the university—including teaching students how to learn; providing professional, moral, and developmental socialization; and certifying professional skills and knowledge—will be managed online. What seems certain is that some amalgam between the traditional university and distance education will survive. In this regard, Burbules and Callister (2000) contend that on-campus, face-to-face learning is not the solution for all students and that consideration needs to be given to what method of teaching is best for what type of student under what circumstances. The types of integration may include the use of small networked groups operating from workstations, large groups attending to a video screen, and individual students working alone using electronic library resources. Certainly, there are many appropriate times to combine use of the Internet with classroom-based education. For example, lectures may still be advantageous to provide an understanding of foundational concepts. They can be transmitted via streaming video over an intranet system, allowing students to revisit difficult segments of the lecture at their convenience (Creighton & Buchanan, 2001).

The modality depends, to some extent, on the information to be learned. The dissemination of highly structured basic content might not require much discussion and may be suitable for a teacher-focused approach (Berge, 1997). Content that is heavily value laden may be more appropriate for peer discussion. It is up to educators to blend teaching modalities and methods in ways that match student needs and capacities to create optimal learning outcomes. We envision a future in which the distinctions between campus-based environments and distributed environments, between classroom-based education and Internet-based education, continue to erode and teaching methods are increasingly tailored to the particular subject matter, group of students, and learning objectives.

Implementing Online Teaching

This book provides the tools to operationalize the institutional, faculty, and student requirements to make the transition from a bricks-and-mortar educational or corporate environment to an online environment. In this regard, Roberts and Jones (2000) propose four models of online teaching: (a) the naive model, which relies on posting lecture notes on the World Wide Web with no opportunities for interaction; (b) the standard model, which draws on the Web's technology to encourage interaction among students and faculty about the course materials; (c) the evolutionary model, which allows the methods of course delivery to remain fluid throughout the term; and (d) the radical model, which dispenses with lectures and relies on interactive groups of students. Although we recognize the need for alternative pedagogies and a variety of teaching methods, the orientation of the chapter authors in this book is primarily in the "radical" camp. The emphasis of the chapters is on student-centered learning—making information, resources, and learning activities available rather than "delivering" instruction. These faculty tend not to lecture. Instead, they provide detailed study guides, along with attached and hypertext-linked resource materials, and make reading assignments from regular textbooks. They design and manage independent and collaborative learning activities that often have an applied dimension and that are related to the stated learning needs of the students. They foster and facilitate student-student dialogue and encourage the development of critical thinking skills.

There are issues to consider at each constituency level: the institution, the faculty, and the student. Institutional issues range from selecting the appropriate technology infrastructure to support online learning, to considering ethical implications of using the Internet (see the chapters by Shapiro and Hughes [Chapter 4] and Agger-Gupta [Chapter 5] in this volume), to coping with accreditation issues now that emerging online educational models cross regional accreditation boundaries. At the faculty level, one cannot assume that faculty who are skilled teachers in a live classroom are necessarily effective teachers in a virtual classroom. The chapter by Palloff and Pratt (Chapter 7) speaks to this issue and offers suggestions regarding faculty training needs for building confidence and success in the online environment. At the student level, the new pedagogy demands considerable maturity and responsibility from "classroom" participants. Successful participation involves time management skills, flexibility and tolerance, and a willingness to elicit and hear feedback from peers as well as professors.

Introduction to the Chapters in the Book

This handbook is organized into two parts and four main sections. The first half of the book addresses changing philosophies and theories of learning. The second half of the book has three sections that cover the practice of online learning. The first section opens with readings that deal with how to develop online teaching programs and learning environments within the university and higher education arena. Chapters in the next section consider the application of theory to practice within the corporate environment. The final section of the book consists of chapters that illustrate the development and implementation of specific courses within the online setting. All of the contributing authors draw on their own personal experiences in teaching adult students using CML in interactive virtual classrooms.

The first group of chapters in the book has a strong conceptual component. In "Presence in 'Teleland,'" Gary Fontaine introduces the VE as "Teleland" and discusses its unique ecology by drawing on both research and his own journey through this "strange land." Fontaine focuses on the importance of having a "sense of presence" in the online classroom and on how that sense of presence can be fostered to generate significant learning outcomes. He builds on our understanding of the phenomenology of space and helps us to think about ways in which to create and nurture virtual spaces to make them conducive to learning. Like other psychological spaces, virtual space, whether it be a learning space or a social space, becomes phenomenological space where we hold our personal map of human interactions. Fontaine recognizes the phenomenology of virtual space and gives hints about ways in which to create bounded spaces for learning. One aspect of classrooms in virtual space is that they come to represent the institution in the student's mind's eye. Schoenholtz-Read (2000) finds that institutional representations held by students at a distance can be powerful motivators of learning .

The next chapter, "Critical Dialogue Online: Personas, Covenants, and Candlepower" by Barclay Hudson, deepens the discussion of virtual space by highlighting the purposes of scholarly interaction and the creative potential that the virtual classroom provides teachers and students. Without visual interpersonal cues, miscommunication can abound. Hudson does a 180-degree turn and illustrates how heightened sensitivity to verbal communication can lead to imaginative methods to facilitate online learning. Hudson notes that criticism can easily convey particular harshness in CMC. Drawing on his own teaching experiences, he offers three specific types of interventions that serve to encourage critical dialogue while minimizing the negative impact of harsh criticism: (a) "personas" to authorize opinions and viewpoints that are otherwise unexpressed, (b) "covenants" in the form of explicit agreements regarding the range and methods of inquiry, and (c) "candle-power" or methods of enhancing the intensity, depth, and intimacy of online forums.

Conversation helps to form the virtual learning space. Using the story of an inflammatory e-mail and its disruptive impact on an academic community, Jeremy Shapiro and Shelley Hughes, in their chapter titled "The Case of the Inflammatory E-Mail: Building Culture and Community in Online Academic Environments," go on to discuss the complex task of building and managing an online learning community given the diverse motives, styles, and preferences of the participants and the realities of CMC. This chapter exposes the technocultural paradigms and social norms that undergird the virtual community and its classrooms. The authors suggest forms of "information literacy" that make learning communities safe environments that recognize the need for informed student, faculty, and administrative participation.

When the boundaries of the virtual classroom and the public nature of Web-based conversations are murky, ethical issues abound. We are in relatively uncharted territory when we consider how to understand the appropriate norms and rules of behavior in the virtual world. The final chapter in Part I, "Uncertain Frontiers: Exploring Ethical Dimensions of Online Learning," was written by Dorothy Agger-Gupta, who illustrates how difficult it is to discern the ethical nature of our actions in the VE. Which sets of rules should apply, especially when rules such as "do no harm" and "protect privacy" may conflict? The chapter describes a number of alternative ethical perspectives and illustrates them with ethical dilemmas bearing on issues such as power, invisibility, confidentiality, surveillance, personal identity, and ownership of intellectual property. We are reminded of the powerful footprints that are left in virtual spaces and of the risks embedded in communication that leaves tracks.

The second part of the book moves from theory to practice. In the first section, on university learning environments, multiple perspectives of program directors, students, teachers, and administrators are reflected. Program implementation, be it online or bricks-and-mortar, requires a vision and a road map. In the first chapter, "The Design and Delivery of Interactive Online Graduate Education," Judith Stevens-Long and Charles Crowell provide us with a vision and map by describing a model master's program in organizational management. Driven by an adult developmental philosophy of learning, the Web-based program includes a rich array of learning spaces—courses and forums or places for students to relate to students, for faculty to relate to one another, and for faculty and students to engage with each other. They point out that program designers are challenged to use Web-based architecture and processes that reflect the learning needs of their students. The authors guide the reader through the steps to develop and manage online programs. With a focus on quality interaction, they discuss software issues, discuss principles of group process and norms, and then guide the reader through a cycle of inquiry that facilitates students' Web-based learning and specifies qualities that lead to good teaching.

Faculty may be eager or fearful to teach in an online environment, and students may be eager or fearful to learn online. In the chapter "Beyond the Looking Glass: What Faculty and Students Need to Be Successful Online," Rena Palloff and Keith Pratt make it clear that not everyone is suited for online teaching or learning. Although personality factors may influence success, so does the need to understand that online teaching and learning require a new pedagogy. Palloff and Pratt use their extensive experience in training online teachers to highlight the psychological and process variables that can make or break a good online teacher. They offer a systematic approach to assess institutional, faculty, and learner readiness as a first step to building online learning programs and courses.

When we actually immerse ourselves in the online learning environment, particularly in text-rich asynchronous dialogue, student and faculty interaction might seem much like a jungle of multiple conversations and activities. Barclay Hudson's chapter "The Jungle Syndrome: Some Perils and Pleasures of Learning Without Walls" provides teachers with jungle navigation tools and references the need to let go of traditional lesson plans. Forum software can give sufficient structure to student and faculty conversations while maintaining a free-flowing and open quality to the interactions. Hudson cites specific features of interactive forum software that facilitate the ability to learn. By making the process manageable, he provides methods to track interactions and introduces the navigational tool of "phaselines." At the same time, rather than trying to conquer the jungle, Hudson encourages teachers to thrive in the environment through the use of "image-based dialogue" and more visually based forms of language that include elements of storytelling and metaphor. He argues that the VE is conducive to alternative and underused forms of interaction and describes a range of dialogic approaches that can stimulate new forms of learning and creativity.

Using a conceptual framework of complex adaptive systems theory, Jim Beaubien's chapter, "Harnessing the Power of Complexity in an Online Learning Environment," offers a systems framework to approach and understand online pedagogy. He describes eight building blocks for course development, pointing out that asynchronous online courses go through stages of development much like the stages of group development. When facilitators or teachers are aware of the group's current stage, they can work effectively to support student learning. However, specific techniques are also needed to make the online course successful. Beaubien asserts that faculty need to pay particular attention to specific kinds of student interaction, and he describes helpful ways in which to respond to each type. By understanding the nature of complex systems, the faculty leader is better able to manage the complexity of online teaching.

When we move to the institutional level, the challenges to administrators are reflected in questions of how to lead a virtual program, provide quality, be cost-effective, and govern effectively. Christi Olson, in her chapter "Leadership in Online Education: Strategies for Effective Online Administration and Governance," contrasts how educational leaders who lead virtual learning environments have goals and tasks compared to those of leaders who manage traditional university programs. She argues that it is critical to recognize the ways in which the two environments and their leadership roles are different. With clearly stated principles to guide administrators, she stresses that the focus needs to be on the quality of the learning experience rather than on technology. In online programs, the one constancy is change, and educational leaders need to focus on four main areas: developing a business model, creating an online leadership presence, hiring and training faculty, and governing the online institution. Olson addresses all of these relatively overlooked areas.

How do students thrive in the virtual classroom? The chapter "Breaking Through Zero-Sum Academics: Two Students' Perspectives on Computer-Mediated Learning Environments" by Shelley Hamilton and Joel Zimmerman, gives us a window into the students' virtual world. Painfully aware from their own experiences in higher education that most students experience a "scarcity mentality" and tend to yearn for scholarly and personal attention and interaction, they suggest that when time, space, and the learning process are reconfigured, new opportunities for learning can emerge that provide students with a rich and intimate learning experience. This does not come automatically; thus, Zimmerman and Hamilton offer specific strategies that can promote deep learning in theory and practice and can break down the "zero-sum academic experience." In particular, they find ways in which to enhance student-to-student collaboration and responsibility and to stimulate the development of the learning community. Their chapter makes us aware that student participation is highly related to the quality of the learning environment.

The next section shifts attention to the corporate learning environment. Each of the four chapters provides specific experiences from corporate consultants and trainers that highlight major issues regarding how to provide training online within a corporate culture. Bruce LaRue's chapter,

"Synthesizing Higher Education and Corporate Learning Strategies," proposes that rapid technological change profoundly affects both the university and the corporation. How to think about what knowledge is needed and how it is to be learned for workers to be productive are his focus. LaRue claims that workers need to develop "epistemological competencies" that will make it possible for them to become the needed "knowledge workers" of the 21st century. Dispersed workers and organizations can join together to form collaborative learning networks to facilitate the growing need for ongoing training. LaRue offers a 4-Plex Model of Networked Learning as a tool for corporate trainers in multinational companies. This unique model provides a practical link between the corporation and the university to enable them to work together to create the knowledge workers of the future.

Multinational and national corporate trainers and consultants know how difficult it is to get busy executives, managers, and employees together for training. Faced with setbacks as a trainer, David Smith, in his chapter titled "Real-World Learning in the Virtual Classroom: Computer-Mediated Learning in the Corporate World," describes his experience in a large electronics corporation slated to grow quickly. Rapid expansion in any business exerts enormous pressure and stress on existing systems and workers, and it often requires immediate behavioral changes. Asked by top managers to create a learning organization as a means to provide ongoing training to managers and employees, Smith developed a program that shifted the traditional lecture format for training to a three-stage program combining face-to-face and online interventions called the One-to-One Value Proposition Workshop. Recognizing that CML is relatively new to most corporations, he provides guidance on how to establish an effective online learning environment.

Under intense pressure to meet earnings targets, most corporate leaders have little time to explore fully how internal and external forces of change affect their leadership and their companies' success. Bruce LaRue and Mark Sobol's chapter, "The Executive Master Class: Cyberspace and the New Frontiers of Executive Education," describes how the authors moved face-to-face executive coaching and training to an online environment to meet the needs of busy executives. They explore how consultants and trainers can respond to ambivalence about and resistance to online interaction by focusing attention on the needs of individual learners. By integrating professional and personal learning needs, the goal becomes how to help work teams develop competencies to deal with rapid change and promote personal mastery. The master class is a carefully constructed online intervention that uses both theory and practice to provide executives with immediate learning and support as well as a way in which to problem solve and resolve misunderstandings that emerge from the need to make rapid decisions. LaRue and Sobol highlight five key learning outcomes, ranging from increased awareness to improved ability to initiate and maintain change.

The development of a learning organization is considered to be one way for corporations to meet the ongoing need to respond to the accelerating influence of technology and change in the marketplace. Mark Neff's chapter, "Online Knowledge Communities and Their Role in Organizational Learning," takes on the difficult task of transforming the corporation into a learning community. Neff gives examples of corporate efforts to become learning organizations and then describes specific methods to facilitate the implementation of corporate communities of learning through the establishment of online learning networks. He offers tools for moderators that support the development and maintenance of corporate knowledge communities.

The final section of the book presents applications of online learning concepts and technologies to specific courses. Creative online teaching methods are illustrated in chapters that cover topics ranging from statistics and research to consulting with health professionals.

When learning crosses cultures and organizational boundaries, instructors need to discover methods by which to engage learners to work collaboratively. Tracy Gibbons and Randi Brenowitz, in "Designing and Using a Course in Organization Design to Facilitate Corporate Learning in the Online Environment," offer a meta-learning model as an experience-based method to help students learn how to work as a team. Translating the language from face-to-face team building into language for virtual team building, principles and processes are illustrated through a step-by-step description of an organization design course that uses virtual teams as the learning vehicle. Facilitation by the instructor requires particular sensitivities and expertise. The authors confront the issue of how to deal with the relationship between theory and practice with adult students who have a wealth of life experience. In so doing, they highlight the limitations and benefits of the online environment.

A different methodology and focus is offered in Barbara Brown's course on virtual leadership. In "Teaching Virtual Leadership: Using the Case Method Online," Brown describes an "event-based seminar" that uses interactive video and forum software to enable future leaders of dispersed global corporations to draw on their work experiences as case studies. The virtual classroom constitutes the environment to study virtual leadership in action. Suggestions on how to use the case study method online and avoid notable pitfalls are presented for educators along with relevant readings.

Teaching statistics online challenges faculty to be aware of their students' strengths and limitations. Pat Hodges and Lynne Saba, in "Teaching Statistics Online," provide a step-by-step description of a multimodal approach to teaching this troublesome topic to graduate students over the Web. This is one of the rare chapters in the book that makes significant use of synchronous, as well as asynchronous, learning tools. The authors present examples of their curriculum, assignments, and methods of interaction including the use of live chat, attention to individual student learning needs, and the significant role of the faculty moderator.

Dean Janoff's chapter, "Health Care Meets Technology: Web-Based Professional Training, Consultation, and Collaboration," presents the forms that professional training can take including certificate programs, continuing education, and professional consultation. Three types of professional training and development are described that combine face-to-face learning with CML. Two examples are from postgraduate training programs for mental health professionals, and the third is an example of a multidisciplinary cardiac rehabilitation collaboration project. In all three situations, participants were busy students and professionals who had limited time for travel to face-to-face training or meetings for project development. Janoff notes that by transferring course discussion and project assignments to online forums, the learning experience increased each group's efficiency, productivity, and learning.

Success in the online environment depends on the creation of safe spaces for conversation, problem solving, and intimacy among students who might never meet. The virtual online space provides metaphorical cafés for human contact and is the virtual version of the face-to-face learning café (Brown, 2000). Based on a course on organizational concepts and methods, Bo Gyllenpalm's chapter, "A Virtual Knowledge Café," outlines a process for establishing virtual online cafés. He focuses on the role of the café host and introduces methods to stimulate and follow multiple conversations simultaneously. The café can expand to a series of cafés with students from different cultures and corporate environments. Gyllenpalm illustrates how student learning derives from assignments that require analysis of conversations that have taken place in cafés. He proposes a model for teachers and trainers to provide virtual spaces within their courses, programs, and learning organizations. The café becomes a place for academic and pragmatic learning as well as a haven for the emotional contact that is so necessary for sustenance in the online community.

References

Beaudin, B. P. (1999). Keeping online asynchronous discussions on topic. *Journal of Asynchronous Learning Network, 3*(2), 1-13. Available: www.aln.org/alnweb/journal/vol3_issue2/beaudin.htm

Beller, M., & Or, E. (1998). The crossroads between lifelong learning and information technology: A challenge facing leading universities. *Journal of Computer Mediated Communication, 4*(2), 1-10. Retrieved April 6, 2001, from http://jcmc.huji.ac.il?vol4/issue2/beller.html

Berge, Z. (1997, May-June). Characteristics of online teaching in post-secondary, formal education. *Educational Technology Magazine*, pp. 35-47.

Bergquist, W. H. (1992). *The four cultures of the academy: Insights and strategies for improving leadership in collegiate organizations*. San Francisco: Jossey-Bass.

Brookfield, S. (1986). *Understanding and facilitating adult learning: A comprehensive analysis of principles and effective practices*. San Francisco: Jossey-Bass.

Brown, J. (2000). *The world café: Catalyzing collaborative learning and collective intelligence.* Unpublished manuscript, Human and Organization Development Program, Fielding Graduate Institute.

Brown, J. S., & Duguid, P. (2000). *The social life of information.* Boston: Harvard Business School Press.

Burbules, N. C., & Callister, T. A. (2000). Universities in transition: The promise and the challenge of new technologies. *Teachers College Record, 102,* 271-293.

Carnevale, D. (2000a, October 27). Social bonds found to be crucial in online education. *Chronicle of Higher Education,* p. A46.

Carnevale, D. (2000b, May 26). U.S. lawmaker questions quality of the online-learning experience. *Chronicle of Higher Education,* p. A51.

Carr-Chellman, A. A., & Duchastel, P. (2000). The ideal online course. *British Journal of Educational Technology, 31,* 229-241.

Cox, R. M. (1999). Web of wisdom: A field study of a virtual learning community. *Dissertation Abstracts International, 60*(5A).

Creighton, J. V., & Buchanan, P. (2001). Toward the e-campus: Using the Internet to strengthen, rather than replace, the campus experience. *EduCause Review, 36*(2), 12-13.

Dabbagh, N. H. (2000). The challenges of interfacing between face-to-face and online instruction. *TechTrends, 44*(6), 37-42.

Daniel, J., & Stevens, A. (1998). The success stories: The use of technology in "out-of-school education." In C. de M. Moura Castro (Ed.), *Education in the information age* (pp. 156-167). New York: Inter-American Development Bank.

Distance learning in higher education. (2000). *CHEA Update, 3,* 1-12. (Council for Higher Education Accreditation) Available: www.chea.org/commentary/distance-learning-3.cfm

Dixon, D. (2001). *Mentoring over distance: The construction of the student-faculty relationship in a doctoral psychology program for mid-life adults.* Unpublished doctoral dissertation, Fielding Graduate Institute.

Doucette, N. (1998). Relieving information overload. *Rough Notes, 141*(2), 26-27.

Drucker, P. F. (1999). *Management challenges for the 21st century.* New York: Harper Business.

Duderstadt, J. (1999). Can colleges and universities survive in the information age? In R. N. Katz (Ed.), *Dancing with the devil: Information technology and the new competition in higher education.* San Francisco: Jossey-Bass.

Eisinger, J. (2000). Education evolution. *Association Management, 52*(13), 52-59.

Fleetwood, J., Vaught, W., Feldman, D., Gracely, E., Kassutto, Z., & Novack, D. (2000). MedEthEx Online: A computer-based learning program in medical ethics and communication skills. *Teaching and Learning in Medicine, 12*(2), 96-104.

Freire, P. (1985). *The politics of education.* South Hadley, MA: Bergin & Garvey.

Gergen, K. (1995). *Technology and the transformation of the pedagogical project* [Online]. Retrieved July 1, 2001, from www.swarthmore.edu/socsci/kgergen1/text12.html

Green, J. (2000, October 23). The online education bubble. *American Prospect,* pp. 32-35.

Gundawardena, C. N., Lowe, C., & Carabajal, K. (2000, February). Evaluating online learning: Models and methods. In *Society for Information Technology and Teacher Education International Conference: Proceedings of the 11th annual conference* (pp. 1677-1683). San Diego. (ERIC No. 444 552)

Halpern, D. (1998, August). Invited address presented at the annual meeting of the American Psychological Association (Division 2), San Francisco.

Hanna, D. E., & Associates. (2000). *Higher education in an era of digital competition: Choices and challenges.* Madison, WI: Atwood.

Harasim, L. M. (1998). The Internet and intranets for education and training: A framework for action. In C. de Moura Castro (Ed.), *Education in the information age* (pp. 181-201). New York: Inter-American Development Bank.

Harasim, L., Hiltz, S. R., Teles, L., & Turoff, M. (1995). *Learning networks.* Cambridge: MIT Press.

Hiltz, S. R. (1994). *The virtual classroom: Learning without limits via computer networks.* Norwood, NJ: Ablex.

Hiltz, S. R., & Turoff, M. (1993). *The network nation: Human communication via computer* (2nd ed.). Reading, MA: Addison-Wesley.

Hiltz, S., & Wellman, B. (1997). Asynchronous learning networks as a virtual classroom. *Communications of the ACM, 40*(9), 44-49.

Institute for Higher Education Policy. (2000, April). *Quality on the line: Benchmarks for success in Internet distance education.* Washington, DC: Author.

Jerome, L. W., DeLeon, P. H., James, L. C., Folen, R., Earles, J., & Gedney, J. J. (2000). The coming of age of telecommunication in psychological research and practice. *American Psychologist, 55,* 407-421.

Johnson, S. D., Aragon, S. R., Shaik, N., & Palma-Rivas, N. (2000). Comparative analysis of learner satisfaction and learning outcomes in online and face-to-face learning environments. *Journal of Interactive Learning Research, 11*(1), 29-49.

Kegan, R. (1994). *In over our heads: The mental demands of modern life.* Cambridge, MA: Harvard University Press.

Lapadat, J. C. (2000, May). *Teaching online: Breaking new ground in collaborative thinking.* Paper presented at the annual conference of the Canadian Society for the Study of Education Congress of the Social Sciences and Humanities, Edmonton, Alberta.

Lovitts, B. E. (2001). *Leaving the ivory tower: The causes and consequences of departure from doctoral study.* Lanham, MD: Rowman & Littlefield.

Maehl, W. H. (2000). *Lifelong learning at its best.* San Francisco: Jossey-Bass.

Maki, R. H., Maki, W. S., Patterson, M., & Whittaker, P. D. (2000). Evaluation of a Web-based introductory psychology course: Learning and satisfaction in on-line versus lecture courses. *Behavior Research Methods, Instruments, and Computers, 32,* 230-239.

Merriam, S. B., & Caffarella, R. S. (1999). *Learning in adulthood: A comprehensive guide* (2nd ed.). San Francisco: Jossey-Bass.

Mick, D. G., & Fournier, S. (1998, September). Paradoxes of technology: Consumer cognizance, emotions, and coping strategies. *Journal of Consumer Research, 25*(2), 123-143.

Noble, D. F. (1999). *Digital diploma mills* [Online]. Retrieved July 1, 2001, from www.firstmonday.dk/issues/issue3_1noble/

Panitz, T., & Panitz, P. (1998). Encouraging the use of collaborative education in higher education. In J. F. Forest (Ed.), *University teaching: International perspectives.* New York: Garland.

Paul, L. G. (1999, September). Thinking together. *Inside Technology Training,* pp. 18-22.

Phillips, V. (Pub.). (2001, January). Dow Jones University goes off-line. *Virtual University Business Digest*, p. 14. Available: www.geteducated.com

Powers, S. M., & Mitchell, J. (1997, March). *Student perceptions and performance in a virtual classroom environment.* Paper presented at the annual meeting of the American Research Educational Research Association, Chicago.

Ragan, L. C. (1998). *Good teaching is good teaching: An emerging set of guiding principles and practices for the design and development of distance education.* Retrieved June 30, 2001, from www.ed.psu.edu/acsde

Roach, R. (2001, January 18). The army marches into online learning. *Black Issues in Higher Education*, pp. 32-33.

Roberts, T. S., & Jones, D. T. (2000, April). Four models of on-line teaching. In *TEND 2000: Proceedings of the Technological Education and National Development Conference, "Crossroads of the New Millennium."* Abu Dhabi, United Arab Emirates.

Romiszowski, A. J. (1998). New technologies for professional education, training, and human resource development. In C. de M. Castro (Ed.), *Education in the information age* (pp. 58-73). New York: Inter-American Development Bank.

Rudestam, K. E., Giannetti, R. A., & Stamm, B. H. (in press). The impact of technology on clinical psychology. In G. Stricker & T. A. Widiger (Eds.), *Comprehensive handbook of psychology: Vol. 8. Clinical psychology.* New York: John Wiley.

Schoenholtz-Read, J. (2000, August). *Interim report on Student Development and Diversity Study.* Unpublished manuscript, Fielding Graduate Institute.

Schrage, M. (1990). *Shared minds: The new technologies of collaboration.* New York: Random House.

Schultz, C. S. (1998, August). Stanford Online: The Stanford University experience with online education. In *Proceedings of the Annual Conference on Distance Teaching and Learning* (pp. 341-345). Madison, WI. (ERIC No. 422 873)

Senge, P. (2000). *Schools that learn: A fifth discipline fieldbook for educators, parents, and everyone who cares about education.* Garden City, NY: Doubleday.

Smith, S. B. (2000). The effectiveness of traditional instructional methods in an online learning environment. *Dissertation Abstracts International, 60*(9A).

Sterling, B. (1992). *The hacker crackdown: Law and disorder on the electronic frontier.* New York: Bantam Books.

Svetcov, D. (2000, September). The virtual classroom vs. the real one. *Forbes*, pp. 50-52.

Talbott, S. (1998, October). Who is killing higher education? Or is it suicide? *Netfuture*, p. 15.

Tinto, V. (1975). Dropout from higher education: A theoretical synthesis of recent research. *Review of Educational Research, 45*(1), 89-129.

Tolmie, A., & Boyle, J. (2000). Factors influencing the success of computer mediated communication (CMC) environments in university teaching: A review and case study. *Computers and Education, 34*(2), 119-140.

Traub, J. (2000, November 19). Online U: How entrepreneurs and academic radicals are breaking down the walls of the university. *The New York Times Magazine*, pp. 88-126.

Turkle, S. (1995). *Life on the screen: Identity in the age of the Internet.* New York: Simon & Schuster.

Wittgenstein, L. (1953). *Philosophical investigations.* New York: Macmillan.

Chapter 2

Presence in "Teleland"

Gary Fontaine

I have journeyed to many "strange lands" over the years, miles, and technologies. I have taught traditional *in-person* courses and training workshops for more than 25 years. Recently, however, many of my academic and professional journeys have been to "Teleland." I have taught courses there face-to-face using the added support of *asynchronous* communication technology (at the University of Hawaii using e-mail and various "Web forums"). I have taught courses in which there was a combination of face-to-face and distant participants using *synchronous* communication technology (the Hawaii Interactive Telecommunication System based on interactive video). Typically, the distant participants in these courses were in several different remote classrooms. And I have taught courses with distant participants alone using asynchronous technology. In these latter courses, the participants not only were distant from me but also were distant from each other without any real classrooms as such (the Fielding Graduate Institute's Organizational Management Program). Often, both the participants and I were physically traveling throughout the world on business during the course as well. Strange lands for sure! This chapter describes some of what I have learned thus far from these journeys to Teleland—both from a growing body of research on them and from my own experience in them.

The Challenges Faced in Strange Lands Anywhere

My own professional focus has primarily been on helping people to deal effectively with more literal strange lands that they encounter on "real" journeys to other companies, cultures, and countries as part of business, diplomacy, service delivery, technology transfer, and education. But a strange land is *any* new or changing ecology, including those associated with the use of new technologies. I have found that journeys to Teleland present the same three key challenges to success (Fontaine, 1997, 2000). The first challenge is coping with our physical and psychological reaction to the strangeness itself—*ecoshock*. The symptoms of ecoshock can include frustration, fatigue, clumsiness, anxiety, paranoia, depression, irritability, and rigid thinking that interfere with adjustment and performance. In strange lands, the ecology changes, the appropriateness of our *normal* or *habitual* ways of doing tasks becomes problematic, and we are faced with the second challenge—developing and implementing strategies to complete the tasks essential for living and working in these new ecologies. With respect specifically to the cultural confrontations with which I most frequently work, given that we expect and are skilled in doing things one way and our hosts in a strange land expect and are skilled in doing them another way, how are we going to do them well together? Do we continue to do them *our way*, try to adopt *their way,* compromise, or develop some new way? I return to this challenge shortly. The third challenge is to maintain the motivation to continue in spite of inevitable frustration, fatigue, ecoshock, and poorer than desired task performance. In my own experience, this challenge is the most important of all because it takes time for ecoshock to diminish and for new strategies and skills to be developed and practiced to get tasks done in the new ecology.

I have previously suggested (Fontaine, 1989, 1997, 2000) that, rather than selecting *specific* strategies based on what has typically been our way, their way, or a compromise, the second challenge requires a more generic strategy of accommodation. With accommodation, these—or frequently other—specific strategies are selected based on what is most appropriate to the new task ecology. These other ways have been labeled "third cultures" (Casmir, 1993) or "third ways" (O'Hara-Devereaux & Johansen, 1994). I have referred to them as "microcultures" (MCs) to emphasize that they most commonly are shared perceptions for completing specific tasks (Fontaine, 1997, 2000).

Microcultures specify how task participants are to negotiate; communicate; teach; make decisions; supervise; delegate; lead; appraise performance; manage; plan; conduct meetings; resolve conflicts; and form, maintain, and dissolve relationships. They specify the meaning of a contract, a treaty, a policy, or an agreement in terms of time, responsibilities, and comprehensiveness. They are "bare-bones" cultures in that they typically include only the minimal number of shared perceptions required for getting the task done acceptably for all parties concerned. In our case, an MC would specify how a particular course in Teleland is to be conducted by the participating teachers, students, and relevant others. To be optimally effective, the course must be tailored to the task ecology in which the participants are interacting. The task ecology includes the characteristics of the participants (their knowledge and skills, national and organizational culture, personalities, objectives, and expectations), characteristics of the course itself (its purpose, novelty, difficulty, and requirements), and characteristics of the broader context (facilities, resources, communication technologies, time available, physical settings, time and time zones, travel, and organizational support). Developing and using MCs is the optimal strategy for effectiveness in strange lands in contexts ranging from international business (Hofner-Saphiere, 1996) to diplomacy (Kimmel, 1989). It is what we need to do if we are consistently going to deal effectively with diversity and meet the second key challenge faced in those lands. I suggest that it is the optimal strategy for teaching in the new and rapidly changing ecologies of Teleland as well.

To some degree, participants (whether international assignees or teachers and students in Teleland) can prepare in advance for the ecology they will encounter through some form of training or preparation. However, the development and use of MCs typically requires knowledge of the task ecology at a level of detail far in excess of what is available in advance. Participants might need to know, for example, the task objectives and their importance from all participants' perspectives; characteristics of the facility in which the task takes place and the available resources; and the participants' personalities, motives, skills, and relationships with each other. To a significant degree, participants must assess what is *necessary* in terms of these or other characteristics, identify a broad range of possible options for dealing with them, and select the most desirable options to constitute an MC "on the spot." The key skill in doing it on the spot is an effective use of *a sense of presence*—the experience we all commonly have in strange lands anywhere in which we have a heightened awareness of everything around us. It is an important part of the "street smarts" we need there.

A Sense of Presence

If you ask people in (or returning from) strange lands about their experiences, they often report a feeling of *immediacy* and a *broad awareness* of everything around them. They report that everything to them is *real* and *vivid* and that they feel very *alive*. They describe a *clarity* of perception and *responsivity* to the world (Fontaine, 1993, 2000). The totality of the experience constitutes this state of consciousness called a sense of presence. It is a state in which we are psychologically present in the immediate task situation and are broadly aware of a range of ecological characteristics of it rather than attending narrowly to a few selected characteristics or to events occurring in other times or places. When engaged in familiar tasks at home, we are often much less than 100% *present* psychologically. Our minds may be occupied by extraneous events so that we are not "tuned in" to the ecology of the immediate tasks. Because so many tasks at home are routine and predictable, we can get by on being less present. The relatively stable and familiar ecology allows general rules for completing various categories of tasks to develop. We need not stay alert for variations in the ecology between successive occurrences of a task. Each task can be successfully completed by applying habitual rules.

But in strange lands, life and work are not so routine. They involve new ecologies. Because so many of them are unfamiliar, we must be aware of a much broader range of ecological characteristics; we do not know which are going to be important. Because so many of them are unpredictable, we rarely have the opportunity for adequate planning. Because task ecologies change so often, we need to monitor them continuously. Because there is always the danger—particularly during times of stress or frustration—of falling back on *habits* from home, we need to monitor our own behavior as well. To be effective in strange lands, we need to be nearly 100% involved or 100% *present!*

Purposeful *attention* involves focusing *narrowly* on a selected set of characteristics of a task ecology, usually those previously found to have been essential for completing the task (e.g., what the teacher in a class has to say). *Presence* involves a broader focus that is more likely to include other potentially relevant characteristics of an ecology (e.g., what the teacher is wearing, which words are chosen, who is looking at whom, the reaction of other students). Presence is less purposeful. It is stimulated by novelty or something like an "orientation reflex." Focused attention is the optimal mode for learning in the familiar task contexts of home; a sense of presence is the optimal mode in contexts that are new, diverse, or changing—strange lands. The key skill for doing things in strange lands is to use the opportunity provided by our typically higher sense of presence to develop the MCs we need to perform effectively.

Presence in Teleland

For most participants, each course in Teleland presents an ecology that is new or different from traditional courses—a strange land. Typically, each is unique relative to other Teleland courses as well in terms of content, technologies, participant characteristics, and so forth. O'Hara-Devereaux and Johansen (1994) present a useful taxonomy of general ecologies of Teleland and the support technologies we find in them:

- ◆ *Same time–same place* (flip charts, films, videos, computer projectors, traditional classrooms)

- *Same time–different place* (synchronous technologies—telephones, videoconferencing, chat rooms, remote classrooms)
- *Different time–same place* (workstations, bulletin boards, teamwork rooms)
- *Different time–different place* (asynchronous technologies—e-mail, voice mail, Web forums, computer conferencing, shared databases, personal [and perhaps mobile] learning sites)

As in any other strange land, in Teleland participants need to develop strategies for meeting course objectives that are accommodated to the particular course. Important ecological characteristics often are those associated with *teaching* versus *training* versus *facilitating* courses; working with *undergraduates* versus *advanced students* (graduates, professionals, managers, and executives); dealing with different course *topics* and *content;* working with different *communication hardware* and *software tools;* and working with varying degrees of *administrative support* and (sometimes) administrative, student, or family *resistance.* As in any strange land, there is no simple "recipe" for success—no universal "best way." Part of the skill of being effective is learning to make those accommodations quickly and well. As with other journeys, some planning can be done in advance, particularly in terms of developing course architecture. But also as with other journeys, doing it well requires skill in the use of a sense of presence.

Although in my work I have used "a sense of presence" (Fontaine, 1989) to describe the state of being psychologically present in the situation in which one is *physically* present, I adopted the term from mentor and colleague Bill Uttal, who was conducting early research on teleoperator systems (the remote operation of undersea recovery and extraterrestrial exploration vehicles; Uttal, 1989). He and others were somewhat ironically using the term "a sense of *remote* presence" to describe the experience of being present *someplace else* (in the remote vehicle being navigated) and were interested principally in the degree to which the experience enhances the operator's performance. The experiential characteristics (e.g., spatial presence, involvement, and realness) have been found to be similar to my own work (Schubert, Friedmann, & Regenbrecht, 1999). Subsequently, the terms "a sense of presence" (Lombard & Ditton, 1997; Welch, 1992), "telepresence" (Lombard & Ditton, 1997), and "virtual presence" (Ditlea, 1990) all have been used to refer to the perception that any mediated experience (e.g., virtual environments [VEs], training simulations, distance education, computer-supported collaboration, videoconferencing, home theater, high-definition television, some amusement park rides) is not mediated—the experience that we are really "there," somewhere. In the case of *virtual presence,* it is the experience of being somewhere that does not "really" exist at all outside of the computer! There is even work on "microtelepresence," the sense of being present in a microscopic world with computer-aided magnification (Ditlea, 1990).

The "somewheres" of interest in this chapter, of course, are the classrooms of Teleland. To keep from getting lost in a maze of terminology, in this chapter I use the term "a sense of presence" to refer to all of the above and try to make clear the specific application of the term to which I am referring.

Lombard and Ditton (1997) define presence as "an illusion that a mediated experience is not mediated" (p. 1). It includes the characteristics of *realism, transportation* ("you are there" or "it is here" or "we are together in a shared space"), and *immersion* ("involved, absorbed, engaged, engrossed"). Witmer and Singer (1998) define it as "the subjective experience of being in one place or environment, even when one is physically situated in another. As applied to a virtual environment (VE), presence refers to experiencing the computer-generated environment rather than the actual physical locale" (p. 225). In both my own work and that of researchers in Teleland, a sense of presence is a characteristic of the psychological experience of the participant rather than of the medium. Thus, it is differentiated from the concept of "social presence" (Short, Williams, & Christie, 1976), defined as the extent to which a medium is perceived as sociable, warm, sensitive, or personal when it is used to interact with others. But certainly, the two are not independent, and presumably the latter would enhance the former. Much of the theory, research, and application of work on a sense of presence is published in the journal *Presence: Teleoperators and Virtual Environments* or is accessible online at www.presence-research.org or http://nimbus.temple.edu/~mlombard/presence/. In this chapter, I try to distill that which has the most implications for distance education.

The Effects of Having a Sense of Presence in Teleland

Research on a sense of presence in all contexts—mediated or not—is still largely in the embryonic stage, and many of the presumed effects are based largely on anecdotal evidence and conjecture. In Teleland, much of the research that has been done has focused on same time–different place ecologies supported by audio, video, (sometimes) tactile, and VE technologies. The effects of interest have been both individual and group learning and performance. There is mounting evidence that an enhanced sense of presence improves both as well as other variables related to performance in distance education (Held & Durlach, 1992; Mania & Chalmers, 2000; Pausch, Shackelford, & Proffitt, 1993; Sheridan, 1992; Whitelock, Romano, Jelfs, & Brna, in press; Witmer & Singer, 1998). Some of these latter variables include arousal (Heeter, 1995; Lombard, Grabe, Reich, Campanella, & Ditton, 1995), enjoyment (Heeter, 1995), involvement (Heeter, 1995), persuasion (Kim, 1996), memory (Ditton, 1997), and motivation to complete the task (Whitelock et al., in press). Involvement, in particular, is likely to be key in both same time–different place and different time–different place ecologies, in part to overcome the distracting effects of the technologies used, an issue discussed later. On the "down side," there is evidence that over time high presence can produce cognitive overload (Whitelock et al., in press). All of these effects taken together likely affect the journey to Teleland in terms of participants' adjustment to the ecoshock encountered, performance on the tasks required, and motivation to continue.

In journeys to the intercultural and international strange lands that have served as my professional focus, the heightened presence appears to occur naturally as a consequence of the novelty encountered. The skill is to make use of it to define the necessary, the possible, and the desirable as I described earlier. In Teleland, however, because of distance and the obtrusiveness of our media, the sense of presence required for optimal performance may more frequently need to be *created*—or at least *nurtured* and *supported*. Thus, in journeys to Teleland, we have an additional challenge.

Causes of a Sense of Presence in Teleland

A variety of conditions appear to nurture a sense of presence in tele-mediated contexts. A selection of those most likely to be relevant to teaching in Teleland is presented next.

Media characteristics. The more completely and consistently all senses are stimulated, the greater the presence (Witmer & Singer, 1998). Clearly, presentation of both visual and audio stimuli is of key importance (Lombard & Ditton, 1997; Whitelock et al., in press). Given that, however, visual display characteristics (when available) appear to have the most impact. These characteristics include image quality and size, viewing distance, proportion of a user's visual field occupied by an image, motion, color, and dimensionality. Hendrix and Barfield (1996), for example, found that presence was higher when head tracking and stereoscopic cues were provided to participants and when the visual display represented a 50- or 90-degree geometric field of view rather than a 10-degree field. Important aural presentation characteristics include quality (frequency range, variations in loudness, and distortion in sound reproduction) and dimensionality. Gilkey and Weisenberger (1995) stress, "Background auditory stimulation may be useful or even critical for achieving a full sense of presence" (p. 364). Lombard and Ditton (1997) suggest, "Adding the smells of food, flowers, or the air at a beach or in a rain forest to the corresponding images and sounds seems likely to enhance a sense of presence" (p. 17); interestingly, so do surprises (e.g., video clips running in picture frames in VE displays or pop-up "help" guides). Fencott (1999) stresses, "Cues and surprises in VEs work together, supporting each other and thus the virtuality they inhabit by seeking to both establish fidelity and catch and retain the attention of the visitor and thus maintain presence" (p. 4). I return specifically to the role of surprises in the virtual classroom later in the chapter. In general, the more the preceding cues support scene realism, consistency with the objective world, and environmental richness, the greater the presence (Witmer & Singer, 1998).

Orientation and movement in space. The more the observers can perceive self-movement and the movement of other people or objects relative to their selves, the greater the presence (Witmer & Singer, 1998). Likewise, the presence is greater the more the participants can modify their viewpoint to change what they see or hear or when kinesthetic cues are provided that the participants' bodies are actually moving in physical space during a mediated experience (e.g., vibrating theater seats to enhance the illusion that the viewers are experiencing an earthquake [Lombard & Ditton, 1997]) and haptic cues (touch or force-feedback) are present as participants encounter other people or objects (Ho, Basdogan, Slater, Durlach, & Srinivasan, 1998).

Freedom from distractions. Both isolation (the degree to which participants are isolated from their physical surroundings) and selective attention (participants' ability to focus on the task stimuli and ignore distractions) facilitate presence. Conversely, interface awareness produced by "unnatural, clumsy, artifact-laden interface devices that interfere with the direct and effortless interpretation of and interaction with a remote or virtual environment diminish presence" (Witmer & Singer, 1998, p. 230; see also Schubert et al., 1999). Lombard and Ditton (1997) likewise suggest, "The medium should not be obvious or obtrusive—it should not draw attention to itself and remind the media user that she/he is having a mediated experience" (p. 19).

Degree of control, interaction, and exploration. The more control participants have over the task environment and their interactions with it, the greater the presence (Schubert et al., 1999; Welch, Blackmon, Liu, Mellers, & Stark, 1996; Witmer & Singer, 1998). Stimuli should be responsive to input by the participants, and noticeable delays between input and reaction diminish presence. Presence is enhanced if the mode of interaction with the environment is natural or well practiced as opposed to artificial or new. Lombard and Ditton (1997) note, "Most writers have either implicitly assumed or explicitly suggested that a major or even the primary cause of presence is the ability to interact with a mediated environment" (p.19). They suggest that the degree to which a medium is interactive depends on (a) the number of inputs from the user that the medium accepts, (b) the number of characteristics of the mediated presentation or experience that can be modified by the user, (c) the range of change possible in each characteristic of the mediated presentation or experience, (d) the degree of correspondence between the type of user input and the type of medium response, and (e) the speed with which the medium responds to user inputs. With respect to the latter, Heeter (1995) notes, "When forced to choose between responsiveness to motion and resolution of images, virtual environment developers are choosing responsiveness as the more important factor" (p. 203).

Nature of the task or activity. The nature of the task or activity (e.g., motor vs. cognitive, learning vs. performance, individual vs. group) is likely to affect the experience of presence, as is the importance, meaningfulness, interest value, and past experience with it (Lombard & Ditton, 1997; Witmer & Singer, 1998). My own work strongly suggests that task novelty and unpredictability in the unfolding of events are key precipitants of presence (Fontaine, 1993), although there is recent evidence that in some contexts predictability and contiguity with expectations may enhance presence (McGreevy, 1994). Clearly, much research and model development is necessary. The earlier mentioned findings with respect to the role of surprises could also be included here. Schubert et al. (1999) find that drama ("the extent to which the environment presents a strong story line, is self-contained, [and] has its own dynamic and unfolding sequence of events" [p. 4]) also contributes to presence.

The number of participants and "copresence." Lombard and Ditton (1997) suggest that, at least up to a point, the greater the number of participants, the greater the presence experienced. The issue as to whether there is some "optimal" number is still largely unexplored. A key, of course, is the degree to which each participant is *aware* of the presence of others in the task or activity. This awareness of being and interacting with others has typically been called a *sense of copresence* (Couch, 1989) or sometimes a *sense of shared presence, sense of togetherness,* or *social awareness*. The more participants are aware of the presence of others and that those others are reciprocating that awareness, the higher the sense of presence (Anderson, Ashraf, Douther, & Jack, 2000; Kaltenbrunner & Huxor, 2000; Steed & Slater, 1998; Thie & van Wijk, 1998), particularly when interactions with them are possible (Schubert et al., 1999). Several studies have examined the variables contributing to the sense of *co*presence (Anderson et al., 2000; Durlach & Slater, 1998; Ho et al., 1998).

Trait and state characteristics of the participants. There are likely to be *individual* and *cultural* differences associated with the experience of presence in Teleland. Some participants might be both more willing and more able to experience presence than are others (Thie & van Wijk, 1998). Lombard and Ditton (1997) suggest, "The identical media form and content might generate a sense of presence in one media user and not in another or might generate presence in the same user on one occasion but not [on] another one" (p. 22). Willingness to suspend disbelief can facilitate "getting into" the experience and overlooking obtrusiveness of the media. Those unfamiliar with technology might be less distracted by its workings than are those closely acquainted with it. More prior experience may lead to more habitual use of media controls and habituation to its distractions and, thus, may facilitate presence. Lombard and Ditton also suggest that the participants' preferred representational system (visual, auditory, or kinesthetic), their cognitive style, the degree to which they "screen" complex stimuli, their level of sensation seeking, their need to overcome loneliness, and their mood can have an effect. Mantovani and Riva (1999) suggest that both the meaning of presence and the experience of it are related to the participants' culture.

Nurturing Presence in Distance Education

Developing and delivering a *good* course anywhere—at home or in Teleland—requires putting it together in a nurturing ecology that consists of talented, motivated participants (e.g., teachers, students, resource persons) with appropriate texts, multimedia and technological resources, and administrative support. As noted earlier, doing all this in today's world, in which many of the ecological characteristics are new or changing, requires building MCs that accommodate a particular course at a particular time. There are no recipes here—no well-marked highways—at least not yet. The theme of this chapter has been that optimizing a sense of presence is a valuable objective in these strange lands of Teleland. A growing body of research suggests as much, and my own experience teaching in Teleland convinces me of the fact. As Gristock (1998) asserts, in effective geographically dispersed teams (which distance education courses must be), knowledge exchange must be "supported by the development of a *sense of telepresence* . . . and *telecommunity* between members . . . , at least for as long as the duration of the exchange" (p. 3). Tammelin (1998) reinforces the point specifically for distance education. The task, then, is to draw on as many clues or tools as we can from research and experience to help us design and deliver the particular course that our journey takes us to next. I next examine some of those applicable to *synchronous* and *asynchronous* course ecologies. I emphasize the latter because, in my view, asynchronous ecologies are likely to be most accommodated to the needs of education, training, and collaboration in a global world.

Synchronous Course Ecologies

Synchronous course ecologies in Teleland can involve same time–different place classrooms connected by interactive audio and video or combinations of those with a same time–same place "traditional" classroom (the teacher presents to physically proximal as well as remote sites in real time through broadcast or cable). Both may also be supported by phone, fax, mail, e-mail, or Web connections with electronic white boards and chat rooms. During recent years, there have been both heavy investments and significant improvements in supportive technology for this ecology, much of which is likely to influence the level of presence experienced. The course architecture (e.g., syllabi, lectures, texts, assignments, evaluations, proximal and distal classrooms, video/audio media) and the degree to which that architecture is accommodated to the ecology of the specific course significantly affect the success of that course. Among the ecological necessities for a course to be effective are that (a) participants be always (or nearly so) physically present in a classroom (somewhere) that can support the appropriate media technologies, (b) they be roughly on the same daily schedule, and (c) they be in proximal time zones. It is also useful for them to have similar backgrounds in terms of course prerequisites and preparation and the same primary language and culture.

The research reviewed earlier and my own experience suggest that in this ecology, the keys to an optimal sense of presence are as follows:

◆ A ratio of high realness and intensity of audio, video, and other display characteristics to distractions associated with the media/computer technology used to produce the displays

◆ A ratio of high interactivity between participants in different sites to those same distractions

In other words, if we can absorb participants in the scene through sensory integrity and interpersonal interactions, then they will forget about the medium through which all of this is occurring. Strangely, an analogy to skin diving comes to mind! When I dive at home in Hawaii, where there is relatively little to see in terms of varied marine flora and fauna (because of isolation, many fewer species have made it there than elsewhere in the Indo-Pacific), I typically become distracted and irritated by the "fog" on my face mask. I constantly find myself spitting on the glass to keep it clear. When I dive in the lagoon in front of our cottage in the Philippines, where there are always new and intriguing sights, I lose awareness of the mask and the faceplate altogether and become absorbed in the scene—same mask, same spit, different show!

The audio and video characteristics reviewed earlier all can play a role in nurturing presence in synchronous courses, including image quality and size; viewing distance; proportion of a user's visual field; motion and color; audio frequency range; and variations in loudness, distortion, and dimensionality. To the degree possible, instructors need to optimize each as budgets support. In my own experience, however, the keys to optimizing presence are big video monitors (consume as much of the field of vision as possible), cameras and monitors that allow participants (certainly the instructor) to perceive self-movement and modify their viewpoints to change what they see or hear, and real-time audio feedback. Monitors—however many—that make up a very small percentage of the visual field both diminish telepresence and interfere with presence in the immediate face-to-face classroom (if there is one). The situation is exacerbated because the image size and depth of field of monitors—at least those that I have had available—generally resolve remote classrooms into some "big heads" of front-row students, with those in back coming through at best as Lilliputians who from time to time raise what appear to be hands (I wonder, "Are they asking a question? Or is that just lint on the camera?").

Although the availability of several monitors displaying different viewpoints (including overhead or other graphic material) can be initially disorienting (especially if there are several remote sites), the freedom to select what to see can certainly enhance a sense of presence. Strangely, this seems particularly true if one can see oneself on one or more monitors as well. There is an interesting parallel here to some of my own work in strange lands that suggests that our sense of presence is enhanced if we perceive that others are attending to us!

Real-time video and audio feedback—consistent across sites—is also key. I can recall one class in which a couple of the remote sites were real time and the other was *slow-screen* video and *real-time* audio. So if I saw a student in the latter classroom raise her hand, I would wonder, "*When* did she do that and in response to *what*?" Or if I heard her say something with exclamation or inquiry, I would turn to look at the student in her monitor, only to find her still smiling and content—yet be struck by whatever was to lead to her query! I might then wonder suddenly whether the comment was delivered instead by somebody in one of the other classes, and in a panic I would look around to the other monitors! And gee, as Lombard and Ditton (1997) suggest, either the scent of her perfume or a breath of fresh air from the window near her would help with presence a bit, too.

A particular challenge in this ecology is handling the audio. It is technically difficult to pick up every student everywhere equally well without everyone having his or her own microphone. So then the problem becomes one of everybody talking over everyone else! Thus, on/off buttons are used to synchronize input. But it is distracting for all but the very experienced to remember to press a button before speaking and then again when finished (remember two-way radios?). The obtrusiveness of the technology can be devastating to presence. You are attending to the button and not present either here or there! And what if you forget to turn off the button and then turn with a joke or obscenity to your neighbor! Over the past decade, those at the Ontario Telepresence Project at the University of Toronto have designed fascinating collaboration environments using unobtrusive computer and media technology to heighten the sense of telepresence (Buxton, 1997). These latter technologies have been integrated in a manner that is ecologically valid in terms of participant "social conventions and mores of architectural location-distance-function relationships" (p. 372). Desks, computers, and imaging devices become one physically and functionally integrated entity. The office or classroom door serves input functions—as a mouse or keyboard might—to indicate to colleagues the availability of the occupant for discourse!

Most recently, same time–different place *collaborative virtual environments* (CVEs) have been developed for computer-supported cooperative work such as meetings and classes (Frecon, 1998; Steed & Slater, 1998). Some use *avatar* representations of participants as they interact with one another in electronic team rooms that mimic the characteristics of physical ones. Frecon (1998, pp. 10-11) describes how these rooms support peripheral awareness (of what other participants are doing to promote coordination), provide for the possibility of chance encounters, offer natural metaphors by mapping participants' understanding of the real world onto virtual counterparts, and provide persistence in recognition that cooperation happens over long periods and involves results from a series of interrelated events. Rooms offer standard collaboration tools such as whiteboards, flip charts, overhead projectors, handouts, and models or prototypes viewable by all. Frecon notes that teams usually elect a room as "theirs" and that members seem naturally drawn toward their room. Current research is examining the requirements for nurturing both effective communication and presence in this state-of-the-art synchronous ecology (Anderson et al., 2000; Rauthenberg, Kauff, & Graffunder, 2000).

There are a number of other issues introduced earlier that are likely to be key for maximizing presence in this course ecology; determining the optimal number of sites and participants are two. But more research and practical experience with them are needed prior to suggesting their impact with confidence. There are yet many shortcomings of this rapidly developing technology. Again, I believe that the key to optimizing presence is to absorb the participants in the scene—wherever that is—through the vibrancy of the presentation, resource media used, or interpersonal interactions between participants. The more this can be done, the more unobtrusive the medium becomes.

Asynchronous Course Ecologies

Asynchronous course ecologies in Teleland involve different time–different place activities in which participants typically access a Web site when it is appropriate or convenient to do so and only for as long as it remains so. Their "classroom" is a computer with Internet access, and they may move from job to home, to airport, to hotel, to plane as participants' lives and work dictate. The same may be true for teachers as well as students. Typically, most or all participants are physically isolated from one another by time zone and distance. The primary medium for interaction is some form of *groupware* or forum software displayed on personal computer monitors, although that may be supplemented again by phone, fax, mail, e-mail, or intermittent scheduled or unscheduled face-to-face contact. This ecology requires groupware that is closely accommodated to course requirements (e.g., access to resources, written assignments, group projects, feedback), a sufficiently high capacity and dependable server, a reliable Internet service provider, reliable phone or cable lines or wireless capability, adequate computer capacity, and participant computer skill. In this ecology, participants need *not* be fully in synchrony in terms of course background or preparation (they can "make up" work when offline). They do *not* have to have the same primary language (they can work on wording offline) or be from the same culture (they can consider and, if necessary, get assistance with intercultural issues offline). It allows for timely silences or absences—built-in pauses in communication—so important for absorption and integration of material, creativity, stress reduction, and deepening connections between ourselves and others (Rubin, 2000; Waterworth & Waterworth, 2000). It is an ecology particularly well suited to education or training for busy students and professionals in our global world. And it is an ecology in which a sense of presence again appears to play a key role in performance (Mania & Chalmers, 2000).

Whereas the burden of nurturing a sense of presence in synchronous ecologies is on the sophistication of technology support, the burden in asynchronous ones is much more on groupware and participant skill. The material just reviewed and my own experience suggest that in these ecologies the keys to an optimal sense of presence are as follows:

◆ High psychological texture for people, settings, work tables, and assignments
◆ High interactivity among an optimal combination of number of participants and tasks and the responsivity of those participants
◆ High meaningfulness and an optimal mixture of predictability, surprise, and drama of course content and activities that foster a merging of proximal and distal settings into "one place"

To the degree that these criteria are met, participants' perceptual worlds are altered such that the "here and now" expands to include the "there and then"!

In the asynchronous course ecologies of Teleland, architecture remains important for supporting course objectives, although components may be somewhat different (groupware forums with topics, replies, and meeting areas against a backdrop of business, office, or home replace proximal and distal classrooms and video/audio media). But in these ecologies, optimizing presence requires going beyond architecture to "interior decorating" the site by spraying *texture* on all of its surfaces, for it is that texture built up in the mental image that each participant has of this "world" that replaces the realness and intensity of the transmitted visual and audio images in synchronous ecologies.

The participants in an asynchronous course all must furnish and decorate the site—even to the "wallpaper"—themselves. It does not come with a technology package. They must provide as much texture as possible. This texture can come in the form of the recall of previous face-to-face interactions among participants; shared experience online with previous courses or the academic program itself; shared experience with the server, the syllabus, course assignments, or texts; or continuing reflections on ongoing world or local events. Meta-communication (communicating about course communication) and communication aimed at building a context of shared experience, expanding interpersonal familiarity and relationships, reducing conflict, and providing support and encouragement—and sometimes humor and perspective—all can be valuable to texturing this distal world to the point where it can be seamlessly integrated into the proximal one. Exchanging small talk or stories of travels, vacations, celebrations, sorrows, hopes, and fears can help to merge the worlds together.

In my own asynchronous courses, I typically have an "Explorer's Lounge" or "Fontaine's Place" or "Babbie's Bar" (named after the author of a research methods text we use [Babbie, 1998] that is, by the way, presented in a manner quite supportive of this ecology). Tammelin (1998) similarly describes the inclusion of "cafés." These "bars," "cafés," or their counterparts can provide "taste," "smell," and "favorite food and drink" (indeed, I sometimes get the impression that participants do mix a *real* drink or prepare *real* food as they are sitting at home or in the office posting their messages!). These "places" provide a bulletin board for course announcements, a table to argue across, an opportunity for social comparison, a voice to console, some space to chat in, a forum to share a joke with, a hall to scream in, or a seam to talk (to anyone) between time zones! This room is by no means the only part of the architecture with texture. Assignment areas, work areas, links, and so forth can be "textured" as well, but the texture of Babbie's Bar after a semester of occupancy is real indeed—at least as much as the bar down the street!

Although the explicit purposes of these bars are as just indicated, their primary (albeit implicit) purpose should be to pull the participants out of their different worlds and into a shared place for a while—to enhance their sense of presence. Tammelin (1998) stresses likewise: "The main purpose of the café conference was to establish a space where the participants could demonstrate their own social presence and sense the presence of the other participants" (pp. 5-6). The techniques I have used for doing so, consistent with the earlier review of the characteristics nurturing presence, can involve presenting participants through topic postings with *novelty* ("The moonrise"—the description of a bloodred moon rising from out of the black Sibuyan Sea one evening before I went online), *surprises* ("A bolt from out of the blue"—an account of my being hit by lightning from a clear blue sky while strolling along the beach drinking coffee in the morning, again just before going online), opportunities for *chance encounters* with important people ("A word from our program director"—the director of our graduate program visited our bar to dialogue about program changes), and *drama* ("The murder"—a traveler found naked and dead on a nearby beach!). All of this in a course on research methodology or, perhaps, on international assignments.

But, of course, to be credible, they all must be *true*! Typically, the other course participants (the students) also make major contributions to this presence-nurturing effort as they post topics from their current lives, for example, about the death of a father, the sickness of a child, a marriage, or a promotion to the new job of organizational "tele-evangelist."

And these stop-the-world experiences cannot simply be scripted and reproduced from semester to semester. Doing so nearly always "shows" to the participants. Rather, the trick is for the instructor to maintain a high sense of presence while participating in the course as well so that the topics flow from real experience and are accommodated to needs stemming from the personalities, experiences, and culture of that particular class. To the degree that I and others with whom I work are successful in evidencing this sense of presence, I have attributed its elicitation variously to dealing with new and highly talented students, dealing with the rapid growth and change of our fields, dealing with new Teleland technologies, and dealing with other new strange lands that we may be encountering as we teach the courses. With respect to the latter, for example, I have often been "on the road" while maintaining a presence in our class via my laptop and a variety of tenuous connections to the Internet. Strange lands indeed!

The example provided in the Appendix illustrates the partial architecture of the Web site for a recent asynchronous course on research methodology that I taught for nine middle and upper level managers in the Fielding program mentioned earlier. The first section presents topics that are associated with the course syllabus, posting areas for assignments, and Babbie's Bar. The second section presents selected topics within Babbie's Bar. Although revealing the actual text of each topic or reply would violate participant confidentiality, the topic titles alone reveal much of the diversity of participant texturing activity. Most topics subsequently received at least several replies from different participants.

I have found that including in the class forum a guest participant (a program administrator or an "outside" resource person) with whom participants have had previous face-to-face contact has a particularly strong effect in weaving proximal and distal realities together. If individual courses can be housed within a broader programmatic ecology that allows or arranges at least occasional face-to-face interaction, then texture is further enhanced. If those face-to-face interactions can also include husbands/wives or bosses/ workmates, then texture is enhanced even more and the distal and proximal realities are integrated further in a Web of the "present." A student in one of Tammelin's cafés noted,

> I feel that at least a few group meetings face to face are needed to create a certain atmosphere. A course where several communication channels are used is very different from a course where only, for example, e-mail would be used to communicate between the participants. If you never see what the others

really look like, it somehow makes it all much more distant and so there will not be the same kind of a connection. (quoted in Tammelin, 1998, p. 8)

Another key to optimizing a sense of presence is just the right amount of interaction between teacher and students and among students themselves to keep this "world" going. Too little input or responsivity from the teacher or students results in most participants fading—or being drawn—into other worlds; too much input inhibits student interaction, and a real but strange world is transformed into a series of Internet lectures or teacher-student dialogues. Note that the key to the timing of interactivity in these asynchronous ecologies is not *immediacy* (the different time–different place ecology does not support that) but rather *sufficiency*. When participants go online, there must be relevant and timely messages for them, and they must have confidence that responses to those messages, or new ones, will be equally timely to the recipients in the not-too-distant future. Participants need a sense of *copresence*. They need to feel that others are really there—that if they cannot catch them in this forum topic today, then they can catch them in the "bar" tomorrow. That is necessary to support the reality that participants share a "present." As indicated previously, maintaining that flow requires some optimal combination of number of participants, task communication requirements, and participant responsivity. My guess is that at this point in our understanding of Teleland, identifying and maintaining that flow is much more an interpersonal art than a science or, perhaps, mostly good luck. We remember those courses in which the optimal levels were obtained, and we forget—and hopefully our students forgive us for—the courses that fell short!

In asynchronous ecologies, distractions from texture or interactivity can inhibit the sense of presence. Intrusions from bosses or coworkers at the office or from spouses or children at home can force Teleland back into a distant reality. Even in an ecology that is based on asynchronous technologies, it can be tempting—but often dangerous—to provide supplementary synchronous ones. For example, if a given participant is not responding quickly to a forum posting, then there can be the temptation to actually telephone. But if the phone rings and rings and rings, or if he or she is there but busy with other things, then the illusion of sharing presence in a course reality can be shattered. The difficulty of trying to use the phone (or other synchronous technologies) to supplement asynchronous technologies can have an impact on presence analogous to the earlier mentioned distracting effect of pushing buttons to sequence audio input in synchronous ecologies.

Asynchronous ecologies place a greater burden on psychologically constructing a broadened sense of place than on being provided with a media-enhanced awareness of one. Developing and/or maintaining a sense of presence in asynchronous ecologies may then require greater sustained effort and, thus, motivation on the part of participants. Although there may be several motives for participants to take such courses, the meaningfulness of either the message (the course content) or the medium (distance education) to professional goals is likely to be key to nurturing presence. In other words, in synchronous ecologies, presence may be high or not based primarily on the quality of the visual/auditory display, distractions, or interactions without much effort required on the part of participants. In fact, if similarities to my own work on presence in "real" strange lands hold true, then focusing attention on *having presence* may have the contrary effect of dissipating it. But in asynchronous ecologies, such effort may be required; it is an ecology that does not "naturally" produce a sense of presence, so it must be constructed and nurtured—with care.

Finally, in asynchronous course ecologies, our rich imaginations are by necessity prompted to paint images of people, places, and events beyond the immediate ones. The sense of presence thus created may well surpass that achieved in synchronous ecologies, which rely so significantly on the image quality and transparency of the support technology—both still somewhat problematic in most courses in Teleland today. Our minds are still better than our monitors!

So Where Are We, Really?

Sense of presence, remote presence, telepresence, and *virtual presence* all are terms referred to in this chapter, all with related but differential meanings. Biocca (1997) says,

> The compelling sense of presence in virtual environments is unstable. At best it is fleeting. Like a voice interrupting a daydream in the imaginal environment, presence in the virtual environment can be interrupted by sensory cues from the physical environment and imperfections in the interface. At one point in time, users can be said to feel as if they are physically present in only one of three places: the *physical environment*, the *virtual environment*, or the *imaginal environment*. (pp. 15-16)

It appears to me that the chief concern in synchronous course ecologies is telepresence or remote presence in the sense that has evolved in research on teleoperator systems. Much remains to be learned, however, especially in how different types of tasks in classrooms affect presence and its antecedents.

In *asynchronous* ecologies, however, the state of consciousness appears more akin to virtual presence or a sense of being present in a place that isn't. But there is a place! On closer examination, a sense of presence in asynchronous ecologies may actually be something like that "old" unmediated (recall that it is the *mind* and not the *media* that appears critical here) sense of presence in strange lands akin to travel abroad. Only it is a very strange land indeed; it is here, there, there, and there. The tentacles of the immediate present extend from the here and now to several "there's" and "then's." It is like expanding a sense of presence to include many selected distal places and times. As Mantovani and Riva (1999) state, "The validity of presence does not consist of simply reproducing the conditions of physical presence but in constructing environments in which *actors may function in an ecologically valid way*" (p. 545, italics added). That is, our presence is where we interact, not necessarily where we physically are!

In today's world, we in fact need to maintain *multiple presences*. As Lipnack and Stamps (2000) stress, "In cyberspace, people do not have to desert old places in order to access new ones. You can simultaneously be in numerous online places, joining new groups while weaning yourself from old ones" (p. 105). Similarly, Kaltenbrunner and Huxor (2000) note that online collaboration requires the following: "One has *a variety of presences*. One can be both in a physical office and engaged in a telephone conversation. In this situation, where is one's presence? It seems to be in both places at once" (p. 2, italics added). Certainly, distance education is centered on just that kind of collaborative work. Both teachers and students need to maintain multiple presences in a variety of courses, teams, and activities—both face-to-face and dispersed. To be optimally successful, then, any given virtual classroom must be "competitive" in nurturing its share of our presence in Teleland.

Appendix: Course Web Page With Topics Opening

Date	Author	Number	Title (replies)
09/15/98	gfontaine	8	bAbble's bAr
09/15/98	gfontaine	7	Project Development Phase #3
09/15/98	gfontaine	6	Project Critique #3
09/15/98	gfontaine	5	Project Development Phase #2
09/15/98	gfontaine	4	Project Critique #2
09/15/98	gfontaine	3	Project Development Phase #1
09/15/98	gfontaine	2	Project Critique #1
09/15/98	gfontaine	1	Course syllabus

Web Page for Topic #8: bAbble's bAr

This is a place (a virtual place, that is, posted as a topic in our course forum) to address team concerns, suggestions, and so forth about our strategies for getting tasks completed effectively in this seminar. Or just a place to drop in for a chat with one another as we explore the study of inquiry and intervention together. While I regularly peruse other topics, I will stop by here most frequently for a break, new ideas, and some companionship. You all are invited to do likewise. We serve coffee, juice, wine, whiskey, shave ice, and cathode ray emissions depending on the time of day and your mood. There is always a dartboard in the corner to take shots at a photo of your current villain (bring your own photo).

Sample of Posted Topics in bAbbIe's bAr With Numbers of First-Order Replies

12/09/98	Aloha for now
12/07/98	RE: Thanks to all and appreciation for Gary's role
12/07/98	HAPPY HOLIDAYS TO ALL—and one last reference
12/06/98	Happy Holidays
12/05/98	Midnight "oil"
12/03/98	See you in February
12/02/98	To B2 from Jan
12/02/98	My turn
11/28/98	My time away
11/28/98	Sounds of silence . . .
11/25/98	Checking in with table mates and the rest of the group
11/24/98	BABBIE'S BAR
11/24/98	Beware of marauding turkeys
11/22/98	Snow!
11/20/98	An engagement!
11/18/98	BABBIE'S BAR
11/18/98	Can't see the meteors for the rain!
11/17/98	And more rain!
11/15/98	Out of touch
11/13/98	NAWLIN'S—BABBIE'S BAR
11/10/98	Suggested reading for organizational change
11/09/98	Pour me a strong one
11/06/98	Aloha Friday
11/04/98	Rain and more rain!
11/02/98	Coffee please
10/30/98	Halloween
10/28/98	BABBIE'S BAR
10/24/98	Variables of all kinds
10/24/98	Am I understanding what "variable" means in the context of research methodology
10/24/98	We're always open
10/19/98	Muggy Mondays
10/17/98	Greetings—and I beg your indulgence . . .
10/15/98	Wow!

10/14/98	Hey Table A, I haven't forgotten you!
10/13/98	Breakfast in the bar
10/11/98	Change and/or spirituality
10/10/98	HELP!!
10/09/98	Aloha Friday
10/07/98	Just a reminder!
10/07/98	Critique #1 comments and such
10/06/98	Clarification on Phase 1 assignment
10/05/98	Greetings from . . .
10/04/98	B2 to front and back tables re: assignments
10/04/98	Time for a joke?
10/04/98	Greetings from sunny Arizona . . .
10/03/98	Off-line Part Deux
10/02/98	Off-Line
09/30/98	Back in Honolulu
09/19/98	Welcome

References

Anderson, J., Ashraf, N., Douther, C., & Jack, M. (2000, March). *A participatory design study of user requirements for a shared virtual meeting space.* Paper presented at the Third International Workshop on Presence, Delft, Netherlands.

Babbie, E. (1998). *The practice of social research.* Belmont, CA: Wadsworth.

Biocca, F. (1997). The "Cyborg's Dilemma": Progressive embodiment in virtual environments. *Journal of Computer-Mediated Communication, 3*(2) [Online]. Available: http://jcmc.huji.ac.il/vol3/issue2/

Buxton, W. (1997). Living in augmented reality: Ubiquitous media and reactive environments. In K. Finn, A. Sellen, & S. Wilber (Eds.), *Video mediated communication* (pp. 363-384). Mahwah, NJ: Lawrence Erlbaum.

Casmir, F. L. (1993). Third culture building: A paradigm shift for international and intercultural communication. In S. A. Deetz (Ed.), *Communication yearbook 16* (pp. 407-428). Newbury Park, CA: Sage.

Couch, C. J. (1989). *Social processes and relationships: A formal approach.* New York: General Hall.

Ditlea, S. (1990, November). Inside artificial reality. *PC/Computing,* pp. 95-102.

Ditton, T. B. (1997). *The unintentional blending of direct experience and mediated experience: The role of enhanced versus limited television presentation.* Unpublished doctoral dissertation, Temple University.

Durlach, N., & Slater, M. (1998). Presence in shared virtual environments and virtual togetherness. *Presence: Teleoperators and Virtual Environments, 9,* 214-217.

Fencott, P. C. (1999, January). *Presence and the content of virtual environments.* Extended abstract presented at the Second International Workshop on Presence, Essex, UK.

Fontaine, G. (1989). *Managing international assignments: The strategy for success.* Englewood Cliffs, NJ: Prentice Hall.

Fontaine, G. (1993). The experience of a sense of presence in intercultural and international encounters. *Presence: Teleoperators and Virtual Environments, 1*(4), 1-9.

Fontaine, G. (1997). *Successfully meeting the three challenges of all international assignments.* Unpublished manuscript, Department of Communication, University of Hawaii. Available: www2.hawaii.edu/~fontaine/manbkweb.html

Fontaine, G. (2000). Skills for successful international assignments to, from, and within Asia and the Pacific: Implications for preparation, support, and training. *Management Decisions, 35,* 635-647.

Frecon, E. (1998, September). Actively supporting collaborative work. *ACCENTS Common European Newsletter* [Online]. Available: www.esat.kuleuven.ac.be/~konijn/accents8.html (Special issue on telepresence and shared virtual environments)

Gilkey, R. H., & Weisenberger, J. M. (1995). The sense of presence for the suddenly deafened adult: Implications for virtual environments. *Presence: Teleoperators and Virtual Environments, 4,* 364-386.

Gristock, J. J. (1998). *Organizational virtuality.* Paper presented at British Telecom Presence Workshop, Ipswich, UK. Available: www.cs.ucl.ac.uk/staff/m.slater/btworkshop/

Heeter, C. (1995). Communication research on consumer VR. In F. Biocca & M. R. Levy (Eds.), *Communication in the age of virtual reality* (pp. 191-218). Hillsdale, NJ: Lawrence Erlbaum.

Held, R. M., & Durlach, N. I. (1992). Telepresence. *Presence: Teleoperators and Virtual Environments, 1*(1), 109-112.

Hendrix, C., & Barfield, W. (1996). Presence within virtual environments as a function of visual display parameters. *Presence: Teleoperators and Virtual Environments, 5,* 290-301.

Ho, C., Basdogan, C., Slater, M., Durlach, N., & Srinivasan, M. A. (1998). *An experiment on the influence of haptic communication on the sense of being together.* Paper presented at the British Telecom Presence Workshop, Ipswich, UK.

Hofner-Saphiere, D. M. (1996). Productive behaviors of global business teams. *International Journal of Intercultural Relations, 20*(2), 227-259.

Kaltenbrunner, M. F. H., & Huxor, A. (2000, March). *Multiple presence through auditory bots in virtual environments.* Paper presented at the Third International Workshop on Presence, Delft, Netherlands. Available: http://yuri.at/marvin/delft/

Kim, T. (1996). *Effects of presence on memory and persuasion.* Unpublished doctoral dissertation, University of North Carolina.

Kimmel, P. R. (1989). *International negotiation and intercultural exploration: Toward cultural understanding.* Washington, DC: U.S. Institute of Peace.

Lipnack, J., & Stamps, J. (2000). *Virtual teams: People working across boundaries with technology.* New York: John Wiley.

Lombard, M., & Ditton, T. (1997). At the heart of it all: The concept of telepresence. *Journal of Computer-Mediated Communication, 3*(2), 1-39.

Lombard, M., Grabe, M. E., Reich, R. D., Campanella, C. M., & Ditton, T. B. (1995). *Big TVs, little TVs: The role of screen size in viewer responses to point-of-view movement*. Paper presented at the annual conference of the International Communication Association, Albuquerque, NM.

Mania, K., & Chalmers, A. (2000, March). *A user-centered methodology for investigating presence and task performance*. Paper presented at the Third International Workshop on Presence, Delft, Netherlands.

Mantovani, G., & Riva, G. (1999). Real presence: How different ontologies generate different criteria for presence, telepresence, and virtual presence. *Presence: Teleoperators and Virtual Environments, 8,* 538-548.

McGreevy, M. W. (1994). *An ethnographic object-oriented analysis of explorer presence in a volcanic terrain environment* (NASA TM-108823). Unpublished manuscript, Ames Research Center, Moffett Field, CA.

O'Hara-Devereaux, M., & Johansen, R. (1994). *Global work: Bridging distance, culture, and time*. San Francisco: Jossey-Bass.

Pausch, R., Shackelford, M. A., & Proffitt, D. (1993). A user study comparing head-mounted and stationary displays. In *Proceedings of the IEEE Symposium on Research Frontiers in Virtual Reality*. San Jose, CA. [Online]. Available: www.cs.cmu.edu/~stage3/publications/93/conferences/ IEEEsymposiumOnResearchFrontiersInVR/handVsHeadUserStudy/paper.html

Rauthenberg, S., Kauff, P., & Graffunder, A. (2000, March). *A realtime implementation of a shared virtual environment system using today's consumer technology in connection with the MPEG-4 standard*. Paper presented at the Third International Workshop on Presence, Delft, Netherlands.

Rubin, A. L. (2000). *The power of silence: Using technology to create free structure in organizations*. Unpublished master's thesis, Fielding Graduate Institute.

Schubert, T., Friedmann, F., & Regenbrecht, H. (1999, January). *Decomposing the sense of presence: Factor analytic insights*. Extended abstract presented at the Second International Workshop on Presence, Essex, UK.

Sheridan, T. B. (1992). Musings on telepresence and virtual presence. *Presence: Teleoperators and Virtual Environments, 1*(1), 120-126.

Short, J., Williams, E., & Christie, B. (1976). *The social psychology of telecommunications*. New York: John Wiley.

Steed, A., & Slater, M. (1998, September). Studies of the behaviour of small groups of users in CVEs. *ACCENTS Common European Newsletter*. (Special issue on telepresence and shared virtual environments)

Tammelin, M. (1998). From telepresence to social presence: The role of presence in a network-based learning environment. In S. Tella (Ed.), *Aspects of media education: Strategic imperatives in the information age*. Helsinki, Finland: University of Helsinki, Media Education Centre.

Thie, S., & van Wijk, J. (1998). *A general theory on presence: Experimental evaluation of social virtual presence in a decision making task*. Paper presented at the British Telecom Presence Workshop, Ipswich, UK.

Uttal, W. R. (1989, December). Teleoperators. *Scientific American*, pp. 124-129.

Waterworth, E. L., & Waterworth, J. A. (2000, March). *Using a telescope in the cave: Presence and absence in educational VR*. Paper presented at the Third International Workshop on Presence, Delft, Netherlands.

Welch, R. (1992, February). *Human adaptation to virtual environments and teleoperator systems*. Paper presented at the Psychology Colloquium series, University of Hawaii.

Welch, R. B., Blackmon, T. T., Liu, A., Mellers, B. A., & Stark, L. W. (1996). The effects of pictorial realism, delay of visual feedback, and observer interactivity on the subjective sense of presence. *Presence: Teleoperators and Virtual Environments, 5,* 274-289.

Whitelock, D., Romano, D., Jelfs, A., & Brna, P. (in press). Perfect presence: What does this mean for the design of virtual learning environments? *Education and Information Technologies.* (Special issue on virtual reality in education)

Witmer, B. G., & Singer, M. J. (1998). Measuring presence in virtual environments: A presence questionnaire. *Presence: Teleoperators and Virtual Environments, 7,* 225-240.

Chapter 3

Critical Dialogue Online

Personas, Covenants, and Candlepower

Barclay Hudson

Critical thinking is fundamental to serious graduate work, and rarely is it a solitary endeavor. In fact, some would argue that the very basis of thinking is rooted in dialogue, drawing on a socially constructed context to endow ideas with meaning. Statements evolve in response to others' ideas and are framed in anticipation of others' reactions. Bakhtin (1981) goes so far as to say that language, social relationships, and even consciousness are based on "dialogic" processes. "To live means to participate in dialogue" (Bakhtin, 1984, p. 293).

Critical Thinking: The Challenge of Taking It Online

Critical dialogue is not the same in a virtual classroom as it is in a Greek marketplace. The online environment poses special challenges and opportunities, and that is what this chapter aims to address. At its best, critical dialogue can engage people in a give-and-take of intense discussion that can break people away from preconceptions and transform their sense of relation to each other. On the other hand, criticism written online can come across as particularly harsh when unmoderated by voice inflections or gestures. Students often don't have the pedagogical skills for constructive criticism, a problem even for seasoned instructors. The result can be a cautious habit of avoiding deep engagement and a retreat into shallow politeness.

The first part of this chapter provides an overview of "critical dialogue," the role it plays in a learning community, and some of the limits and special challenges posed by the online environment. I mention seven elements of critical dialogue—most of them having a role in distance learning, but some calling for special and unusual forms of online communication. The rest of the chapter focuses on practical ways to foster critical dialogue using three illustrative devices that are very different but complementary. These devices—personas, covenants, and candlepower—are included here because they can be implemented without extensive preparation or special skills. They can be used independently, but they are also synergistic, invoking different elements of critical dialogue that are themselves mutually reinforcing.

Critical Dialogue: Seven Variations on a Theme

Dialogue consists of a shared exploration of thought processes that lie behind ideas, looking not just at the logic and data in isolation but also at the human needs and relationships that underlie the issues at hand (Bohm, 1996, pp. 6-7). Critical dialogue is more problematic, having many definitions and connotations and often getting lost in unproductive debates about its own ground rules, with some group members looking for shared assumptions as a point of departure and others engaging in "critical analysis" of those assumptions from the very start.

"Dialogue analysis" has emerged as a field of its own, beginning during the 1970s, drawing on ethnographics, linguistics, psychology, logic, sociology, philosophy, and even artificial intelligence (Schwitalla, 1994). Taking an interdisciplinary perspective, Weigard (1994) concludes that dialogue becomes especially interesting and fruitful when there is a switch in the implicit rules, a rupture in habitual assumptions, through the introduction of new voices bringing new "modalities" such as irony, pathos, humor, and exaggeration, or taking "time out to speak off the record" (pp. 29-30). These switches are inherent in the devices of "left-column" voices and personas, which I address shortly.

By considering various meanings of critical dialogue, we can make the ground rules clearer for each approach, telling people when we switch the rules and selecting the form of dialogue most suited for a particular purpose. As Cheyne and Tarulli (1999) emphasize, there are profoundly different traditions of dialogue that come into play depending on one's purposes, each of them illuminating different possibilities. So it is important to begin by asking, "What kind of dialogue is this?" I mention seven possibilities here.

1. *Personally directed feedback* is probably the most common version and the first that comes to mind. The very word *critical* has overtones of skepticism and intimidation. Still, there are techniques that can greatly improve feedback, both in its substance and in the way people experience it. LaPelle (1997) makes the case that under the right conditions, people can thrive on performance evaluations. Later in the chapter, I describe some techniques and settings that support constructive critical feedback.

2. *Critical analysis* is typically addressed to the work of third parties outside of the dialogue itself, as in "literary criticism" or the work of music critics and political commentators. The tone can be nasty or nice, but the student can feel relatively safe because the criticism is directed principally at someone else (e.g., Shakespeare, Dewey). Nevertheless, the student is never off the hook for self-examination because reflective critical thinking involves scrutiny not only of others' arguments but also of one's own reasoning and assumptions.

3. *Critical thinking* can mean several things—a mind-set of scientific rigor (Feynman, 1988, 1998; Shapiro & Hughes, 1997, pp. 5-8), or simply systematic reasoning (Cederblom & Paulsen, 2001). It has been described as "asking the right question" (Browne & Keeley, 2001) but also as "solving the right problem" (Mitroff, 1998). Some authors look at critical thinking as a way of getting outside the box of conventional ideas (Andolina, 2001; Bassham, 2001; Ruggiero, 2001) or as a deliberate mind-set of "exploratory consciousness" (Peterson, 1998). Others see it as "reflective judgment" and "intellectual growth" (King & Kitchener, 1994), which can be extended to the idea of "meta-learning" or learning how to learn. Some authors treat critical thinking more narrowly as a technique of debate (Missimer, 1995; Reinard, 1991; Waller, 2001; Warnick & Inch, 1994). But Bohm (1996) considers this inappropriate, contrasting dialogue (a shared search for meaning) with the more adversarial process of debate or "discussion"—a word whose root meaning is to "cut apart" or dissect, lifting things out of context for sake of argument, with appeal to higher reason and authority.

4. *Critical theory* goes to the deeper context of the dialogue—the cultural, political, and economic framework that sets the stage. Here, language is seen to be inescapably ideological, shaping the way people think (Bakhtin, 1981). The focus is a critique of society, but with special attention to psychological and cultural challenges facing the very process of dialogue (Berry, 1990; Bodi, 1988; Ellul, 1954/1964; Roszak, 1972, 1992). In this sense, dialogue involves a "double-loop" narrative (Argyris, 1999, pp. 67-90), which is self-reflective and self-critical. Whether the starting point is critical theory, deconstructivism, or postmodernism, the dialogue itself addresses the way in which social discourse constructs the perception of reality.

5. *Dialectical theory* is a particular kind of critical theory, both a method of inquiry and a description of social processes. It often invokes a grand theory of how things work and can be prone to excluding other methods and other worldviews (Hindery, 2001). Its strength, as a form of critical dialogue, comes from always saying "Consider the opposite" because it emphasizes the polarities and evolution of oppositions, the confrontation of thesis and antithesis, arriving at synthesis (Isaacs, 1999, p. 50). This can take many forms such as Hegelian or Marxist theories or Eastern worldviews, for example, as illustrated by the God/Goddess Shiva, who is inseparably both the Creator and the Destroyer. The problem is how to keep an open mind while employing such theories because they are built on tightly interlocked methods, assumptions, conclusions, and social agendas. This conceptual lumpiness can constrain open dialogue, which of course would be true of other highly elaborated worldviews or paradigms (Kuhn, 1962).

6. In terms of *dialogue as action,* the ability to speak with an authentic "voice" depends on the clarity of one's identity in the context of practical choices of action available, much as a theatrical troupe will create a particular stage setting and linguistic repertoire and set of roles that delimit the possibilities of character development in a play (Lawrence & Phillips, 1998). The *action* basis of critical inquiry can be traced back to Bacon's 17th-century insistence on empirical investigation and inductive science, challenging the a priori method of medieval scholasticism. More recently, we have social experimentation, ranging from controlled experiments such as the Hawthorne plant studies on worker productivity to social reforms and "action research," putting heavier emphases on community participation and dialogue as integral to the research (Coghlan & Brannick, 2001; Franklin, 1999; Sherman & Torbert, 2000; Szecsy, 1995; Toulmin & Gustavsen, 1996). The tradition of participatory action research includes early work by Kurt Lewin, Donald Schön, and Chris Argyris (Argyris, Putnam, & Smith, 1985; Lewin, 1946/1999; Schön, 1983). William Torbert's "action inquiry" is one of the latest and most compelling theories in this tradition; it goes beyond Argyris's notion of single-loop learning (simple feedback and correction) and double-loop learning (changes in models of reality and strategies and desired outcomes) to a third level—personal transformation (Fisher, Rooke, & Torbert, 2000; Franklin, 1999, p. 41). The goal is not just awareness per se but also testing of awareness in new experience. As Bailie (1995, p. 49) puts it, awareness is not sufficient unless it engages the will to act.

7. Regarding *critical consciousness, social justice, and democratic structures,* Bailie (1995) identifies "critical communication scholarship" as a distinct form of dialogic inquiry in which institutions and human relationships are examined in terms of "history, power, and struggle" (p. 33). Here, the goal is to emancipate language through greater diversity of voices and

through experience-based storytelling that can challenge the abstractions of conventional beliefs or academic language. This resonates with Freire's (1981) view of education as "conscientization" aimed at students' development of a capacity to perceive "social, political, and economic contradictions and to take action against the oppressive elements of reality" (p. 19). There is some very eloquent writing on the importance of language for liberationist causes (Greenwood & Levin, 1998; Horton, 1998; Rahman, 1993), yet this is not just an intellectual tradition but rather a history of sustained social experimentation, as seen in the Mondragon cooperatives in Spain (Morrison, 1991), the micro loans in Bangladesh (Yunus, 2001), and the New Deal cooperatives founded by the Agricultural Resettlement Administration (Banfield, 1951; Duggan, 1937).

At this point, I want to bring the discussion of critical dialogue back into the context of adult learning and begin by suggesting that all seven versions of critical dialogue just listed have direct application to the distinctive needs of adult learning online as compared with instruction of children in a traditional classroom.

Critical Dialogue and Andragogy: The Different World of Adult Learning

The link between critical dialogue and adult learning has been constructed in some detail by Malcolm Knowles, who has been a chief proponent of "andragogic" learning, or learning designed specifically for adults, as distinct from child-directed pedagogy. Knowles (1978) points out that the term "andragogy" was first coined in 1833 by a German grammar school teacher, Alexander Kapp. Subsequent 19th-century references were mostly in opposition to Kapp's ideas, but in 1921 they resurfaced at the Academy of Labor in Frankfort, Germany, and slowly gained strength in Europe until 1966, when the University of Amsterdam established a doctorate in "andragogues." During the late 1970s, Knowles brought the concept to the United States (Knowles, 1978). At about that time, adult learning programs took on a new impetus and new roles in the context of social liberation movements, both in the United States (e.g., at the Highlander Folk School [Collyer, 1996, pp. 45-55; Horton, 1998]) and overseas, in the ideas of educators such as Paolo Freire, who emphasized that learning involves being challenged and socially engaged, not just being filled as an unconscious vessel (Freire, 1981).

But Knowles (1978) also points out that the basic premises of andragogy apply to the great teachers of ancient history—Lao Tzu and Confucius in China, the Hebrew prophets, Aristotle, Socrates, Plato, Euclid, Cicero, and Quintilian—emphasizing that education is a process of discovery by the learner, involving learning by doing and observation, and is grounded in civil life as well as in verbal skills as a basis for dialogue and critical analysis.

Knowles relates how these traditions were overturned with the establishment of monastic schools during the 7th century. Reading became focused on rote learning and transcription of sacred literature. Emphasis turned to obedience, efficiency, and unquestioning adherence to the orthodox faith as taught by a priesthood. The concept of learning from one's own experience, through engagement with the world at large, came to be seen as "pagan" and a threat to approved ideas—a form of learning that became not only neglected but even forbidden (p. 54). This monastic tradition is reflected even in today's schools, where students are not encouraged to learn from dialogue among themselves but instead are encouraged to derive their education from the authority of teachers and books in a context where talking among themselves is discouraged.

Premonastic forms of andragogy can be found in Native American traditions of dialogue, which placed great emphasis on learning from observation of the natural environment, on speaking skills, on absence of literature-based authority, and on debate of social issues in open councils. Inter-tribal conflicts were not uncommon, but the forms of council for mediation were fairly consistent across North America, and part of this tradition was a respect for differences in beliefs (Bierhorst, 1974; Johansen, 1982; Mander, 1991, chap. 12).

Critical Dialogue Online: Protecting the Online Psyche

Critical dialogue online can have the effect of bruising participants' egos. Online commentary leaves its trail in a lasting writing record, like that of a court reporter, and if differences of opinion arise the vague presence of an online forum audience can seem like a jury weighing an accusation. This oversensitivity may seem irrational and is not typical of most situations, but it is more likely to arise where personal relationships are new and undefined, before group expectations and "culture" have congealed, or where the purposes and ground rules of the forum are vague. In practice, of course, most critical dialogue is not intended as personal criticism, yet it seems widely recognized that online critique tends to come across as relatively harsh in computer-mediated communications when compared with face-to-face situations that can be softened by visible cues and inflections (Brookfield, 1987, pp. 22-23; Porter, 1996, p. xi). In graduate seminars, moreover, a great deal of feedback comes from other students, who often lack the experienced teaching skills to provide critical feedback in a way that feels comfortable to the "target" audience. Even in a conventional setting, graduate students can feel deeply hurt by critique, no matter how appropriate and sensitive the instructor's approach.

The sharpness of online criticism is not just from a lack of visual and vocal "buffering" to soften the message. Most of us have discovered that online communication is far from a "flat" medium (Brown, 1998). In fact, it can be a very powerful medium for conveying subtexts. Usually, the subtexts are intentional, and most people seem to naturally develop a repertoire of skills in conveying humor, emotion, caring, poetic allusions, multiple meanings, and richness of personal experience expressed in concise symbolic references—forms of expression that are usually quite absent from traditional academic analysis. By the same token, however, the power of conveying intended messages brings with it the power to convey unintended ones. Most people have had the experience of being "burned" online. And once burned, twice shy, so people tend to err on the side of being self-consciously supportive of each other rather than risk conveying hurtful remarks in the course of critical dialogue.

From his work at Harvard University on neuropsychology, Peterson (1998) sees the brain as having two distinct functional systems: one that handles the things we understand and are comfortable with and the other that deals with the things we do not understand. The unknown represents chaos, vulnerability, and disruption. To protect us from the intense discomfort of the unknown, people invent a structure of artifacts, drawn from culture and beliefs, that correspond to a form of "territoriality" that needs to be defended against the chaos beyond the walls. Peterson observes, "Because people are capable of abstraction, the territories we defend can become abstract. Belief systems—the familiar 'abstract territories' we inhabit—literally regulate our emotions. When a threat arises to a key belief, the emotional consequences can be devastating" (quoted in Lambert, 1998, p. 20). When thoughtless comments are added to the mix, that possibility of "emotional devastation" becomes more immanent. One doctoral student reflected on his experience with virtual teams:

> Usually I am amazed at how well I can coordinate with teammates while separated by so much time and distance. . . . [But] occasionally I am dismayed at how even well-intended communications can bring a chain of reaction and overreaction that seems to bring out the worst in all involved and leave team members bewildered and hurt and work unattended. (Bonnevier, 1999, p. 5)

Bonnevier (1999) sees this as a reciprocal process, with small changes in the tone of the dialogue bringing out different personality aspects (or "selves") of each group member that feed back into the tone of the group as a whole—a process that he describes in terms of "the social construction of the self in virtual teams."

I began work on this chapter focused on the problem of how to avoid the sting of critical dialogue given that online forums somehow seem to magnify people's sensitivities. My initial goal was to find "cruelty-free" methods of online dialogue without losing the rigor of constructive criticism and critical analysis. The deeper I looked into the problem, however, the more I began to think that this was the wrong problem to attack. First, although the problem of distress from criticism is very real, it arises quite rarely, especially in a community of adult learners. Second, the difficult and painful character of critical dialogue may be unavoidable for achieving understanding in ways that call for a reevaluation of oneself and a letting go of protective illusions or complacency. Sometimes, painful realizations just cannot emerge with sugar coating.

As I began to monitor my own online courses for clues, it became clearer that the more serious problem of criticism was not the level of pain but rather the opposite difficulty, which lies in people's avoidance of confrontation through polite exchange. Students themselves have pointed this out:

> It's very tough to provide constructive feedback in this [online] type of forum because you have no idea how the person on the other end will receive the feedback. [But] when I think back about the feedback I've received, . . . it's been when people push me a little bit . . . that really adds value. (J. Shulkin, Fielding Graduate Institute forum posting, May 4, 1999)

So the main problem becomes one of not avoiding all pain but rather managing it better in a way that allows people to remain fully engaged in terms of both personal interaction and in-depth critical thinking. The idea is not to avoid the strain but rather to "feel comfortable with discomfort" at a level controlled by the student and not just by the instructor. "Flaming" is always a possibility, but there are fairly strong inhibitions against emotional outbursts in a context where the participants are adults and (in most cases) experienced professionals who have had practice in dealing with difficult clients and bosses. Moreover, remarks are almost never made anonymously; instead, they are made as part of a group. Especially important, the asynchronous format allows time for counting to 10 and for remembering the rules of "netiquette." Much depends on deliberate attention to confrontation as a "learning experience" rather than as a "fight or flight" situation.

Online learning also tends to be more sensitive to the needs of cross-cultural understanding—not just making oneself understood but taking the extra step of guarding against misunderstandings. At the Fielding Graduate Institute, we are dealing with adult learners from around the world—Hong Kong, Brussels, South Africa, Alaska, and Australia, to mention a few locations—all mature adults and a good mix of professionals spanning the private, public, and nonprofit sectors. Faculty are similarly distributed around the world. Our courses are explicitly designed to include issues of "decentralized intelligence," individual differences, diversity in groups, and structural inequalities that arise in a globalized economy. We attempt to address most topics from these multiple perspectives. And we often probe the depth of cultural and intellectual confrontations and contradictions, beyond the simple aim of fostering balance within diversity.

As adults, most of these students have the self-confidence to work constructively in a group without the undergraduate's tendency to sometimes slip into strident tones as part of establishing an identity. Many have had long exposure to alternative cultures and varied work environments. Their aim is not simply to continue academic study as an extension of college but to challenge conventional thinking in a setting that supports that effort. They seek critical learning and are impatient with academic platitudes. They enter graduate work in mid-career for the opportunity of grappling openly and candidly with issues that cannot be addressed elsewhere, including the workplace.

Some Devices for Critical Dialogue Online: Personas, Covenants, and Candlepower

The rest of this chapter is aimed at suggesting some specific practical devices to promote critical dialogue online in ways that also protect against the peculiar harshness of online confrontation. All of the devices are designed for asynchronous forms of communication as practiced in the online forums at Fielding. Comments and responses are posted sequentially in a text-based forum, allowing everyone random access to multiple topics and threads of dialogue that may be unfolding simultaneously and staying visible over the entire 11-week course. Each forum typically has about a dozen participants. These courses have been designed from scratch for online critical dialogue and reflect several years of sharing best practices with colleagues. Each of these devices draws on theory from literature and Web documents. Primarily, however, they stem from my own experience and that of other faculty in the master's program in organizational management at Fielding.

Next, I quickly summarize the three devices I have in mind and then go into more detail:

1. First is the use of "personas" that can give voice to opinions and perspectives that are otherwise silenced. Both students and faculty can take these character roles, sometimes in prestructured ways and other times spontaneously. There are several variations, including the use of left-column voices. Their effect is to establish a constructive tone for dialogue—a lightened mood for dealing with serious issues, allowing alternative views to be expressed in a way that feels separated from person-to-person attack and defense.

2. The second device involves explicit prior agreements on the scope and methods of inquiry—a "covenant" for critical dialogue that is not unique to online pedagogy but is especially important for groups working in this context. Covenants are vital because the best dialogue and the best criticism penetrate deeply into not just the minds but also the feelings of those engaged. Participants make themselves vulnerable to new ideas and to each other, and this can result in painful encounters—not just as an occasional side effect but embedded in the most productive results of the process. The goal then becomes

not painless inquiry but rather the capacity to enter the dialogue willingly, with a certain amount of personal control over the process, allowing a greater measure of "resilient vulnerability."

3. A third factor is the enhancement of "candlepower," a term I use to describe the surprising intensity, personal depth, and intimacy that can arise in an online forum. In essence, one is working in the dark, with attention highly focused—and people highly engaged—within a small patch of light where the narrative takes place. In asynchronous dialogue, words linger, thoughts are not interrupted, and errors of spontaneity are forgiven by the chance for rewrite. The very limitations of a purely text-based forum—its inability to command instant feedback, to touch all of the senses, and/or to replicate traditional classroom pedagogies—far from being a drawback, turn out to be a great advantage.

The rest of this chapter focuses on the three devices in turn. Each device contributes to all of the several facets of critical dialogue just mentioned. All involve "storytelling" in the sense of personal involvement, evocation, and setting of context. They all involve a departure from business as usual, a sense of risk taking, and a quality of speaking off the record in exploring ways to get outside the box. Each can be used independently and implemented without much advance preparation or special software besides the bulletin board format of an asynchronous forum.

On the other hand, the three devices differ in some important respects that make them complementary. These differences are summarized in Table 3.1.

Personas for Online Critical Analysis

Use of personas for critical dialogue is an exercise in role-playing. A persona is sometimes defined as a "dramatic, fictional, or historical character." But real people, too, carry around various personas within them—some intentional, some unconscious, and occasionally in conflict. An adult student especially has a keen appreciation of carrying around several roles at once, with multiple involvements as student, team partner, family member, economic provider, boss, employee, and colleague.

Even in the same role, one's persona changes in reaction to personalities of others engaged. As Bonnevier (1999) notes,

> I have noticed [in] online communications that different situations and different senders bring out different people in me. E-mail from one boss calls out a reflective and supportive me. E-mail from my other boss calls out a to-the-point, bottom-line guy. From my wife—a playful, can't wait to get home me.

TABLE 3.1 Comparison of Devices to Promote Critical Dialogue Online

	Personas	*Covenants*	*Candlepower*
Application	One assignment or perhaps several involving rotating roles	Single intensive event, usually face-to-face at start of program	Spontaneous moments in evolution of discussion threads
Role of instructor	Define roles to be played and basic scenario	Facilitate session or series of sessions	Set tone and act as model for deepening issues
Mood and tone	Playful, thoughtful, questioning, Socratic	Respectful, probing, supportive, celebratory	Evocative, self-revealing, a "dance of the mind"
Content and objectives	Attention to loaded issues such as diversity and stakeholder perspectives; cross-culturalism; interplay of personality, organizational role, culture, and technology	Trust and resiliency, addressing fears; norms on feedback, responsibilities, and sensitivities; crises as opportunities; willingness to feel "comfortable with discomfort"	Usually tangential to formal assignments; emotional literacy; authenticity; self-discovery; finding one's voice; spontaneous, synergistic creativity
Getting outside the box	Standing in another's shoes; left-column voices; role-playing allowing many degrees of freedom for evolution of dialogue; humor	Removing blockages to trust; clarity of group identity, distinct from other groups and norms	Leaving room for mystery; dialogue via unspoken subtext; asynchronous engagement at any inspired moment
Safety net elements	Role-playing, not taking criticism personally; humor.	Support for risk-taking failures (not just success); posting of norms (always in view online); clarity about version of "critical dialogue" in play	Informality; absence of judgment

Some senders start a resistant, rather unsympathetic response in me even before I read their message ("Oh no, not him/her again"). Or a cautious me ("Hmmmm—they didn't answer my last question—wonder why"). (p. 5)

Bonnevier finds that working with personas has increased his sensitivity to these different aspects of his own personality, the different forms of resourcefulness they each bring to the table, and their inherent limitations.

The persona devices mentioned here are illustrative only, but they are selected with the aim of requiring little advance preparation or pedagogical baggage. They draw out student creativity on a "minimalist" stage, avoiding elaborate construction of scenarios. Use of personas in my own courses takes place primarily in the setting of an 11-week course dealing with organizational structures and cross-cultural settings. It addresses cross-national differences (Trompenaars, 1994) but also issues of cultural diversity *within* organizations (Collins & Porras, 1994/1997; Morgan, 1986; Schein, 1992). Thus, students are primed to think in terms of multiple perspectives for critical analysis and to recognize the tug between the need for cultural alignment and the need for diversity. The course is divided into several phases, each phase typically revolving around one of the core readings. During the first week of each phase, 2 or 3 students (from a group of 6 to 10) independently post a summary critique of the same book or article, including their own critical evaluations. During the following week, the remaining students post a criticism of both the reading and of the earlier book reviews posted by their partners.

These follow-up critiques are made in the voice of an assigned persona residing in a vaguely defined country—say, Galitia—into which the group has been "parachuted" at the beginning of the course. One persona might be Khaldun, the Galitian minister of culture; Rinzai, the chief executive officer of a multinational corporation based in that country; Tallala, a rural cooperatives agent with a concern for preserving viable traditional economies and social structures; or Arafar, an investigative journalist and intellectual. These personas are predefined by the syllabus and remain constant, but students rotate from one role to the next as the course progresses from one phase to another. Importantly, the course syllabus provides only the barest (50- to 100-word) sketch of each persona and of the "host country" setting, with the rest being left for students to develop in ways that best address their own issues.

Students can take it from there with little other guidance. Occasional reminders may be needed to keep people from adding unnecessary detail and local color to a persona or host country setting; a simple sketch is sufficient as a frame for substantive issues. Critical thinking starts with the book reviews, then goes deeper in the next round of persona-based critiques, and then goes even deeper in the debriefing comments during the third week. In this final round, students usually revert to their own voices but sometimes stay in the voices of personas that have proven strong in articulating an issue.

A Variety of Functions Served by Personas

The use of personas adds to critical dialogue in a variety of ways that are mutually reinforcing. As a way of providing feedback, persona voices allow students to express critical ideas more forcefully and clearly, without apologies, and with less fear that the recipients will take the criticisms as ad hominem attacks. Speaking through a persona lets students give (and take) criticism with a more overt understanding of differences between the parties engaged. Effective criticism (and effective feedback) needs to be based on a mutual understanding of these differences, and the personas help to bring them into play on an explicit and conscious basis.

Role-playing also serves as a way of analyzing the readings (and other partners' book reviews) from multiple cultural and situational perspectives. By contrast, most academic critiques implicitly build on reflecting Western male academic and corporate world perspectives. Use of personas brings home the point (made often in the readings) that there is no one theory or framework of interpretation that applies to all situations. Rather, one needs to consider a spectrum of viewpoints reflecting not just diversity of cultural and organizational settings but also value premises, functional missions, and even personality traits.

Use of personas brings home another point about handling situations in the context of organizational management: You have to play the hand you're dealt. Students don't choose their role or the country into which they are parachuted for the course duration. They can question anything they want, but they need to become conscious of doing it "in context" of their culture, organizational setting, and career role. The use of personas forces attention to concrete situations as the basis for criticism, with discussion revolving around the pragmatic meaning of ideas for their impact on local communities (e.g., Galitia) and specific implications for personal action. Discussion does not get lost in conceptual models or broad and meaningless generalizations about, say, the benefits and costs of globalization. It directs attention to specific contingencies of problems and solutions.

In the role of persona, and charged with evaluating a particular situation (or text, concept, or technology), the student is led to a way of thinking that C. Wright Mills calls "the sociological imagination." It is an approach that stresses the interplay between history and biography, relating "the most impersonal and remote transformations" of the world at large to "the most intimate features of the human self and to see the relations between them" (Mills, 1959, p. 7). This focuses attention on the interplay between social structures that define public issues at large and people's direct experience of "personal troubles" within (p. 8). This contrasts with traditional forms of criticism that tend to separate ideas from their social context and history, based on a somewhat outdated view of objectivity that posits a "neutral" analyst separated from what is being observed.

Use of personas draws attention to the importance and power of language and specifically to the possibility of choosing different voices to open up different issues. Whereas most academic writing encourages a "neutral" language (discouraging the subjective voice beginning with "I"), the use of personas encourages ideas to be expressed in a more consciously acknowledged subjectivity, using a tone of voice that serves an aware intent. It reveals that each of us carries inside a repertoire of voices, each attuned to a particular role and attitude—but most of them preempted by academic formalism.

This personalized "voicing" of individual differences can end up creating a stronger sense of solidarity within the group (Bates, 1999). I suspect that comes from breaking down the unspoken concern of many groups: "Do I belong? Am I up to the standards? Am I going to put my foot in my mouth?"

Putting oneself in another's shoes can be unexpectedly self-revealing, tapping into thoughts and feelings from outside the normal academic subject matter. As one student said, "It is amazing how much you can learn about yourself when you're pretending to be someone else" (K. Caesar-Beaubien, Fielding forum posting, December 2, 1997). Another student reflected,

> I discovered a nasty little surprise about me. When I took on the persona of Tallala, I could easily imagine her. . . . But Makjubar meant nothing to me. I couldn't feel him, understand what he was interested in, or comfortably speak for him. I couldn't relate. This really got me thinking about my inter-action with real people. Do I subconsciously give value to some and not to others because of my ability to *relate* to them? Do I bring that to my inter-actions within my organizations? . . . This course has been different than I expected, and I really struggled with the personas. But that struggle may have been the part . . . that provided the greatest insight. (J. Post-Darnell, Fielding forum posting, April 27, 1999)

These remarks illustrate the importance of Bakhtin's insights into the importance of confrontation among different language frameworks or "heteroglossia." As Bakhtin (1995) sees it,

> Utterances acquire meaning only in dialogue, which is always situated in a social-cultural context where a multiplicity of different languages intersect (political, technical, literary, interpersonal, etc.). From this emerges a conception of personhood where *we author ourselves in dialogue with others and subject to the reinterpretations they give us.* (italics added)

The same happens at a more conscious level in exposures to other national cultures. As Hampden-Turner (1993) puts it,

> We talk about culture shock, but the shock may be strongest from seeing exposed and explicit and accepted and powerful in others what is suppressed or tacit or unconscious—but nevertheless deeply part of—our own culture. The shock of looking into a mirror after a life of no mirrors. (p. 2)

Use of personas is a way of agreeing to suspend the usual psychological and interpersonal baggage that goes with academic criticism. The effect is to shatter the monoculture (or monotheism) of acceptable academic ideas and demeanors, ridding the group's docility before an implicit standard. Short of "de-schooling society" (Ivan Illich's phrase), personas allow one to explore beyond academic conventions in addressing social issues.

Personas help to engage a playful element in social criticism, not just making it more fun but also making it more creative and less likely to set up defensive responses. This taps into the spirit of improvisational theater, which employs specific techniques for "making the other guy look good" and "seeing with big eyes" (Johnson, 1998). Some of the best persona responses start with a preface that reminds everyone of this half-serious, half-playful context. For example, one student began his critique with the comment,

> Folks, please go into this with your sense of humor intact and forgiveness in your hearts. It took me a while to begin thinking like this Arafar character, but when I got into it, well, he just took over before I even knew what was happening. My voice changed, my ears got pointy, and my fangs came out. There was no stopping it. HE wrote the commentary you are about to read. . . . I'll be myself again next week when we get into the debriefing comments, but until then, watch out for Arafar. He's scary, and I truly hate this character. P.S. to Karen: Arafar thinks you're American. I tried to tell him you were Canadian, but there's no reasoning with this guy. (paraphrased from J. Zimmerman, Fielding forum posting, October 14, 1997)

How easily do students adapt to the role of an assigned persona? I haven't done any systematic evaluation of this, but my impression is that only 1 or 2 out of 10 students in a group will feel somewhat uncomfortable with role-playing in the first round, but even that resistance is usually gone by the end of an 11-week course. As one student posted in the online café,

> Julia, You asked how it was to write in persona. Very strange! Tallala has taken this task to heart, while I seem to be along for the ride. I see the humor in Khaldun's comments, but Tallala takes it all so seriously. Could this be sanctioned schizophrenia? It will be interesting to see how Tallala evolves. (J. Post-Darnell, Fielding forum posting, March 14, 1999)

Personas as Faculty Assistants

Personas can serve as faculty "assistants" for online seminars. In my own experience, personas serving in this role have emerged fairly spontaneously, as if self-invited, without elaborate introduction or even clear authorship. Some personas have evolved out of characters mentioned in student café postings, who then become adopted by the group for an entire course:

> Tough day, a lot of stress, we're behind on deadlines, and my section is part of the problem. But I get home, make some tea, and log in to the forum. Dave comes in with Manfred, our 3-year-old Lab, still a puppy-spirit, all wagging tail and wet kisses. He doesn't care if I screw up or save the world, he treats me the same, he's always there for me. Slurp! (K. Axtman, Fielding forum posting, June 6, 1999)

For a while in this forum, "Slurp" becomes a frequent sign-off for messages of empathy for exasperating situations and issues.

One of the first personas to emerge in a more "full-time" role is a guy named Major Max Harsh, who essentially barged into the middle of one of my own attempts to provide gentle feedback and took over the job of insisting that a thesis topic had to be manageable and needed to have a single message: "You can't build a bridge until you decide what river you want to cross. You need to get from A to B. So show me on the map: If A is your problem, and B is your solution, exactly what are you talking about?"

Max works for the Corps of Engineers, and he wants things stated clearly, concisely, and with the practical objective always in mind. "Don't expect the literature review to tell you where *you* want to go. And don't do a bunch of reading until you know exactly what message you want the reading to support. Be a scientist; start with a clear hypothesis." In the thesis project course, he becomes the "heavy," while I cling to the role of good guy—enthusiastic, supportive of going further and deeper into the topic, suggesting new readings, encouraging divergent interpretations. Max growls in the background about deadlines, keeping it focused, and getting rid of the "sissy jargon" that shields people from having to deal with the real world. He has a sign on his wall: "Learning something worthwhile is painful. Life is painful. Stop whining. —Freud & Buddha."

By the end of the thesis course, students bring up Max more frequently than I do, especially as the thesis development course shifts from divergent inquiry to convergent inquiry and from exploration of ideas to consolidation of research design for hypothesis testing. A student often knows what is needed and looks to Max for the push to get focused. For this, Max can become an ally on the student's side, even if he remains a grouch. Max might get on his bulldozer and flatten the local bookstore: "Stop reading. If you don't know what your message is by now, more books won't help. Just get it on paper. Say something useful to my 14-year-old niece in words she can understand."

The power of Max—or any persona—is the power of horror movies, evoking more by what is unseen and unsaid than by what is made explicit. If personas work, it is because they can speak on this level of subtext. Their presence becomes especially real in the candlepower luminosity of online media, which I describe later.

Left-Column Voices

Left-column thinking can be used independently of personas, but it seems to work just as well—and often more forcefully—within a role-playing exercise. Left-column thinking is one of the methods used by David Bohm's Dialogues Group in Britain (Bohm, 1996; Bohm, Factor, & Garrett, 1991) and is described by Argyris (1999) as "the left- and right-hand column case method" (pp. 61-63). The left-column exercise is also presented in *The Fifth*

Discipline Fieldbook by Senge, Kleiner, Roberts, Ross, and Smith (1994, pp. 246-252). The starting point is the notion that in every conversation or group, there are things that people express openly, while other thoughts and feelings are withheld. The function of a left-column exercise is to provide a safe way—a sanctioned peephole—to reveal what is hidden.

The technique is very straightforward. You simply draw a line down the center of a blank page, and in the right column, you write what you would normally say in a conversation. In the left column, you enter what you might be thinking but normally keep to yourself:

> I've never gotten along with the Dutch, but I'm sure as heck not going to say that here in the forum because Pat will be offended, and it sounds prejudiced, even though it's simply describing my own experience. (paraphrase of Fielding forum posting, May 14, 1999)

Most online forums do not provide a way of writing in two columns, so left-column voices (or LCV) can be simply given a prefix or a bracket, interjected among normal right-column remarks:

> Perhaps our countries are not so different if one compares our slums with yours or our suburbs or universities or nightclubs.
>
> [LCV: I wonder if Barclay will think my comment is insensitive—I see a lot of books on his Suggested Readings list that take a Third World perspective. But I think we're doing some kind of "noble savage" number with the ethnic personas, projecting all our human wisdom and spirit onto the Third World and assigning all human greed to the Americans.]
>
> Interesting point—do you have a book or Web source I can use to go deeper? [LCV: I'm disturbed by your reaction. You seem to be really defensive about transnational enterprise and bitter about "ignorant management consultants." Strong stuff. What's happening?]

Why are people willing to express their "hidden thoughts" openly in this kind of exercise? Partly, it seems, because the "rules of the game" are stated clearly, and the risks of self-revelation are shared by everyone on the same basis. (This is one foundation of the "working covenant" for critical dialogue that I talk about next.) Another factor is the playful element at work; people can reveal their own thoughts, but in a voice that is different from the academic formal tone of the right-hand column. The left column is expressed in a vernacular that has an "off-the-record" quality, not meant to be judged, but listened to carefully, and valued for its authenticity as opposed to its conformity with accepted norms.

Left-column voices inject a conscious form of dialectical thinking—the direct questioning of one statement with its hidden opposite—which is one of the major foundations of critical analysis. As McWhinney (1992) puts it, dialectical thinking is a process that comes from "getting people to let go of one truth to explore another" (pp. 169-171). Letting personas loose in the forum helps to support one of the distinctive features of adult education, which is a break from the notion of an academic hierarchy with one voice—the instructor's—at the top. With personas, the voice of authority dissolves into multiple voices, often giving contradictory advice, requiring the student to exercise the important art of "polarity management" (Johnson, 1992). This awareness of contradiction and contradictory voices is a form of "stereoscopic vision" (Senge et al., 1994), which is also an important basis for critical dialogue aimed at shared exploration rather than criticism geared to attack and defense.

Covenants for Critical Online Dialogue

A covenant generally means an agreement that has a strong psychological and cultural component and is based on a sense of equality among the parties, as opposed to a legal contract between persons of differing rank or power. DuPree (1989) describes covenantial relationships as "bonds that fulfill deep needs and give work meaning" (cited in Axtman, 1999, p. 21).

The act of coming together with a common purpose is itself a kind of covenant. The Latin root of *covenant* means literally a "coming together," whereas in Old French *convenir* meant "to agree," and later English usage added the meaning of "convocation" in pursuit of a shared interest. The covenant may be written or spoken, but it can also be largely implicit, based simply on role modeling in much the way that national or ethnic or corporate cultures are transmitted. According to Parker (1998), covenants are made "not so much by what we say, but by what we do" (cited in Axtman, 1999, p. 22).

The notion of covenant applies well to online critical dialogue; it suggests a convocation that people enter, not based on a formal contract, explicit rules of debate, or elaborate preparation, but simply arising from a "coming together" with a simple, clearly understood purpose in mind. *Covenant* also has the connotation of making a promise that reflects on one's conduct and way of being, both as a person and as a member of a gathering or community. The word *covenant* is also a legal term, but that is not its intended meaning here. The objective here is not something compelled but rather something inviting. The "promise" of critical dialogue is something both simple and radical because it needs to serve both for moment-to-moment behavior and as a reflection of self-development, identity, and life purpose. This is expressed well in Betty Reid Soskin's principle: "The way to change the world is to be what we want to see" (cited in Parker, 1998).

From Fear of Isolation to Trust in the Group

A covenant is important because if it is not made explicitly for a shared intention, then other frameworks will come into play unseen and haphazardly, either reinforcing the status quo or imposing the agenda of the most forceful speakers. Especially in a newly formed group, the framework will tend to be governed by issues of fear, status, protection of safe retreats, or imposition of safely controlled areas of expertise. The choice of language—and the choices of the questions raised—will happen for private or unseen agendas.

A deliberate covenant provides a clearer choice of language, a more deliberate focus of issues, and more inclusive participation in establishing the framework of working together. It shifts the emphasis from a defensive mode of "What can I say?" to a more open stance of "What can I hear?" Listening is usually the neglected half of communication. The mix of hearing and speaking and anticipating reactions is fundamental to all discourse, but especially in the conscious establishment of a framework for dialogue. A covenant makes explicit what Bakhtin sees as the very basis of language: The word is a two-sided act, determined equally by the speaker and listener, a shared territory. Power is always in play, but it can be threatening (asymmetric and implicit), or it can be explicit with a shared purpose (Bakhtin, 1981, 1995).

As sensitivity and experience increase, a perception of shared meaning emerges in which people find that they are neither opposing one another nor simply interacting. There is no imposed consensus, nor is there any attempt to avoid conflict. No single individual or subgroup is able to achieve dominance because every single subject, including domination and submission, is always available to be considered (Bohm et al., 1991, p. 4).

Simple Examples and Simplicity Are Vital

Peck (1993) talks about the importance of simple "civility" as the basis of community, making the case that spirituality of some kind is needed as the basis for civility itself. A covenant draws on similar principles. To be operational, a covenant needs to be boiled down to essences for easy recall in the heat of the moment. Like corporate purposes and mission statements, they have to be very simple, very rooted in fundamentals (Collins & Porras, 1994/ 1997). *Have fun, work hard, be kind.*

Our brains are capable of handling only a few ideas at any one time—perhaps around seven (Miller, 1956). In the midst of critical dialogue, when a group gets deeply and effectively into the spirit of it, the guidelines need to be simple and internalized, based less on a set of constant reminders or special techniques and more on a set of understandings reached prior to entering into the process—the stuff of a covenant. The idea is a pre-flight checklist, *before* the moment of takeoff, that lets the group quickly switch to auto-pilot.

Adult learners usually have the basic habits of civility needed for online dialogue, but there are some specific tips for respectful listening that may be especially useful for cross-cultural dialogue and encouragement of diversity in viewpoints. One such list, developed by Saphiere (2000), has been created through an international online group of professional interculturalists. Other, more general lists of netiquette abound (Shapiro & Hughes, 1997; Shea, 1994; University of New Mexico, 1998; Wabash College, 1995). A good summary checklist is provided by Beizer (1999, p. 86), drawing on Simmons's (1999) *A Safe Place for Dangerous Truths,* Ellinor and Gerard's (1998) *Dialogue,* and Isaacs and Jones's (1995) *Foundations for Dialogue.* Beizer's (1999) list includes the following:

- Speak personally. Own your own feelings, thoughts, and judgments.
- Be specific.
- Don't try to convert others. Respect individual differences. Encourage diversity.
- Listen without resistance or judgment. Acknowledge and affirm each speaker.
- Speak only when moved to do so.
- Suspend assumptions and certainties.

Three additional guidelines in Beizer's list have special relevance to critical dialogue and to the way it is supported by the asynchronous format:

- Slow down the inquiry.
- Speak to the center (rather than to one another).
- Talk in sequence (no interrupting).

In the asynchronous format, an unsettling (or seriously upsetting) message from someone else can be set aside, allowing time to "count to 10" before replying. Apart from simply waiting to calm down, the response can be framed by questions aimed at self-reflection: "How am I misinterpreting what he intended? What is his cultural context and agenda—and my own, for that matter?" Or one might ask, "Why is this suddenly not working—what's missing? Hmmm, well, for one thing, we've lost a sense of humor here. Is there any way to bring that back in?"

Resilient Vulnerability

Although a covenant invites participants to place their trust in the group, it does not shy away from confrontation on difficult issues. Critical dialogue entails a tension between the "tough" side of critical engagement—the confrontation of thesis and antithesis, the knocking of ideas and heads, the encouragement of dissent and scientific skepticism—and the "caring" side of the process through a spirit of collaborative exploration, active listening and open-mindedness, and appreciation of seeing things from another person's perspective.

The "critical" side is understandably painful if one is on the receiving end, giving rise to defensiveness that defeats the spirit of dialogue. But the caring and collaborative part can also be painful to the extent that it digs deeply into questions of identity, blocked consciousness, thwarted self-actualization, and our unconscious roles in oppression of others. Critical dialogue might *have* to be painful to achieve the kind of insights and break-throughs that are the most valuable. If the aim is primarily to avoid pain, then the dialogue too easily falls back on superficial politeness, numbing of attention, or paths of retreat. The goal, then, can't be simply to avoid pain; instead, it should be to stay clear-headed and committed to the process in the midst of discomfort and to avoid the defensiveness that cuts off dialogue and critical insights. But if the aim is to preserve a state of openness, then we have to find ways of endowing our heightened vulnerability with *resilience*.

Pulley (1997) talks about this kind of resilience in *Losing Your Job— Reclaiming Your Soul: Stories of Resilience, Renewal, and Hope,* as does Higgins (1994) in *Resilient Adults: Overcoming a Cruel Past.* In the context of promoting critical dialogue, "resilient vulnerability" is not aimed at over-coming trauma or working on long-term strengthening of character. It simply serves as the orientation of a covenant to set the stage for critical dialogue, whether it is used in the "tone" of opening remarks, provided through role models, incorporated into a more explicit set of ground rules, or made part of an initial bonding experience for preparation of the group.

There are various methods one can use to prepare a group for openness to other viewpoints. What they have in common is the reinforcement of a basic understanding to be "comfortable with the discomfort" of exploring what is usually avoided.

Explicit and Implicit Covenants

The explicit aspects of a covenant are probably less powerful than the implicit ones. Explicit covenants are important, of course, visible in ancient and venerated parchments and serving as milestones of new undertakings. For students in their first encounter with a new learning environment, explicit guidelines are usually welcome, and discussion of norms can be a functional keystone in creation of the working community. Especially in adult learning groups, these norms can derive from students' own experience and sense of identity and purpose. The result is not a list of do's and don'ts but rather an articulation of expectations, a recognition of individual differences, and a willingness to be challenged. In an online environment, these norms can be posted, always just a single click away, and they can be elaborated continuously with accumulation of experience.

Yet it may be the implicit elements of a covenant that count for most in the end. Whatever is made explicit—a code of ethics, a loyalty oath, a list of sanctions—can end up preempting and working against the impulse that people willingly bring to the group. Regulations can be annoying not just for offenders but also for those who act ethically for the intrinsic good of it. The function of a covenant, then, is not necessarily to codify something new but to give recognition to things that people have already brought to the community and to celebrate them.

An implicit covenant has some other advantages. It allows instinct to guide the process. It is flexible in adapting to the culture and circumstances of any particular group. It avoids interruption in the stream of group thought, and it can minimize interference from any facilitators involved. Most important, it *trusts* participants to engage their own management skills and instincts. Like athletic peak performance, the ideal state is reached by letting go of self-conscious control—getting beyond the need for it—to let experience and instinct take over.

To achieve its true potential, online critical dialogue needs to take the process back from learning facilitators, or traditional pedagogues, and embed it in the group itself—work invisibly as part of the substance of the dialogue. In a more explicit "managed" form of covenant, there is always some ultimate source of authority outside the group, no matter how unobtrusive (Butler, 1999; Pegau, 1999).

Emergence of Trust

A little trust leads to some information sharing, then more trust, in a dynamic spiral (Butler, 1999, pp. 219-220; Rogers & Roethlisberger, 1952, pp. 47-48). Rogers's research on small groups showed that the decisive element for trust is the conscious act of suspending judgment about others as people and instead seeking understanding "from the *other's* point of view." That shift "can be initiated by one party, without waiting for the other to be ready," or "by a neutral third person, provided he can gain a minimum of cooperation from one of the parties" (Rogers & Roethlisberger, 1952, p. 47). Then,

> The dropping of some defensiveness by one party leads to further dropping of defensiveness by the other party . . . [until] communication tends to be pointed toward solving a problem rather than toward attacking a person or group. . . . These defensive distortions drop away with astonishing speed as people find that the only intent is to understand, not to judge. (p. 48)

Sampson (1993) sees this embracing of differences as a process of "celebrating the other." Bakhtin (1990) elaborates on this by asking,

> In what way would it enrich the event if I merged with the other, and instead
> of one there would be now only one? And what would I myself gain by the
> other's merging with me? If he did, he would see and know no more than
> what I see and know myself. . . . Let him rather remain outside of me, for in
> that position he can see and know what I myself do not see and do not know
> from my own place, and he can essentially enrich the event of my own life.
> (p. 87)

Listening for Mystery and Surprise

In his essay "Shakespeare and the Listener," White (1986) poses the
question: If I say I had a good conversation with X today, what does that
mean? It means we each pulled the other into a new idea or feeling or understanding that wouldn't have been possible without the other. It means a personal experience with an unexpected outcome—discovering something
together. But it starts with the power of listening, for "What we *hear* is what
enables us to *speak*. . . . It is the listening function which is, far from being passive, of prime creative importance in determining the direction and future
course of a conversational interaction" (p. 125).

Indeed, dialogue, at its best, is not constrained by the initial "givens," or
guided by managers of critical dialogue as a "technique," but instead opens
doors to the kind of learning where *information consists of surprise.* Claude
Shannon, one of the founders of information theory while working at Bell
Labs during the 1940s, defines information in terms of uncertainty about the
next message to be received. This is counterintuitive, but the higher the
uncertainty or surprise, the greater the new information or "surprise value"
contributed by the communication (Coffman, 1997; Shannon & Weaver,
1998). Communication that brings out nothing unexpected can only confirm
what we already know, deepening the ruts of unquestioned thought habits.
These habits can become constraining, as Coffman (1997) points out, not
only in terms of what we perceive but also in defining "the circumference of
our being." With too much order, predictability, and stasis, "we have no window left in our lives for information to intrude—to stir things up and make us
doubt, challenge, practice, fail, and learn again." We need messages that provide us with the raw materials to grow and evolve, and for that, they need to
surprise us out of compliance.

So perhaps we can say that listening itself, as the root of dialogue, consists
of a willingness to be surprised through anticipation and search for surprise.
This in turn might have two quite distinct foundations. One is scientific:
the willingness to suspend assumptions and certainties and to maintain a
spirit of inquiry (Marquart, 1996, p. 61). In Feynman's (1988) view, the
essence of science is the willingness and freedom to doubt, which was "born
out of a struggle against authority in the early days of science" (p. 245). Scientific progress comes from a "satisfactory philosophy of ignorance" that

recognizes "the openness of possibilities. . . . If we want to solve a problem that we have never solved before, we must leave the door to the unknown ajar" (pp. 247-248).

Feynman (1998) maintains that one of the great heritages of Western civilization is "the scientific spirit of adventure" or

> the adventure into the unknown, an unknown that must be recognized as unknown in order to be explored, the demand that the unanswerable mysteries of the universe remain unanswered, the attitude that all is uncertain. To summarize it: humility of the intellect. (p. 47)

Feynman (1998) sees in that humility the very basis of effective discourse and the basis of democracy itself. "The writers of the Constitution knew of the value of doubt, which provided an 'openness of possibility,' so that uncertainty is seen as an opportunity for people, some day, to find another way beyond our own powers to imagine" (pp. 49-50). "We have plenty of time to solve problems. The only way that we will make a mistake is that . . . impetuously we will decide we know the answer" (p. 57).

But even within the more "objective" field of science, critical dialogue finds its power in something that goes beyond anything usually found in "managed discourse." Feynman's (1988) "philosophy of ignorance," as he calls it, provides a door to the experience of mysteries, which is for him a "particular type of religious experience" available to serious scientists. A good scientist, he maintains, will see that "the imagination of nature is far, far greater than the imagination of man. [We] turn over each new stone to find unimagined strangeness leading on to more wonderful questions and mysteries—certainly a grand adventure" (pp. 242-243).

Doris Lessing makes the similar case about the power of the written word derived from its unresolved quality. There is a power in ambiguity, which leaves a continuing open dialogue between writer and reader, even if the text is from a book of a long departed author. For Lessing (1973),

> A book is alive and potent and fructifying and able to promote thought and discussion *only* when its plan and shape and intention are not understood, because that moment of seeing the plan and shape and intention is also the moment where there isn't anything more to be got out of it. (p. 22)

If the purpose of dialogue is to find *meaning*, then the goal is not the arrival at a fixed point of understanding but rather the sustaining of a process. Meaning is not static but exists only within the process of its own development. Berger and Mohr (1982) put it this way: "Without an unfolding, there is no meaning; meaning is a response, not only to the known but also the unknown; meaning and mystery are inseparable, and neither can exist without the passing of time" (p. 15). This is reflected, too, in the Zen approach to understanding. Zen teaches nothing; it merely enables us to wake up and become aware (Cleary, 1995).

Intensive listening and response is always an invitation to mystery, leading to surprise and unforeseeable outcomes. This is reflected in the title of Johnson's (1998) recent Fielding thesis, *The Power of Not Knowing What Comes Next,* a study of applying improvisational theater processes to organizational groups. Improvisation produces the same unpredictable, unscripted, and powerfully creative process that comes out of critical dialogue when a group takes off on its own path. To be sure, even improvisation has its own techniques and conventions, but it cannot have the self-consciousness of a facilitator-managed process. Instead, in the parlance of complexity theory, it follows the model of a "self-organized" system (Kauffman, 1995; Wheatley, 1992).

A covenant is thus important for adult online education, not only as a foundation for community among people geographically dispersed but also to provide a coherent point of departure for continued emergence of trust and acceptance of differences, which are at the heart of critical dialogue.

Candlepower:
The Value of Critical Subtraction

Online dialogue is quite different from discussions found in traditional classrooms or problem-solving teams in the workplace. The pitfalls are deeper and the cues are fewer. But the journey can go farther and faster than most people imagine. Computer-mediated communication, even on the level of pure text, is not a flat medium any more than staring into a fireplace or listening to campfire stories is a flat experience for lack of audiovisual aids. The limited field of a computer screen can actually deepen the focus of concentration and the power of imagination, just as conversation can deepen over candlelight. I think of this as the candlepower of online critical dialogue. It entails the exploratory mood and evocative context for people to work in the shadows of half-understood issues and cast a light of their own making.

Candlepower is shorthand for a surprising quality of online dialogue— the intimacy it creates among participants. Even in a forum with a dozen participants, posting a message can *feel* as if there is only one other person involved. The mind's eye narrows the audience to a particular other, like a face seen across a candlelit table, with the rest of the space in shadows. Intimacy is a widely reported quality of the experience (Brown, 1998; Negroponte, 1995; Porter, 1996; Stevens-Long, 1999). Perhaps this should not be such a surprise. Wives of ARPANET (Advanced Research Projects Agency Network) builders during the early 1970s used to log on late at night and talk among themselves at scattered university sites, never meeting face-to-face but deeply engaged in discussion that touched on their personal lives. That suggests, at least, that intimacy is not dependent on having the latest in sophisticated software features.

To me, online intimacy has been a great and pleasant surprise given my general disappointment with the shallow and erratic conversation of typical chat rooms. Back during the 1960s, I spent a whole summer doing statistical analysis at the Harvard Economic Research Project, feeding racks of IBM cards into a balky IBM 7090 computer the size of a small room. Twenty years later, I was working with CAD-CAM systems. Neither system hinted at the possibility of intimacy.

But with online asynchronous communication, everything changes. Here, you become intensely focused on one thing, the person behind the screen. Your attention is fixed on the conversation or topic or Web search of your own choice, without interruptions. You can linger on particular words, which do not fade as they do in ordinary conversation but instead remain in place. Or you can speed-read conversations that don't engage you until you find one that does. You choose where to pick up the narrative and when to continue the exchange. You enter a zone tailored to your own rhythms and gravitations. You are unconcerned with your appearances or theirs. You are not in a public academic space where the natural habits take over—to judge and be judged, to show off what you know, or to make an impression.

Brown (1998) labels as a myth the "impersonality" of computer-mediated instruction. Referring to her own experience, she states,

> There is a type of intimacy achievable between students and teachers in this medium that is quite extraordinary. . . . I believe this intimacy results from a sense of shared control and responsibility, commitment to collaboration and dialogue, and increased willingness to take risks in communications with others online. . . . The text-based forum network also forces one to make one's thoughts very explicit. . . . As one administrator put it: "In an online environment, words matter. . . . Words are everything."
>
> People's feelings can be hurt [more easily online], so more time and effort are put into explaining meanings and supplying detailed contextual background to enhance mutual understanding. Thus, writers get to know one another intimately. (p. 3)

Brown (1998) also sees as a myth the view that computer-based learning is a "flat medium" for dialogue. On the contrary, Brown points out, an asynchronous computer-mediated forum can simultaneously carry several threaded conversations, each in many layers of depth, with the dialogue starting between two people and branching with new participation of others.

The appearance of candlepower varies from one forum to another, but there are a number of contributing factors that can be controlled, and for this reason I call it a "device" rather than simply a spontaneous phenomenon or a built-in aspect of online dialogue. Several factors come into play, including some that have already been mentioned. One is the conscious formation of a covenant within the group already mentioned. Another is the application of basic principles of andragogy drawing on the depth of experience and maturity of intellect found among adult learners.

A third factor is the use of *asynchronous* communication because this format allows a unique double-loop character of response—one that is both spontaneous and reflective—in contrast to chat rooms and other real-time exchanges. The candlepower of online learning draws on a thoughtfulness and reflective sharing that is missing both from the lockstep focus and steady droning of traditional classroom pedagogy and from the intensive, time-accelerated nature of real-time exchange online. For most people, the candle-power of computer-based education is a surprising feature of the experience. Yet it is missing from most online curricula, both because traditional pedagogy does not seek it out and because the conditions that bring it into play have not been well understood.

Different people construct online intimacy in ways and degrees of their own making, but I think that there are some recognizable factors at work, which I will describe briefly. Individually and collectively, they have the effect of reducing the influence of contextual "friction" that impinges on dialogue. Each provides a way of becoming fully involved in the moment, relatively free of self-conscious guidance from pedagogy or other facilitation by outsiders or the intrusion of technology.

In some respects, it is a matter of reducing particular distractions, resulting in a much improved ratio of signal to noise. But when all of these factors come together, it amounts to a "critical subtraction"—a shedding of constraints and distractions that work against critical dialogue in traditional classrooms. The resulting candlepower can be dim or bright, but failure to recognize its qualities and advantages can result in misguided attempts to boost online technology capabilities and management "tools" at the expense of this intimacy.

The Asynchronous Moment

Asynchronous conversations have a paradoxical quality to them—a sense that "someone is always listening" (Pratt, 1996, p. 116) and that the dialogue is maintained independent of normal time and space constraints. They also allow for individual differences in the ways in which people like to communicate—even the person who says, "I am an expert procrastinator and am able to practice my skills at my leisure" (Pratt, 1996, p. 116).

Something not so obvious about asynchronous work in a group is that it seems to narrow the focus into a dialogue between just two people in the present moment. Asynchronous dialogue can *feel* like an off-the-record, closed-door conversation. The effect of asynchronous online dialogue is to focus on a particular person as audience. Your own words arise from a kind of continued listening to the words of that person, regardless of when they were actually posted. A thoughtful person might believe, "I am a slow thinker, but online that problem goes away. I don't have to be good at repartee; it feels like the other person is always there, waiting, and I can use my strengths of cognition and mulling" (paraphrase of a student comment reported by Pratt, 1996, p. 116). One reason why Internet conversations *feel* safe is that your side of the conversation is literally taking place on your own turf—at home or wherever your computer happens to reside. You can reach out anytime you wish and shut off even faster.

As part of a genuine dialogue, asynchronous postings let you draft comments quickly and spontaneously, with the juices flowing, keeping your intuition and personal context in play. Time and space become nonfactors; the dialogue comes to you, at your terminal, at the time you choose. Like a small candlelit table at a restaurant, asynchronous communication creates a time and space of your own choosing. It bestows the flexibility to post at any hour, working around the time-space dictates of work, family, and other obligations.

Online dialogue usually preserves the entire thread of a discussion in a text record. Asynchronous dialogue takes advantage of this capacity, allowing anyone to go back and reinterpret earlier remarks or pick up an earlier idea and apply it to a new topic. It also provides a more structured and well-documented basis for critiquing earlier points or building the case for an idea, drawing on multiple contributors, so that criticism becomes a joint endeavor rather than a polarized argument.

Stronger Signal, Less Noise From Academic Machinery

One factor contributing to candlepower is its ability to keep attention focused on substantive content without the distraction of ancillary processes associated with higher education. There is no commuting to campus, no parking problems, and no dead space in lectures or in waiting for everyone to show up. There is no waiting in lines for registration, no signing up for appointments with the instructor, and no arrangements to attend to for dorm life and campus activities. To be sure, there are dozens of online "extracurricular" programs in the form of café discussions, community halls, user groups, work groups, and research collaborative sites. But each site is only a click away, and exiting is just another click. Clark Kerr, former president of the University of California, once described his role as dealing primarily with issues of parking, student sex, and athletic programs. None of those intrudes very significantly on online learning.

Information theory tells us that one of the key measures of effective communication lies in a high ratio of "signal to noise," which indicates the strength of substantive content against the background chatter (Coffman, 1997). Online critical dialogue provides a very high ratio of signal—in substantive discussion—relative to the noise of academic machinery found on a traditional campus.

The Fullness of Silence

Asynchronous dialogue allows uninterrupted pauses and silence and "shadow space" for thoughts to come to the surface, as if simultaneously authored by speaker and listener. This helps to create a sense of reciprocity and cooperation, based on collaboration rather than competition, and social skills apart from academic ones. This is very different from the real-time jostling of ideas in a chat room. One student talked about the forum as a place for critical inquiry that can "keep the deep water still and clear" (E. Franklin, Fielding thesis group forum, May 1999). Another referred to the "wonderful starkness of just pure thought." Asynchronous dialogue brings into play the spaces and messages of silence in a way that is often lost on Americans. As Ruch (1989) points out in his cross-cultural study of communication styles, "In many cultures, silence is used very effectively in the course of conversation; Americans, on the other hand, rush to fill silence, talking when they should wait patiently" (p. 28).

The American tendency to rush conversation, to fill in silence, and even to interrupt others in the middle of a thought comes across as rudeness in many other cultures, but it can also handicap Americans because it causes them to miss most of the message. Pascale and Athos (1981) make a similar assessment:

> Americans listen in an evaluative way, accepting or rejecting ideas presented, which leads to fatigue and listening shortcuts so that they absorb only about 30 percent of the message. [By contrast,] The Japanese practice "less-ego listening": They hold "principle" in abeyance, regard themselves as one among others in the situation, and thus achieve easy accommodation with the circumstances of the meeting. This situational ethic enables the Japanese to air different views without falling into a duel of personalities. (pp. 130-131)

In a more local context (for American educators at least), the "council" format of Indian meetings has received considerable attention as a basis for school discussion, being less formalistic than traditional debate formats and giving more opportunity for everyone to speak without interruption. A salient feature of the council is the rule not to interrupt the speaker. To European-origin Americans, the phrase "I have spoken" sounds pompous, but it is simply the speaker's way of saying, "Well, that's all I wanted to say. Your turn now, and I will give my full attention to your own thoughts. Take your time." This is different from typical chat room conversation, where multiple voices are simultaneously in play, somewhat disjointed and unfocused but always impinging on the "social construction" of the conversation.

Americans especially, compared to Europeans, love to interrupt; it shows interest and enthusiasm as well as collaboration in joint development of ideas. This tendency to interrupt can greatly annoy Europeans (as Fielding faculty based in Europe sometimes remind us). And it is especially rude in council format, where eloquence of speech, cadence, storytelling, and image building are highly valued and where pauses and silence are used for emphasis. Americans love to fill silences with words, and that puts a special burden on the management of critical dialogue in this culture.

American grade schools sometimes make use of a "talking stick" that is passed around as a reminder not to interrupt the person who holds it while speaking. A talking stick, although coming into more frequent pedagogical use, would probably seem childish, inefficient, and manipulative in an adult seminar or a corporate meeting. But *asynchronous online dialogue* provides a built-in device serving exactly the same purpose. Here, nobody interrupts you, giving you all of the time you need, including time to review your words against your intentions and make adjustments until it feels right. In this entire process, your audience remains before your mind's eye, and when the moment comes when it feels right to say, "I have posted," it somehow *feels* as if the audience is right there.

The Power of Sensory Deprivation

Online forums are highly limited in many respects; they don't touch all the senses, and they can't command immediate responses. But that can be an advantage. Other senses, drawing on the powers of experience and the imagination, may come to the surface and take over. Once on a field trip, I injured both eyes, which were bandaged during my plane trip home. The temporary state of blindness brought an unexpected awareness of things usually beyond my normal perceptions—the slope and texture of floors; the heat from surfaces that were sunlit; the sense of distance to walls and ceilings from sound echoes; the awareness of smells; and the inflections, accents, and feelings behind spoken words. Perhaps people have a similar range of sensitivities about the subtext of other people's written words, but they are distracted from that awareness by the preemptive strength of visual clues in face-to-face conversation or in vocal inflections on the telephone. In academic and business contexts, too, conventional syntax and jargon tend to mask the personalization of language. But asynchronous online dialogue provides more freedom to add subtext and more time to absorb it.

There are many studies about the high percentage of communication that is nonverbal (93%, according to Mehrabian, 1981, p. 44), with the majority of "information" transmitted through visual clues such as body language, facial expression, and vocal inflection. Perhaps, however, these numbers may be misleading. Many of those "nonverbal" cues may stem not from visual or auditory inflections but rather from subtleties in the use of language that most people are barely aware of using or hearing. These subtexts come closer to the surface through the "vernacular" mode of online dialogue—with its mix of spontaneity and thoughtfulness—in words usually directed to a particular person but tapping into the shared meanings evolving within a small group.

The importance of those quickly evolved subtextual meanings can be glimpsed when someone enters the group late in the process unaware of them. One student, reflecting back on earlier courses, reported,

> The next semester was a stark contrast from the first. . . . For the first time, we encountered conflict within our group. [A] classmate arrived late in the semester and upset the norms that had already been established within the group. He tried to take charge and [a few weeks later] provided some biting, harsh feedback to another member of the group [that seemed] unprofessional. (D. Moore, Fielding forum posting, July 8, 1999)

In the absence of other signals, one's attention shifts to a richer interpretation of cues within the written text, going deeper into the layers of meaning behind words. This does not require formal training in "communication skills," but it does call for the full exercise of people's innate capacities for listening and responding.

Again, Americans may be at a disadvantage here. The skill of seeing "behind the message" based on the sender's *personality and intent* is a skill that does not come naturally to our culture. Edward Hall's studies indicate that Americans (along with most Northern Europeans) are members of a "low-content culture," meaning that they place great confidence in *words* for conveying information but discount the broader context of a message—who it came from and under what circumstances (Hall, 1977). Online dialogue helps to reintroduce those "high-context" elements, allowing greater attention to the subtext of the other person's words and situation, in a way less possible in the give-and-take of a real-time discussion.

Trompenaars (1994) agrees with Hall's (1977) assessment, based on his own research on cross-cultural differences. Trompenaars uses the terms "diffuse" and "specific" for high- and low-context cultures, but his point is the same. Americans have trouble dealing with the "whole person" in their business dealings but focus on a particular role segment. Americans can be relaxed, garrulous, and friendly in part because they are relating on a thin "public layer" that is "not a very big commitment. You 'know' the other person for limited purposes only" (Trompenaars, 1994, p. 80). On other layers, Americans are comfortable with not telling, not asking, and skimming over any implicit layers of subtext.

Online asynchronous dialogue reestablishes the possibility of working more effectively and sensitively at the level of subtext. Our skills may be rudimentary, but our innate ability to deal on this level may be far more than we normally realize because so few other opportunities have been afforded or encouraged. Research on perception suggests that our sense of vision gives us power to discriminate among more than 7 million colors and 300,000 tones (Geldard, 1953, p. 53). Undoubtedly, the mind can also discriminate meanings and subtexts with great subtlety, but we lack objective instruments for measuring the gradations, the dimensions are less fixed, and until now the emphasis of schooling has been on low-context subject matters, where subject matters are diced into objective unambiguous bricks of information, separate from the personalities of the people who discovered or validated those facts. Online critical dialogue reconnects the word with the speaker by focusing the candlelight of dialogue on subtext without the distraction of other sensory inputs.

Farr (1991) points out that, paradoxically, another person's physical presence can lead to a psychological distancing. The other person becomes an "object," he argues, "because the skin is such a compelling boundary from a visual perspective" (p. 253). Regardless how much information may be missed or misinterpreted in the words of a conversation, an even stronger effect of confusion and uneasiness stems from the *physical* presence and unconscious signals between two conversants. Body language and facial expression send powerful messages, all the more powerful because the messages are usually unconscious.

If we take this evidence at face value, then we have an interesting result: Far from diminishing the power and accuracy of messages, the online format of dialogue that strips away visual images has the effect of purifying and strengthening the transmission of information and meaning, in effect by eliminating the extraneous confusion of unconscious, random, and inaccurate signals that are sent by one's physical presence. Again, there is a dramatic improvement in the ratio of signal to noise.

Another "purification" is the freedom that online dialogue provides from the complex (and again unconscious) process of interpreting *auditory* signals. The power and sophistication of auditory filtering is illustrated by cultural differences, even in the same household. For example, some kids seem to need rock music to study, whereas adults need silence even for rudimentary thinking. Another example is what McGregor and White (1986) call the "cocktail party effect," whereby "it is normally possible to follow a selected conversation even though the total loudness of the other conversations seems greater" (p. 4). In this process, the auditory filtering system is "judge, juror, [and] witness" for what the mind extracts, absorbing a considerable amount of mental energy. But an online dialogue needs none of that; the need for auditory filtering, and its intrusion on the intended meaning of the speaker, is completely absent. In this way, too, the signal-to-noise ratio gets a significant boost.

Conclusion: Critical Dialogue Is Not Managed but Rather Cultivated

The devices described in this chapter can be used independently, each with minimal preparation or special skills. Each comes in more elaborate versions, but I have tried to focus on the simpler ones. In the end, however, the sources of powerful critical dialogue can remain elusive and beyond rational construction. It cannot be directly managed like an assembly line or lab experiment; it cannot be taught like a history lesson or math skill. It emerges from an exchange of language that engages people on many levels. What our experience is telling us is that this language—and this depth of personal engagement—can become even more powerful in the setting of adult, asynchronous online learning. As Casaus (2000) puts it in his thesis, the deliverable ends up being more than the assignment: "The deliverable is yourself" (G. Casaus, Fielding thesis forum group, November 2000).

Critical dialogue at its best, especially among online adult learners, has some of the elements of a good joke. It is a form of storytelling—a paced unfolding narrative in a somewhat mysterious process that defies normal logic but leads to a satisfying surprise. Equally important is a sense of fun. That may seem frivolous, but "having fun" is a remarkably frequent theme among the mission statements of visionary companies researched by Collins and Porras (1994/1997, pp. 70-71). Sony, for example, was founded in 1945 with no clear product in view—it did not even settle on electronics for nearly a decade—but it was very clear about its purpose. It aimed at nourishing the "sheer joy" of developing wonderful products of a quality that would help to establish Japan's worldwide reputation for excellence and not just the export of cheap and unreliable toys.

The same vision might well serve us as online educators. In this revolutionary new world of adult-oriented distance-free learning, critical dialogue might do worse than to follow the slogan that used to appear on the masthead of *The Old Mole*, a radical paper of the 1960s: "A revolution without joy is almost not worth the trouble."

References

Andolina, M. (2001). *Critical thinking for working students*. Albany, NY: Delmar.

Argyris, C. (1999). *The learning organization* (2nd ed.). Malden, MA: Blackwell.

Argyris, C., Putnam, R., & Smith, D. M. (1985). *Action science*. San Francisco: Jossey-Bass.

Axtman, K. (1999). *Working covenants: Generation X's quest for meaningful work.* Unpublished master's thesis, Organizational Design and Effectiveness Program, Fielding Graduate Institute.

Bailie, M. (1995). Critical communication pedagogy: Teaching and learning for democratic life. In M. Bailie & D. Winseck (Eds.), *Democratizing communication?* (pp. 33-56). Cresskill, NJ: Hampton.

Bakhtin, M. M. (1981). *The dialogical imagination* (M. Holquist, Ed.). Austin: University of Texas Press.

Bakhtin, M. M. (1984). *Problems of Dostoevsky's poetics* (C. Emerson, Ed. and Trans.). Minneapolis: University of Minnesota Press.

Bakhtin, M. M. (1990). *Art and answerability*. Austin: University of Texas Press.

Bakhtin, M. M. (1995). Bakhtin. In T. Honderich (Ed.), *The Oxford companion to philosophy.* Oxford, UK: Oxford University Press. Retrieved February 15, 2001, from: www.xrefer.com/entry/551383

Banfield, E. C. (1951). *Government project.* Glencoe, IL: Free Press.

Bassham, G. (2001). *Critical thinking: An introduction.* Mountain View, CA: Mayfield.

Bates, B. (1999). *Mining meaning with the power of paradox: How differences enhance spirituality and community.* Unpublished master's thesis, Organizational Design and Effectiveness Program, Fielding Graduate Institute.

Beizer, B. (1999). *New perspectives on organizational change: Rethinking resistance at the edge of chaos.* Unpublished master's thesis, Organizational Design and Effectiveness Program, Fielding Graduate Institute.

Berger, J., & Mohr, J. (1982). *Another way of feeling.* London: Writers and Readers Publishing Co-op.

Berry, W. (1990). *What are people for?* San Francisco: North Point.

Bierhorst, J. (Ed.). (1974). *Four masterworks of American Indian literature.* Tucson: University of Arizona Press.

Bodi, S. (1988). Critical thinking and bibliographic instruction: The relationship. *Journal of Academic Librarianship, 14*(3), 150-153.

Bohm, D. (1996). *On dialogue* (L. Nichol, Ed.). New York: Routledge.

Bohm, D., Factor, D., & Garrett, P. (1991). *Dialogue: A proposal.* Gloucester, UK: Hawthorn Cottage. Retrieved February 2001 from http://world.std.com/~lo/bohm/0000.html

Bonnevier, B. (1999). *The social construction of self in virtual teams.* Unpublished manuscript, Human and Organization Development, Fielding Graduate Institute.

Brookfield, S. D. (1987). *Developing critical thinkers: Challenging adults to explore alternative ways of thinking and acting.* San Francisco: Jossey-Bass.

Brown, B. M. (1998). *Digital classrooms: Some myths about developing new educational programs using the Internet.* Unpublished manuscript, San Jose State University.

Browne, M. N., & Keeley, S. M. (2001). *Asking the right questions: A guide to critical thinking* (6th ed.). Upper Saddle River, NJ: Prentice Hall.

Butler, J. K., Jr. (1999). Trust expectations, information sharing, climate of trust, and negotiation effectiveness and efficiency. *Group and Organization Management, 24,* 217-238.

Casaus, G. (2000). *The ventriloquist: Finding one's voice in community.* Unpublished master's thesis, Organizational Design and Effectiveness Program, Fielding Graduate Institute.

Cederblom, J. B., & Paulsen, D. W. (2001). *Critical reasoning: Understanding and criticizing arguments and theories* (5th ed.). Belmont, CA: Wadsworth/Thomson Learning.

Cheyne, J. A., & Tarulli, D. (1999). *Dialogue, difference, and the "third voice" in the zone of proximal development.* Earlier version retrieved February 15, 2001, from: www.arts.uwaterloo.ca/~acheyne/zpd

Cleary, T. (1995). *Zen essence: The science of freedom* (C. Thomas, Ed. and Trans.). Boston: Shambhala.

Coffman, B. S. (1997). *Weak signal research, Part II: Information theory*. [Online]. Retrieved August 16, 1999, from: www.mgtaylor.com/mgtaylor/jotm/winter97/infotheory

Coghlan, D., & Brannick, T. (2001). *Doing action research in your own organization*. Thousand Oaks, CA: Sage.

Collins, J. C., & Porras, J. I. (1997). *Built to last: Successful habits of visionary companies*. New York: HarperBusiness. (Original work published 1994)

Collyer, J. R. (1996). *Independent and inclusive leadership experiences in relation to critical consciousness and social structure*. Unpublished doctoral dissertation, Fielding Graduate Institute, Human and Organization Development Program, Santa Barbara, CA.

Duggan, R. P. (1937). *A federal resettlement project: Granger Homesteads*. Doctoral dissertation, Catholic University of America, School of Social Work.

DuPree, M. (1989). *Leadership is an art*. New York: Dell.

Ellinor, L., & Gerard, G. (1998). *Dialogue: Rediscover the transforming power of conversation*. New York: John Wiley.

Ellul, J. (1964). *The technological society*. New York: Vintage. (Original work published 1954)

Farr, R. (1991). Bodies and voices in dialogue. In I. Marková & K. Foppa (Eds.), *Asymmetries in dialogue* (pp. 241-258). Hemel Hempstead, UK: Harvester Wheatsheaf.

Feynman, R. P. (1988). The value of science. In R. P. Feynman, *What do you care what other people think?* (pp. 240-248). New York: Norton.

Feynman, R. P. (1998). *The meaning of it all*. Reading, MA: Addison-Wesley.

Fisher, D., Rooke, D., & Torbert, W. (2000). *Personal and organizational transformations through action inquiry*. Boston: Edge\Work Press.

Franklin, E. (1999). *Executive revolution: Transforming leaders to transform the organization*. Unpublished master's thesis, Organizational Design and Effectiveness Program, Fielding Graduate Institute.

Freire, P. (1981). *Pedagogy of the oppressed*. New York: Continuum.

Geldard, F. A. (1953). *The human senses*. New York: John Wiley.

Greenwood, D. J., & Levin. M. (1998). *Introduction to action research: Social research for social change*. Thousand Oaks, CA: Sage.

Hall, E. T. (1977). *Beyond culture*. Garden City, NY: Doubleday.

Hampden-Turner, C. (1993). *Seven cultures of capitalism*. Garden City, NY: Doubleday.

Higgins, G. O. C. (1994). *Resilient adults: Overcoming a cruel past*. San Francisco: Jossey-Bass.

Hindery, R. (2001). *Indoctrination and self-deception or free and critical thought?* Lewiston, IL: E. Mellen.

Horton, M., with Kohl, J., & Kohl, H. (1998). *The long haul: An autobiography*. New York: Columbia University, Teachers College Press.

Isaacs, W. (1999). *Dialogue and the art of thinking together: A pioneering approach to communicating in business and in life*. New York: Currency.

Isaacs, W., & Jones, M. (Eds.). (1995). *Foundations for dialogue* (design of a seminar to be presented to Motorola Inc.). Cambridge, MA: DIAlogos.

Johansen, B. E. (1982). *Forgotten founders: How the American Indian helped shape democracy*. Boston: Harvard Common Press.

Johnson, B. (1992). *Polarity management: Identifying and managing unsolvable problems.* Amherst, MA: HRD Press.

Johnson, D. (1998). *The power of not knowing what comes next.* Unpublished master's thesis, Organizational Design and Effectiveness Program, Fielding Graduate Institute.

Kauffman, S. (1995). *At home in the universe: The search for laws of self-organization and complexity.* New York: Oxford University Press.

King, P. M., & Kitchener, K. S. (1994). *Developing reflective judgment: Understanding and promoting intellectual growth and critical thinking in adolescents and adults.* San Francisco: Jossey-Bass.

Knowles, M. (1978). *The adult learner: A neglected species* (2nd ed.). Houston, TX: Gulf.

Kuhn, T. S. (1962). *The structure of scientific revolutions.* Chicago: University of Chicago Press.

Lambert, C. (1998, September-October). Chaos, culture, curiosity: Turf wars of the mind—The emotional path to success. *Harvard Magazine,* p. 20.

LaPelle, N. R. (1997). *Thriving on performance evaluation in organizations.* Unpublished doctoral dissertation, Human and Organization Development Program, Fielding Graduate Institute.

Lawrence, T. B., & Phillips, N. (1998). Commentary: Separating play and critique—Postmodern and critical perspectives on TQM/BPR. *Journal of Management Inquiry, 7,* 154-160.

Lessing, D. (1973). *The golden notebook.* London: Granada.

Lewin, K. (1999). *The complete social scientist: A Kurt Lewin reader* (M. Gold, Ed.). Washington, DC: American Psychological Association. (Original work published 1946)

Mander, J. (1991). *In the absence of the sacred.* San Francisco: Sierra Club Books.

Marquart, M. (1996). *Building the learning organization.* New York: McGraw-Hill.

McGregor, G., & White, R. S. (Eds.). (1986). *The art of listening.* London: Croom Helm.

McWhinney, W. (1992). *Paths of change: Strategic choices for organizations and society.* Newbury Park, CA: Sage.

Mehrabian, A. (1981). *Silent messages* (2nd ed.). Belmont, CA: Wadsworth.

Miller, G. A. (1956). The magical number seven, plus or minus two: Some limits on our capacity for processing information. *Psychological Review, 63,* 81-97.

Mills, C. W. (1959). *The sociological imagination.* New York: Oxford University Press.

Missimer, C. A. (1995). *Good arguments: An introduction to critical thinking* (3rd ed.). Englewood Cliffs, NJ: Prentice Hall.

Mitroff, I. (1998). *Smart thinking for crazy times: The art of solving the right problems.* San Francisco: Berrett-Koehler.

Morgan, G. (1986). *Images of organization.* Newbury Park, CA: Sage.

Morrison, R. (1991). *We build the road as we travel: The story of the Mondragon worker-owned cooperatives.* Philadelphia: New Society.

Negroponte, N. (1995). *Being digital.* New York: Vintage.

Parker, R. (1998, June). *What they dreamed to be ours to do: Lessons from the history of covenant.* Paper presented at the general assembly of the Unitarian Universalist Association, Berkeley, CA. Retrieved August 21, 2001, from www.uua.org/ga/ga98/jun29parker.html

Pascale, R. T., & Athos, A. G. (1981). *The art of Japanese management.* New York: Simon & Schuster.

Peck, M. S. (1993). *A world waiting to be born: Civility rediscovered.* New York: Bantam Books.

Pegau, S. (1999). *Working the communication to trust, and trusting the communication to work.* Unpublished master's thesis, Organizational Design and Effectiveness Program, Fielding Graduate Institute.

Peterson, J. B. (1998). *Maps of meaning: The architecture of beliefs.* Cambridge, MA: Harvard University Press.

Porter, D. (1996). *Internet culture.* New York: Routledge.

Pratt, H. K. (1996). *The electronic personality.* Unpublished doctoral dissertation, Human and Organization Development Program, Fielding Graduate Institute.

Pulley, M. L. (1997). *Losing your job—reclaiming your soul: Stories of resilience, renewal, and hope.* San Francisco: Jossey-Bass.

Rahman, M. A. (1993). *People's self-development: Perspectives on participatory action research.* Atlantic Highlands, NJ: Zed Books.

Reinard, J. C. (1991). *Foundations of argument: Effective communication for critical thinking.* Dubuque, IA: William C. Brown.

Rogers, C. R., & Roethlisberger, F. J. (1952). Barriers and gateways to communication. In *Business classics* (pp. 44-50). Cambridge, MA: Harvard Business Review Press. (*Harvard Business Review,* Reprint No. 52408)

Roszak, T. (Ed.). (1972). *Sources: An anthology of contemporary materials useful for preserving personal sanity while braving the great technological wilderness.* New York: HarperColophon.

Roszak, T. (1992). *The voice of the earth.* New York: Simon & Schuster.

Ruch, W. V. (1989). *International handbook of corporate communication.* Jefferson, NC: McFarland.

Ruggiero, V. R. (2001). *The art of thinking: A guide to critical and creative thought* (6th ed.). New York: Longman.

Sampson, E. E. (1993). *Celebrating the other: A dialogical account of human nature.* Boulder, CO: Westview.

Saphiere, D. H. (2000). Online cross-cultural collaboration. *Training & Development, 54*(10), 71-72.

Schein, E. H. (1992). *Organizational culture and leadership* (2nd ed.). San Francisco: Jossey-Bass.

Schön, D. (1983). *The reflective practitioner: How professionals think in action.* New York: Basic Books.

Schwitalla, J. (1994). The concept of dialogue from an ethnographic point of view. In E. Weigard (Ed.), *Concepts of dialogue, considered from the perspectives of different disciplines* (pp. 15-35). Tubingen, Germany: Max Niemeyer Verlag.

Senge, P. M., Kleiner, A., Roberts, C., Ross, R., & Smith, B. (1994). *The fifth discipline fieldbook: Strategies and tools for building a learning organization.* New York: Currency Doubleday.

Shannon, C. E., & Weaver, W. (1998). *The mathematical theory of communication.* Urbana: University of Illinois Press.

Shapiro, J. J., & Hughes, S. K. (1997). Think critically and expand your intellectual horizons. In J. J. Shapiro & S. K. Hughes (Eds.), *Getting started in the community of scholars: Tips and suggestions* (pp. 5-8). Santa Barbara, CA: Fielding Graduate Institute.

Shea, V. (1994). *Netiquette.* San Francisco: Albion Books. Retrieved September 1, 1999, from: www.albion.com/netiquette/corerules.html

Sherman, F., & Torbert, W. R. (2000). *Transforming social inquiry, transforming social action.* Boston: Kluwer.

Simmons, A. (1999). *A safe place for dangerous truths: Using dialogue to overcome fear and distrust at work.* New York: John Wiley.

Stevens-Long, J. (1999). *The design and delivery of interactive on-line graduate education.* Santa Barbara, CA: Fielding Graduate Institute.

Szecsy, E. (1995). *Reflective dialogue and hermeneutics in research: Mapping community out of diversity* [Online]. Retrieved March 8, 2001, from: www. interactivities.org/home/elsie/papers/reflect

Toulmin, S., & Gustavsen, B. (Eds.). (1996). *Beyond theory: Changing organizations through participation.* Philadelphia: John Benjamins.

Trompenaars, F. (1994). *Riding the waves of culture: Understanding diversity in global business.* Chicago: Irwin.

University of New Mexico. (1998). *Netiquette.* Web site paper edited with added suggestions by Shelley Hughes, Fielding Graduate Institute. Available on Fielding Web forum: www.fielding.edu

Wabash College. (1995). *Wabash College (Indiana) netiquette Web site* [Online]. Retrieved September 1, 1999, from http://jade.wabash.edu/wabnet/info/netiquet. htm

Waller, B. N. (2001). *Critical thinking: Consider the verdict* (4th ed.). Upper Saddle River, NJ: Prentice Hall.

Warnick, B., & Inch, E. S. (1994). *Critical thinking and communication: The use of reason in argument* (2nd ed.). New York: Macmillan.

Weigard, E. (Ed.). (1994). *Concepts of dialogue, considered from the perspectives of different disciplines.* Tubingen, Germany: Max Niemeyer Verlag.

Wheatley, M. J. (1992). *Leadership and the new science: Learning about organization from an orderly universe.* San Francisco: Berrett-Koehler.

White, R. S. (1986). Shakespeare and the listener. In G. McGregor & R. S. White (Eds.), *The art of listening* (pp. 124-151). London: Croom Helm.

Yunus, M. (2001). *Banker to the poor: Autobiography of Muhammad Yunus.* Dakka, Bangladesh. (Available from Vedams eBooks (P) Ltd., 12A/11.W.E. Area, P.O. Box 2674, New Delhi, 110 005, India; e-mail: vedams@vedamsbooks.com)

Chapter 4

The Case of the Inflammatory E-Mail

Building Culture and Community in Online Academic Environments

Jeremy J. Shapiro
and Shelley K. Hughes

When people think about developing online academic environments or virtual campuses, their focus is primarily on the World Wide Web, for the emergence of the Web has certainly been the decisive innovation in creating such environments on a global scale. The ability of the Web to simulate a rich and variegated space; to connect to nearly infinite resources; to house lectures, conversations, cafés, documents, slide presentations, movies, music, and questionnaires; to be interactive; and to make all of this accessible to anyone with a browser and an Internet connection is undoubtedly a revolution in the history of the humanly constructed environment in general and in education in particular. The Web-based online environment is a far cry from the university lecture and seminar rooms that have changed little since the 12th century.

E-mail, nevertheless, is so fundamental to the communication fabric of life in cyberspace—it is still by far the major use of the Internet—that it

"You've got mail."

provides instructive material for the understanding of online culture and community and enables us to put some of their features under the microscope, as it were. A recent e-mail brouhaha in an online academic environment will lend itself to consideration of some of the complex cultural and community issues that sometimes manifest themselves in marked forms there. It started with an e-mail message that some experienced as inflammatory, progressed through a rash of angry messages, and culminated in the temporary suspension of e-mail lists and a faculty member's threat to resign. We should add that this incident occurred in our own environment, and we were involved both as participants and as observers.

About 10 days before the November 2000 U.S. presidential election, a faculty member sent an e-mail message to the faculty and student e-mail lists of the graduate program in which he teaches, stating his reasons for believing that people who are political Greens should vote for Democratic candidate Al Gore rather than Green candidate Ralph Nader. All told, the initial message went to about 400 students and faculty. This message led to a flurry of e-mail messages—several dozen over the next several days—many of them angry or excited and several of which accused the faculty member of violating an implicit ethical code regarding faculty behavior toward students. Some of these messages, in turn, were also sent to the faculty and students of another, equally large graduate program, which increased the number of people who entered the melee. The faculty member who initiated the exchange felt so offended by the angry responses, which he experienced as "hate mail," that he announced that he would resign from the institution (this decision was later rescinded after a "cooling off" period). Some students were so distressed about some of the messages that they received in the course of the fracas that they requested to be removed from mailing lists that are part of the administrative infrastructure of the institution. The spreading of distress eventually led to the temporary suspension of the mailing lists entirely.

With a few exceptions, the messages were not about political issues of the presidential campaign. They were primarily about issues central to culture and community in an online environment, such as the cultural norms that are to govern it, its definition of the boundaries between private and public, and its information structure. We return to these issues, as they manifested themselves here, later in the chapter. First, we must look more generally at the nature of online culture and community; the challenges to developing them; alternative approaches to doing so; and the larger social context as it enters into the online situations confronted by educators, administrators, information system developers, and students wanting to make online education work optimally for all those concerned.

The Larger Context

In a social world increasingly shaped by algorithms, the mechanical procedures that computers are so good at carrying out, there is no algorithm for building culture and community in online academic and educational environments. For better or worse, it requires the ongoing monitoring and analysis of the fabric of institutional life in which social and technological threads are woven together in complex, concrete, unrepeatable, and sometimes confusing and contradictory ways. The combination of several trends has brought about a situation where, both in the larger society and in academic environments, one can no longer take for granted what it means to have community or a common culture—trends such as rapidly changing technologies; changes in higher education such as the increasing number of adult and returning students in colleges and universities, the spread of corporate education, and the trend toward the convergence of education, business, and entertainment; and major social and cultural changes such as the globalization of the economy, the informatization of work, and the increasingly multicultural environment. Students, faculty, and administrators come together with a multiplicity of beliefs and values about what kind of culture, and what kind of community, is real, desirable, or possible. Consequently, culture and community must be built or developed, and not simply in one fell swoop but rather as an ongoing process. It is this process that we would like to illuminate through consideration of the case of the inflammatory e-mail.

The situation we have briefly described, of multiple and sometimes radically conflicting values and beliefs, implies that the individuals who come together to build culture and community, either online or offline, will be doing so with rather different conceptions of what culture and community are, what forms of culture and community should exist in an academic or educational environment, what values should underlie them, and what norms should govern them. Furthermore, as we elaborate later, divergent paradigms govern the theory and practice of information systems development, so that there is not just one way in which to conceptualize and act on such a system. Therefore, there is no value-neutral or purely administrative or technical way of building culture and community. This is what we perceive to be the weakness of the otherwise helpful literature that already exists on this subject (Kim, 2000; Palloff & Pratt, 1999; Rheingold, 2000). Although containing useful technical and practical tips, it tends to assume that we already know, or that there already is consensus about, what community is and that we just need to be wise or astute in making it happen. It assumes consensus on how one goes about creating and interacting with an information system. But in an academic environment that for two decades has been the site of the so-called "culture wars," how could it be simple to develop culture? In a society where there are profound ideological differences about the nature and value of community—and where these differences mark students and faculty at our schools—how could one even know what to aim at in building an online community? The technological environment is relatively new, changes constantly, and directly affects how people communicate and interact, often in ways that are not well understood. How can these not fully understood, not fully controllable communication tools be used constructively to help develop culture and community in such a conflicted, or at least turbulent, context? And when those who work with information systems come from orientations as different as engineering and community organizing, or as different as business and academia, how can one lay down neutral rules for improving the human dimension of an online environment?

Humans Are Hard-Wired for Face-to-Face

We share in the visible broad energy and enthusiasm of many individuals, universities, corporations, government agencies, and cultural commentators for the development of computer-mediated communication (CMC) and its extension into many domains of life—from education through telecommuting and commerce to intimate relationships—and the proliferation and frequent success of such communication in these domains. At the same time, it also seems that humans are severely impaired with regard to their ability to interact naturally in the text- and image-based computer and network spaces that are still the predominant form of online environment. There is reason to think that we humans are neurologically "hard-wired" for face-to-face interaction in which bodily and emotional communication are the infrastructure, or at least the constant context, of verbal communication. This is so forcefully, compactly, and eloquently stated by Turner (2000) that we quote him in full:

At the behavioral level, the evidence [for the disposition of our brain toward face-to-face interaction] is clear each and every time humans interact: ritualized openings, repairs, and closings of encounters; extensive use of body positioning and countenance to communicate meanings; and heavy reliance upon facial gestures and voice intonations to communicate emotional states. When any of these signals is missing or is produced in an inappropriate way, interaction becomes strained, even if a constant flow of instrumental verbal chatter continues. For language alone, without an accompanying array of nonverbal, emotional clues first used by our hominid ancestors to strengthen social bonds, cannot sustain the flow of an interaction. Without the more primal, visually based language of emotions, interaction becomes problematic along several fronts: Individuals are not sure how to frame the encounter in terms of what is to be included and excluded; they are not sure of the relevant norms and other cultural systems to be employed; they are not sure of what resources, especially the intrinsic ones so essential to interaction, are to be exchanged; they are not sure if they are really a part of the ongoing flow of interaction; they are not sure if they can trust others to do what they are supposed to do; they are not sure if they can predict the response of others; and they are not sure if they can even presume that they subjectively experience the situation with others in similar ways. (p. 121)

All of the problems identified by Turner are no strangers to online environments and can turn into obstacles to effective communication and to a sense of being part of a community.

Because we depend on emotional bodily communication, conducting effective, humane, and fulfilling communication in online environments would be challenging even against a stable background of beliefs about and orientations toward culture and community in the larger society. Those involved would need to work in an ongoing way to maintain the flow of interaction so that it was interpersonally inclusive and made people feel visible, recognized, and understood. In face-to-face interaction, much of this work is done intuitively and habitually using methods into which people have been socialized. Consequently, people are often not even aware that it is being done. The need to engage in deliberate and conscious work becomes clear when certain kinds of differences or breaches occur. As Turner (2000) reminds us, "If there is disagreement over relevant cultural symbols, over understandings about the social structural demography, positions, or ties, and over meeting transactional needs, then interaction soon disintegrates, arousing potentially disassociative emotions like anger, fear, and sadness" (p. 152). Even in face-to-face contexts, considerable effort might need to be extended to maintain or restore understanding and community in the face of such disagreement. When we consider that academic environments are likely to contain or generate such disagreements and that online academic environments are marked by the absence of the social and emotional resources on which we have come to rely face-to-face, then building culture and community online can be demanding. If there is any level of interpersonal or cultural diversity, difference, or conflict that can lead to gaps in understanding, then our work, as people familiarly say, is cut out for us.

Of course, not every online setting is fraught with disintegrative tendencies or is a communicational headache. Computer-mediated courses, discussions, and public spaces are thriving everywhere. But in the words of the Internet "guru" of online or virtual community, Howard Rheingold, "All online social systems are challenged by human social foibles and technological bugs that tend to split groups apart" (Rheingold, n.d., p. 23). That is why those responsible for online educational settings and those who participate in them need to be aware of the issues we have mentioned, take them into consideration in the design and structuring of these settings, and have some experience in or orientation to dealing with typical communication and technical problems and some methods for responding to them. They also need to pay attention to these issues in an ongoing way, both to maintain constructive interaction and to be able to engage in activities of reflection and problem solving when misunderstandings or difficulties arise. This is especially true because, as has long been noted by participants and observers, communicational or cultural misunderstandings in online interaction sometimes develop in a significantly nonlinear fashion. From what seems like one moment to the next, a slight misunderstanding can turn into a flare-up of anger. The posting of one message that is not responded to can lead to the individual who posted it feeling totally unrecognized or ostracized. If in this chapter we focus especially on understanding communicational problems and gaps or breaches in community, it is because we believe that it is there that reflection, action, and intervention can make the most difference in building culture and community online.

There are two principal levels at which it is possible to focus on cultural and community issues: that of the individual class, course, or seminar and that of the larger institutional environment within which it (usually) resides. A course is a little micro-community of its own, with its own distinctive culture, and educators are beginning to realize that online education is not primarily about course delivery or content delivery but rather about creating learning environments or learning communities in which content delivery is just one component. This means attending to the course *as* a learning community. Usually, a course is embedded in an academic institution or a corporation with its own culture, and aspects of the institutional culture that have nothing to do with course content, such as drinking on campus at a college or employee motivation in a corporation, have a major effect on the individual learner and the immediate learning environment. The university or corporation is, in turn, part of the larger social environment, with its distinctive culture or (usually) cultures that affect the institution and the individual course in many ways. This means attending to trends and tensions in both the institutional culture and its social context as part of shaping benign learning environments. In the perspective from which we view information systems and educational environments and which we lay out briefly in what follows, the micro-context (in this case the course, class, or seminar) and the macro-context (the institution as well as the larger social environment) are seen as intertwined and interdependent. Hence, our focus is not on courses per se but rather on learning environments.

Paradigms of Information Systems Development

An online academic environment is a particular kind of information system. Just as communities themselves are the sites of wide-ranging and sometimes intense differences, so is the practice of information systems development. Indeed, there are significant divergences in the values, theoretical perspectives, and orientations to action that can be adopted. As already indicated, some of the now rapidly accumulating literature about online culture and online community is naive about its own assumptions or perspective, operating as though there were only one way in which to conceptualize and act in this domain.

Hirschheim and Klein (1989), adapting a well-known taxonomy of sociological theories, identify four different paradigms used in the development of information systems, each with its own values, conceptual scheme, theoretical tradition, sociopolitical stance, methods, and system developer role: the (a) functionalist (with the developer as expert), (b) social relativist (with the developer as facilitator), (c) radical structuralist (with the developer as partisan), and (d) neo-humanist (with the developer as emancipator or social therapist) paradigms. This scheme can be summarized as in Table 4.1.

Despite the limitations of this schematic and oversimplifying model, which Hirschheim and Klein (1989) acknowledge, it lends itself at least to raising to a higher level the analysis of what is involved in developing online community and culture. It is useful for educators or administrators working in this area to locate themselves in the context of these paradigms because their values, conceptual frameworks, and sociopolitical stances will have a major impact not only on their field of action and type of intervention but even on their definitions of the system itself. As Hirschheim and Klein emphasize, the different paradigms do not even agree on the elements used in defining an information system. For example, a functionalist defines the elements of an information system as "people, hardware, software, rules (organizational procedures) as physical or formal objective entities," whereas a social relativist defines them as "symbolic structures affecting the evolution of sense, the making and sharing of meanings, and metaphors" (see Table 4.1).

TABLE 4.1   Paradigms of Information Systems Development

Paradigm	Developer Archetype	Systems Development Proceeds	Elements Used in Defining Information Systems	Examples
Functionalism	Expert or platonic philosopher king	From without, by application of formal concepts through planned intervention with rationalistic tools and methods	People, hardware, software, rules (organizational procedures) as physical or formal objective entities	Structured analysis, information engineering
Social relativism	Catalyst or facilitator	From within, by improving subjective understanding and cultural sensitivity through adapting to internal forces of evolutionary social change	Subjectivity of meanings, symbolic structures affecting evolution of sense, making and sharing of meanings, metaphors	Ethnographic approaches
Radical structuralism	Warrior for social progress or partisan	From without, by raising ideological conscience and consciousness through organized political action and adaptation of tools and methods to different social class interests	People, hardware, software, rules (organizational procedures) as physical or formal objective entities put in the service of economic class interests	Trade union-led approaches
Neo-humanism	Emancipator or social therapist	From within, by improving human understanding and the rationality of human action through emancipation of suppressed interests and liberation from unwarranted natural and social constraints	People, hardware, software, rules (organizational procedures) as physical or formal objective entities for the technical knowledge interest; subjectivity of meanings and intersubjectivity of language use in other knowledge interests	Critical social theory

SOURCE: Adapted from Hirschheim and Klein (1989, p. 1210).

To stay within the confines of a book chapter, we do not discuss what building culture and community would look like according to each of these paradigms. Rather, we stay with our preferred one, the neo-humanist paradigm. Unlike its role in the others, in the neo-humanist paradigm, systems development proceeds "from within, by improving human understanding and the rationality of human action through emancipation of suppressed interests and liberation from unwarranted natural and social constraints" (see Table 4.1). We would add technical constraints to this list because of the way in which they are interwoven with social and natural ones.

The neo-humanist paradigm is grounded intellectually in critical social theory, especially the work of Habermas (1984, 1988, 1990, 1994) and those influenced by it, such as Alvesson and Willmott (1992), who have extended it to the arena of organizations and management; Forester (1992), who has applied it to the detailed analysis of communicational transactions; and Bentz and Shapiro (1998), who have incorporated it into processes of mindful inquiry. This work is relevant to information systems development and building online community through its emphasis on the following:

◆ The perspective of a person who is part of and engaged with the situation, mindful of her or his own experience and role and aiming at human betterment

◆ The nature, importance, and logic of procedures for arriving at genuine, unforced mutual understanding; at rational unforced consensus; and at norms that derive from that understanding and consensus—what this approach refers to as "communicative rationality"

◆ The recognition that this logic of mutual understanding and rational consensus differs from the logic of control, efficiency, and predictability (technical/strategic rationality); each is legitimate in its own domain, but problems arise when one is applied to the other, especially when the world of mutual understanding and shared experience is "colonized" by the principles of control, efficiency, and predictability

◆ The interlocking of communication structures with visible and invisible power structures as well as with the structure of work and technology, so that improving communication has technical and political implications, and changes in technology and power have communicative implications

◆ Affirming egalitarian and democratic values; looking at the potential in a situation for increased freedom, happiness, and justice; and sustaining utopian ideals

◆ Paying attention to what is historically and culturally unique about the situation being analyzed and recognizing that the broadest social and historical trends and tensions, such as the globalization of the economy, are present in even the smallest of human interactions

◆ Using a systemic approach, with special attention to a system's internal contradictions, especially those between what is espoused and what is practiced and between visible and invisible power structures

◆ Exposing unequal power relations and revealing that what is put forward as the common good may really serve special interests

◆ Finding ways in which to undo or weaken distorted communication, illegitimate power, and repression and to counteract the closing off of possibilities for communication (e.g., encouraging "noise" to break socially structured silences)

Clearly, there is a value conflict between this approach and the functionalist paradigm, which corresponds to the prevailing ideology of advanced industrial society and many organizations, whose emphasis is often on productivity, efficiency, throughput, output, and measurement, even in education. We should add that the choice of paradigm for information systems development may itself be affected by the type of educational environment that is at hand. The neo-humanist paradigm seems particularly suited to the shift occurring at many institutions toward learner-centered education. Whether driven by a philosophical commitment to the autonomy of the individual or the market-driven orientation toward "the customer," the learner- or student-centered approach implies taking seriously students' perspective on their own learning and its environment and, to whatever extent possible, fitting the environment to their needs rather than fitting them to the environment. Because the neo-humanist paradigm (in this regard like the social relativist paradigm) takes seriously all points of view within the system, including learners', rather than regarding them just as input to be managed, it fits with this educational approach. Ironically, however, because graduate education is increasingly driven by the demands of workplace relevance—more than 50% of all graduate students in the United States are now in the workforce—it is sometimes the students themselves who bring the criteria of productivity, efficiency, and output into education and who experience themselves as having "not enough time" for humanistically oriented exploration.

The neo-humanist paradigm in information systems development dovetails with two other traditions: participatory action research (Park, 1993), in which members of a community or group engage in a process of learning more about their social situation so as to change it in the interest of increased social justice, and the participatory design of information systems (Schuler & Namioka, 1993), in which users are regarded as primary or important shapers and designers of the information system and work processes of which they are or will be a part so as to ensure that the system meets their needs and aids their work rather than the other way around.

All of these approaches converge in advocating and encouraging a partic-ular mode of critical, creative, and reflective engagement with one's own institutional and informational environment. They all either assert or imply that we—the educators, administrators, and system developers—do not indeed build or create community and culture. Rather, we work with the community and culture that is there to make it more rational, meaningful, productive, satisfying, humane, democratic, and (in education) enhancing of learning. At certain points and in certain situations, we might need to take leadership and initiative, but in general, we need to act as particularly respon-sible and effective members of the environments that we inhabit. This some-times means articulating needs and interests that are located in them but not expressed, and it sometimes involves making proposals or taking actions. In the neo-humanist paradigm, however, one is always working within a human/technical environment rather than doing something to it. Its princi-ples are not a set of mechanical procedures to be applied to an online educa-tional setting but rather guidelines to be interpreted creatively by actors or members who inhabit it. As Rheingold (n.d.) writes, "Communities can't be manufactured, but you can design the conditions under which they are most likely to emerge and encourage their growth when they do" (p. 20).

There are two areas in which we find critical social theory and the neo-humanist paradigm weak for analyzing and engaging with online culture and community. The first is that of the concrete issues that present themselves as values and choice alternatives and preferences in communities and groups. Perhaps because of its focus on the macrostructure of modern society, critical social theory is underdeveloped in the area of small-group and community processes. It is useful for those trying to build culture and community online to be aware of some of the concepts and tools that have been developed to capture cultural preferences and differences about fundamental cultural and social issues (e.g., Hofstede, 1997; Parsons, 1977; Slater, 1976). These define dimensions or axes along which cultures vary, such as from hierarchy to equality with regard to authority structure, from cooperation to competi-tion in people's interpersonal orientation, or from engagement to detach-ment with regard to how people relate to their world. Each culture embodies a preference for a specific point along these axes, although not every individ-ual within a culture prefers the same point as the general or average norm or preference of his or her culture. This approach helps us to see, articulate, and work with cultural differences within or among groups. It also means recog-nizing that some of these differences are genuinely antagonistic or mutually exclusive. For example, it is difficult or impossible to have a short- and long-term orientation simultaneously. This does not mean, however, that a group cannot work out a method or perspective that enables individuals with differ-ent values to coexist or cooperate.

The educator or administrator working with an online culture may want to ask about himself or herself, about a specific group (e.g., class, seminar), about the online community as a whole, and about different individuals or interest groups within it, "Where am I [is it, is he/she, is his/her cultural background] located along the following dimensions or axes?"

hierarchy	↔	equality
community	↔	competition
engagement	↔	detachment
dependence	↔	independence
risk taking	↔	risk avoidance
masculinity	↔	femininity
emotionality	↔	emotional neutrality
short-term orientation	↔	long-term orientation
universalism	↔	particularism
majority	↔	minority
task orientation	↔	process orientation
self-disclosure	↔	self-concealment

Although these do not exhaust the dimensions identified by students of difference that affect groups and organizations, we believe that they are particularly useful for working with online communities. Simply by formulating the differences and preferences that exist within a community, the educator or facilitator can enhance mutual understanding by making incomprehensible differences become comprehensible and, therefore, also discussable. We omit from consideration the entire domain of group behavior and group process that involves unconscious motivation and the "group unconscious" (i.e., the sorts of antagonisms and distresses that are studied and dealt with by professionals with experience in group psychotherapy and group dynamics). Although this domain certainly affects behavior in online communities, and although group psychotherapeutic and group dynamics experience and skills can be helpful in dealing with issues that arise there, they lie outside of what can be expected of the educator or administrator without professional training in group work.

The second underdeveloped area of critical theory is that of ecology and design, that is, of understanding the online environment as a habitat in which the physical, or in this case the technical, features of the system affect or mediate human behavior and experience. Despite the valuable insights provided by ecological and behavior theory (Hiss, 1990), we find the most useful approach to this area to be not that of ecological or sociotechnical theory and research per se but rather the approach to design and habitat represented by the work of Alexander and his associates (1977). Their book, *A Pattern Language,* sensitizes us to the way in which all features of human habitation, from the layout of zones and regions in a city down to the location of doors and windows in a house and the design of a bed or bookcase, have major ramifications for the quality of life in an environment and for the organization and experience of human interaction within it. Alexander and his associates observe, for example, that the maximum distance across public squares or plazas in many beautiful old cities correlates closely with the maximum distance at which an individual can make out the details of a human face. Being sensitized to the ways in which the built environment shapes experience and life is particularly valuable for work in online environments, for two reasons. First, many of the familiar guideposts of the physical world are missing. In this cyberspace, moreover, computer and network tools play the role of physical objects in physical space—as markers of boundaries, as resources, as shapers of attention, as stimuli, as obstacles, as creators of closeness or distance. Second, as the first generations living and working in these environments, our observations and sensitivities can, it is to be hoped, shape them creatively and constructively.

Pervasive Social Trends

Central to the neo-humanist paradigm is the notion that even the smallest social unit is also a microcosm of the larger society. There is a tendency among technophiles and naive commentators to consider online environments as though they were self-contained. In this view, they can also serve as oases or refuges, somehow immunized against the rest of the world, an attitude symbolized in the famous *New Yorker* cartoon (Mankoff, 2000) of the dog sitting in front of a computer and saying to another dog, "On the Internet, nobody knows you're a dog" (p. 68). As Wellman and Gulia (1999) point out about this approach,

> Much of the analysis that does exist is parochial. It almost always treats the Internet as an isolated social phenomenon without taking into account how interactions on the Net fit with other aspects of people's lives. The Net is only one of many ways in which the same people may interact. It is not a separate reality. People bring to their on-line interactions such baggage as their gender, stage in the life-cycle, cultural milieu, socioeconomic status, and off-line connections with others. (p. 650)

Through this baggage—through people's involvement in multiple social worlds and networks—it is only natural that important social and cultural issues and tensions migrate from the larger society into online environments. Of course, there are places in cyberspace where some individuals go to escape from some of the limitations of their everyday social identities—where they can assume alternate identities, act out different gender roles, and so on (Dery, 1996; Turkle, 1995). And many individuals in text-based online environments, where they are not seen physically and communicate only via text, have had experiences of being temporarily liberated from social constraints in the sorts of communication or interaction in which they have engaged (an experience that may vanish when videoconferencing over the Internet becomes more widespread). Nevertheless, most available research (see, e.g., Smith & Kollock, 1999) shows that existing social differentiations, such as those of race and power, persist in online communities. And it makes sense that, in online educational environments where students and faculty participate as major ongoing activities, they are present with major aspects of their preexisting selves, including identities, social group memberships and backgrounds, and biases.

As Polanyi (1966) points out with regard to tools in general, it is natural that, in the early stages of their use, the physical and technical features with which people interact are in the foreground of awareness. As tool use becomes habitual, these features fade into unawareness, and instead their intended uses and objective purposes become more prominent. In the early phases of computer and network use, their technical surfaces may obscure the human relationships that they mediate, and they are perceived *as* technology. As they become increasingly "transparent to the user," their human and social context and impact become more prominent and visible. This is well symbolized by another *New Yorker* cartoon (Mankoff, 2000, p. 58), which depicts a man and a woman saying firmly to a bespectacled boy in their living room, "We're neither software nor hardware. We're your parents."

In our observation, there are a few core, complex social and cultural issues of the present that inevitably shape the nature of culture and community in any particular online academic or educational environment and make them into contested fields and concepts. Tensions, divergences, confusions, and conflicts in online communities often arise around these core issues from the larger society. Because they are pervasive in the larger society and globally, and not merely in a particular nation, they can be expected to surface in any academic community—virtual or physical. They will be familiar to most readers, both personally and intellectually. Some of them overlap and intertwine. And because they are fundamental "contradictions," or sources of conflict and tension in society, they come with no easy resolution; they may be dilemmas to be lived rather than problems to be solved, at least in the short run (Farson, 1996). What we believe to be core issues are as follows:

◆ Multiculturalism, meaning here not only the awareness and validation of individuals with different racial, ethnic, cultural, and gender backgrounds but also the question of whether and to what extent any particular cultural or group background should be privileged or taken for granted as normative either epistemologically (e.g., in the role given to the culture of "dead White European males") or as the basis for the communicative and cultural norms of the educational environment. Multiculturalism can be interpreted either in a liberal way as tolerance of or openness to "diversity" or in a radical way as a subversion of the predominance or "hegemony" of a particular culture.

◆ The extension of the principles of instrumental, strategic, and technical rationality—of means-ends thinking, control, productivity, efficiency, predictability, quantifiability, and profit—that govern business, bureaucracy, and technology to areas of life that have been organized around principles of communicative rationality (i.e., of mutual understanding, shared culture and experience, and personal expression) and, in higher education, of the pursuit of knowledge and cultural creation. This is what Habermas (1988) refers to as the issue of the "system" versus the "lifeworld" or the "colonization of the lifeworld." This tension affects both the nature and quality of academic community as well as the value and goals ascribed to learning. It governs the extent to which education and learning should be subordinated to instrumental, business, technical, and credentialist considerations or should be open-ended, exploratory, and humanistic—whether they should be fundamentally oriented toward skill enhancement and problem solving for "the workplace" or should encourage goals and aspirations that transcend it. As we have already pointed out, the large number of graduate students who are in the workforce often come to their university programs with a set of business- or work-related goals that moves the issue of "system versus lifeworld" squarely into the everyday reality of higher education.

◆ The relative weight assigned to individualism, on the one hand, and collectivism or community, on the other. Slater (1976) points out that individuals and cultures need both autonomy and dependence—both individuality and community—and that particular cultures may be weighted more toward one or the other pole. American culture, for example, is so focused on individualism and autonomy to the exclusion of interdependence and embeddedness that it is a "pursuit of loneliness." Furthermore, as Bourdieu (1998) argues, currently the world as a whole, through the global extension of the logic of the market to all provinces of social life, is being subjected to "a program of the methodical destruction of collectives" in which the individual as economic actor is given pride of place over collectives, communities, associations, and groups. This has implications for individualistic versus collaborative models of learning and for the norms that govern action and discourse in the educational environment.

How the educator or administrator relates to these issues—or to a context in which these issues are active—will have a major impact on the culture of the online educational environment.

The Case of the Inflammatory E-Mail

We pointed out at the beginning that building culture and community online involves analyzing and monitoring in detail the fabric of institutional life, and it is in this spirit, and with the larger context in mind, that we return to the case of the inflammatory e-mail. While it does not by any means raise all of the larger issues that we have discussed, it is instructive nevertheless.

Of course, every example has its own specific qualities that make it what it is and resist generalization. As local background of the case at hand, it is useful to know that all of the several hundred students in each of several graduate programs are automatically added to programwide e-mail lists that are used only occasionally and in a limited way. These lists differ from many Internet e-mail lists in that their members do not join them voluntarily but rather are added by the institution's administrative staff and removed when they either graduate or drop out. Thus, they are a captive audience, even though that is not part of the local definition of the situation and is usually not relevant given that the list is used infrequently. There are usually between a half dozen and a dozen messages per list each month. Communication designed for a list of 400 students clearly differs from that in an online seminar of 8 students.

Typical messages to the list include administrative announcements; requests for bibliographical information; faculty or administrative requests for student input or interest regarding intellectual or administrative projects; a faculty member notifying the program of a change in e-mail address; or an administrative assistant informing students that a faculty member's computer is down and that, as a consequence, he or she would not be able to communicate for several days. On entering the program, students are encouraged not to use these mailing lists for personal discussions or for communications that would be of interest or relevance to only a small subset of the student body and instead are encouraged to use online bulletin boards (forums) or more narrow group mailing lists for this purpose. Some typical messages from one of the lists should give a sense of what list members regard as "normal" or acceptable communication:

> Please pardon the intrusion. I am looking for realistic novels about men at mid-life, either making the passage or later reflecting on it. An example of the genre might be Wallace Stegner's last two—"Crossing to Safety" and "The Spectator Bird." Your suggestions would be appreciated.

> Faculty member Harrison Smerdyakov is alive and well after knee surgery and receiving messages at 702/555-0226. He will not be up on e-mail until August 21st. Thanks.

> I highly recommend Butterfly, an independent film that was recently released (Spanish with American subtitles). It is about freeing the human spirit from oppression and reminded me in many ways of our school.

> Enjoy,
> Rosa Vorian, student
> P.S. I also posted this message on the program forum in case anyone would like to discuss further.

A typical e-mail sequence on one of these lists was a query sent out by a faculty member to students soliciting input about the program's research training, several subsequent messages from faculty and students containing ideas and suggestions in response, and finally a message from the initial faculty member saying that an online forum (bulletin board) conversation about this had been initiated, so that those interested could continue the discussion while keeping those not interested from receiving unwanted e-mail.

As background, one also ought to know that the student body consists of adult professionals who have decided to pursue graduate degrees, in programs with a very substantial online component as well as occasional face-to-face contact, while continuing to live and work in their usual environments and social contexts. Importantly, as is increasingly characteristic of members of online communities and social networks, many of them are also members of other online environments, groups, or social networks, which means that neither their personal identity, nor social behavior, nor CMC is defined principally by either this particular e-mail list or this particular social group, the graduate program in which they are students. Thus, they are what we all are becoming—"limited liability members of several partial communities rather than fully committed members of one all-embracing community"—according to Barry Wellman, a preeminent scholar of technologically mediated social networks (Wellman & Hampton, 1999, p. 170).

GMOTL: Get Me Off This List!

The first issue was visible in the well-known hysterical Internet positive feedback loop "get me off this list" phenomenon (for which we have coined the acronym GMOTL). In this phenomenon, inexperienced individuals do not know how to unsubscribe from a list. They then send urgent or impassioned messages to other list members, rather than to the list manager software, asking to be removed from the list, leading other inexperienced members to "reply all" to these messages, resulting in list members receiving more unwanted messages, which in turn sets off even more desperate and often angry requests to be removed from the list and other angry responses, sometimes reducing communication to a rather primitive level. For those who have never experienced GMOTL, here is an example from the situation under discussion:

> Please take me off the list!!!!
> Please take me off the list!!!
> PLEASE take me off the list!!!
> Thank you and have a nice day.
> Zorena Livingston

Here is a sample response in this case (capitals in the original):

DEAR ALL, MUCH WORSE THAN POLITICAL E-MAILS ON THE LIST ARE THE COUNTLESS RESPONSES TO THAT INCIDENT. ALL YOU COMMENTERS PLEASE MAKE SURE THAT YOU DON'T SEND YOUR COMMENTS TO ME. I AM NOT INTERESTED TO HEAR ANYTHING OF ANY SORT ABOUT ANYTHING. CLEAR? THANKS.

This points both to the way in which participants in CMC can "show greater . . . emotional swings than those talking face to face" (Wellman & Hampton, 1999) and to the impact of individuals' computer literacy on the tone and substance of their communication. People's unfamiliarity with a medium or difficulty in navigating in it can affect their experience of the medium and the nature of their social interaction. In this event, the positive feedback loop, which produced an amplification both in the number of GMOTL messages and in the intensity of the emotions, led to something unheard of at this institution: the temporary suspension of the e-mail lists to prevent further escalation and distress. It should be noted that, given the way in which the lists were set up, the procedure for unsubscribing from them was not generally known or easily visible and was almost never used. This apparent "no exit" situation surely added to or caused the intensity of members' receiving unwanted messages. Because this situation had occurred infrequently in the past, and because the institution wanted all students to be available via an e-mail list for essential administrative communication, administrators did not immediately come forth with the standard response in Internet environments, which is to point people to the procedure for leaving the list. In the Internet as a whole, GMOTL and users' frustration about it have become so widespread that many e-mail lists now end each message to the list with instructions for unsubscribing.

GMOTL is an excellent starting point for consideration of problems in online community and culture, first, because of the way in which human communication and technology, in their intertwinement, can be at cross-purposes with one another, and second, because this clash can have wide-ranging emotional and interpersonal consequences. It is probable that most of those wanting to unsubscribe from the mailing list were trying to do "the responsible thing" in asking to be removed from it. However, because they did not do so in the technically appropriate way, they provoked a widening pool of emotional distress. Correspondingly, the recipients of the messages, instead of responding to them as technical problems, mistook them as personal offenses or inappropriate behavior deserving of blame or outrage. That these interchanges could generate such intense reactions points to some of the unusual qualities of online environments.

Cultural Norms and Technocultural Paradigms

The second issue was discussion of the appropriateness of sending political messages on or to this e-mail list—in other words, of the cultural norms of the list. Furthermore, because a significant portion of the institutional life of this graduate program occurs through CMC, discussion of the norms of the mailing list was immediately also a discussion of the norms of the academic community. So one student wrote,

> I would like to go on record as being vehemently opposed to any students using this school for their own political agenda. I find it offensive, inappropriate, and downright tacky! I am here to further my education, and I resent receiving e-mails from anyone that have absolutely nothing to do with the school per se. I also feel that the faculty should have some kind of policy against any person attempting to capitalize on students with his/her politicking!

Another replied,

> I think that a university e-mail account is the most appropriate place to get political information—especially a university that deals with psychology and human organizations. What could be more "political"? What a terrific way to make the connections between individual effort and social policy and change, in a practical way so that we can all contribute to improving our lives through political action.

Here, as in many online environments, participants might not have explicitly negotiated or contracted about either the communicational norms and ground rules or, more important, about the root values and beliefs that are to govern it. In this particular academic environment, as in many others, there are fundamental disagreements about the nature of the academic community itself, of the boundaries between private and public, and of the boundaries between educational and social or political matters.

Of course, differences about social norms, values, and boundaries exist in many human groups. But current information technologies raise special issues because implicit norms are built into them, at least as users experience them and conceive of them. When one participant wrote, "Perhaps there are those that feel that their e-mail boxes are akin to private property, to which they are only willing to permit entry to those they approve of," he was surfacing the important fact that technical tools are not merely neutral conveniences but rather are embedded in cultural and social meanings that shape how they appear to the "users." We may all have e-mail boxes or accounts, but if I think of mine as private property and you think of yours as a public communication vehicle, then we are not using "the same" tools; rather, the same tools appear within different "technocultural paradigms" (Mowshowitz, 1985). A technocultural paradigm "is not discernible in the intrinsic features of technology and transcends particular actors.... [Technocultural paradigms] provide model uses, designs, and implementations to a community of decision-makers" (p. 105).

Everyday language misleads us. In the everyday language of both contemporary culture in general and information technology professionals in particular, we are surrounded or confronted by a multiplicity of neutral technical tools and objects—computers, modems, network cables, software applications, cellular phones, and so on—which we "use" and of which we are mere "users." As Mowshowitz (1985) shows us, however, what exists is almost always a tool plus a technocultural paradigm taken together. Moreover, there can be divergent paradigms for the same tools. Thus, discourse about the technology and its uses needs to be deconstructed to reveal the paradigm, the taken-for-granted cultural and social meanings that are attached to the tools and objects, that always shape their meaning for actual humans, and that can easily lead to conflict and misunderstanding because of the differences between them.

Meta-issues

The third issue—really a set of issues—was visible in an ongoing meta-discussion of where and how to conduct such a political discussion about the election in the online environment. As in most institutions, here the online environment is actually an assemblage of a variety of technological resources, which in current practice range from e-mail lists and newsgroups through bulletin boards and Web-based groupware to synchronous media such as chat, whiteboard, and videoconferencing. An online environment is not a simple unity but rather a complex one. Sometimes a single online course will use a combination of media and communication tools, and a member of an institution with a significant online component is likely to be part of several online sub-environments within the same institution. Just as a face-to-face community consists of multiple institutions with their own norms—the norms of communication at work are different from those at home, which in turn are different from those in bars, restaurants, and places of entertainment—so online communities operate according to different norms in their different computer-mediated spaces. Different media or computer tools, partly by convention or tradition and partly because of their intrinsic features, seem to favor or disfavor particular kinds of communication and of interpersonal ties. What is appropriate in an e-mail sent to a few individuals may be inappropriate in a message sent via e-mail to a group or mailing list, and what is appropriate to any e-mail context may seem inappropriate in a public Web-based forum or bulletin board and vice versa.

When one combines this consideration with the fact that participants in CMC sometimes also interact with their CMC partners face-to-face in other contexts, creating or even identifying the relevant cultural and social norms can be a complex matter. It has often been observed that participating in multiple online environments contributes to the formation—or at least the manifestation—of multiple identities or personalities corresponding to these different environments (Turkle, 1995). This is clearly correlated with the way in which different computer- and network-mediated environments are also different cultures, with their own norms, symbols, values, rituals, and practices. Accordingly, resolving issues about culture and community requires meta-communication about both cultural differences and the appropriate uses of the technologies that themselves affect these differences. It may also involve dealing with the special character of collisions among the multiple personalities generated by these complex multidimensional environments and among the diverse norms of different parts of the same institution. For example, sometimes individuals who have had frequent or intense exchanges in a Web-based discussion group or via e-mail—who might even consider themselves to be friends or intimates in those contexts—will find themselves in the same face-to-face environment and not even acknowledge each other's existence, as though their intimacy online had no bearing on their face-to-face relationship. This can be distressing when one person expects such acknowledgment and the other does not provide it. The first person can feel rejected or that "something is wrong" because of expecting that the relationship in one domain will extend to another, while the second person is oblivious of any problem simply because of not sharing that expectation. People can be confused about the appropriate sort of language (e.g., polite, familiar) to use in an interaction because of having used language in one domain that does not seem to transfer naturally to another. Hence, in online environments, it is important to surface, articulate, and discuss these expectations and any conflicts that exist with regard to norms and the definition of roles.

In the context that we have been discussing, the meta-communicative discussion had three foci: the ability to delete messages, the use of e-mail lists versus Web-based discussion forums, and (perhaps most peculiar but also most important) whether such meta-communication should take place at all.

To Delete or Not to Delete: Who's in Control?

As an instance of how fine-grained technological issues become and how they affect human interaction, the issue of the "deleteability" of messages is illuminating. A principal source of contention—and of emotional outbursts—in the controversy about the use of a general e-mail list for political messages was that to some members of the community, the fact that they received unwanted messages at all made them feel persecuted, whereas to others, the fact that anyone can easily delete any message that they receive means that by definition there can be no problem of unwanted messages. In the words of one participant,

> For those that don't like the topic or tone, I suggest the delete button. Having an e-mail address will always open you up to some level of communication

you don't like/approve/want. However, e-mail, unlike the phone, is a window on the world, and the world is not always neat and orderly.

This points to the subtle ways in which cultural and community issues are interwoven with matters of computer literacy in particular and information literacy in general (Shapiro & Hughes, 1996). It is probable that some students receiving messages from the e-mail list either did not know how to easily or automatically delete them or felt that they were obligated to read them, so that for them the receipt of messages constituted a burden in a way that did not hold for the more experienced (or more cynical). In computer-mediated environments, "the same" environment, "the same" phenomena, and "the same" issues appear quite differently to people with different levels of technical skill and familiarity. A person who is learning to drive an automobile may experience a street as a chaotic and dangerous environment, with automobiles and pedestrians flying toward her or him in unpredictable, uncontrollable, and frightening ways, whereas an experienced driver may perceive the same street as a calm and ordered environment. Likewise, a new user of particular software or a new member of a particular computer-mediated environment may perceive herself or himself as beset by a large number of chaotic and disturbing stimuli requiring attention and response, whereas an experienced user or member may have a greater subjective sense of control induced by the skills to bring about such control. That is why, in the present case, a technically astute faculty member even sent out instructions as to how students could create an e-mail filter that would delete all unwanted messages automatically, hoping that this would bring about the sense of control that some experienced as missing.

It is likely that greater familiarity with e-mail software, and a greater sense of autonomy with it or control over it, would have solved the problem of unwanted e-mail messages for some people. It would not, however, resolve the tension between opposing values about whether the world is, or should be, neat and orderly. One person's "neat and orderly" is another person's "messy and chaotic," and when one considers the interplay of personal and cultural values—for there are cultural, as well as personal, differences in conceptions of order and chaos, public and private, open and closed, and so on—one can begin to grasp one of the challenges of building culture and community in an online educational environment.

There are also multiple layers of cultural lag with regard to the methods people adopt to handle different communication vehicles. For example, an individual who has habituated herself or himself to receiving and throwing out physical paper "junk mail" delivered by the postal service, without emotion, might not have developed the same emotional neutrality about getting junk e-mail. In addition, of course, the subjective meaning of different media may differ for different people. E-mail, because it arrives on one's computer, may be experienced as more "inside" of one's private space than is postal mail. To someone else, postal mail may seem more private because the address is handwritten and the stamp has been physically canceled.

In a culture that is in the course of technological change, which reaches different individuals at different moments in time, there is also a sort of life-historical cultural lag with regard to different individuals who are at different points in the process of adapting to a new technology and assimilating it into their lives. Partly in accordance with the phases identified by Rogers's (1995) theory of the diffusion of innovation, and partly because of life-historical and social accidents, one individual may be just learning a new technology while another is already abandoning it for a subsequent one or has just worn it out from use. In the world today, there are people who are just beginning to use e-mail in their leisure time and experiencing the excitement of connecting with long-lost and distant friends and relatives, while others have been using it for a decade for work and spend each day trying desperately to cope with literally hundreds of messages on which their professional future or financial security depends. People who were part of the early noncommercial phase of the Internet may be despondent about its commercialization, whereas others have no conception of that phase. With this diversity of background, experience, and orientation, the members of an online community may be separated by vast differences that are not easily visible in public communication but that forcefully shape individuals' experience of what is going on in that environment and what it means to them.

The issue of the "deleteability" of messages also points to a deep and important consequence of the extension of information and communication technologies into daily life, one that has scarcely received adequate treatment in either popular or scholarly literature: the breakdown of communication barriers and the elimination of silence. In an article in the *New York Times,* Friedman (1999) predicts that the major social problem for developed nations during the 21st century will be "overconnectedness," an anxiety that will result when "everyone will be able to be connected all the time, everywhere" (p. A17). Friedman points out that "time and distance provide buffers and breathing space in our lives, and when you eliminate both you eliminate some very important cushions." One result is that "the boundary between work and play disappears" (p. A17). Perhaps the major difficulty in analyzing developments and prescribing methods and solutions in online education is precisely one of cultural lag. Many enthusiastic educators, software developers, and other leaders in the field had their initial experiences of online learning and developed their enthusiasm for it during a time of minimal connectedness. Thus, they are often thinking about it within the attitude of "bringing connection to the unconnected," whereas by the time their programs and software are set up and their advertising copy is written, they may be confronting a population of the overconnected who already have mental calluses from the barrage of digitized information they receive from multiple sources on a daily, hourly, or even minute-by-minute basis and no longer have the enthusiasm and pioneering orientation of the innovators and leaders in the field.

Finding the Right Place

The second focus of the meta-discussion was moving the discussion to a Web-based online forum. To some people, there is a significant difference between two sorts of messages: those that one receives automatically— and, as it were, involuntarily—via e-mail and that are stored in one's own e-mail box on one's own computer and those that are posted and stored in a public place on a Web site to which one must "travel" to read them. As Messerschmitt (1999) points out, one task of configuring CMC for a group is finding the right balance between "push" and "pull" information because push information, which arrives relatively uncontrolled, is invasive, whereas pull information, such as notices on a Web page that one has to go to, can be overlooked and "requires more attention and conscious activity" on the individual's part. There are differences both in how they are experienced and in how the norms governing them are perceived. To some, an unwanted e-mail message is an invasion of privacy and would be more appropriate in a public place where privacy is not expected. To others, the very fact of having to go to a Web site makes such supposedly public messages de facto nonpublic by virtue of the arbitrariness of whether people actually see them or not. To them, it is precisely by going to everyone on an e-mail list that these messages become public. As the previous participant remarked in the present case,

> Someone suggested moving this to the community issue board. Some may gasp at this, but I admit publicly that I rarely if ever check that board, and I would have missed this discussion. Please, for my sake, don't move it to obscurity. It will die after a couple of posts by the same small group that frequents the boards most often. At least out here in public, there seems to be more of an opportunity for us "lurkers" to throw in the odd comment.

To some, in other words, the repeated proposal by others to relieve those who felt persecuted by moving the discussion to an online forum—which is the cultural norm for handling such issues in this particular academic environment—was really a way in which to kill the discussion or to remove it from the public realm. Thus, the most mundane and operational technical solutions or policies can be seen to have social and political agendas or implications. Within this same group of people, some defined e-mail as public and bulletin boards as private. For others, precisely the reverse was true.

Furthermore, the meaning and value of the public sphere in higher education in general and in online academic environments in particular is itself controversial, partly because of the issue of individualism versus collectivism that we discussed earlier. Is the public realm—for example, an online forum, bulletin board, chat space, or e-mail list—merely a place for individuals to pursue their own individual and instrumental goals? Or is it a place for the building of group or institutional understandings, discourse, culture, and norms? Do individuals in online educational environments have responsibilities to the group or community of which they are a part—to a public that is larger and broader than they are—or does the public realm exist only to help individuals pursue their own private purposes?

These questions can arise in some form in any social group. But the single most radical impact of current information and communication technologies on society, culture, politics, and personal life at present is precisely their redefining the lived experience of public and private and the radical dislocation of the boundary between them. In a world where it is impossible to sit in a doctor's office or café without listening to someone else's conversation on a cellular phone, where more than half of all businesses read their employees' e-mail, where individuals are having sexual intercourse in their own homes and broadcasting their activities to millions of viewers over the Internet, and where it is possible to "steal someone's identity" via technological means and impersonate her or him remotely, centuries-old meanings of private and public are being fundamentally recast. The very conceptions of public and private are in crisis. Under these circumstances, it is quite unlikely that any collection of individuals will enter a group, class, or community with identical experiences, definitions, and values regarding them.

In the actual situation that we have been analyzing, two solutions were adopted to the problem of experiencing public messages as an invasion of privacy or personal space (partly as a consequence of our suggestions and direct involvement): first, an admonition to use Web forums for messages to the whole community, and second, the creation of additional, separate, "opt in/ opt out" mailing lists for each graduate program, not for the delivery of administrative messages but rather only for those students and faculty who were both interested in public discussion and willing to delete unwanted messages. Because of the way in which the evolution of culture is itself part of the hermeneutics of culture—that is, because new developments make us reinterpret the past and even experience it differently in retrospect—an interesting sidelight on the entire incident was cast by the development of the new separate mailing lists. They came into existence under different conditions and with a different "contract," or set of shared understandings, on the part of their subscribers. For one thing, membership was by voluntary self-subscription. In addition, those who joined did so with an explicit belief in the value of public discussion and an explicit understanding that individuals would delete unwanted messages rather than complain about them. And they knew that they could unsubscribe if and when they wished, especially because, following current Internet practice, each message from the new list ended with instructions as to how to unsubscribe. These repeated brief instructions not only gave people an easy exit from the list, they also had a quasi-ethical subtext—that the individual subscribers were on this list of their own free choice and that what happened there was their own responsibility.

One of these new lists rapidly evolved into an active and intense online group. Only about 35 of the 400 students in one of the programs joined the list, as did a few faculty members. A few days after the group started, one list member used a sexual metaphor in commenting on the presidential election, and a fair amount of humor crept into the group discussion, creating an atmosphere of "anything goes." Apparently, this combination of circumstances made list members feel that they could communicate in a more intimate, personal, and engaged manner, and they exchanged more than 1,600 messages during the course of the next 3½ months on topics ranging from the presidential election, to problems in developing doctoral research proposals, to the recent deaths of relatives of some list members. Several stated that they had found on the list a kind of "community" that they had been missing and wanting in their previous experience, both on the larger group mailing list and in the institution in general. This points to the ways in which the explicit and shared understanding of group norms on the part of people who want deep communication and community can help to bring them about online. It also serves to remind us of the limits to this in official contexts and confirms what has long been observed by students of group dynamics in face-to-face groups—that a small number of people can, through their reactions, hinder or prevent open communication in a group, even if it is desired by a majority. It is also important to note that a few individuals, both students and faculty, eventually removed themselves from this new list, either because they did not feel comfortable with the tone of the conversation or because they did not want to be on a list that sent out so many messages.

A valuable and cautionary insight is provided by an accidental "experiment" that occurred in this situation. Because two graduate programs of roughly equal size were involved in the original brouhaha, an opt in/opt out list was created for each, with identical technical features. Yet while one evolved into the garrulous and intimate group already described, the other led to practically nothing. That is, by the time the first group had 40 members and had exchanged 1,672 messages, the other group had 16 members and still had not exchanged a single message. We suspect that the differences resulted from the differences between the professional cultures of the two groups as well as the personalities of those who joined, a reminder not to generalize from purely technical characteristics to human consequences.

Meta-communication and Double Binds

Perhaps the most striking meta-communicative feature of the e-mail flurry set off by the political message was the extent to which the most vocal and emphatic messages, those that were written in imperative sentences and uppercase type, seemed directed more against those who were discussing the propriety of political discussion than against those who were engaging in it—indeed, against the legitimacy of reflecting or meta-communicating at all—for once the initial message (about voting for Gore rather than Nader) had been sent, there were in fact only one or two more about the election itself. The articulate, thought-out messages were, regardless of their position, about the nature of academic community and the appropriateness of political discussion. In other words, they were meta-communicative in nature. We know, from a long-standing intellectual and research tradition originating in Bateson's double-bind theory (Bateson, 1972; Sluzki & Ransom, 1976; Watzlawick, Beavin, & Jackson, 1967), that the solution of interpersonal problems is directly bound up with the possibility of communicating about them (i.e., meta-communication), just as the impossibility or prohibition of communicating about them leads to stasis and alienation in a group or psychosis in the individual as a way of managing irresolvable conflicts. The most virulent messages here were not about receiving political propaganda; rather, they followed immediately, and seemed to be responses to, messages discussing the norms of the e-mail list itself. This was particularly true of the previously mentioned "I AM NOT INTERESTED TO HEAR ANYTHING OF ANY SORT ABOUT ANYTHING," which was addressed not only to the list but also to the two individuals who had written the most articulate arguments for and against discussing political issues on the list. In other words, they appeared to express the attitude, "I do not want to be a member of a group that discusses or publicly reflects on the norms of the group itself."

Taken to its logical conclusion, such an orientation traps those who hold it in the very predicament they are trying to escape because they have no means of reflecting on the situation and considering alternatives, options, or solutions. And in this situation, that is precisely what happened to some participants, indeed to those who chose the simplest and most obvious technological solution—hitting the "reply to all" button. Like the sorcerer's apprentice, they set off a vicious cycle of an increasing number of unwanted messages, bringing about the very thing that they wanted to escape. The consequences of this extreme anti-meta-communicative, anti-reflective attitude show clearly why meta-communication and reflection are so important in building culture and community in online educational environments. Perhaps because most online communication is denuded of the indirect nonverbal meta-communication that is so prominent in face-to-face communication, it is particularly prone to misunderstanding and miscommunication and thereby requires more intentional, explicit, and articulate meta-communication. This is why, as has been so often pointed out, online communicators sometimes resort to "emoticons" (i.e., graphic representations of human faces smiling, frowning, etc.) to function as nonlinguistic meta-communicative devices. It would be a rather important consequence of CMC if its very limitations led to a compensatory flourishing of meta-communication.

Yet people cannot be "forced" to reflect or meta-communicate; rather, they can only be shown the impact of not doing so. This impact, moreover, will differ depending on the meaning of the particular "limited liability" environment to the individual, which will not be the same for different individuals. Therefore, we cannot assume an equal interest in meta-communication on the part of all members of an online group. We need to think ourselves into the situation of the person who does not wish to meta-communicate. In an intimate relationship or in psychotherapy, this unwillingness may be regarded as a defense mechanism. However, in an online community of diverse individuals of different social backgrounds, it may mean something quite different. It is conceivable that the person who wrote "I AM NOT INTERESTED TO HEAR ANYTHING OF ANY SORT ABOUT ANYTHING" is an individual with a family under financial stress, who is working two jobs, and who is in graduate school to receive a credential that will alleviate her or his situation, with a predominantly instrumental and credentialist approach to getting a degree. For this person, the activities of a community that discusses large issues in an open-ended way, indeed anything other than taking and passing courses, may seem like a luxury that is beyond her or his possibilities. These activities may strike the person as the pastime of idle rich students, flaunting their freedom to indulge in such activities. Or the student may come from a family or cultural background in which meta-communication was taboo. The point here is that the neo-humanist perspective involves understanding all of the positions in the situation, not just the ones that the neo-humanist prefers.

The Information Structure of the Online Environment

Finally, the fourth issue to surface in the vortex of e-mail communication about the incident was the information structure of the online community itself, that is, how in a community of geographically far-flung individuals with different levels of involvement in the community and its technology one could even find out what the norms and ground rules actually are. As someone asked in an e-mail,

> I wonder if there is, somewhere, a posting that specifies the uses to which the student/faculty mailing lists can be put to. If so, then we who are on those lists should abide by those guidelines as though they were a contract for our inclusion on those lists. I do not know if such guidelines exist, and if they do, I obviously do not know where to find them. If someone does, would they kindly either reproduce and add them to this mailing or at least send out the [URL] so we can check them out.

Regardless of how involving an online educational environment may be, its normative structure can sometimes seem either opaque or invisible, even when embodied in written rules and guidelines that are posted in known places, as in the environment referred to here. The reasons for this are worthy of detailed consideration and research. Here we note only that people both navigate through Web sites at their own will and import into one environment assumptions and norms that are derived from others. This can make it easy for the norms, even when explicit, to slip by the participants. Because there is no standard format or structure for an online environment, there is no standard "place" for the location or display of its norms, even if they have been formulated. Those who remember their ancient history will know what a decisive step it was in the evolution of civilization when the laws of the city were first written down—chipped into walls, such as the ones still visible in the Cretan town of Gortyn—so that in matters of dispute people could go down to the wall and read the laws themselves. During recent years, the FAQ (frequently asked questions) document has begun to take on some of that function in computer- and network-mediated environments, even though FAQs are still largely technical in content. There are, of course, many policy documents online. But a formal policy, often formulated with an eye to possible future legal protection or litigation, is not a statement of norms. What is needed is something like a FANQ (frequently asked normative questions) or a FASQ (frequently asked social questions) in a publicly identified place.

Even a FANQ, however, presupposes a subjective orientation toward finding out the norms and taking them into account in one's behavior. How many people read the privacy policies of the companies from which they buy on the Internet or the legal and copyright stipulations that appear on their screens when they install software? For many people, cyberspace is still their personal "wild west" of liberation from social constraints. This may be even truer of people who have not grown up in online environments. In any case, this issue focuses our attention not only on the special need to clarify and articulate the norms of the online educational environment but also on the need to then make them visible and public in adequate ways. In the situation at hand, we did in fact create and send out a message trying to articulate the norms of this particular institutional and online culture and pointing to existing documents available online that set out the sort of norms and guidelines that were being requested.

The fact that, in the case of the inflammatory e-mail, there actually were such guidelines already available online, although their locations were not generally known, points to another important matter. Individuals in any particular online environment will have been there for different lengths of time and with different histories, which are sometimes less visible online than in face-to-face groups or communities. These differences in history make for different "stocks of knowledge" (Schutz, 1970), which in turn create important differences in how the online environment is perceived, experienced, and known and in how people interact in it. In face-to-face communities, people have a sense of when people enter the community and leave it, who is a newcomer and who is an old-timer, and so on, and this knowledge becomes associated with people's perceptions of even the physical appearances of others. In Japan, small children in their first year of school wear specially colored clothing, so that people who see a child dressed this way on the street will know that this child might need some special attention or help in getting across a street, finding her or his way, and so on. Although these kinds of differences can be visible and can be made known in online groups, they might not be, and consequently, knowledge that could be shared might not be. The very assumption of equality that has been hailed as a virtue in online interactions can also efface relevant history and differences, the knowledge of which could make interactions more cooperative and result in communicating information that otherwise remains invisible.

Some Tentative Lessons

In general, information literacy and computer literacy are defined as competences that inhere—or should inhere—in an individual to serve her or his goals. A few years ago, we developed an expanded and now widely used conception of information literacy as consisting of seven dimensions (Kirk, 2000; Shapiro & Hughes, 1996):

- *Tool literacy:* the ability to understand and use the practical and conceptual tools of current information technology that are relevant to education and the areas of work and professional life that the individual expects to inhabit
- *Resource literacy:* the ability to understand the form, format, location, and access methods of information resources, especially daily expanding networked information resources
- *Social-structural literacy:* knowing that and how information is socially situated and produced
- *Research literacy:* the ability to understand and use the information technology-based tools relevant to the work of today's researcher and scholar
- *Publishing literacy:* the ability to format and publish research and ideas electronically, in textual and multimedia forms, to introduce them into the electronic public realm and the electronic community of scholars
- *Emerging technology literacy:* the ability to adapt to, understand, evaluate, and make use of—in an ongoing way—the continually emerging innovations in information technology
- *Critical literacy:* the ability to evaluate critically the intellectual, human, and social strengths and weaknesses, potentials and limits, and benefits and costs of information technologies

At the time, we recommended that education for information literacy focus on all of these dimensions. Now that an increasing portion of an increasing number of individuals' lives is spent in online social networks and environments, it is becoming clear that this and other conceptions of information literacy are deficient through neglect of a vital competence area—that of communication, interaction, and interpersonal behavior in the world of cyberspace. This eighth dimension of information literacy could be called "online community literacy" or, following Habermas's (1970, 1984) notion of communicative competence, "online communicative competence."

The notion of communicative competence in general denotes individuals' ability to construct interpersonal intersubjective relationships of shared meaning and understanding through their communicative acts in the dimensions of defining a shared objective reality, acting according to interpersonally valid norms, and expressing their own subjective reality. Competent communication includes what Schutz (1970), in line with Mead's notion of the construction of the self through communication, calls the "reciprocity of perspectives," that is, individuals' ability to "relativize" their own perspectives in relation to those of the persons with whom they communicate. Through the reciprocity of perspectives, the individual recognizes that, just as a partner in communication is an "other" to her or him, or part of the periphery of the individual's own self-centered world, the individual is an "other" to that partner, or a peripheral person in the partner's self-centered world. Maintaining the reciprocity of perspectives in communication requires communication partners to continuously adjust their egocentric perspective to take account of the other's. Indeed, it requires a synthesis that incorporates and transcends both. When I sit across from you, not only do I know implicitly that what is to my left is to your right, I also know implicitly that neither of these directions is absolute. They are always relative to someone.

In online environments, communicative competence involves recognizing that in CMC, interpersonal actions are mediated by the computer and network structures and tools through which they take place; that is, the processes of constructing an interpersonal world, as well as the world that is constructed, are affected and shaped by those structures and tools. Competent communication in face-to-face situations involves awareness both of context and of impact, for all communication has an implied reference to the context in which it takes place and some kind of acknowledgment of the way in which that context enters into what is communicated. This includes the famous "definition of the situation," in which communicators define and experience themselves as sharing a context. Competent communication also involves the awareness of impact—that precisely through my communication and action, I am affecting those with whom I communicate. Indeed, being competent in this way is part of what we mean and assume in thinking of someone to be rational, adult, and sane. Nevertheless, it is possible to be communicatively competent in general (i.e., to be a rational, sane adult person in the general social world) without being able to translate this ability into competence within online environments. Thus, a generally rational sane adult might not automatically know how to be so in cyberspace (just as it is said of some rational sane adults who learn how to drive that they are a "terror at the wheel"). Conversely, of course, it is possible to master computer communication tools without being communicatively competent in this interpersonal sense. That is why we think that it makes sense to identify online communicative competence as a separate dimension or skill area and to concentrate on it educationally, that is, to focus on the intersection of communicative competence and computer and network tool use as an area for development in both individuals and groups.

Developing online communicative competence is shaped by social, cultural, psychological, and technical factors. It cannot be taught like a technical skill or an aggregate of information. It is quite likely that particular cultural and social environments may be more or less favorable to it. It may be, for example, that a culture such as that of the United States, which emphasizes the individual over the community and, as Slater (1976) argues, is pathologically individualistic to the point of denying individuals' interdependence, may make it harder for individuals to become communicatively competent online or community literate. Nevertheless, we believe that it would be prudent for educators to spend time on online communicative competence, which goes well beyond "netiquette," in orientation programs for new students and in courses in computer and information literacy. It would also be useful to devote some time to it in online courses as well as to prepare FANQ and FASQ documents and make them available in known places.

Over and above these specific educational activities, how can the neo-humanist, emancipatory, or critical information systems developer, educator, or administrator contribute to the development of community literacy and online communicative competence in her or his environment? We believe that central to this role is aiming at and modeling a particular sort of meta-communication—an ideal rational discourse in which all of the technical, social, cultural, value, and psychological interests at play in the situation, as well as the technology through which they are shaped and mediated, would be represented and articulated in a reflective process. In this process, mutual understanding and reflection would also make possible shifts in people's positions, views, and interpreted needs, such that a new genuine consensus and a new configuration of the system could be arrived at. The neo-humanist actor must aim at such a discourse, even if it is impossible, while understanding and trying to educate the community about *why* it is impossible in the particular situation. The neo-humanist actor should try to act in a way that best mediates between the constraining and enabling factors to move the system in the direction of such a state, choosing from a repertoire of possible actions and techniques to create this movement—educational and informational comments and documents, policy proposals, process comments, humor, alliances, conspiracies, assistance to individuals, negotiations, psychological and cultural interpretations, imaginative and innovative actions, surrealist or absurd gestures. In any actual situation, power structures and inequalities, patterns of distorted communication, psychological deformations, and skill deficits may severely curtail what can be done. But there is almost always something that can be done.

References

Alexander, C., Ishikawa, S., Silverstein, M., Jacobson, M., Fiksdahl-King, I., & Angel, S. (1977). *A pattern language: Towns, building, construction.* New York: Oxford University Press.

Alvesson, M., & Willmott, H. (Eds.). (1992). *Critical management studies.* Newbury Park, CA: Sage.

Bateson, G. (1972). *Steps to an ecology of mind.* New York: Ballantine Books.

Bentz, V. M., & Shapiro, J. J. (1998). *Mindful inquiry in social research.* Thousand Oaks, CA: Sage.

Bourdieu, P. (1998, December 8). The essence of neo-liberalism (J. J. Shapiro, Trans.). *Le Monde Diplomatique* (English-language edition). Available: www. en.monde-diplomatique.fr/1998/12/08bourdieu.

Dery, M. (1996). *Escape velocity: Cyberculture at the end of the century.* New York: Grove.

Farson, R. (1996). *Management of the absurd: Paradoxes in leadership.* New York: Simon & Schuster.

Forester, J. (1992). Critical ethnography: On fieldwork in a Habermasian way. In M. Alvesson & H. Willmott (Eds.), *Critical management studies* (pp. 46-65). Newbury Park, CA: Sage.

Friedman, T. (1999, August 10). The Y2K social disease. The *New York Times,* p. A17.

Habermas, J. (1970). Toward a theory of communicative competence. In H. P. Dreitzel (Ed.), *Recent sociology #2* (pp. 114-148). New York: Macmillan.

Habermas, J. (1984). *The theory of communicative action: Vol. 1, Reasons and the rationalization of society* (T. McCarthy, Trans.). Boston: Beacon.

Habermas, J. (1988). *The theory of communicative action: Vol. 2, Lifeworld and system: A critique of functionalist reason* (T. McCarthy, Trans.). Boston: Beacon.

Habermas, J. (1990). *Moral consciousness and communicative action* (S. W. Nicholsen, Trans.). Cambridge: MIT Press.

Habermas, J. (1994). Three normative models of democracy. *Constellations, 1*(1), 1-10.

Hirschheim, R., & Klein, H. K. (1989). Four paradigms of information systems development. *Communications of the ACM, 32,* 1199-1215.

Hiss, T. (1990). *The experience of place.* New York: Knopf.

Hofstede, G. H. (1997). *Cultures and organizations: Software of the mind* (Rev. ed.). New York: McGraw-Hill.

Kim, A. J. (2000). *Community building on the Web: Secret strategies for successful online communities*. Berkeley, CA: Peachpit Press.

Kirk, T. G., Jr. (2000). *Information literacy in a nutshell: Basic information for academic administrators and faculty* [Online]. Retrieved June 22, 2001, from: www.ala.org/acrl/nili/whatis.html

Mankoff, R. (Ed.). (2000). *The New Yorker book of technology cartoons*. Princeton, NJ: Bloomberg.

Messerschmitt, D. G. (1999). *Networked applications: A guide to the new computing infrastructure*. San Francisco: Morgan Kaufmann.

Mowshowitz, A. (1985). On the social relations of computers. *Human Systems Management, 5*, 99-110.

Palloff, R. M., & Pratt, K. (1999). *Building learning communities in cyberspace: Effective strategies for the online classroom*. San Francisco: Jossey-Bass.

Park, P. (Ed.). (1993). *Voices of change: Participatory research in the United States and Canada*. Westport, CT: Bergin & Garvey.

Parsons, T. (1977). *The evolution of societies*. Englewood Cliffs, NJ: Prentice Hall.

Polanyi, M. (1966). *The tacit dimension*. Garden City, NY: Doubleday.

Rheingold, H. (n.d.). *The art of hosting good conversations online* [Online]. Retrieved November 18, 2000, from: www.rheingold.com/texts/artonlinehost.html

Rheingold, H. (2000). *The virtual community: Homesteading on the electronic frontier* (rev. ed.). Cambridge: MIT Press.

Rogers, E. M. (1995). *Diffusion of innovations* (4th ed.). New York: Free Press.

Schuler, D., & Namioka, A. (1993). *Participatory design: Principles and practices*. Hillsdale, NJ: Lawrence Erlbaum.

Schutz, A. (1970). *On phenomenology and social relations: Selected writings*. Chicago: University of Chicago Press.

Shapiro, J. J., & Hughes, S. K. (1996). Information literacy: Technical skill or liberal art? Enlightenment proposals for a new curriculum. *EDUCOM Review, 31*(2), 31-35.

Slater, P. (1976). *The pursuit of loneliness: American culture at the breaking point* (Rev. ed.). Boston: Beacon.

Sluzki, C. E., & Ransom, D. C. (1976). *Double bind: The foundation of the communicational approach to the family*. New York: Grune & Stratton.

Smith, M. A., & Kollock, P. (Eds.). (1999). *Communities in cyberspace*. New York: Routledge.

Turkle, S. (1995). *Life on the screen: Identity in the age of the Internet*. New York: Simon & Schuster.

Turner, J. H. (2000). *On the origins of human emotions: A sociological inquiry into the evolution of human affect*. Stanford, CA: Stanford University Press.

Watzlawick, P., Beavin, J. H., & Jackson, D. D. (1967). *The pragmatics of human communication: A study of interactional patterns, pathologies, and paradoxes*. New York: Norton.

Wellman, B., & Gulia, M. (1999). Net surfers don't ride alone: Virtual communities as communities. In M. A. Smith & P. Kollock (Eds.), *Communities in Cyberspace* (pp. 167-194). New York: Routledge.

Wellman, B., & Hampton, K. (1999). Living networked in a wired world. *Contemporary Sociology, 28*, 648-654.

Chapter 5

Uncertain Frontiers

Exploring Ethical Dimensions of Online Learning

Dorothy Agger-Gupta

Sitting in her kitchen in Wisconsin, with her children finally asleep, Linda—an accountant, single mother, and graduate student—turns on her computer and logs on to an online seminar on global leadership. She reads the entries posted by the professor, a public policy expert who lives in Texas, and the other student members of the seminar: a retired U.S. Air Force captain in Virginia, a banker in Brazil, a social worker in Boston, a teacher in Tokyo, and a lawyer in San Francisco. Linda posts her paper on the online forum and responds to the comments of other students. She switches to the university's online open forum, where she reads some contentious dialogue about the university's recent hiring decision. She chooses not to join in. A notice pops up on her screen inviting her to join in a live text chat with two students who entered the graduate program with her last year: a nurse in Sweden and a police officer in Alaska. They ask her for help in understanding a difficult statistics problem. Linda turns on the log function of the chat room to save the text on her home computer. After 15 minutes of online discussion, Linda says goodbye and leaves the chat room. She checks her e-mail and is disappointed that she has not yet received a reply from her professor on a question she e-mailed over a week ago. She wonders whether the professor is upset with her question, disappointed in her work, or just too busy to answer. Linda sends an e-mail to one of her online friends, complaining about the faculty member's lack of response. She scans her other e-mails, annoyed at the number of messages that are being broadcast to all students at her university. She deletes some without reading them, frustrated at spending her time clearing out these "extra" e-mails. It takes more than an hour to review and respond to the remaining e-mail from others at the university, from colleagues at work, and from her family and friends. When Linda finally logs off of the Internet, she leaves a virtual world where time, space, culture, and even identities are untethered by the constraints of the "real world." She continues to work on her computer, scanning the text she has saved from these live chats, and notices a pattern of increasing tension between two participants. This pattern suggests a new model for online conflict that might be relevant to Linda's research. She wonders whether to try out her new qualitative analysis software to analyze this text and further develop this model. Two hours after turning on her computer, she turns it off.

Linda opens her text and begins her assigned reading. She is exhilarated and exhausted by her online world, and she worries about keeping this world in balance with the reading and writing demands of her studies and with the pressures of her other roles as a professional, mother, and volunteer to youth sports. She knows that she has to leave behind some "real life" roles to make time for her life in her virtual learning community. But she does not know which ones.

Overview

This chapter explores the ethical dimensions of online learning. Ethics are involved wherever there is social interaction that involves choice, action, and impact on others. Internet-based technologies have extended the scope of ethics into online forms of social interaction among people who share affiliations but might never meet face-to-face. When we migrate well-established forms of human endeavor, such as education and learning, into virtual environments, the ethical dilemmas that emerge are often unrecognized or unacknowledged.

Although we have a long tradition of ethical theory and research, in practice we tend to rely on goodwill and "caring for others" as guiding principles when faced with personal and professional ethical dilemmas. This approach is much like traditional folk medicine; it may be appropriate for some situations but inadequate for subtle yet far-reaching dilemmas involved with online learning that include social interaction among people who never meet. In virtual education, ethical dilemmas are often unrecognized because of the subtle yet pervasive nature of computer technologies as well as the hidden nature of the impact of actions on others whom we never see.

Most theoretical models of ethics were developed to address choices in a face-to-face world, where we assumed we could "know" the impact of our actions. Traditional models, although based in different and sometimes conflicting underlying principles, all assume a linear world in which we can either use a logical framework for assessing the inherent ethics of a choice of action or follow a logical sequence for determining the probable consequences of a choice of action. The nature of online learning is based in a global arena, unseen results, and nonlinearity in which the impact of a few words or a "small" action can have unpredictably large, widespread results.

Competency in recognizing and addressing ethical dilemmas of online learning involves understanding the pervasive yet hidden nature of computer technologies such as logical malleability, invisibility, privacy, and confidentiality. Our roles as online educators and students are linked to our ethical responsibility. Ethical issues associated with power, autonomy, self, and personas are exacerbated in online environments. Issues of copyright and ownership of intellectual properties remain unresolved for virtual environments that bypass national boundaries. The subtly persuasive power of computer-generated script may dominate a virtual environment. As teachers and students, we share a responsibility to better recognize and understand the ethical nature of our online learning places.

Introduction to Ethical Dimensions of Online Learning Communities

Information and communication technologies are an integral part of cultural forces that influence the nature of a society (Bonk & King, 1998; Hobart & Schiffman, 1998). Online discourse and virtual learning are manifestations of rapid technocultural changes, serving to redefine education and to create new systems for learning.

Classroom-based education promotes schedules and structures because specific classrooms need to be allocated at specified times. Standardization is supported by people teaching side by side. Although there is a differentiation between "classroom learning" and "homework learning," the classroom teacher is responsible for enforcing the rules of both.

By contrast, many effective models of online learning do not attempt to transfer the rules and norms of classroom-based education into virtual environments. Rules are different when the teacher and students do not meet in a classroom in pre-arranged blocks of time. Online learning may involve collaboration, sharing, and discovery among people who never meet face-to-face. Collaboration and sharing of information are often encouraged. As students access an ever-expanding universe of knowledge via the Internet, teacher-supplied content may be replaced by students' self-discovery, knowing what questions to ask, and knowing how to locate relevant knowledge (Haythornthwaite, Kazmer, Robins, & Shoemaker, 2000; Palloff & Pratt, 1999).

As in any new frontier, these changes create a void of behavioral norms that is now being filled by rapidly designed laws, regulations, rules, and standards. Policies, standards, and cultural norms about learning are reformulated to address new issues in online learning. The rules of engagement in online learning appear seductively similar to those of face-to-face education. It is tempting to ignore change and apply our favored understandings and effective practices from classroom-based learning.

Issues of ethics in online learning go beyond questions of right and wrong, and they address far more than ethical dilemmas. Ethical choices inform our actions and become silently embedded in our culture. Rapid technological changes fuel explosive scenarios that far outdistance our comfortable ways of understanding ethical choices. "Every social institution and psychological effect of modernity, let alone the market-spawn economic interests, militate[s] against all effective change of direction" (Bauman, 1993, p. 217). By ignoring the ethical dimensions of online learning, we become more vulnerable to the unintended consequences of our choices that may impact social values, cultural norms, and dominant rule sets of learning (Fisher & Wright, 2001).

The choices and actions of every person involved in online learning are important. In the world of networked communications that form the framework for online learning, even the "weakest" links of people and ideas are important for the complex whole to thrive (Watts, 1999). During the emergence of complex systems, there are leverage points at which even the smallest actions may have profound effects (Holland, 1995, 1998).

We need to be able to develop trust in each other as we build new systems of learning. "One component of ethical pioneering is making an assumption of trust and operating on that assumption until the evidence indicates that more caution is required" (Morgan, 1999, p. 153). Values matter in this new frontier, but also needed is competency in understanding the unique nature of virtual communication, where differences in culture, cues, timing, and dispersion may be difficult to discern yet affect the nature of online learning (Schweizer, Paechter, & Weidenmann, 2001).

Theoretical Views of Ethics

Ellen is engaged in a private online seminar in human development at a local college. Many of the students work during the day, and the online seminar gives everyone a chance to learn and engage in dialogue outside of normal class times. At the beginning of the seminar, all participants agreed to keep all of the dialogue confidential because some of it was expected to be of a confidential nature. One of the participants revealed that she was having an affair with a man whom Ellen recognized as the husband of one of her friends. She copied the student's comments onto her hard drive. The following day, the student returned to the forum and deleted her comments about her affair and

TABLE 5.1   Four Ethical Belief Systems

	Situational	
Relativism		Pragmatic sensibility
Choice Itself _____		_____ **Future Impact of Actions**
Deontological theories		Consequentialism
	Logical, Theoretical	

asked all of the other participants not to mention it to anyone. Ellen decides to keep the original comments on her computer.

The foundational values of educators in North America have deep roots in a long tradition of Western academia. Understanding ethics in online learning involves deliberate attention to traditional foundations, recent developments in ethical theorizing, and the unique attributes of online learning (Althauser & Matuga, 1998).

Traditional ethical theories assume proximity and neighborhoods, worlds in which we could know—through logic—either the ethics of an action itself or the impact of an action. Recent developments in ethics have a greater appreciation for the importance of intuition, stories, and determinants such as culture and professional roles in determining the ethical implications of an action (see Table 5.1).

In the virtual world of online learning, it is difficult to discern the ethical nature of our actions. "Modern technology has introduced actions of such a novel scale, objects and consequences that the framework of former ethics can no longer contain them" (Jonas, 1974, pp. 7-8). Our awareness of ethical issues often ends when we are satisfied that we have addressed the needs of those near and dear to us—or at least those who are within our immediate sphere of connection (Bauman, 1993). In online learning environments, the "immediate sphere of connection" may extend around the world and include people we might never meet face-to-face.

A discussion of ethical issues needs to address ways in which to reconcile multiple truths. Whereas classical philosophical discourse articulates differences among theoretical bases of ethical belief systems, other pragmatic and professional ethicists focus on the situational context. Ethical rules describe the specifics of what we should and should not do. Codes of ethics are sets of rules, often created by institutions or professions to guide their members in consistency of ethical choices. When closely scrutinized, they often lead to paradoxical dilemmas. "Do no harm" and "protect privacy" can be difficult to follow when protecting the privacy of one person can cause harm to another person. The reconciliation of multiple truths can be through elevating one truth above another or through narrative lenses that embrace the tensions and differences. When ethical rules conflict, ethical principles help to guide the balancing of the choices. Finally, ethical theories provide the foundation of underlying beliefs that provide the rationale for all ethical choices (Newman & Brown, 1996).

There are fundamental differences in the nature of these underlying belief systems that guide us in evaluating ethical dilemmas. Consequentialism (including forms of utilitarianism) claims that the rightness or wrongness of an action can be determined by the consequences of the action itself. Deontological theories base the rightness or wrongness of an action on the nature of the action itself. A third approach, relativism, claims that there are no universal truths but that the rightness or wrongness depends on the context, culture, and unique circumstances of the action itself (Johnson, 1985).

Differences also emerge in the nature of the values that underpin these belief systems. Utilitarianism, which bases rightness on maximizing total happiness, ranges from individual happiness to considering the happiness of all peoples both living and of future generations (Smart, 1986). Ethical choices in online learning would intend to create the most positive learning community for all current and future peoples. Contractualism is based on informed agreement: "An act is wrong if its performance under the circumstances would be disallowed by any system of rules for the general regulation of behavior which no one could reasonably reject as a basis for informed, unforced general agreement" (Scanlon, 1986, p. 43). Existential ethics may be viewed as an approach that forces people to go beyond their social roles, taking responsibility for their own lives, "striving to be clear-sighted about the implications of our involvements, and acknowledging our indebtedness to the wider community" (Guignon, 1986, p. 88).

Although many belief systems suggest that all peoples are similar and should share ethical belief systems, pragmatic sensibility recognizes that different people have different experiences that influence their beliefs. Yet we all share an obligation to act to make the world a better place, even though we know that "better place" is an unreachable ideal and that we may have very different views of what that better place would look like (Dewey, 1984, p. 218).

Pragmatic sensibility is based in the ideas of two American philosophers: John Dewey and William James. It has three core concepts: transiency, pluralism, and meliorism. Transiency supports the sanctity of individuals and the importance of all of our decisions (McDermott, 1986, p. 122). We share an obligation to keep in mind the ever-unreachable ideal as we honor the importance of each daily decision. A second core concept, pluralism, acknowledges that knowing is based in unique experiences that produce multiple traditions of what should and should not be done. "Moral pluralism is at the center of political pluralism. . . . Most of our difficulties emerge from misunderstanding, condescension, and arrogance, none of which [is] salutary for building a genuine moral community throughout the world" (p. 125). The third concept is meliorism, in which "we effect no ultimate solutions yet strive to make things better" (p. 126). The consequences of what we do matters. There are no absolute ends—we are always in the process of becoming—yet we need to use our ethics wisely to understand the impact that our actions will have in changing circumstances.

Most approaches to ethical choices are based in logical reasoning and situational analysis involving rule sets and explicit values. A few alternate approaches to ethical choices reject both logic and situation as having any ultimate authority and offer narrative reasoning as a rigorous and appropriate way in which to address complex issues.

Narrative logic is a powerful approach for building an ethical belief system for people with different values, traditions, and experiences by developing a shared understanding of the potential consequences of an action. It is based on the strength of that understanding that comes from telling stories of anticipated outcomes—and listening to the stories of others. Narrative logic is particularly well suited for online environments in which people share learning experiences while living and working in different locations with diverse cultures. Through narration, we can share our stories of what we believe to be the consequences of specific actions, and we can better understand whether the outcomes are likely to be what we intended. "While logic is good for describing what is, narrative is good for exploring what could be and for figuring out what should be" (Artz, 2000, p. 77). With narration, a diversity of belief systems give rise to different stories of perceived consequences of choices and actions. Through this diversity of stories, we can come to better understandings of our deep differences in ways that support the development of a richer story that reflects our multiple truths and experiences and helps us to create, together, a better world through our online learning communities.

Professional Ethics in Online Learning Communities

Several members of a university's online community are engaged in a spirited online dialogue, using a forum and chat service provider not associated with the university. The online dialogue was created by faculty and students who wanted to converse in an arena that was free of the restrictions of the university's forum guidelines. Participants are also able to invite their non-university colleagues to join in the dialogue. At times, the conversation becomes focused on the politics, personalities, and relationships of the university's administra-

tion. A student relays her version of a statement by a particularly controversial professor regarding a highly sensitive and volatile issue.

There are some participants who "lurk" in this forum, copying material from the discussions, without indicating their presence, to develop their own studies of this community. One participant copies and distributes the student's version of the professor's controversial statement to several others who are not part of the forum, including potential students, the university's administrators, and personal friends who she believes would be interested in the conversation. All of the copying, distributing, and analysis of the conversations is occurring without the knowledge of the participants themselves. The faculty's comments are rapidly spread through multiple newsgroups and become a shared story—globally. The professor begins receiving e-mails from around the world criticizing his "words." His purported statement is used as an example by news commentators about the disintegration of our society. The professor in question denies the specifics of the comments. Furthermore, he maintains that the overall impact of this misstatement, which has been dispersed around the world, absolutely misrepresents him, his values, and his intent. His rebuttal and attempts to reclaim his reputation receive little attention in the online, rapidly dispersed grapevine.

People in professions have unique powers. "It is because professionals have this power to affect the world that imposing obligations on them to behave in certain ways is justified" (Johnson, 1985, p. 25). Professional ethics assume that professional roles matter (MediaMoo, 1997). When you assume the role of a professional, the codes of ethics established for that profession matter, going beyond that of an individual (Johnson, 1985). Professional ethics provide explicit guidance for people engaged in similar professional roles. "Clinical pragmatic ethics" focuses on doing what one's profession has trained one to do (Lowenberg & Dolgoff, 1988). Most professionals tend to rely on their intuition, past experience, conventional behavior among colleagues, and professional codes of ethics as the basis for ethical decisions (Newman & Brown, 1996), with little reflection or debate on ethics beyond support for "good intentions."

There are differences between institutional responsibilities and individual responsibilities. Frankena (1986) suggests three ethical questions that an institution needs to address: "1) What should our laws require, forbid, or permit[?]; 2) What should our positive social morality require, forbid, or permit[?]; and 3) What should be the rules and ideals of other social institutions[?]" (p. 314). Issues of personal ethics are outside the purview of the institution. The challenge for online communities is to differentiate what should and should not be permitted within the institution while still supporting the rights of individuals to assert their own ethical beliefs.

Newman and Brown (1996), in addressing the ethical conflicts inherent in situations that embody differing ethical belief systems, propose a guiding framework for ethical decision making that is based on Kitchener's (1984) ethical principles: "respecting autonomy, avoiding undue harm, doing good, being fair, and being faithful" (Newman & Brown, 1996, p. 5).

Professional Ethics for Faculty in Education

Professional codes of ethics in educational institutions often delineate the responsibilities of faculty to defend their own freedoms while upholding the freedoms of others, to respect the dignity of others, to respect the rights of others to express diverse opinions, to support intellectual freedom and honesty, and to create a learning environment for students that supports learning and equity in the student-teacher relationship (Sterling College, 2000).

Sumsion (2000), in a reflective log of her initial year as a college professor, found that the professional code of ethics that she was required to sign was insufficient and messy in its ambiguity. She developed a bounded form of an ethics of caring that included a measure of being present in the moment— to balance the nurturing with professional accountability. "Embracing presence as a pedagogical practice . . . holds potential for enacting a commitment to caring as a foundation of professional practice without perpetuating the disadvantages associated with women's traditional nurturing roles" (p. 167).

The Unique Ethical Responsibilities of Online Learning Professionals

> *On the university's private Web site, there is a forum for discussing university issues. Several students are engaged in an online conversation about a dean's decision regarding dismissal of a faculty member, suggesting that these actions were based in personal biases rather than the faculty member's academic record. Using e-mail, several faculty members and administrators exchange comments about this dialogue by the students, question the motives of the students, and discuss any potential actions to take with the students.*

Does freedom of speech, highly valued in an academic environment, extend into online environments, or does the university have a legitimate right to intervene with material posted on the university's Web site? When two faculty members share information about a student using any form of electronic media, the student has a right to access that information. When two students discuss a faculty member using e-mail, the faculty member has no similar right. The professor has rights only when the students post false and damaging information about him or her in a forum that is more broadly accessible by members of the learning community (Carlson, 2001). In a 2001 decision by the U.S. Supreme Court, the court expanded university rights further by letting stand a 2001 ruling by the U.S. Court of Appeals for the Fourth Circuit in Richmond, Virginia, that supported a university administration's right to prohibit employees, including faculty, from viewing sexually explicit material on the Internet without the approval of their supervisors (Foster, 2001).

The ethical dilemmas confronting the teacher in online environments are embedded in the understanding of the very meaning of education, of the university, and of the teacher. The nature of online environments directly affects the nature of teaching. If we treat online educational environments as places for not only the "filling of the pail" with information but also the "lighting of the fire" of learning, then we make ethical choices.

> If the teacher, if anyone, is to be an example of a whole person to others, he must first strive to be a whole person. . . . His life is full of risks, but risks he has the courage to accept because, like the explorer, he learns to trust his own capacities to endure, to overcome. (Weizenbaum, 1976, p. 280)

Reading text on a computer screen, in isolation from others, raises questions about the construction of meaning, of values, and of understanding in virtual environments. Do educators have a professional responsibility to monitor the construction of meaning in collaborative online environments? If so, then how? As Zuboff (1984) remarks when considering meaning making in learning workplaces, "Meaning cannot be tacitly assumed [or] remain implicit in action. Instead, people have to talk about what they think and why. This kind of interaction introduces new psychological demands and implications for social relationships" (p. 204).

Ethical Dimensions of Information and Communication Technologies

> No uniform causal relation stands out between the technologies of information and the ages they demarcate. . . . Technology exists in dynamic interplay with culture, shaping and being shaped by it. Thus, in some instances, technology may foster new forms of information, while in others, it is fostered by them. (Hobart & Schiffman, 1998, p. 5)

Online learning is growing within a globally accessible, fertile environment that is nourished by a confluence of computer and network-based technologies, creating ethical dilemmas that are more extensive and uncertain than the familiar dilemmas in face-to-face learning. Online educators and students have become affiliated strangers, linked together by power and play, joining other actors during the transition period of technologically engineered and globally fueled social change. Ethics in online learning involves attention to the ultimate social implications of this transformation (Fisher & Wright, 2001; Hobart & Schiffman, 1998).

The confluence of technologies is not ethically neutral. It is imbued with the values and intentions of those who fund, design, develop, manage, and use them. Together, we are as the gods of antiquity, creating the rules for new worlds—sometimes with serious intent and other times with playful abandonment. The discipline of computer ethics has a rich, if brief, history, stemming from a need to develop ethical foundations for the human dilemmas made possible by new technologies. Much of the field of computer ethics is inductive, derived from case studies (Floridi, 1998) written by people who understand the social engineering aspects of technology.

Online discourse, as represented by text, does not consider the time differential between messages. It is unable to acknowledge the experience and meaning of those whose words are represented but who are participating on their own computers in fully separated environments.

> The language of computer-mediated communication is more ephemeral than ordinary written texts (it has therefore been defined as written speech); it is not intended for people uninvolved directly in interaction, and it loses part of its sense and meaning when re-read afterward by neutral observers. (Paccagnella, 1997, p. 15)

Online ethical dilemmas require thoughtful and open debate and dialogue. There is no attempt here to propose simple frameworks for resolving difficult dilemmas. Any such framework is mired in its own assumptions and values. "A system of moral philosophy put to such uses (for hard choices) is like a magician's hat—almost anything can be pulled out of it, wafted about, let fly" (Bok, 1979, p. 57).

Power and Play

> Among the e-mail messages streaming into his e-mailbox, Tim reads that a new version of his favorite online adventure game has just been released. With this version, he and his virtual teammates will be able to create more elaborate avatars (graphical representations of people) for their online escapades. He reads a message from an online news service describing how hackers from several countries are conducting a real-life cyber-battle and are disrupting the computers of their respective governments. Tim is intrigued by a provocative note from a woman in his online class who invites him to join in an "extracurricular" encounter in a private online chat room. It is easy for Tim to be fully immersed in the online world that is hidden from his "real" life.

Both power and play are embedded in the foundation of our computer technologies. Alan Turing and John von Neuman, the primary computer architects of our age, were concerned with the power of logic and the thrill of play. They "yoked" logic to electronic circuitry, creating power from information as well as early versions of poker-based game theory and computer chess. "And both toyed with the computer as a plaything in its own right. Their interest reveals deeper, more culturally rich levels of play, which connect the determinism of the computer's symbols and operations to the sensory world of experience" (Hobart & Schiffman, 1998, p. 204).

Logical Malleability, Invisibility, and Subsumption

What gets measured is what counts in an organization. In the software that manages the course records in the university's database, the only number that is counted in determining a faculty member's workload is the number of students who complete an online course. The database software that was used to create the course records allows only one faculty member to be linked to a course. The course tracking software has no measure of the quality, quantity, or timeliness of the faculty member's engagement with the students. In the department's annual reports, the productivity and effectiveness of the department as a whole, as well as of individual faculty members, are determined by the number of courses taught and the number of students who complete each course.

The penetration of the computer into homes and offices during the second half of the 20th century introduced several key ethical issues that are part of the nature of computer technology: logical malleability, subsumption, and invisibility. As computers are ingrained as necessities in our society, these ethical dimensions remain as powerful, but often unnoticed, influences in our lives.

Logical malleability refers to the fundamental task and ability of computers—to take inputs, shape the inputs with a set of programmer-defined logics, and create an output. We become the gods, creating the rules of the game. There is no logic that is "right" or "wrong." There is only the set of directions that is established within the computer's internal connections. During the early days of the computer, human programmers created these rule sets. Computers have evolved in complexity to where these rule sets may be designed to continuously evolve into new rule sets. Programmers establish the nature of computer applications, choosing the forms of logic to use to select, filter, and manipulate data and then to store, transfer, and selectively distribute information according to any schema of format, media, and audience (Kling, 1974; Moor, 1989, 2000b).

The power of logical malleability is that we rarely question data that appear on computer screens because the logic remains invisible to us. We have come to depend on computer-generated information; to do otherwise is no longer an option. The malleable logic that controls the computer's systems is within the purview of the programmer and is invisible to both the sponsor and the user of the system. As a society, we are way past the time when we could question this instrumental reasoning of the computer (Weizenbaum, 1976). Knowingly or unknowingly, we fully accept it as part of ourselves.

Subsumption occurs as one set of logical components is subsumed into subsequent components. The decisions that are made early in the development of a program continue forward as the initial program becomes a subset of larger programs. Some of our most prominent technologically related disasters, such as that of the Challenger, are directly attributable to the subsumption of faulty decisions into larger, ultimately disastrous decisions (Gleason, 2000). The ethical questions become increasingly complex. Who is responsible when faulty choices are made that then become part of larger decisions? We are left with contaminated choices that are not directly traceable to the originators. Online learning environments are composed of countless subsumed components that may have a major social impact yet be increasingly difficult to address and monitor.

Invisibility is present when people interact with computers without being aware of the underlying software logic that determines what appears on the screen. Computer-generated "information" has a pernicious potential for delusion that accompanies the freedoms of online learning. During the mid-1960s, Joseph Weizenbaum, a professor of computer science at MIT, authored a software program, ELIZA, that analyzed text and presented replies that appeared to maintain a conversation, mimicking a Rogerian therapist. Weizenbaum was trying to demonstrate that language could be understood only in contextual frameworks. He was shocked when people became emotionally involved with the computer, believing that the machine was actually understanding them. Many psychiatrists believed that software would yield an automated form of psychotherapy (Weizenbaum, 1976).

Privacy, Secrecy, and Confidentiality

When Lisa was attending an academic conference with her colleague, Harry, she was still engaged in online teaching. As she prepared for that evening's online seminar, Lisa's computer broke down. Harry let her borrow his laptop for the evening. Lisa was able to plug her zip drive into Harry's computer. As she was searching for some references, she noticed several files with her name. Curious, she opened them up. Without ever asking Lisa for permission, Harry had accumulated, catalogued, and stored on his computer all of her online postings, as well as all of her e-mail messages, for the past several years. He was using text analysis software to analyze all of her messages. Lisa was shocked and angry. She realized that he had legitimate access to everything she had posted. But she felt that he had misused his legitimate access. He had violated her trust and was probing into her personal self in ways that she had not authorized.

Our unprecedented ability to gather, organize, and analyze data has changed the very nature of our society. Information on individual purchases, library and video rentals, medical records, real estate transactions, telephone numbers, and online dialogue represents examples of the growing amount of information that is quickly gathered and permanently stored, creating intimate personal profiles, usually without our awareness or authorization. Information can be gathered and used to generate new information on a scale unimaginable prior to the advent of computers.

> *There is a man who follows every movement of Jill, using hidden cameras and monitoring all of her actions, conversations, and communications. He never interferes with Jill's activities and never causes her physical harm. Her privacy is lost, but she does not know it.*

Do we have a right to control who can access information about ourselves? In a computerized society, we have limited ability to control this information or to know whether others access it. If our rights are based in a "control/restricted access" theory of privacy that allows access to information based on needs and relevance (Moor, 2000a), then those who have the authority to determine needs and relevance have power over others. In online learning environments, who holds this power? Is there an ethical responsibility to inform others when such information is gathered?

Secrecy involves the power to control the flow of information (Bok, 1979). Whereas advocates of freedom on the Internet argue that secrecy is anathema to true democracy, others fiercely defend their rights to keep secret information from becoming publicly accessible. Do members of an online learning community have unlimited freedoms to share information? When hate-based messages are posted on a university's forum, is there a responsibility to monitor or control the flow of information?

Confidentiality is the ability to set and preserve boundaries around secret information (Bok, 1989). In education, confidentiality is protected by law and policy. We rarely question codes of confidentiality as they preserve the secrecy of students' records, grievances filed against faculty, administrators' salaries, and private online seminars. Yet in the online world, the power to impose confidentiality may be abused and used to keep relevant information secret or hidden from those who would otherwise have rights to it. "One name for professional confidentiality has been the 'professional secret.'" Such secrecy is sometimes mistakenly confused with privacy, yet it can concern many matters that are in no way private but that someone wishes to keep from the knowledge of third parties (Bok, 1989, p. 119).

Instances of secrecy and confidentiality often appear so innocuous that they are accepted without question. Access to the information is controlled by those with administrative, technical, or other forms of power. There is rarely any challenge to the power or right to keep information secret. Online seminars are closed to nonparticipants. Faculty evaluations, student information, and administrative dialogue all are kept confidential.

The ability to maintain personal secrets, and the choices over when and to whom to reveal secrets, may be fundamental to our sense of professional identity. But the power to control secrets—to maintain confidentiality—can become the power to conceal wrongdoings.

> These risks are great when control over secrecy is combined with personal unscrupulousness; greater still when it is joined to unusual political or other power and to special privileges of secrecy such as those granted to professionals; and greatest of all when it is in the hands of government leaders. (Bok, 1989, p. 282)

Surveillance

> *Harry is mapping all of the conversations posted on the university's Web site, including all open forums, minutes of meetings, documents, and schedules. He is developing a software tool that will illustrate who is speaking to whom, when, how frequently, and on what topics. He is investigating the creation of different forms of community building among university colleagues, including the building of political coalitions to enforce or disrupt the status quo and personal coalitions to create communities of interest.*

The power of unnoticed surveillance is omnipresent, available to anyone who has access to electronic text. Software developed and marketed by Ari-Pekka Hameri creates self-organizing maps to illustrate the communication dynamics among individuals. It reveals the closeness with which people work together and graphically illustrates differences in self-discipline and creativity ("Big Picture," 2001, p. 75). A call for papers by the Association for Computing Machinery (2001) asks, "What will happen when our machines stop thinking for us and start thinking about us?"

Because our current technologies are just the initial steps toward a more intimately surveyed future, our comfortable ways of understanding privacy might no longer be relevant. Colleges are finding that the benefits of wireless communication—immediate unfiltered access from any space within the reaches of the wireless network—also create problems of privacy, security, and unauthorized surveillance as the networks are easily penetrated, with the penetration remaining undetectable with our current technologies (Olsen, 2000).

Anonymity and Personal Identity

> *A debate emerges about "lurking" on online seminars—reading the text of the dialogue without informing the participants and saving the text on one's computer. Although the communication software has a function that allows all readers of the text to be identified when they read the discourse, some members of the university object, saying that they have the right to read the discourse anonymously.*

The university has a "tip box" for anonymous complaints about faculty and staff. When the university decided to migrate the physical box to a Web-based forum, there was a great deal of concern about the need for assurance of anonymity. The university has installed software that strips the user name of the respondent from the posted message. However, this information is retained in a "protected" file, where it can be accessed. Only a few administrators and technical managers are aware of this file.

In an online seminar, students and faculty assume pseudo-identities to explore the role of self in discourse. Jim recognizes that all of his assumed personas generate different responses, even though the issues that they raise, or the ideas that they propose, are similar. In his other online exchanges, he continues to experiment with multiple personas and soon discovers that he can generate heated exchanges with some personas, ambivalence with others, and compliance with his ideas with one particular persona.

In online learning environments, there are many questions regarding anonymity and identity. Do we have a "right" to know who comes into the room, or can we allow access via one-way "mirrors" with which people can read and copy the conversation without giving any trace to the participants that they have been eavesdropping? Is "dropping by" similar to classroom observers who "sit in" but do not participate?

What is the impact of anonymous comments when the identity of one participant is not known by the others? Is it enough to know that participants who are using pseudonyms are members of the university? Or must their identities be revealed before they are allowed access to public forums? Does the identity of a "whistle-blower" need to be disclosed? What if anonymity is being used to cover up abusive behavior for which one does not want to be accountable? Can institutional policy allow anonymity but prohibit abusive and illegal discourse online (Moor, 2000b)?

The scenario of Linda's evening, at the beginning of this chapter, reveals multiple personas and different roles. The autonomous self is seen by many to disappear, replaced by a mosaic of multiple selves (Kolko, 2000)—or by a meta-self co-created by several participants engaged in online discourse (Turkle, 1984, 2000). When people assume multiple online personas to explore selves that remain hidden in concrete realities, "slippages often occur in places where persona and self merge, where the multiple personae join to comprise what the individual thinks of as his or her authentic self" (Turkle, 2000, p. 132). Our forays into alternative personas open opportunities to experiences that are inaccessible in our "real" worlds, to understand multiple perspectives, and to allow personal transformations that are blocked in other encounters. "Without a deep understanding of the many selves that we express in the virtual [environment], we cannot use our experiences there to enrich the real" (p. 141).

The online environment raises new questions about the importance of privacy to identity and self. When we display multiple personas online, we go outside of the socially constructed boundaries that guide our "real world" relationships. People who enact alternate online personas are sometimes shocked when others respond to the exposed persona, often feeling angry, vulnerable, and personally violated (Palloff & Pratt, 1999). Many people find it easy to reveal intimate secrets online. Sexually explicit material thrives online. In online research, Witmer (1997) found that the majority of respondents were not concerned about privacy as they interacted on unmoderated, sexually explicit newsgroups. "Respondents tended to feel personally and technologically secure in their CMC [computer-mediated communication] and felt that they had little or nothing to lose if their activities were discovered by unintended others" (p. 11).

The Persuasive Power of Computer-Generated Script

> [Writing] will cause people to trust to the external written characters and not remember of themselves. . . . They will be hearers of many things and will have learned nothing.
>
> —Plato (5th century B.C.)

The power of persuasion in online learning is a critical ethical issue. The impact of an immediate global audience is to generate more controversy, speculation, and dialogue with varying degrees of validity and reliability. In the summer of 2000, two anthropology professors received page proofs of a book that alleged serious misconduct by two prominent scientists. The professors sent e-mail messages to colleagues, intending to open a forum for dialogue about this issue, prior to the book's publication. The news spread rapidly, inflaming worldwide dialogue, charges, and countercharges. The author revised some of the book in response to the issues that were raised.

> Fierce and inconclusive debates on e-mail lists are nothing new in academe, of course. But in this case, reports, research memos, and press releases sent by e-mail and posted on Web sites became the primary source of scholarly grist. While academics wondered, "Can this be true?," Internet-savvy scholars fed that hunger for information. (Miller, 2001, p. A14)

The social psychology of persuasion suggests several human tendencies that matter: reciprocation (if you give me something, then I feel obliged to give you what you are asking for), the need to appear to be consistent (if I agreed to a similar request earlier, then I want to be seen as consistent and am more likely to comply), social validation (we comply with requests when we know that others have already complied), liking (we support the requests that come from people we like), authority (we follow those who we presume have authority), and scarcity (the more unique something is perceived to be, the more we tend to value it). These values seem to reflect the key components in effective persuasion (Cialdini, 2001). In the case of the response to the e-mail message regarding the anthropologist's research, these factors came into play in an explosive manner. People responded to the unexpected information. As scholars, they needed to appear consistent. The flood of e-mail responses created an impression of a massive social response.

The issue of liking is curious. We might join forces with others because we want to show our great displeasure at someone we do not like. Hence, the power of persuasion on the Internet can often be a rallying around a hated idea or person. Authority in the academic world comes from affiliations to particular universities, journals, and associations and from conveying the impression that one has rigorously followed the standards of a particular profession. The role of scarcity involves timeliness in academia. Ideas are perceived as most important if they are among the first to be issued. The number of immediate e-mail responses was great, feeding into the critical mass of social validation.

Ownership of Intellectual Property

> During an online seminar using an asynchronous forum, students and faculty develop a new theoretical model. Several months later, the professor publishes a journal article claiming ownership of the theory that emerged during the chat dialogue.

> An online synchronous chat among students delves into personal issues as participants share facts and emotions about their personal, professional, and social lives. A few years later, a member of this seminar publishes articles that include some of these stories.

> The university develops a process for enabling multilanguage dialogue on its forums. It chooses to maintain ownership of this process. In spite of the university's order, the students who developed the process are disseminating the details of the process on the Web and encouraging educators in underdeveloped countries to copy and use this process so as to better access Web-based conversations that are conducted in English.

Who "owns" online conversations on forums? Our traditions of intellectual ownership seem increasingly irrelevant to online communication. The tensions inherent in the issues of ownership of intellectual property in the United States originated from the dual purpose of the U.S. copyright acts, which are designed both to serve the public through promoting science and the useful arts and to protect the rights of authors (Goodwin, 2000). This foundation for considering ownership is called into question in an era of global networks, flowing information, and online collaboration.

The institution is responsible for establishing its core intellectual property policy. Within the institution, this policy then extends to ownership of a distance learning course, the rights of faculty and students within that course or seminar, access rights to the seminar, potential liability (including copyright infringement liability) for the institution and faculty associated with the course, and accreditation and international policy implications as the participants are located globally (American Council on Education, 2000).

When a paper is posted on a Web site, the paper is assumed to be owned by the person who wrote it, and full acknowledgment must be given for every use of the content and ideas in the paper. To copy the words of another without authorization and acknowledgment is condemned as plagiarism in all of Western academia. Collaborative papers are suspect because they do not clarify who contributed which piece. The structure of Western education is based on separation of people into categories. "As they educated themselves in self-government, the European bourgeoisie succeeded in excluding the non-literate, the non-affluent, and the non-male" (Habermas, 1989, p. 51).

Creativity and innovation are not viewed as social acts in our laws, even though the creative process may be seen as occurring in multiple modalities from a sole creator through a collective process (LeFevre, 1987). Collaboratively developed intellectual property is troublesome to Western notions of ownership because property laws of ownership still seek definitive linkages between the product and specific owners of the product. When the value of a product comes from use, including copying and modification, Western perspectives on ownership are no longer viable (Johnson, 1985, 2000).

Of special interest to online learning environments are the challenges of real-time MUDs (multi-user domains) and MOOs (object-oriented MUDs). In these online spaces, people converse in real time, assuming a variety of personas. They participate in collaborative learning, storytelling, and community building. The foundation of our notions of ownership—that of a distinct self as a solo creator—is challenged by this real-time environment. This Western notion of an autonomous self is superseded in the MUD environment, where multiple personas interact to create new realities. Ownership of material is collaboratively regulated (Kolko, 2000; MediaMoo, 1997).

When people converse using real-time text and collaborate using computer-mediated communication, it is difficult to categorize the text because it often entails a hybrid of speech and writing (Kolko, 2000). The difficulties in determining authorship, property, and even text in computer-mediated conversations require more relevant laws than currently exist associated with copyrights (Post, 1996). "It is precisely the interweaving of selves that occurs in MOO environments that makes the question of intellectual property a thorny one" (Kolko, 2000, pp. 259-260). The U.S. Supreme Court has ruled that Internet speech is entitled to First Amendment protection but has given conflicting opinions as to whether the discourse is written or spoken (Kolko, 2000).

Unresolved issues of online discourse, both synchronous and asynchronous, will become more complex in the near future as technology further blurs the lines between written and spoken discourse. Wireless technologies will further complicate the issues as voice, text, visuals, and graphics are simultaneously transmitted on the Internet.

Immersion virtual reality is becoming more accessible. Through this technology, people who are physically dispersed can share a virtual space and "interact" directly as they navigate their shared space. Their movements—even eye movements—can connect directly, creating a shared reality that exists in cyberspace but is experienced within each participant's own self only so long as it exists relationally. This shared reality, co-created by dispersed participants, may soon dominate online interaction. Current understandings, laws, and ethics are inadequate to navigate in this relational environment.

Conclusions

> Concerning society in the year 2000, . . . the most remarkable predictions concern the transformation of educational methods and the problem of human reproduction. Knowledge will be accumulated in "electronic banks" and transmitted directly to the human nervous system by means of coded electronic messages. . . . What is needed will pass directly from the machine to the brain without going through consciousness. (Ellul, 1964, p. 432)

There is no pretension here that ethical dilemmas dominate our thinking. We are so deeply engaged in the development of our new forms of online learning that it is difficult to justify taking time out to consider the ethical implications—no matter how profound—of our choices in creating our learning environments. Yet the ethical dilemmas persist, ever the more powerful through their subtle and unobtrusive manner. As our nature is more intertwined with the reasoning of our computers and technologies, we have less opportunity to engage in dialogue and debate about the ethical implications of our acquiescence to an unplanned future (Ellul, 1964; Weizenbaum, 1976).

Issues that dominated in the past, such as privacy and confidentiality, persist. But emerging issues of self and identity, of authorship, of relational spaces and relational selves, of ownership of property, and of the work and play of collaboration are revealing greater complexity in the interconnected world of online learning.

The "stuff" of information is created by our human minds, is influenced by our collective technologies, and has a unique meaning in each era and culture. Beginning with the joining of the oral world with the literate world, the participative nature of information was established. Technologies have always affected the nature of society itself (Hobart & Schiffman, 1998). We can only glimpse at the ways in which our new technologies will be affecting learning in the years to come (Fisher & Wright, 2001; Hobart & Schiffman, 1998).

Appendix: Resources

http://ethics.acusd.edu/index.html	Ethics updates edited by Lawrence M. Hinman
http://www.ethics.ubc.ca/resources/computer	Centre for Applied Ethics, University of British Columbia
http://ezinfo.ucs.indiana.edu	Association for Practical and Professional Ethics
http://condor.depaul.edu/ethics/ethg1.html	On-line Journal of Ethics

References

Althauser, R., & Matuga, J. M. (1998). On the pedagogy of electronic instruction. In C. J. Bonk & K. S. King (Eds.), *Electronic collaborators: Learner-centered technologies for literacy, apprenticeship, and discourse* (pp. 183-208). Mahwah, NJ: Lawrence Erlbaum.

American Council on Education. (2000). *Developing a distance education policy for 21st century learning* [Online]. Retrieved March 21, 2000, from: www.acenet.edu

Artz, J. M. (2000). Narrative vs. logical reasoning in computer ethics. In R. M. Baird, R. Ramsower, & S. E. Rosenbaum (Eds.), *Cyberethics: Social and moral issues in the computer age* (pp. 73-79). Amherst, NY: Prometheus Books.

Association for Computing Machinery. (2001). ACM1 conference, beyond cyberspace: A journey of many directions [conference announcement]. Retrieved from: www.acm.org/acm1

Bauman, Z. (1993). *Postmodern ethics.* Oxford, UK: Blackwell.

The big picture. (2001, January 6). *The Economist,* p. 75.

Bok, S. (1979). *Lying: Moral choice in public and private life.* New York: Vintage.

Bok, S. (1989). *Secrets: On the ethics of concealment and revelation.* New York: Vintage.

Bonk, C. J., & King, K. S. (Eds.). (1998). *Electronic collaborators: Learner-centered technologies for literacy, apprenticeship, and discourse.* Mahwah, NJ: Lawrence Erlbaum.

Carlson, S. (2001, January 19). North Dakota professor sues former student and a Web site over allegations in an article. *The Chronicle of Higher Education,* p. A33.

Cialdini, R. B. (2001). The science of persuasion. *Scientific American, 284*(2), 76-81.

Dewey, J. (1984). *The quest for certainty: The later works* (Vol. 4). Carbondale: Southern Illinois University Press.

Ellul, J. (1964). *The technological society* (J. Wilkinson, Trans.). New York: Vintage.

Fisher, D. R., & Wright, L. M. (2001). On utopias and dystopias: Toward an under-standing of the discourse surrounding the Internet. *Journal of Computer-Mediated Communication, 6*(2), 13. Retrieved September 6, 2001, from: www.ascusc.org/jcmc/vol6/issue2/fisher.html

Floridi, L. (1998, March). *Information ethics: On the philosophical foundation of computer ethics.* Paper presented at the ETHICOMP98, the Fourth Inter-national Conference on Ethical Issues of Information Technology, Erasmus Uni-versity, Netherlands.

Foster, A. (2001, January 19). Supreme Court rebuffs professor's challenge to a Vir-ginia law on Internet use. *The Chronicle of Higher Education,* p. A31. Available: http://chronicle.com/weekly/v47/i19/19a03101.htm

Frankena, W. K. (1986). Moral philosophy and the future. In J. P. DeMarco & R. M. Fox (Eds.), *New directions in ethics: The challenge of applied ethics* (pp. 299-318). London: Routledge & Kegan Paul.

Gleason, D. H. (2000). Subsumption ethics. In R. M. Baird, R. Ramsower, & S. E. Rosenbaum (Eds.), *Cyberethics: Social and moral issues in the computer age* (pp. 56-72). Amherst, NY: Prometheus Books.

Goodwin, M. (Ed.). (2000). *Wild, wild Web.* Amherst, NY: Prometheus Books.

Guignon, C. (1986). Existentialist ethics. In J. P. DeMarco & R. M. Fox (Eds.), *New directions in ethics: The challenge of applied ethics* (pp. 73-91). London: Routledge & Kegan Paul.

Habermas, J. (1989). *The structural transformation of the public sphere.* Cambridge, UK: Polity.

Haythornthwaite, C., Kazmer, M. M., Robins, J., & Shoemaker, S. (2000). Commu-nity development among distance learners: Temporal and technological dimen-sions. *Journal of Computer-Mediated Communication, 6*(1), 30. Retrieved September 6, 2001, from: www.ascusc.org/jcmc/vol6/issue1/haythornthwaite.html

Hobart, M. E., & Schiffman, Z. S. (1998). *Information ages: Literacy, numeracy, and the computer revolution.* Baltimore, MD: Johns Hopkins University Press.

Holland, J. H. (1995). *Hidden order: How adaptation builds complexity.* Reading, MA: Addison-Wesley.

Holland, J. H. (1998). *Emergence: From chaos to order.* Reading, MA: Addison-Wesley.

Johnson, D. (1985). *Computer ethics.* Englewood Cliffs, NJ: Prentice Hall.

Johnson, D. (2000). Should computer programs be owned? In R. M. Baird, R. Ramsower, & S. E. Rosenbaum (Eds.), *Cyberethics: Social and moral issues in the computer age* (pp. 222-235). Amherst, NY: Prometheus Books.

Jonas, H. (1974). *Philosophical essays: From ancient creed to technological man.* Englewood Cliffs, NJ: Prentice Hall.

Kitchener, K. S. (1984). Intuition, critical evaluation, and ethical principles: The foundation for ethical decisions in counselling psychology. *The Counselling Psychologist, 12*(3), 43-56.

Kling, R. (1974). Computers and social power. *Computers & Society, 5*(3), 6-11.

Kolko, B. E. (2000). Intellectual property in synchronous and collaborative virtual space. In R. M. Baird, R. Ramsower, & S. E. Rosenbaum (Eds.), *Cyberethics: Social and moral issues in the computer age* (pp. 257-281). Amherst, NY: Prome-theus Books.

LeFevre, K. B. (1987). *Invention as a social act.* Carbondale: Southern Illinois University Press.

Lowenberg, F., & Dolgoff, R. (1988). *Ethical decisions for social work practice* (3rd ed.). Itasca, IL: F. E. Peacock.

McDermott, J. J. (1986). Pragmatic sensibility: The morality of experience. In J. P. DeMarco & R. M. Fox (Eds.), *New directions in ethics: The challenge of applied ethics* (pp. 113-134). London: Routledge & Kegan Paul.

MediaMoo. (1997). *MediaMoo symposium: The ethics of research in virtual communities.* [Online]. Retrieved October 6, 2000, from: www.cc.gatech.edu/~asb/mediamoo/ethics-symposium-97.html

Miller, D. W. (2001, January 12). Academic scandal in the Internet age: When a furor broke out in anthropolgy, e-mail was more powerful than peer review. *The Chronicle of Higher Education,* pp. A14-A17.

Moor, J. H. (1989). How to invade and protect privacy with computers. In C. C. Gould (Ed.), *The information Web* (pp. 61-62). Boulder, CO: Westview.

Moor, J. H. (2000a). Moor: Toward a theory of privacy. In R. M. Baird, R. Ramsower, & S. E. Rosenbaum (Eds.), *Cyberethics: Social and moral issues in the computer age.* Amherst, NY: Prometheus Books.

Moor, J. H. (2000b). What is computer ethics? In R. M. Baird (Ed.), *Cyberethics: Social and moral issues in the computer age* (pp. 23-33). Amherst, NY: Prometheus Books.

Morgan, E. (1999). *Navigating cross-cultural ethics: What global managers do right to keep from going wrong.* Boston: Butterworth Heinemann.

Newman, D. L., & Brown, R. D. (1996). *Applied ethics for program evaluation.* Thousand Oaks, CA: Sage.

Olsen, F. (2000, October 13). The wireless revolution. *The Chronicle of Higher Education,* p. A13. Available: http://chronicle.com/weekly/v47/i07/07a05901.htm

Paccagnella, L. (1997). Getting the seats of your pants dirty: Strategies for ethnographic research on virtual communities. *Journal of Computer-Mediated Communication, 3*(1), 15. Retrieved September 6, 2001, from: www.ascusc.org/jcmc/vol3/issue1/paccagnella.html

Palloff, R. M., & Pratt, K. (1999). *Building learning communities in cyberspace: Effective strategies for the online classroom.* San Francisco: Jossey-Bass.

Post, D. (1996). "Clarifying" the law of cyberspace. *American Lawyer, 18*(3), 115. Available: www.temple.edu/lawschool/dpost/clarifying.html

Scanlon, T. M. (1986). A contractualist alternative. In J. P. DeMarco & R. M. Fox (Eds.), *New directions in ethics: The challenge of applied ethics* (pp. 42-57). London: Routledge & Kegan Paul.

Schweizer, K., Paechter, M., & Weidenmann, B. (2001). A field study on distance education and communication: Experiences of a virtual tutor. *Journal of Computer-Mediated Communication, 6*(2), 16. Retrieved September 6, 2001, from: www.ascusc.org/jcmc/vol6/issue2/schweizer.html

Smart, J. J. C. (1986). Utilitarianism and its applications. In J. P. DeMarco & R. M. Fox (Eds.), *New directions in ethics: The challenge of applied ethics* (pp. 24-41). London: Routledge & Kegan Paul.

Sterling College. (2000). *Sterling College's code of professional ethics* [Online]. Retrieved October 16, 2000, from: www.stercolks.edu/offices/acad_aff/code.htm

Sumsion, J. (2000). Caring and empowerment: A teacher educator's reflection on an ethical dilemma. *Teaching in Higher Education, 5*(3), 167.

Turkle, S. (1984). *The second self: Computers and the human spirit*. New York: Simon & Schuster.

Turkle, S. (2000). Who am we? In R. M. Baird, R. Ramsower, & S. E. Rosenbaum (Eds.), *Cyberethics: Social and moral issues in the computer age* (pp. 129-141). Amherst, NY: Prometheus Books.

Watts, D. J. (1999). *Small worlds: The dynamics of networks between order and randomness*. Princeton, NJ: Princeton University Press.

Weizenbaum, J. (1976). *Computer power and human reason: From judgment to calculation*. New York: Freeman.

Witmer, D. (1997). Risky business: Why people feel safe in sexually explicit on-line communication. *Journal of Computer-Mediated Communication, 2*(4), 11. Retrieved September 6, 2001, from: www.ascusc.org/jcmc/vol2/issue4/witmer2.html

Zuboff, S. (1984). *In the age of the smart machine: The future of work and power*. New York: Basic Books.

Part **II**

IMPLEMENTING ONLINE LEARNING

A. Programs/Environments: University

Chapter 6

The Design and Delivery of Interactive Online Graduate Education

Judith Stevens-Long
and Charles Crowell

Computer-mediated learning presents one of the greatest opportunities and most important challenges ever faced by educational institutions. A bold statement—but also a striking reality. Computers have been used in the classroom for decades, and educational software has become a staple of the middle-class library. However, the delivery of coursework and degree programs over the Internet, aptly defined as computer-mediated learning (CML), is a relatively new development. More significantly, like any paradigmatic change, the early initiatives in CML have more in common with past practice than with new practice. In the case of computer-mediated inquiry, this is particularly the case. Much of what is currently touted as computer-mediated coursework is really an effort to literally transfer face-to-face classroom instructional practices into a different (virtual) medium. By way of illustration, the conventional formulation of the theory for CML builds from the historical conceptualization for "distance education." Indeed, computer-mediated inquiry is still often characterized by that latter appellation.

There is a long and relatively rich history to the development of distance education. It began during the late 19th century with the efforts of Anna Ticknor, who created a society in Boston in 1873 to instigate educational opportunities for women by the distribution of printed materials through the mail and the use of correspondence (Ticknor, 1897). Subsequently, the Chautauqua College of Liberal Arts recognized education by correspondence in 1883. Visual instruction, including "lantern slides and motion pictures," was added to the repertory of correspondence education during the period from 1910 to 1920.

In 1932, the University of Iowa began experimenting with using television to transmit instructional courses. After World War II, television became another mode of delivery for correspondence study. Its entrance, and interest by the Ford Foundation, marked a renewal in the field. The doctoral research of Gayle Childs examined the effectiveness and reliability of correspondence study as an educational method (Childs, 1949). In 1956, Childs determined that there were no appreciable differences in student achievement between instruction in regular classrooms and instruction by television or a combination of television and correspondence study. Parsons (1957) showed only borderline differences in achievement between correspondence and conventional classrooms. Nonetheless, by the mid-1960s, much of the interest in instructional television had waned. The Ford Foundation shifted its earlier support to public television. According to Reiser (1987), much of that shift was driven by the poor quality of instructional programming, which attempted to solely replicate classroom lecture by a teacher.

More recent initiatives capture a diversity of instructional media approaches. Many colleges and universities offer courses that use institutional intranets for instruction as well as closed-circuit television, video, CDs, and external Web-based resources such as WebCT (for more detailed discussions, see, e.g., Moore & Kearsley, 1996, and Nasseh, 1997). Notice the emphasis on media and the absence of any emphasis on new pedagogical models. The pertinence of the preceding brief history of distance education is that the educational model has remained basically the same throughout approximately 130 years. The pedagogy has remained an independent study model that has consistently adopted new communication technology (instructional radio, instructional television, later videotape, and now the Internet) to shorten the communication time between instructor and student, but those technology-based efficiencies have been largely both singular and unidirectional (applied only to the linkage from the instructor to the student). New technology sped up information transfer to the student; it allowed, in some forms, for more facile, concurrent access to a larger learner population.

Technology was used primarily to address distance issues as well as distribution and concurrence problems. Radio and television were used to broaden access to the correspondence study model by offering concurrent distribution to widely dispersed populations of learners and compressing time through a more rapid transmission in the linkage to the student. Television provided more visualization but little more. With the introduction of e-mail and the Web, bidirectional communication became prevalent, but throughout, the basic learning pedagogy remained the same. In other words, the instructional model for distance education, although with more illustrations and more broadly distributed over time, remained largely the same: an exchange of correspondence intended to replicate classroom inquiry.

The significance of this pedagogical model, represented in distance education, is that it defines a historical instructional paradigm that has remained intact, a paradigm that established and maintained the context and conceptual boundaries for interpretation and innovation of ideas and new practices in learning. Then something happened (i.e., the convergence of low-cost, widely distributed computing power in personal computers; the World Wide Web; HTML; and Web servers). It is not at all surprising, then, that much of contemporary, so-called computer-mediated inquiry is "shrink-wrapped" workbook- or textbook-style material that the student is expected to download, read, and respond to by either taking a test or writing a paper before uploading the finished product. The professor receives it, grades it, may offer some feedback, and eventually the student receives credit for a course. Such instructional methods do not constitute a change from earlier distance education models; they attempt to replicate the conventional face-to-face classroom and feature little more than greater speed of transmission.

That said, some college or university courses are accompanied by online discussion groups or chat features, but few institutions have attempted more interactive Web-based approaches, and even fewer have tried to mount an entire degree program using interactive Web-based methodology based on a theoretical foundation. We will argue that the modality for instruction (the Web) requires not only different instructional conceptions and methodologies but also different learning practices by instructors and students.

The master's program in organizational management (OM) offered by the Fielding Graduate Institute is one of the first interactive Web-based degree programs available on the Internet, and this chapter outlines some of what we have learned from designing, developing, and delivering the program. In addition, we have taught individual computer-mediated undergraduate- and graduate-level courses for more than a decade, have tried a variety of experiments, have made a great many mistakes and achieved many successes, and applied what we have learned to the design of the OM program.

At the foundation of the OM program is a new pedagogy for learning in a virtual environment (VE). Importantly, we believe that these learnings can be readily generalized to the work of dispersed teams in organizations and to the development of any virtual training, work, or organizational learning environment. This chapter covers the architectural and process considerations in the development and management of an online instructional design.

Delivery System: Software and Architecture

Developments in conferencing software over the past 5 years have made it possible to engage in a truly interactive way on the Web. In contrast to the earlier unidirectional models of distance education, conferencing software (or "groupware") has introduced multidirectional communication between instructor and students and between students and students as well as a variety of features that support learning.

In the OM program, we chose to use AltaVista Forum (now called SiteScape); however, there are now several good centralized forum and groupware programs that offer similar features and functionality. (For more discussion here, see, e.g., the very informative Web site by David R. Wooley at www.thinkofit.com/webconf/index.htm.) What is critical in choosing such software is that it offers "threaded" conversation in a format that is well organized and readily accessible to the user.

In our use of AltaVista Forum, students enter a Web page environment that contains a discussion page on which topics are listed in a column at the far left-hand side of the page. In general, faculty use these topics to list assignments over the course of the quarter, and students post their assignments as "replies" to these topics. One might think of these replies as running in rows across the page, while the topics are listed in a column on the far left of the page. In our courses, each student reads the work of the other students and provides feedback. These responses are listed as replies to the student papers. The instructor may then respond to these replies, noting which ones are particularly interesting or useful. All of the student papers, replies to them, instructors' comments, and so forth on one assignment are nested under the topic in which the assignment was described.

As an example, let's say that the assignment was to post a reaction to a particular set of readings. (Please note the "inverted tree" structure of the replies. The lines indicate the sources [or "branches"] on which the replies comment.)

TOPIC #1: Today's Assignment

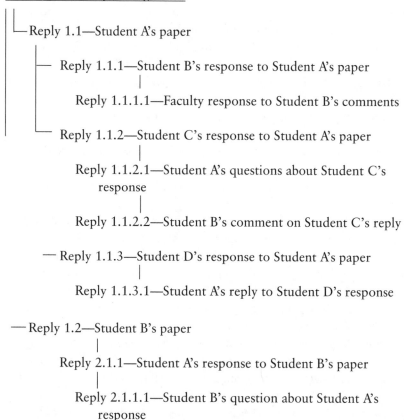

—Reply 1.1—Student A's paper

    — Reply 1.1.1—Student B's response to Student A's paper

        Reply 1.1.1.1—Faculty response to Student B's comments

    — Reply 1.1.2—Student C's response to Student A's paper

        Reply 1.1.2.1—Student A's questions about Student C's response

        Reply 1.1.2.2—Student B's comment on Student C's reply

— Reply 1.1.3—Student D's response to Student A's paper

        Reply 1.1.3.1—Student A's reply to Student D's response

— Reply 1.2—Student B's paper

        Reply 2.1.1—Student A's response to Student B's paper

        Reply 2.1.1.1—Student B's question about Student A's response

Although we have indicated a small number of replies to each paper, it is possible to post any number of replies to each topic at each level. In this way, long discussions may occur on a given topic, but the class may go forward to new assignments as well. Clearly, it becomes quite important for students to "follow the thread" and not start new topics or new reply levels out of turn. We have also learned that it is helpful for students and faculty to be careful and clear in naming their topics and replies so that the relationship between a particular topic and the current reply is clear.

At this juncture in our program, we use as many as five levels of replies to one assignment. However, continuing the discussion of a particular assignment over a long period creates the same kind of problem in cyberspace that it creates in the traditional classroom: The instructor has difficulty in moving forward with the rest of the course. Cyberspace has the advantage, however, of allowing formal and informal discussions to occur simultaneously (albeit asynchronously). Here is where the notion of "architecture" is relevant.

Faculty have designed their forum or classroom spaces in a variety of ways. The most general approach is to use the topics for the posting of assignments but to reserve several topic categories for ongoing, less formal conversations. One topic may be designated as the "café." Under this topic, continuing conversation about an assignment or a reading may go on throughout the term without "cluttering up" the classroom. The café may also be used for discussion of information, readings, and problems that come up outside of particular assignments. "Guest faculty" may interact with students in the café, or special hyperlinks may be posted to Web sites that may be useful for some of the students but not required for the course.

Faculty may also use a topic heading as an office space in which they answer the usual "office hours" questions about assignments, grades, and other administrative or advising topics. Another topic may serve as a space for discussing "process issues." That is, the structure of the course or the assignments, or problems that people are having in giving or receiving feedback, may be brought up in this space without disrupting the threads of conversation about particular assignments. Some faculty use spaces on their own private Web sites as well to store hyperlinks and reading lists or other pieces of assignments that they wish to keep permanently. Because technical issues are often a matter of periodic concern, we have also found it useful to create library and laboratory topics. The classroom spaces for any particular term are "archived" at the end of the term.

In the OM program, we also provide public spaces (forums) where students from all of the classes come together for general discussions about curriculum issues, program delivery suggestions, evaluation of programwide initiatives, and other student-initiated issues. We call this the "Community Hall," and students are informed at the time of orientation that they must check in to the Community Hall on a regular basis. All syllabi for new courses are posted in the Community Hall, new faculty are introduced there, and students are surveyed about their curricular needs there. It is critical that important information be available through a community space, and only through that space, if the students are to identify with the program as a whole and, even more importantly, sustain the functionality of the virtual inquiry. Forums may also be used for hosting faculty discussions and committee meetings.

This structure may seem elaborate, but it is actually created and maintained easily. We suggest that the availability, ease of use, and practical functionality of such features are the criteria by which one should evaluate different conferencing software or groupware choices. This structure has the advantage of creating a "location" in cyberspace that offers all of the physical locations available in the traditional classroom and institutional setting (e.g., the classroom, the café or lounge, the faculty offices, the auditorium and public spaces). Cyberspace has the added advantage, however, that many conversations ordinarily held privately (e.g., the discussion clarifying an assignment during an office hour) but helpful to all can be posted in a public space. Furthermore, it is possible to carry on informal simultaneous discussions that do not disrupt the class.

Although structure and architecture are central issues in designing the cyber-classroom, issues of process and the unique developmental opportunities of the medium have also captured our attention. Three sets of principles have directed our efforts to guide process over the years. These are the principles of group process, principles of adult education, and principles of human development. The work we have done is most clearly applicable to the education, training, and development of adults in educational institutions and contemporary organizations that integrate knowledge acquisition with the strategic function, but we also believe that most of what we have learned can easily be translated into educational design for secondary school students. Creating a learning environment on the Internet is a generalizable task, and the successes of such efforts inform all subsequent attempts.

Principles of Group Process

In extending the work of Bion (1959) on group process, Stevens-Long (1994) suggests that group process and function can be adequately described through the use of two dimensions: role structure and boundary. Role structure refers to the set of behaviors that are deemed appropriate for various members of a group—in case of the classroom, for students and teachers. Boundary refers to the limits of membership and the degree to which information may flow into the group environment from the outside or out from the group. In most face-to-face teaching environments, roles are very clearly structured. The teacher is in charge of "delivering" the learning through lecture or through the design of experiential learning exercises. The teacher is expected to outline his or her "learning objectives," and the students are to manifest these objectives as outcomes through the transformation of their behavior and understandings. Membership in the group is completely described by the roster, and the physical boundaries of the setting help to define the boundary of the group.

In the computer-mediated classroom, boundaries are defined not by physical space but rather by the structure and timing of participation. Because there is no way in which to monitor who might "sit in" on a class (e.g., anyone in the student's home environment might well be privy to the setting), issues of confidentiality and trust have to be negotiated. Structure, process, and in some cases even issues of identity itself all must be carefully planned and monitored. Because there is no physical "there" there, the space has to be consciously constructed.

For example, we are sometimes asked, "How do you know that the person enrolled in the course is the person who is doing the work?" Of course, this assumes that in the face-to-face classroom one knows that the person who shows up in the classroom is the person to whom the work will be credited (and we cannot be certain about that). Actually, we believe that the interactive environment provides more assurance that the same person is doing all of the work than do most traditional educational settings. Students are called on to engage in a continuous dialogue with other members of their class. All students are required to participate in both doing assignments and providing feedback to other participants. These requirements create a surprisingly intimate learning environment, as others of our faculty have noted (Brown, 1998).

All students are required to be online twice a week. They may need to post a paper or to post comments on the work of other students. They may be engaged in an ongoing dialogue with the professor or with other students. They may be coaching or consulting other students. There are a variety of forms that participation may take. What is essential is that the nature and frequency of participation must be clearly specified by the faculty member or facilitator. We have found that clear deadlines and well-defined assignments are critical to new students in this medium and for achieving high-quality learning and decision-making outcomes.

In the OM program, 3 days of face-to-face contact, mostly devoted to computer and software training as well as to the setting of norms for communication, constitute the primary orientation for the students. Students begin subsequent terms without further face-to-face contact. Therefore, information about participation, deadlines, assignments, and other expectations must be contained in online interactions. Such information is critical not just to the level of work in a course but also to creating the instructional or decision-making space itself. Students need to know that there is a place, a structure, or a group that is waiting for their participation. Immediate feedback from the facilitator and other members of the group establishes the viability of the environment. Most of the course syllabi for the master's degree in organizational design and effectiveness require that every student respond to the work of every other student in his or her study group. Courses are divided into study groups of six to eight people, and the instructor interacts with each group at least twice a week. Students are provided with feedback on both the quality of their own work and the quality of the feedback and support they give to other students.

It has been our experience that for most adult students in this environment, anxiety is high not only about their own ability to accomplish graduate-level work, often after long hiatuses from education, but also about whether they can succeed in a VE. Immediate feedback and clear rules of participation are critical to allaying such anxieties and getting on with the work. Our architecture also provides students with immediate access to administration through e-mail for similar purposes. On the other hand, we have restricted access to broadcast e-mail so as to maintain boundaries. Boundaries in the electronic environment are highly permeable, and the rumors and contagion that often plague electronic environments can be more readily controlled if the rules for making complaints and getting help are clearly considered in developing the program. Our network administrator filters all broadcast e-mail, sending it to the program director for approval before allowing it to enter the program environment.

Membership in the group must be carefully contained. Broadcast e-mail is a way in which people can breach the "walls" of the classroom. Likewise, the rules for participation of administrators and staff have to be negotiated. Although administrators and staff have access to all of the classes, permission for visits is obtained through e-mail to the instructor. Students and faculty need to feel that they have privacy from administrative oversight and from other members of the community who they might not even know are "watching."

A course may be divided into several study groups (sections) of five to eight students each. Only members of a given study group of a course typically have access to the work done in that study group. Because students often discuss their personal or workplace experiences, confidentiality is the norm. Tight boundaries around membership also ensure optimal participation in the home group. It is our experience that under most circumstances, permitting students to enter other groups (even with permission) can dilute the intensity of participation in the home group, create fuzziness around who is allowed to participate, and encourage invidious comparisons. All of these distract from the quality of the work that students post in their home groups. Occasionally, an instructor may "import" a particularly good piece of work from one study group to another or may copy a discussion from one group to another.

The electronic environment offers a number of process challenges that are linked to particular competencies. Certainly, there are technical competencies that students develop as a function of using their computers as their primary learning space. They have to become accustomed to dealing with problems of interface, with information technology infrastructures that are not always optimal; they must find their way through the Internet to school, and most of the courses require some roaming and research on the Web. In addition, they must function in novel social ways that are completely and uncompromisingly explicit. Most of the subtle nonverbal cues that we rely on for the interpretation of daily interactions are unavailable in cyberspace, and students must learn to compensate for that. A more complete description of the effects of the absence of nonverbal cues in computer-mediated environments can be found in Crowell (1997). This compensation involves the explicit setting of new norms and the development of new social competencies.

New Norms and Behaviors

When group process is portrayed in terms of stage development, it is common to describe the first stage as one devoted to "norming," that is, to the development of the rules of engagement that will characterize the processes of the group. We have found, in developing classroom and work team structures, that this phase is critical to the continued participation of group members and is central to determining the quality of subsequent work. Training and preparation, particularly time spent face-to-face prior to the initiation of project work, is best spent consciously establishing and clarifying the norms and expectations for online participation.

It might well be argued that if this phase of the work were done consciously in any setting, then groups would be more productive and less conflicted. However, in virtual teams, it is doubly important because many of the physical and nonverbal cues that promote process discussions will be missing subsequent to training or orientation. Furthermore, the norms and behaviors ordinarily expected in the work setting are rather different from those required by the VE.

For some, the norms we advocate require the development of new competencies, particularly because the work must be accomplished in writing. This applies to the teacher or facilitator as clearly as to the student or team member. Although asynchronous computer-mediated communication (CMC) eliminates some troublesome face-to-face norms (e.g., no one needs to keep a straight face or show up at the same time as everyone else), it offers its own unique challenges and benefits. Face-to-face orientation and training sessions highlight the following norms:

◆ Minimal frequency of log-on is required. In the courses we have designed, the specified minimum is twice a week. Participants are expected to post regular assignments and comment on the work of others on a regular specified schedule. In a dispersed team, time must be designated in a standard way (e.g., Greenwich Mean Time, Pacific Standard Time). For example, all postings on a particular topic might be expected by 12 a.m. PST.

◆ It is expected that work will be composed offline and sent as an attachment from a word processing program or as a cut-and-paste entry. This requirement is related to the more abstract norms of thoughtful articulation and reflectivity noted in what follows.

◆ A premium is placed on thoughtful articulation. Words are everything in this medium, and members need to spend the extra moment or two required to express themselves accurately and to review their work before posting it. In this medium, all communications become a permanent public record, and team members are held accountable for their words in a way that does not happen so clearly face-to-face.

◆ The medium provides an opportunity for team members to reflect on the problem, the assigned reading, or the responses of others. Immediate reactions are unnecessary. Although it is imperative that members keep up with the schedule of postings and respond in a timely fashion, it is expected that the asynchronous character of the dialogue will permit greater thoughtfulness.

♦ Affective disclosure is expected. Because the medium does not offer ordinary cues to social orientation that we take for granted in face-to-face contact, team members must explicitly indicate emotional tone, tentativeness/certainty, investment, motivation, and the like. Although icons have come into regular use (:() along with the creative use of punctuation (!!!???), we advocate that team members take a moment to think about their emotional and intellectual stance in a more elaborate way ("I'm not sure this is the best way to express this idea, but here goes . . ."). Parenthetical commentary ("is this too abstract?") helps the receiver to interpret and respond to the message in ways most likely to support the work without long process-related digressions.

♦ All documents and postings must be read as a prerequisite to participation. Entering a discussion without knowing the background is as disruptive in the VE as it is face-to-face.

♦ Postings should be substantial. This requires a subtle shift from face-to-face interaction and might not seem intuitively correct to the beginning team member. We have found, however, that lots of responses of the "atta boy," "good work," or "thanks" variety simply make it harder to follow a threaded discussion. It takes as much time to enter and check out the "atta boy" posting as it does to check out the critical comment, and nonsubstantive postings clutter the classroom environment.

♦ Equity agreements should be made by the team prior to beginning the project work. Although anonymous VEs enhance the power of less powerful members, the status, gender, and prestige of team members are often known to all members. Explicit norm setting about the requirement that all members respond to all postings or that all members read all documents and postings can support the equity balancing effect of the medium.

♦ Methods and deadlines for decisions and conclusions must be clear to all members. If members are to work by inclusion and consensus, then the rules for minimal participation and consensus must be explicit. Will complete agreement be required? If someone stands outside of consensus, can the work of the team still go forward? Will members be allowed to block consensus? By what date must members lodge objections?

♦ Notice of absence must be posted. If members cannot meet the requirement for participation (e.g., twice a week), then they must notify the group. Members should be encouraged to explain absences and make return dates explicit so that assistance can be given, if possible, and the group can discuss how to come to conclusion in the absence of a member.

♦ The process for making decisions in the absence of members must be explicitly discussed. We do not support delaying most decisions when members are missing or reopening decisions when missing members reappear. At least at the outset, proceeding with members in absentia is much more likely to reinforce norms of participation.

♦ Provisions for a safety net should be discussed. What happens if the system "crashes"? How will the work proceed in the event of a disaster? What is the responsibility of members for backing up their own participation, and how will data be recovered if the central server is damaged or destroyed? We create specific plans for the use of fax, phone, or face-to-face engagement in the event of system failure at the individual, team, and system levels.

♦ The moderator must model acceptable communication and demonstrate that risk taking is safe. Here the role of the teacher/facilitator is radically different from that in the traditional setting. The teacher/facilitator is neither neutral nor simply authoritative. He or she must not only present a model of reflective articulate thinking but also demonstrate the kinds of affective disclosure that are appropriate, the sort of feedback that is expected, and the level of support and collaboration that is required for the work of the team.

Members of virtual groups need to remember that socialized behavior often deteriorates when there are no face-to-face cues and that this happens in a seductive way. Members need to realize that this is likely to happen to them—not just to other people—and that increased consciousness and deliberation about communication is the only way in which to compensate. We have also found that the ordinary pace of the traditional classroom is not as effective when people are required to do the kind of reflection and interpersonal work that we are asking them to do. Over the years, we have developed a way of thinking about structuring assignments and syllabi that is better suited to this environment than the ordinary classroom week-by-week approach.

Cycle of Inquiry

We have learned to construct class assignments using a deliberate, protected learning cycle that permits students more time for reflection, evaluation, and synthesis. This model was developed by Crowell (1997). In general, the faculty member or facilitator organizes the new knowledge to be acquired, the topic to be discussed, or the decision to be made into modules that can be readily assimilated. The concept is that students or members of a team work with segments of information that can be readily managed in terms of their complexity and cognitive difficulty. Those segments are then offered in a defined and highly structured time frame during which students are expected to pursue the following activities:

Initial informational segment (assignment)
> *Student activity:*
>> First sequence: read/reflect/write (post) response
>> Second sequence: read the postings of others/reflect on them/write (post) response

(an intentional break)

Second informational segment (assignment)
> *Student activity:*
>> Third sequence: read/reflect/write (post) response
>> Fourth sequence: read the postings of others/reflect/write (post) a synthesis of the entire discussion

The duration of the time frame is based on time to read/write/reflect/react and rest over the course of 10 days to 2 weeks, depending on the complexity of the topic. Because time frames may run through weekends, rests of 2 or 3 days need to be scheduled. The assignment is conceived of as an ongoing interaction with several iterations and redundant "loops" that yield a deeper comprehension of the material rather than as a module that is initiated and completed in the course of a week. Students need time to engage in older discussions, to read and react to the work of others, and to review earlier thoughts on a related subject.

In addition to the reflective character, several iterations, and redundant loops that characterize this cycle of inquiry, this model for learning and decision making also includes a literal physical break in the activity. The earlier versions of this model did not allow for such a respite, and in its absence, irresolvable conflicts arose for some participants between study requirements and concurrent work, family, and community commitments. Because the broadest efficacy for this learning model requires the participation of all parties, the quality of subsequent dialogue, mastery of complex topics, and achievement all suffered. In the OM application of this model, we intentionally introduce a physical break to allow learners to meet competing work, family, and community obligations and, where necessary, to catch up on their reading and related assignments.

It is critical to make the deadlines associated with reading and posting and the break explicit so as to maintain qualitative outcomes and support the efficacy of computer-mediated inquiry. The requirements and expectations for students need to be clearly established, thoroughly articulated, and broadly distributed. If people do not respond in a timely way, then the work of the whole class falls behind schedule, the didactic effects of the model fail, and the entire process begins to resemble a poor effort to replicate face-to-face inquiry in a virtual medium. Although occasional "work-arounds" are possible, making many exceptions effectively dilutes the learning outcomes for the entire class. Many of the faculty deduct percentage points or half grades on assignments when the work is late.

Many of the norms we have been discussing are basic not only to good teamwork, regardless of venue, but also to the principles of adult education as we have adapted them for use in a VE. Because computer-mediated education appeals to working adults with busy lives, our students tend to be older than those in more traditional classrooms. Our approach to computer-mediated inquiry has been to integrate into it the principles of adult education. Lecture is discouraged and, for all practical purposes, is not a functional adaptation in a virtual medium. The instructor may write a paper or direct students to his or her existing body of work, but posting lectures is not particularly productive. Learning is enhanced and strengthened through the interests and workplace problems that students bring into the classroom, particularly when situated in the dialogical context used in conferencing software that we deploy.

Adult Education and Facilitation

It is our experience, as Fazio (1993) also suggests, that some college faculty feel insecure and even threatened when they first encounter much older graduate students who bring a wealth of life and work experience to the classroom. The students enrolled in the OM program include director- and vice president-level managers from many different large organizations. A basic principle we have embedded in the program is that the work experience and prior knowledge of these people constitute an important learning resource. Students are encouraged to share their practical wisdom and workplace challenges both in the process of raising questions to be addressed in our courses and in contributing to the dialogue by which answers are produced.

Building on the work of Malcolm Knowles (Knowles & Associates, 1984), we have conceptualized teaching in this environment as facilitation, permitting much more student interaction and collaborative learning. Like Knox (1986), we believe that teaching adults means respecting them as joint partners in their own learning process. We have adopted the term "andragogy" after Knowles (1980, 1984), who emphasizes movement through the educational process toward self-directedness, the use of life experience as legitimate knowledge, and the critical place of practical application in the education of adults.

In the VE as we use it, facilitating means several different things. First, it means creating a structure for the course and clarifying expectations not only with regard to assignments, deadlines, and the usual syllabus content but also with regard to process. Students are expected to read each other's work, to critique, to question, and to analyze. They are expected to give feedback on both content and how it is communicated. They may also be expected to pay attention to and comment on the process they are using. All of this has to be explained by the instructor.

Second, facilitation means commenting on student work, giving both individual- and group-level feedback. Individual feedback might be quite similar to the kinds of feedback that one gives in a traditional course, but often it is shared online, particularly where the instructor wants to recognize outstanding work and underscore model feedback. Group-level feedback refers to commenting on the direction of the discussion, raising questions that the group seems to have ignored, offering expert opinion, and referring the student to further resources. Group-level feedback may also be given on the process (e.g., how the work of the class is going, whether we are able to collaborate, general comments on the kinds of feedback that are useful). Instructors may summarize, redirect, and encourage discussion.

In contrast to conventional face-to-face instruction, the computer-mediated medium itself is instructive. Because the OM program is inter-active, it provides an opportunity to learn *about* the medium. Through their participation in various courses facilitated by different instructors, students come to see what works and what does not work; what is exciting and what is mundane; and how VEs might be developed, managed, and facilitated. Here, in this limited sense, the medium does become part of the message.

Learning about the medium occurs not only through participation but also through the efforts of the instructor to highlight student engagement with the medium. Facilitation here means pointing out how effective electronic communication differs from ordinary written communication or face-to-face engagement. The OM program has also (unintentionally) offered a lesson in handling electronic emergencies. For example, 1 week after the program was launched, America Online experienced a "crash" of its system. Many of our students were "stranded" or unable to "get into" the Web. Instructors modeled how to frame such events and how to create work-arounds, and they continued including all members of the class in the on-going work of the group.

Facilitation also means helping to contain the anxiety of students about the medium. It means providing safety in cyberspace. How the instructor handles his or her own computer emergencies is extremely important. When the instructor complains online and blames the system or program without making an effort to model crisis behavior, all existing problems in the system are amplified. When the instructor uses his or her own problems as a basis for more learning and greater collaboration, students are able to contribute to the learning of the group and sometimes even solve the instructor's problem. Such a crisis can empower students rather than disable them.

The characteristics of good instructors in the online environment are both similar to and different from traditional faculty. One needs, of course, to look for content expertise and the ability to engage student interest. In our particular case, we are also looking for faculty who can respect and use the work and life experience of mature students in a collaborative relationship. In addition, however, the instructor has to be able to construct a presence online and be willing to cope with the everyday exigencies of the environment. In the America Online crisis, one of our instructors gave students the analogy of "snow days" in school and reminded them that they might well have to cope with similar problems in any Web-based work environment. How could they manage it? Instructors have to be able to take advantage of real events and address the real problems that students experience in the medium.

Finally, we have found that few instructors really know whether they are going to be comfortable and satisfied in the medium until they have had some experience. Some simply realize that the rewards they find in teaching are quite dependent on face-to-face contact with students. Some cannot create a strong presence online. Some are *too* present, interfering with student participation and reflection. Finding the right fit among the instructor, the medium, and the goals of the program becomes a complex problem. We have instituted rather clear faculty probationary periods during which that fit is tested. Immediate long-term commitments on the part of either the institution or the instructor are probably premature at this stage of development.

Human Development

In planning the future of distance education, many conceive of recreating face-to-face engagement at a distance. High-speed networks already allow for the transmission of real-time video. The only obstacle to replicating face-to-face engagement appears to be the cost and the current limited distribution of high-speed networks. We would like to pose an argument for the unique developmental properties of a non-face-to-face computer-mediated education.

As Anderson (1997) argues in *The Future of the Self,* or as Gergen (1990) suggests in *The Saturated Self,* cyberspace makes it possible to construct one's identity in a uniquely conscious way. In chat rooms around the globe, people use gender-ambiguous names, switch genders altogether, rewrite their own histories, or adopt fabricated identities. These phenomena create an opportunity to experience the extent to which we live in a socially constructed world where one's sex, race, status, and so on determine how others respond.

In normal development, the growth of identity is primarily an unconscious process. Computer-mediated communication allows some aspects of that process to become more explicit for adolescents and adults. In a similar way, students appear to become more conscious of the ways in which knowledge is socially constructed. In a Web-based classroom such as ours, they offer various interpretations of the same materials to each other. They are required to read and comment not only on the text but also on the meanings that others draw from the text in a systematic way.

Furthermore, because all interactions are written, asynchronous, and sustained over time, students have the opportunity to contribute in more thoughtful ways. They are explicitly given time to reflect on and interpret the remarks of others. Everything they post in the classroom remains posted for the entire term. Other students and the instructor are able to review past discussions or to look at the remarks of any contributor again. Our preliminary analysis suggests that classroom discussions are much more reflective under these conditions than in the ordinary face-to-face setting.

Finally, in cyberspace, everyone's voice is equally loud. Everyone speaks without interruption. What impresses others is the idea itself or the way in which it is communicated rather than the frequency or volume. The voices of individuals who are ordinarily underrepresented in face-to-face discussion are as frequent as those who are used to speaking up. In fact, because all students are required to participate equally, underrepresented voices may take on a special value because they have not been heard before. Dominant interpretations can be challenged. We have certainly seen that the voices of students working and living in Europe, Asia, or Africa make unique contributions to the work of the group.

It is a great advantage of the medium that students are not taken from their ordinary working and living environments to obtain an education. The problems that students encounter in their everyday lives with work and family constitute opportunities for their learning in the VE. In our dialogical approach to learning, there is a much greater opportunity for making constructive use of the day-to-day applications that anchor knowledge in the concrete world. Students are able to test their insights, bring the results back to "class," reevaluate their learning, and retest it. They can continue a conversation regarding a particular problem or application over very long periods of time through the use of the café configuration. They can come back to a discussion that may have taken place a month earlier and reevaluate it in the light of new data. The discussion remains in place so long as the students find it valuable.

The instructor must keep in mind that students are learning more than the material at hand. They are also learning how to construct themselves in the medium, how to communicate with others, how to give and take feedback, how to collaborate, and how to design the very structure of their own learning. They are encouraged to comment on the design of the course and the assignment. Their feedback is taken seriously, not only at the classroom level but also at the program level. The Web offers unique opportunities to be a real-time learning organization as well as an academic program. We hope to model much of what we want to see in the external world.

Like many other leading-edge organizations, we are building the rocket while we are riding it. Our students have many opportunities to cope with change, crisis, and even chaos in the medium as well as with the definition and redefinition of the curriculum and the delivery system. Such "meta-learning" is all the more explicit because it is not conducted in the face-to-face setting where much of what we communicate is less intentional.

There may come a time in the not-so-distant future when the current level of communication networks and technology is replaced by video and audio transmissions that seem more like everyday reality and, therefore, more comfortable for many. It is possible that much will be lost when this happens. Current conditions offer a unique opportunity to recognize how the medium of communication itself affects the construction of the self, reality, and knowledge. This is one of the most important of the learnings we have taken away from our work so far. Distance learning programs that depend on the use of television and shrink-wrapped or packaged content miss this opportunity entirely.

According to Torbert (1993), graduate or postformal adult education should embrace capacities for empirical operational learning, for abstract hypothetical learning, and for subjective self-knowledge. It must provide the opportunity to coordinate thought, action, and outcomes. It must invite students to improve not only their analytic competence but also their competence as professionals, and it must encourage the cycle of feedback and new initiatives. A mature graduate education is designed to take students beyond the stage of formal operations as described by Piaget and into the realm of systems thinking (Commons, Armon, Richards, & Schrader, 1989). We believe that Web-based education provides an unprecedented opportunity to meet the requirements of postformal education.

References

Anderson, W. A. (1997). *The future of the self: Inventing the postmodern person.* New York: Jeremy P. Tarcher/Putnum.

Bion, W. F. (1959). *Experiences in groups.* New York: Basic Books.

Brown, B. M. (1998). Digital classrooms: Some myths about developing new educational programs using the Internet. *T.H.E. Journal, 25,* 56-59.

Childs, G. B. (1949). *A comparison of supervised correspondence study pupils and classroom pupils in achievement in school subjects.* Doctoral dissertation, University of Nebraska.

Commons, M. L., Armon, C., Richards, F. A., & Schrader, D. E., with Farrell, E. W., Tappan, M. B., & Bauer, N. F. (1989). A multidomain study of adult development. In M. L. Commons, C. Armon, & F. A. Richards (Eds.), *Adult development: Vol. 1. Comparisons and applications of adolescent and adult development.* New York: Praeger.

Crowell, C. (1997). *A 10-day learning cycle model for computer-mediated inquiry.* Occasional paper, Institute for Computer-Mediated Learning, Communication, and Research, Putney, VT.

Fazio, J. (1993). *Instructional imperatives of the adult student in the undergraduate institution.* Unpublished dissertation, Fielding Graduate Institute.

Gergen, K. (1990). *The saturated self: Dilemmas of identity in contemporary life.* New York: Basic Books.

Knowles, M. A. (1980). *The modern practice of adult education from pedagogy to andragogy.* New York: Cambridge University Press.

Knowles, M. A., & Associates. (1984). *Andragogy in action.* San Francisco: Jossey-Bass.

Knox, A. B. (1986). *Helping adults learn: A guide to planning, implementing, and conducting programs.* Englewood Cliffs, NJ: Prentice Hall.

Moore, M. G., & Kearsley, G. (1996). *Distance education: A systems view.* Belmont, CA: Wadsworth.

Nasseh, B. (1997). *A brief history of distance education* [Online]. Retrieved June 14, 2001, from: www.bsu.edu/classes/nasseh/study/history.html

Parsons, T. S. (1957). A comparison of instruction by kinescope, correspondence study, and customary classroom procedures. *Journal of Educational Psychology, 48,* 27-40.

Reiser, R. A. (1987). Instructional technology: A history. In R. Gagne (Ed.), *Instructional technology: Foundations.* Hillsdale: Lawrence Erlbaum.

Stevens-Long, J. (1994, June). *The application of decision-making theory and theories of adult development to diagnosis and intervention in group process.* Paper presented at the meeting of the International Society for the Psycho-analytic Study of Organizations, Chicago.

Ticknor, A. E. (1897). *Society to encourage studies at home.* Cambridge, UK: Riverside.

Torbert, W. (1993). Cultivating postformal adult development: Higher stages and contrasting interventions. In M. Miller & S. Cook-Greuter (Eds.), *Transcendence and mature thought in adulthood.* Boston: Rowman & Littlefield.

Chapter 7

Beyond the Looking Glass

*What Faculty and Students Need
to Be Successful Online*

Rena M. Palloff and Keith Pratt

Oh, Kitty, how nice it would be if we could only get through into looking-glass house! I'm sure it's got, oh! such beautiful things in it! Let's pretend there's a way of getting through into it somehow, Kitty. Let's pretend the glass has got all soft like gauze, so that we can get through. Why, it's turning into a sort of mist now. I declare! It'll be easy enough to get through. (Carroll, 1871, p. 181)

Those in higher education are seeing the move to online distance education as both a blessing and a curse. Many administrators view it as a way to increase flagging enrollments and extend the reach of the institution or, in simple terms, as an easy way to maximize profits. Many students view online courses as a more convenient way to go to school and even sometimes as an easier way to earn credit. Faculty given the responsibility to develop and teach online courses, however, might not see online education in such a positive light.

There are a significant number of faculty who are sincerely interested in online education and its possibilities. Early enthusiasts are exploring alternative ways of teaching in this environment. However, some faculty have been told that they *must* develop and teach online classes. They are being given no choice in the matter. Many feel lost, not even sure where to begin. Others have heard that the key to success is content; simply migrate the content that has been taught in the face-to-face classroom into the online classroom, and all will be well. Others learn how to use the software that is designed to teach the course and think that this is all they need to know to move successfully to the online environment.

The result of these false assumptions is the development of courses that are poorly conceived and lack interactivity, taught by faculty who are frustrated by their inability to get students involved. A likely outcome is low enrollment or attrition from online courses and programs. Unfortunately, faculty are rarely provided with training in the pedagogical skills they need to teach online. A 1999 survey of 60 faculty members conducted at Arkansas State University yielded results that appear to be the norm of faculty experience, as 90% indicated that they needed substantially more preparation time to develop a course and 75% had not participated in any additional training opportunities other than what they needed to understand the online technology (Dickinson, Agnew, & Gorman, 1999, p. 1). Given these statistics, it is no wonder that research into retention in online courses shows upward of 50% dropout rates (Carr, 2000) and that many faculty view online learning as a poor and inferior stepchild of higher education.

In this chapter, we do not intend to deliver a message of gloom and doom. We believe that if faculty are trained in pedagogical methods that lend themselves to the online environment, and if students are effectively oriented to online work, then the result can be highly interactive courses that lead to successful achievement of learning objectives and a sense of satisfaction on the part of faculty and students alike. This chapter explores some of the ways in which faculty and student development can be accomplished to achieve these goals.

Working With Faculty to Develop a New Pedagogy

> In another moment, Alice was through the glass and had jumped lightly down into the looking-glass room. . . . Then she began looking about and noticed that what could be seen from the old room was quite common and uninteresting, but that all the rest was as different as possible. . . . "They don't keep this room so tidy as the other," Alice thought to herself. (Carroll, 1871, pp. 183-184)

Teaching online requires faculty to move beyond traditional models of teaching and to adopt new practices that facilitate student learning. Some faculty resist this notion, however, thinking that it must be possible somehow to retain the lecture/discussion model of teaching in the online medium. Unlike the face-to-face classroom, where such methods may be successful, in online distance education a lecture simply becomes another article that students need to read. Although the advent of streaming audio and video has made it possible for instructors to deliver lectures to students who have the technology to receive them, students, when asked where they derived the most benefit from an online class, have noted that they often bypassed online lecture material and went directly to the discussion board, where they were able to interact with the instructor and their peers about the subject matter (Feenberg, 1999; Palloff & Pratt, 2001). Thus, in online learning, attention needs to be paid to promoting interactivity and the development of a sense of community within the student group to achieve successful learning outcomes.

Even the most seasoned faculty in the face-to-face classroom, however, might not intuitively know how to build interactive courses online. The skills involved in delivering a course using interactive facilitative means—which we term "electronic pedagogy"—can be taught, but these skills are often overlooked when faculty are trained to teach online. Questions that need to be addressed as faculty learn about online teaching are as follows: What does it really mean to be a "guide on the side" or a "learning facilitator" rather than an instructor? How does an instructor successfully make the transition required to teach an online course so that students become empowered learners and take charge of the learning process? Is it possible to develop every instructor into a good online instructor? How can institutions discern the difference between those who will do well online and those who will not, be they faculty or students?

Not all faculty are suited for the online environment, and academic institutions are making some serious mistakes when they make their decisions about who should teach. Choices about who should teach online are often based on faulty criteria; it is usually either someone who is considered a content expert or someone who is deemed entertaining in the face-to-face classroom who is chosen. Brookfield (1995) notes that often the most popular faculty, who get the best course evaluations, are the ones who are able to entertain. Being entertaining does not translate so well online, where one's personality is reduced to text on a screen. Focusing on faculty who are content experts may present a problem. Although they may know their subject matter well, they might not have, or might not have been taught, the facilitative skills required for online teaching.

Personality characteristics of successful online faculty may differ from those of successful classroom faculty. Research by one of the authors reveals that it is the introverted student who does particularly well online (Pratt, 1996). We believe that this finding generally applies to introverted instructors as well. In the online environment, facial and body language cues are removed from communication. The introvert, who can be inhibited by these cues in face-to-face communication, generally appears far more extroverted online and frequently becomes quite verbal and interactive. The ability to take time, reflect, and present himself or herself through text serves the introvert well. Self-consciousness diminishes when the instructor is out from under the physical scrutiny of students. On the other hand, the extrovert, who generally establishes presence quickly through verbal and social connection, may have more difficulty in the text-based online environment. Taking time to reflect is not the forte of the extrovert, who tends to process ideas out loud at the time they occur. The responses received help the extrovert to formulate and refine his or her ideas. Consequently, the asynchronous online environment, with its absence of immediate feedback, can be frustrating to the extrovert.

> People who are introverts are more adept at creating a virtual environment because they can process information internally and are less outgoing socially. It is more comfortable for an introvert to spend time thinking about information before responding to it. It is more difficult—but not impossible—for extroverts to interact this way, perhaps because they have less need to. Extroverts tend to feel more comfortable processing verbally and in the company of others. (Palloff & Pratt, 1999, p. 22)

Consequently, it can be assumed that the instructor who might not be an entertainer in the face-to-face classroom, yet who has subject matter expertise, is flexible, and is open to the development of a more collaborative way of teaching, may be the better candidate to develop and deliver online courses.

We have found that successful instructors are willing to give up a fair degree of control in the teaching and learning process. They are able to empower their learners and build a learning community. An instructor who is willing to use collaborative, active learning techniques and ideas, and who allows for personal interaction, brings in real-life examples, and builds reflective practice into teaching, is a good candidate for teaching online. The open and flexible instructor needs support, however, to make the transition to the online classroom successful. This support rests in training and mentoring.

Training to Support the Transition

Faculty cannot be expected to know intuitively how to design and deliver an effective online course. Although courses and programs about the use of technology in education are emerging, and attendance at conferences on the topic is growing markedly, faculty have not been fully exposed to the techniques and methods needed to make online work successful. Current software applications make it easy for faculty to simply transfer material to a course site. The lure to do this is complicated by the fact that institutions, which may view online distance learning as their lifesaver during times

of on-campus declining enrollment, are now registering such large numbers of students in online classes that the burden on faculty is enormous.

Training faculty to help them get started and to support their ongoing teaching online does help. In our experience, creating a mentoring relationship through the pairing of faculty who are more experienced online with those who are just starting helps to break down barriers and provides real concrete examples of what works and what does not. The University of Central Florida has established a comprehensive faculty development program that addresses four key areas of readiness: the institution, faculty, courses, and learners. The areas can be used to generate the following checklist to help institutions and faculty evaluate which aspects of their program or courses need attention.

Institutional Readiness
- The course or program is a good fit with the institution's character and mission.
- There is a good fit with learner characteristics of the institution.
- There is a clearly articulated mission and strategic plan.
- There is demonstrated faculty interest.
- There is a robust campus infrastructure to support courses and programs.
- There is leadership for the initiative.
- There is a commitment to faculty support.
- There is a commitment to course and program support.
- There is a commitment to learner support.
- There is a commitment to assessment.

Faculty Readiness
- A willingness to learn
- A willingness to surrender some control over class design and teaching style
- An ability to collaborate with peers
- A willingness to change the traditional faculty role
- An ability to build a support system
- Patience with technology
- An ability to learn from others

Course Readiness
- A demonstrated faculty understanding of the technology in use
- A demonstrated understanding of the pedagogy required for online teaching

◆ A demonstrated understanding of the logistics of the course production process

Learner Readiness

◆ Determined through informed self-selection

◆ An ability to take responsibility for one's own learning

◆ An access plan (i.e., has access to a computer and software at home or has a plan for accessing them) for taking the course

◆ An awareness of one's own learning style

◆ Technical skill—an ability to build a support system

◆ An ability to deal with the uncertainties of using technology to take courses (Truman-Davis, Futch, Thompson, & Yonekura, 2000)

Online training courses are another useful way to deliver training to faculty who will be teaching online. In an online training course, the best practices involved in online teaching can be demonstrated. The best practices relate to the activities of teaching and learning and not to the technology itself. In an online faculty development course, faculty can experience firsthand what it is like to be both an instructor and a student in the process. In our experience, the courseware to be used in the development and delivery of courses should be the software used in the training. The course should be long enough so that faculty can be encouraged to develop the skeleton of a course or even one lesson that other participants can critique. The facilitator of the training should model good techniques for building a learning community within the course and for empowering the participating faculty to explore both the medium and the material. We have found that it is best to include in online training faculty who will imminently teach their first online courses. Faculty who are about to teach online are highly motivated to learn good techniques for doing so. Faculty who are simply interested but will not immediately be using the training might not participate to the same degree. When the group is made up of those who will be teaching online immediately and those who are simply interested, those who will not be teaching online in the immediate future do not feel as compelled to comply with participation expectations for the course. They may drop out and create frustration for those who stay with the training and who depend on the group to learn how the online learning process works.

The following are some final reflections on a professional development course. It was conducted over 4 weeks and focused on the development of an effective learning community within the context of an online course. The group was composed of 35 faculty members, instructional designers, and student affairs personnel, all of whom wanted to understand and experience the impact of online learning on the students with whom they worked. The group members were given reading assignments about online teaching and learning. Then they were asked to engage with one another and to reflect on the concepts presented. They were asked to commit to participate in the discussion at least twice weekly during the 4-week course. They were also encouraged, through the discussion questions, to apply the concepts discussed with concrete examples from their own work. Representative faculty participants described their training experiences in the following ways:

> I found this course to be an intensive online experience as my regular workload was increasing. I found myself working overtime in the normal workweek digesting information and responding to the academic content, as well as the personal contact, while trying to participate in the course to learn from my colleagues. I was able to experience firsthand a possible online experience for our new online education program at the college and to extrapolate, albeit slowly, some of the issues raised in the postings to my ever-changingworkplace. Participating in a college committee involving faculty and administrators involved in online education, I felt I could give a student perspective [on] the institution's online education program. Personally, I was excited and pleased to learn some new technical skills. I found myself having new respect for these students as they work with me and I try to interpret the requirements, rules, [and] culture of this new medium with them.

> I enjoyed my experience with this online course. Although I was not able to participate in the discussion threads very much these last 2 weeks, I have learned from the experience. As I work with students who are taking or planning to take an online class, I will be better able to advise them [regarding] time commitments, strong self-motivation, realistic expectations, etc. While I learned from the experience without necessarily jumping into every discussion, I'm not being graded. :-) The students do need to be concerned with what is expected of them in terms of participation. It has been enjoyable to begin learning about this new learning environment!

> Overwhelming. Confusing. And yet enlightening. I think I have learned that what sometimes may seem like a well-structured experience on my end may not be so from the perspective of my students. Ultimately, they as a group need to organize their environment in a way that makes most sense to them.

> I have learned that online learning takes a lot of time, but I enjoy writing and reading the writing of others. . . . I've learned what it might feel like to be a new online student who was anxious about where and how to post assignments. . . . I realize if students are frustrated in the beginning of the class, it might affect their performance in the class. . . . I've also learned how important it is for online teachers to find other online teachers to share their teaching experiences with and the need for us to find, explore, update, and do research in this field.

The reflections of these instructors indicate that significant learning came out of their experience of being students online. The experience will likely assist them in developing courses that are more responsive to the needs of learners. The faculty have seen what it is like from the other side of the looking glass. This is invaluable learning—learning that is difficult to convey in face-to-face training.

Developing New Techniques

Bates (2000) notes that in institutions where best practices in the implementation of technology are followed, faculty development focuses on teaching and learning and not on the technology itself. There is little doubt that faculty are in need of developing skills in computer literacy before they can move into teaching online. However, as we have been emphasizing, the focus in faculty development should be on pedagogical methods and not on the software in use.

When presented with instructional design principles that promote interactive delivery appropriate to online teaching, faculty will often ask, "Where is the lecture?" An appropriate response to this question is presented by Lytle, Lytle, Lenhart, and Skrotsky (1999), who state, "Lectures are important and certainly numerous in higher education, but are not necessarily any more valuable in the learning process than any other learning tool" (p. 58). Incorporated into faculty training and development, then, should be concrete ways in which content can be presented without the use of lectures. Some of the techniques can include the following:

- Creating Web pages that contain no more than one screen of text and graphics
- Collaborative small-group assignments
- Research assignments asking students to seek out and present additional resources available on the Internet and in books and journals
- Simulations that mimic real-life work applications of the material discussed, such as asking a group to become a work team to develop a proposal on a given topic to be submitted to a fictitious company
- Asking students to become "experts" on a topic within the scope of the course and to then present that topic to their peers
- Asynchronous discussion of the topics within the scope of the course material being studied
- Papers posted to the course site
- Limited use of audio and video clips (Palloff & Pratt, 2001, p. 43)

What is important is to encourage and support faculty in thinking outside the box in terms of developing creative ways to present course content, keeping in mind the technology to which students are likely to have access.

Yet another critical factor in faculty training is to help them develop sensitivity to student needs and expectations as they enter the online environment. Just as faculty struggled in their online faculty development course to understand how online learning works and what is expected, students will not intuitively know how to function in an online course. In addition, learning online poses new challenges to students who previously have been exposed to traditional learning models. We now turn our attention to what it takes to assist students in becoming effective online learners and how faculty can help them with the process.

Learning to Learn Online

There was a book lying near Alice on the table, and while she sat watching . . . she turned over the leaves to find some part that she could read, "for it's all in some language I don't know," she said to herself. . . . "Why, it's a looking-glass book, of course! And if I hold it up to the glass, the words will all go the right way again." (Carroll, 1871, p. 190)

Students are, for the most part, unaware of the demands that online learning will place on them as learners. They generally enter an online class with traditional expectations, that is, that the instructor will "teach" and they will "learn" from the material the instructor provides. They do not know that the instructor is less visible in the learning process and that the instructor role is one of facilitator rather than of traditional teacher or lecturer. They also have not been told that the online learning process is less structured and demands significantly more input from them as learners to make it successful. Consequently, it is important that the instructor convey this information to students prior to beginning an online course. Many times difficulties emerge when students have differing sets of expectations from the course and the instructor and little or no attempt is made to clarify expectations at the outset.

Students generally enter an online program with the expectation that a course will be more attuned to their needs as learners. This may mean that the course is more convenient for them due to distance or work and family demands. Or it may mean that they do not like large classroom situations and prefer the potential for increased instructor-student interaction.

Because students enter online programs and courses with expectations that might not match the realities of online learning, some institutions are creating online courses to teach students about online learning, and some are even mandating that students complete an introductory course before embarking on other online classes. Some incorporate mandatory face-to-face orientations to online programs and courses, involving both computer training and training in what it means to learn online and how to be an effective online student. The assumption behind all of these approaches is the same: To maximize the educational potential for both the online classroom and online students. We must pay attention to teaching our teachers how to teach and teaching our learners how to learn when teaching and learning are virtual.

As with faculty training, conducting student training online allows students to experience online learning before they take an actual course. Regardless of the means by which the training is conducted, the following should be included in a student orientation to online learning:

- The basics of logging on to the Internet, including the use of a browser, accessing the course site, using course management software, saving and printing material found online, basic Internet searching, and e-mail

- Understanding what is required to become a successful online learner, including time requirements and time management

- The differences between a face-to-face course and an online course, including the role of the instructor and the roles of students as well as expectations about how students will be evaluated

- Interaction between the instructor and students and among students

- How to give feedback to other students

- Appropriate interaction and communication, including the rules of "netiquette"

- How to get help when it is needed (Palloff & Pratt, 2001, pp. 123-124)

Providing an orientation course might not resolve all of the issues for students as they make the transition to the online classroom. But it certainly can help to provide a clearer understanding of the differences in the type of educational experience they are about to undertake and can help to clarify expectations. Following up with a written guide to online work, whether in hard copy or placed on the institution's Web site, can help to reinforce this learning. When concerns or complaints regarding expectations arise, students can then be referred back to the guidelines that are readily available to them to help them understand the online teaching and learning methods and processes.

If the institution cannot provide student training about how to learn, then suggestions for how to learn online become the responsibility of the faculty who are delivering courses. Ways in which faculty can orient students include the following:

- Hold a face-to-face, hands-on orientation, if possible, to show students the course site and discuss online learning.
- Provide an orientation to the course on the course site or as a first discussion item.
- Provide students with a list of frequently asked questions and responses to those questions.
- Place basic information about how to navigate the course site on the welcome screen or course home page.
- Send an e-mail message to each student enrolled in the course containing orientation information. (Palloff & Pratt, 2001, p. 43)

Regardless of how student orientation occurs, it needs to be considered an important element in the development of the course. Unfortunately, it is often overlooked. Including this information in faculty training, especially if faculty have the ability to participate in their own online courses, can create an awareness of just how important student orientation is.

Changing Roles and Relationships

Alice watched the White King as he slowly struggled up from bar to bar, till at last she said, "Why, you'll be hours and hours getting to the table at that rate. I'd far better help you, hadn't I?" . . . So Alice picked him up very gently and lifted him across. (Carroll, 1871, p. 188)

One final issue that faculty and student development should touch on is the changing nature of faculty-student relationships created by the more facilitative methods used in online teaching. The student enrolled in higher education today, whether online or in traditional institutions, is less likely to be the 18- to 21-year-old seeking a one-time educational experience. Instead, today's student is likely to be an adult returning to school to obtain the knowledge and skills needed to compete and advance in the workforce. The adult student, therefore, is more likely to be a lifelong learner embarking on the beginning of what may be a learning process that results in the pursuit of multiple degrees, courses, or certifications (Bates, 2000). Although their previous educational experiences have been traditional—meaning that the instructor is the expert with knowledge and wisdom to impart and that the student has only to receive—the lifelong learner is looking to enter a partnership that results in the achievement of specified learning objectives.

The partnership that these students seek is not only with an instructor but also with student colleagues and with an academic institution that understands and tries to meet their needs. There is a movement occurring in the academic world; academic institutions need to be increasingly responsive to those they serve, resulting in a shift from the traditional faculty-centered institution to a learner-focused one. In this context, the relationship between faculty and students will change as well.

In the online classroom, the most effective means of achieving learning outcomes is the use of active learning techniques that encourage students to become empowered learners. The fully engaged, active learner is likely to bring new demands to the learning situation. The online environment can be a great equalizer, and the online classroom can become the place where faculty and students partner to achieve learning objectives through interactive, self-empowering means (Harasim, Hiltz, Teles, & Turoff, 1996; Palloff & Pratt, 1999, 2001). Bates (2000) notes,

> Modern learning theory sees learning as an individual quest for meaning and relevance. Once learning moves beyond the recall of facts, principles, or correct procedures and into the area of creativity, problem solving, analysis, or evaluation (the very skills needed in the workplace in a knowledge-based economy, not to mention in life in general), learners need the opportunity to communicate with one another as well as with their teachers. This, of course, includes the opportunity to question, challenge, and discuss issues. (pp. 13-14)

Rather than be threatened by the shift in the faculty-student relationship, faculty can be challenged by the change and embrace it. Faculty, too, are lifelong learners. The changing relationship between faculty and students serves to expand the network through which faculty can learn. We always believe, as we enter a new online course, that we have as much to learn from our students as they do from us, and we find this to be an exciting element of our online work that we welcome.

Life on the Other Side of the Looking Glass

> "Your Red Majesty shouldn't purr so loud," Alice said, rubbing her eyes and addressing the kitten respectfully, yet with some severity. "You woke me out of oh! such a nice dream! And you've been along with me, Kitty—all through the looking-glass world. Did you know it, dear?" (Carroll, 1871, p. 341)

When faculty and students are provided with good training and support for online teaching and learning, the likely outcome is excitement about new ways of teaching and learning. There is enthusiasm about the meeting of learning objectives in deep and meaningful ways. When courses are designed and delivered with interactivity in mind, a shift occurs as learners become more empowered and discover that the learning in an online course comes from other students and not solely from interaction with the instructor. In fact, when courses progress well, the instructor often learns as much from his or her students as students learn from the instructor. The reflection of one of our students at the end of an online course demonstrates this shift:

> I wanted to take another opportunity to thank each of you for your partici-
> pation in this course. I remember when I first joined the program, . . . [other
> students] talked about the importance [that] their colleagues played in their
> success in the program. I had no idea of the significance of those statements,
> or the degree to which they were true, until I experienced it for myself.
> Thank you all for this tremendous contribution to my development. —Jane

Jane's reflection is the type we hope to see at the end of a course. It gives us an indication that the planning and delivery of the course was effective not only in achieving learning objectives but also in moving students toward what we consider to be real learning—a shared creation of meaning and knowledge.

When instructors and students are able to reap the benefits of a well-designed online course, the end result is excitement about what is possible in the online realm and about the new relationships that are developed between instructor and student; among students; and among instructor, students, and knowledge creation. The resultant excitement about learning helps to stimulate new creative approaches to online teaching and demonstrates that there is, in fact, the possibility that life beyond the looking glass is not a dream but a reality with great potential.

References

Bates, A. W. (2000). *Managing technological change*. San Francisco: Jossey-Bass.

Brookfield, S. (1995). *Becoming a critically reflective teacher*. San Francisco: Jossey-Bass.

Carr, S. (2000, February 11). As distance education comes of age, the challenge is keeping the students. *The Chronicle of Higher Education* [Online]. Available: http://chronicle.com/free/v46/i23/23a00101.htm

Carroll, L. (1871). *Through the looking glass, and what Alice found there*. New York: Macmillan.

Dickinson, G., Agnew, D., & Gorman, R. (1999). Are teacher training and compensation keeping up with institutional demands for distance learning? *Cause/Effect Journal, 22*(3). Available: www.educause.edu/ir/library/html/cem9939.html

Feenberg, A. (1999, September-October). No frills in the virtual classroom. *Academe*, pp. 26-31.

Harasim, L., Hiltz, S. R., Teles, L., & Turoff, M. (1996). *Learning networks*. Cambridge: MIT Press.

Lytle, S., Lytle, V., Lenhart, K., & Skrotsky, L. (1999, November-December). Large-scale deployment of technology-enhanced courses. *Syllabus*, pp. 57-59.

Palloff, R. M., & Pratt, K. (1999). *Building learning communities in cyberspace: Effective strategies for the online classroom*. San Francisco: Jossey-Bass.

Palloff, R. M., & Pratt, K. (2001). *Lessons from the cyberspace classroom: The realities of online teaching.* San Francisco: Jossey-Bass.

Pratt, K. (1996). *The electronic personality.* Unpublished doctoral dissertation, Human and Organizational Systems Program, Fielding Graduate Institute.

Truman-Davis, B., Futch, L., Thompson, K., & Yonekura, F. (2000). Support for online teaching and learning. *Educause Quarterly, 2,* 44-51.

Chapter 8

The Jungle Syndrome

Some Perils and Pleasures of Learning Without Walls

Barclay Hudson

The "jungle syndrome" is inherent in adult online learning. It arises from the best aspects of adult education, breaking away from the lock-step regimentation of traditional pedagogy. The online library is not a reading list but rather the Internet, a space without boundaries or center or maps. Issues and purposes emerge from group dialogue as much as from a lesson plan. Critical thinking becomes more important than knowledge content. Learning is aimed at getting out of intellectual boxes rather than staying within the conventions of a particular discipline and subject focus.

These gains, however, can come at a cost. The jungle syndrome involves a form of information overload, especially from the open-ended and evolving conceptual framework used for assimilating information. Traditional pedagogy avoids this by constant reference to prepackaged, compartmentalized lesson plans—everything in its place, all questions answered, all purposes spelled out, all outcomes predetermined, all learning neatly channeled into exam-based assessments.

Adult online learning turns all of this on its head. Getting rid of rigid teaching structures and lesson plans puts the learner (and teacher) into unfamiliar territory. The central "texts" are not drawn so much from books as from personal experience and lifelong learning and the voices of collaborative exploration. Even if one starts with a clear set of objectives and assignments, the path soon leads to a place of unexpected encounters and detours until the familiar landmarks disappear entirely. This kind of challenge is entirely different from traditional education. Here, when things are moving ahead most powerfully, we become lost in a way that is both transformational and fearful. It calls on us to think about learning in a different way and to find ways of understanding outside the frame of received knowledge.

At its best, then, adult online education challenges students to the point where they become overwhelmed. At various unpredictable stages in the process, learning fills the mind to the point of saturation and incapacity to go further. Solutions come not from "knowing the right answers" but rather from developing personal and group skills in *managing* information—not just data but also relationships and interpretive frameworks that have meaning for a particular group. The same holds for faculty as well as students. The teacher cannot remain outside the process and simply observe how people struggle to find the right path. The teacher is along for the expedition, offering knowledge resources and keeping basic course purposes in view but, even more important, conveying survival skills, a sense of exploration, and respect for what the jungle can do—both positive and negative.

In this chapter, I start by describing the jungle syndrome in a little more detail. Then I briefly review some jungle navigation tools in terms of (a) software features for learning forums and (b) design and presentation of individual courses.

In the second half of the chapter, I turn to a quite different approach, where the goal is not to tame and civilize the jungle but rather to provide better tools for thriving in it. The focus is on use of "image-based" dialogue—the use of concrete, visually oriented forms of language, which I consider one of the most critical and underappreciated aspects of online learning. This approach has elements of storytelling and metaphor, but it is also reflected in scientific method, including the systematic use of thought experiments. Verbal imagery has powerful applications offline as well, as an antidote to the abstractness of many academic concepts. But for online learning, it is especially valuable, and for learning in a jungle environment, it becomes almost indispensable.

Into the Jungle

I can illustrate the jungle syndrome with a memory. My first teenage summer job was in Montana, working for a guide and outfitter named Ray Guthrie. I started by going with Ray on a 2-day climb into the mountains with a pack train of horses, bringing supplies to a high camp. Near the destination, Ray turned to me in his saddle and asked, "Know where you are?"

"Well, I guess, sort of," I said. Ray nodded, and a while later he said, to my horror, "Okay, then, I might have you take the horses back down while I stay up here a couple of days to get things set up."

It was a truly awful moment. In truth, I had paid little attention to the way we had come or how to get back out. I felt so completely lost, I didn't even dare to admit it. For the entire rest of the summer, I made a point of memorizing every feature of landscape I laid eyes on—every ridge line, trail fork, and patch of vegetation.

Adult online learning raises this question, too—"Know where you are?" It's unstated, but it comes up more often than we probably realize because it is easy to get disoriented by the multiple simultaneous threads of online dialogue. Yet nobody likes to admit being lost or falling behind, so the problems and the anxiety usually go unexpressed. Being lost connotes lack of alertness, poor attention to the group, mental slowness, or lack of discipline—a failure to stick with the pack. Losing touch with the class taps into the atavistic fear of a teacher calling on you in class to answer a question when your mind has been a million miles away on other things.

"Jungle syndrome" was the term used first by Alberic Augeard, a Belgium-based graduate student in our online master's program in organizational management, whose virtual campus is part of the Fielding Graduate Institute based in Santa Barbara, California. "It feels like a jungle," Augeard once posted, speaking frankly about it.

> I'm lost. There are so many threads of discussion going on at once, I constantly feel that I'm missing something important. Every time I sign on and start to comment on a point, there's so much that has already been said. Maybe someone has already covered the point I want to make, and I'll just seem redundant, or unprepared, or uncaring about other people's contributions. The more systematic I am about trying to keep track, the more I'm aware of new comments all over the forum, and the less prepared I feel to catch up. Where to start? How to synthesize? How to make it all manageable? How to get a coherent grasp on all these themes? (Fielding Graduate Institute forum posting, April 1998)

Those issues come not just from Augeard but from many voices over the years, both students and faculty. Verbal expressions of the jungle syndrome vary, but there is a recognizable subtext in common—a feeling of angst, a sense of exclusion or alienation, when the group seems to be moving ahead beyond your own ability to keep up. There is frustration about the open-ended format of discussion, which flows so easily beyond the boundaries of lesson plans, and fear of stalling for good behind the snowballing of postings unread. Late with an assignment, most people will tend to withdraw into a kind of self-exile as protection against exposure and accountability. But in adult online learning, the sense of separation and disorientation seems to go deeper. There is a feeling of missing out—a sense that forum conversations are going off in some wonderful directions that elude you. There's also a feeling of guilt at not holding up your own end of a conversation, or of being unresponsive to others you care about, in a tenuous virtual community where reciprocal caring is highly valued.

One of the simplest remedies is to acknowledge the problem openly and give a name to it. This can help to shift the issue from a personal shortcoming (the syndrome) to the situation that created it (the jungle itself). As often as not, the naming of it spreads the burden around. "You think it's *you* furthest behind? Well, that's a relief. I thought it was just me." In fact, the jungle syndrome seems to come in unpredictable little epidemics, affecting everyone in the same given course one year and disappearing the next.

Importantly, the jungle syndrome can arise most acutely among the "best" people—those most conscientious about being responsive, most thoughtful about relationships, and most concerned about seeing "the big picture" rather than settling for fragments.

For adult learning, the easiest solution is the one most important to avoid. This is the temptation of reverting to lock-step, surprise-free lesson plans and the other props of traditional pedagogy. The jungle is not a sign of things going wrong but rather a sign of things going right—getting outside the box of predetermined problems and solutions, text chapters, and correct answers on an exam.

The other options are more challenging but ultimately more rewarding, and they go to the heart of adult online learning. The tougher solution is to discover in the jungle itself the deepest form of learning and the most transformative capabilities of the learning community. There is no real possibility of personal and cognitive transformation without disorientation, no learning without going through a place of confusion, and no true community without starting from a place of being lost.

Online Education as a Microcosm of Changes in the World at Large

The jungle isn't unique to learning forums, but it appears in the larger world of business and social relations. Organizations seem to be shifting away from monolithic, hierarchical, clearly delineated, well-focused entities striving for order and predictability. Instead, they are evolving toward organizational flatness and decentralization, striving for flexibility and management of change and structures that are indistinct at the edges through a closer symbiosis with clients, vendors, and partners. The lines of communication, the compartments of dialogue, and the categories of issues are becoming overlapped and blurred. Entity and identity are less predetermined, more created in the moment, and more contextually based. Management theory is moving decisively toward a view of organizations as evolving distributed networks rather than clearly bounded entities (Hamilton, 1998; Handy, 1994, chap. 4; Reynolds, 1999; Slater, 1999).

Just as postmodern critical theory would have it, the heart of an organization is becoming less a matter of neatly drawn organization charts and more a matter of "social construction" or a matter of self-organization (Kauffman, 1995; Mintzberg & Van der Heyden, 1999). Identity is not a given; it is a problematic—a growing focus of concern. Change on any level, whether individual or organizational, revolves around the evolution of identities, especially through emergence of a new shared purpose. Dialogue is a critical part of this. And all of this holds true not only for organizations at large but also for learning in a classroom.

It is truest of all for adult online education, where the object is to treat students not as passive repositories of facts and ideas but as learners going beyond factual information. Adult learners are interested in personal evolution and change in their jobs and workplaces. They are interested not just in what they learn but in how they learn, not just in the classroom but in everyday experience and in the world of connectivity outside formal education, not just in skills and work roles but in self-identity, not just in addressing issues but in finding their voice—and not just their own voice but also a distinctive voice that emerges with a trusted group in the form of dialogue.

This, then, is the larger context for the jungle syndrome. It arises because the neatly organized compartments are dissolving and because the lesson plans are no longer conveniently packaged in approved textbooks. If the goal is learning and change, then the way is no longer clearly mapped. If the journey is to be a group venture, then the role of a single leader, out in front showing the way, no longer applies. Everyone gets lost together or found together.

Jungle Navigation 101:
Software Needs of Adult Learning Forums

Recently, I served on an institute-wide committee charged with upgrading our software for online learning—a very educational experience. We reviewed shortcomings of the existing system, wrote specifications for vendor bids, evaluated about two dozen vendors to create a short list, and then looked closely at three vendors, including hands-on tours of their learning forums.

Some surprises emerged. First, it became apparent that even the smallest technical features can make a big difference in the way people collaborate within forums. Some software is designed to help people navigate "within the jungle" of self-organized discussion threads, whereas other vendors aim at trying to re-create the familiar environment of a traditional campus, complete with links to sororities and fraternities; scheduled campus activities; libraries; parking administration; entertainment and sports ticket sales; chat rooms; hot links to "cool" Web sites; and, of course, "classrooms" organized around assignments, grades, and grade curves. Traditional pedagogy aims at clearly defined, modularized packages of knowledge, spoon-fed and re-flected back faithfully in quizzes. By contrast, adult learning is far more open to paradox and uncertainty, with shifting boundaries of focus emerging from collaborative, self-organized projects.

Technology as Mirror and Manager of Culture

These kinds of built-in software features reveal a deep divide between adult education and traditional pedagogy. Choices that at first seem quite technical turn out to be deeply embedded assumptions about the way people learn and about the underlying culture of learning. You don't always appreci-ate the nature of your own culture until you see how it differs from other approaches.

In most commercial learning software, the model "campus" is designed around administration functions, social activities, and student assessment and grading, but in adult online learning the focus is almost entirely on the discussion forums. To be sure, adults also deal with assignments, but the real work derives from their personal resourcefulness, their ability to link per-sonal experience with concepts from the literature, their depth of critical analysis, their ability to see things in cross-cultural perspective, their contri-bution to group problem solving, and their ability to hear and deal with issues raised by others. Exams have no part in this, and grades are almost never mentioned except briefly in the syllabus, where grading criteria are described in terms of substantive course objectives and students are often invited to add their own criteria. In short, students are treated like adults.

For adults, the trappings of a traditional campus not only are irrelevant but even can appear condescending and juvenile. Most features of today's commercial "distance learning" software are an attempt to re-create the full richness of an undergraduate or high school campus, but in ways that often functionally detract from focus on substantive learning discussions—just as happens on real campuses. Traditional "campus-model" software is pat-terned on a culture of pedagogy rooted in classroom lectures and lesson plans that are controlled, bounded, internally consistent, and top-down—just the opposite of the intense self-organized dialogue that distinguishes adult learn-ing at its best.

Basic Navigation Tools

Because of the open-ended, student-centered nature of adult learning and the lack of regimentation in lesson plans, adult learning software needs to provide a more powerful set of navigation features, many of them missing from the mainstream products aimed at more conventional classrooms. The basic navigation tools that I've found most helpful are these:

- A "home page" for each forum, with major topics displayed as a single list. This provides a consolidated portal to weekly assignments, resource materials, the syllabus, informal "café-type" meeting places, administrative bulletins, and special topics that can be added by either faculty or students.

- A "search" button for words or phrases used anywhere in the forum, with additional search capabilities for posting dates and author. The retrieved items are displayed in a list, each showing the subject heading, author, and posting date.

- An "unseen" button that lists all postings not previously viewed. Also included is a way to relabel any posting to be "saved as unseen" or "marked as if seen."

- A minimal number of standard navigation buttons such as "help," "next unseen," "next/previous topic," and "next/previous reply."

- Automatic numbering of topics in hierarchical order, along with display of posting date and author. A numerical tag such as 3.5.2 helps not only in making shorthand reference to another person's work but also in allowing quick access to that numbered topic through a "search" button. Even better is a display function that shows a nested list of ascending subject heads, each providing a hyperlink to the original text:

  3.—Main topic for Week 3: Critical review of Alton's "Culture" (Hudson, 3/21/99)

  3.5—Becky's critique: Alton is caught in a white male European box (Sailor, 4/2/99)

  3.5.2—True, but at least he opens the door to other boxes (Grant, 4/3/99)

- A "tracker" feature. Assuming that students and faculty need to monitor several forums on a daily or weekly basis, a tracker window is very useful as a way of showing, in a single screen list, how many "unseen" postings are at each of these high-priority forums. Each user can select which forums to include in the tracker and can make this site the main portal for hyperlink access to any of the other sites visited regularly.

The Virtues of Minimalism

Another lesson from our software evaluation exercise is minimalism—the value of keeping the software uncomplicated. At first, we thought that we could customize available software to better suit our own needs and learning culture (take the "sorority" site, relabel it, and link it to the Library of Congress catalog?). But it turns out that customization of software packages becomes very expensive and can result in software conflicts, voiding of service warranties, and maintenance problems down the road. It's a little like trying to make a sports car out of a sports utility vehicle by lowering the suspension.

It's not just a matter of paying for features that won't be used. The extra features mean extra work navigating several screens to reach a particular forum. One can always create personalized shortcuts and display options, but this has disadvantages. It calls for a degree of familiarity with computers that adults are less likely to have than are teenagers, and it creates different "mental maps" among students as to where they come together, how to get there, and how to find other linked resource material. In a virtual group, if each student creates a customized version of the forum space, it can lead to confusion or miscommunication ("Oh, you're using that display option? No wonder you didn't see my posting. Try turning on the 'unseens' feature.").

A minimalist approach resists the urge to use software with many layers of features (e.g., frames, graphics, animations, attachments, audio files). A substantial number of students in our program are participating from overseas, some of them with slow connections, older versions of hardware and operating systems, and a mix of Mac and PC platforms. Many are communicating from airports and hotels, and even a few seconds of waiting for useless frames and buttons to load can be maddening. If the software comes with a host of extra features built in, then at least there should be simple a way to turn them all off to optimize speed of connection and navigation.

This is especially important if we care about diversity in the learning community and refrain from insisting that everyone has to stay on the cutting edge of technology. One of our students, Mike, resides in South Africa, and he walks seven miles to use a village-owned vintage PC equipped with a slow modem, a fragile phone connection, and a rudimentary Internet service provider. Every time a software vendor tries to sell us on a technical refinement from its latest vision of a virtual campus, I ask myself, "Will this help Mike? Or will it simply make it tougher for him to get quickly into the heart of the discussion, post his comments, download everything new, check for special bulletins needing immediate reply, and sign off without a screen crash?"

Jungle Navigation 102: Individual Course Design

Although software selection is an institution-level decision, individual faculty have their own choices to make at the level of course design. Here, too, adult learning forums call for some structural elements that may depart from traditional classrooms.

Phase Lines

First, there is greater value in providing well-bounded "phases" and rest points—every 2 or 3 weeks—for courses that are intensive but built on open-ended structures. Some students, no matter how diligent, get behind or lose track of the many threads of discussion. Where one student's work depends strongly on input or feedback from another, one can build in redundancy, ensuring that if one student falters, then another's work covers much the same ground. But there often remains a growing sense of falling behind and a snowballing of unmet obligations. In part, this is because adult learners often have other major events going on in their lives. More important, however, the kinds of issues addressed in adult learning are not neatly bounded and prepackaged into textbooks, and all students—the most serious ones especially—will be aware of unresolved issues lying always just beyond the edge of the question at hand. The "phase lines" provide a resting point or a clearing in the jungle for catching one's breath.

Phase lines are analogous to the watertight bulkheads of a ship. The point is not to count on everything being controllable and watertight, but to know the importance of letting go of some things to keep the rest intact. The door is slammed shut on discussion in progress, and the phase compartment is abandoned, with all efforts then refocused on the tasks ahead. It can be frustrating, almost painful, to have thoughts cut off "in midsentence," but those discussions, if really valuable, will reemerge by themselves, either as whole new topics, or in café banter, or woven into later assignments, often with a kind of clarity and energy beyond anything normally associated with an assigned task. Unfinished communications have a kind of pregnancy. They can jumpstart the next work session better than thoughts brought to full closure. They tantalize and stir input from the subconscious. They have sticky edges that connect with other material. They provide "white space" for other audiences to fill in. The importance of all this for adult learning is that in this kind of forum, cultural subtext is always in play, whereas formal learning structures are open to question. "Walls are meant to be penetrated. Boxes are there to be gotten out of."

Phase lines allow important breaks—like stepping on the clutch of a car to allow a shifting of gears or like NASA's built-in holds for a launch countdown. The human mind needs time to integrate things, this perhaps being one of the imperative reasons for sleep time. As one student, Annmarie Rubin, noted about the process of writing a thesis, "There is an important tension between unraveling your topic—giving it time to realize its full potential—and meeting deadlines" (Fielding forum posting, May 18, 2000). It is a creative tension, part of the process. Taking a day off from writing can make it much more productive when you come back.

Adult collaborative learning has much in common with thesis writing. It is not spoon-fed problem solving and knowledge assimilation but rather a process of finding and sharing information from almost limitless information resources and, above all, learning the skills of *making that process manageable*. Unlike traditional classroom work, this is a process of meta-learning or learning how to learn. It involves skills of problem formulation and problem manageability, not just problem solving. It means setting up information structures, not just using the structure provided by a textbook; evolving and exchanging skills, not just applying taught skills to one's own work; using heuristic exploratory analysis, not just algorithms supplied by the curriculum; constructing and testing models, not just absorbing them from others; seeing performance in terms of group outcomes rather than personal outcomes; and creating action maps, not just following directions. In these ways, every adult learning course has elements of a thesis-writing project, whatever other kinds of learning are involved.

Topic Lists

In a jungle-like environment, any orientation device can make a big difference. For example, clarity of topic lists and reply headings take on more importance. My own practice is to always make Topics 1 through 11 correspond to Weeks 1 through 11 of the course schedule. Even if some weeks call for taking a break or independent work, the topic provides a regular milestone of progress. Beyond that initial list, I also use topics as opening-day placeholders for basic resources such as the course syllabus, bibliographies, administrative bulletins, and the student café. Once the course begins, additional topics can be added by anyone, and these are usually focused on substantive issues arising from the ongoing dialogue. Keeping all of these topics together in a single list provides a map of the major landmarks for the entire course. Consolidated in this way, everything in the forum is covered by the "search" and "unseen" functions of the software.

I also ask students to be very concrete in their subject headings for each posting; for example, instead of the label "Another idea," using "Becky, why not apply Senge's Principle of Leverage?" This way, Becky can scan unseen postings and immediately see the ones directed to her, while anyone else with an interest in Senge or leverage will also be alerted.

Importance of Personal Voice

Apart from topic structure, another important basis for orientation is a clear sense of other individual "voices" in the forum. Every classroom has personalities, but among adults these are distinguished by a richer base of personal and professional histories. Online, being part of the group can't come from physical presence in a classroom; instead, it comes from an awareness of who else is there by the distinctive features of each person's online voice.

Instead of traditionally bland academic voice for online posting, I like to encourage conversational language, including the use of "I" and "we" and "you" instead of impersonal statements. I look for students' references to other people's contributions, willingness to express uncertainty and vulnerability, and constructive questions—"That's where I got lost, when you mentioned Lawrence's work on postmodern critiques of TQM [total quality management]," or "You really jolted me when you referred to counseling as a kind of oppression. How did you arrive at that? Because that might explain some reactions that I've noticed, too, in those kinds of counseling sessions," or "That works for me. But how would you explain it to my 14-year-old son? Or to a farmer in Bangladesh?"

Jungle Navigation 103: The Power of the Verbal Image

Outside of English literature classes, not much is said about the use of metaphors as a device for organizing ideas, explaining relationships, focusing group attention, and holding concepts up to scrutiny by a group. But metaphors can do all of these things, and in the virtual world of online dialogue, their role is especially important. Even more than words and language, visual images play the key role in organizing information into coherence. Wenger (1999) claims, "The greater part of our information and experiences is stored in our brain, not in words but as sensory images. In fact, 80% of the brain is involved with handling these richer, more immediate visual responses."

Brann (1991), too, argues that imagery is not just an adjunct to language and serious thinking but actually forms the core of it. We spend as much of our lives imagining as we do dealing with words, yet for formal education, images are treated as "nonexistent" (p. 4). Images are a "pivot between sense and intellect" (p. 6), with "figurative language" providing extra dimensions to description, in terms of meaning, and addressing factors that can be increasingly clarified but never resolved in full (p. 18). Images allow for a kind of "internal theatre" where ideas engage and affect each other, whether in one's own mind or in group interaction (p. 5).

I want to look at "verbal images" from several perspectives. How can they help information management online? How do they promote dialogue? How do images apply to the study of organizations and behavior? Do they have a role in scientific analysis, or are they strictly limited to humanistic studies? Do they address limited concepts, or can they open doors to critical inquiry about mind-sets deeply buried in culture and hard to access without use of images? What differences arise between use of verbal metaphors and visual graphics in support of image-based dialogue?

I start with the role of metaphors for information management because this problem applies so directly to navigating virtual spaces and working without classroom walls.

Information Overload—And It's Only Just Beginning

There is a problem of information overload that won't go away. To paraphrase Parkinson's Law (Parkinson, 1957/1964), *information grows to fill the space that can contain it*. Every new generation of desktop computer adds speed and memory, but the amount of information and the number of access channels grow even faster. In an ongoing study of Internet use, the UCLA Center for Communication Policy (2001) recently noted that the population of Internet users tripled in the year1997 and grew fivefold between 1997 and 1999, from 19 million to 100 million.

In the year 2000, the number of online documents passed the 1 billion mark, and the Internet's capacity to carry information doubles every 100 days. Every 24 hours, the content of the Web increases by more than 3.2 million new pages. Late in 1999, with the turn of the millennium, the total number of hits on U.S. Web pages alone passed the mark of 1 billion per day. In 1998, while 101 billion pieces of paper mail were being delivered, e-mail messages surpassed this number 40 times over—to a level of about 4 trillion. (UCLA Center for Communication Policy, 2001, pp. 4-5).

To sort through all of this, the best computer you will ever possess is the 2-pound wet processor perched on top of your spinal cord known as the brain. The power of the information age is only as great as your cognitive power to pull all of the pieces together into a coherent picture that you can then share with others. It is a matter of seeing patterns, making connections between ideas and data, appreciating what has meaning and application, and making critical discernment about what does or doesn't belong in the picture one has in mind. The brain has a billion years of experience in doing just that. No other piece of hardware or software comes close.

Image as Memory Device

Information storage, whether as text of forum discussion threads or in personal memory, can serve only as well as the system used for recall and retrieval of that data. Lewis Thomas puts it nicely: "It isn't so much that I forget things outright, I forget where I stored them. I need reminders. . . . Lacking landmarks, I cannot be sure that the snatches of memory still lodged in my brain have any reliability at all" (Thomas, 1983/1985, pp. 1-2).

Mnemonics are the techniques of remembering, an art that goes far back in history. Cicero advocated attention to physical things and locations in oratory, not only to make language more vivid to the audience but also as a memory aide to the speaker. Cato's rules of rhetoric gave similar advice: "Cleave to things, the words will follow" (Brann, 1991, p. 283). During the Renaissance, without printing presses, image-based systems for storing memories were developed to a high art. These were based on mental maps consisting of an enduring visualized landscape having ordered spaces set at midrange, with fixed and regular framing elements such as columns, entries, halls, and architectural nooks. The landscape and frame were kept dimmed so that particular objects to be remembered could stand out in a bright and dramatic light, portrayed in vivid and sometimes lurid novelty.

An example of this technique is the device used by Leonardo da Vinci, as depicted in Jack Dann's novel, *The Memory Cathedral* (Dann, 1995). As da Vinci gets older, his memory can no longer keep track of all the things he has learned and accomplished, so he builds in his mind's eye a cathedral where they can be stored and retrieved at will. Each detail of architecture captures a remembered experience or collection of knowledge. Each area within the cathedral—nave, pulpit, transept, cloister, alter, sacristy—is devoted to a field of accomplishment such as art, science, war machines, or love. One of Dann's purposes in writing fiction of this kind is to give the reader access to a kind of history and imagery that could "give the reader his or her own experience, one that could be drawn on like personal memory" (Dann, 2000). This description would serve equally well for the role that metaphors can play in adult online education.

More recent work on memory puts more emphasis on *kinetic* images, the kind that depict things in motion or interacting. A special issue of the journal *Daedelus* (Fall 1985), "The Moving Image," was devoted to this point. When an image is endowed with a component of motion, this helps it to interact with other images following in a sequence, helping to establish remembered relationships with other ideas, like the clustered elements of a story line or notes of a song. Kinetic motion in the image also makes it more likely to be recalled from the fringes of memory, just as the human eye tends to pick up small motions most quickly through peripheral vision.

New York City hosts an annual competition of student teams in feats of memory about information fed to them—long numbers, series of images, poems, portraits matched with names. Teams that win consistently rely on use of image-based "tags" applied to each thing to be remembered. A portrait of Bill Hatcher, say, is remembered because his hair can be imagined to look like a bird's nest, with the bill of a small chick breaking out from a hatching egg. The very absurdity of the image can be helpful, jogging the brain to take notice and remember this item for its distinctiveness.

Image, Group Memory, and Dialogue

Memory is important for individuals participating in groups, but images have an even more powerful function in the way they serve *group* memory and group dialogue. Metaphoric images provide a clearinghouse for "transactive memory" (TM), which Rulke and Rau (2000) define as "a group memory system that details the expertise possessed by group members along with an awareness of who knows what in the group" (p. 373). Transactive memory is important for self-management and performance because it provides a means to make best use of team members and the resources that each brings to a task. It has special value for groups newly formed, but good TM also contributes to group learning over time.

Metaphors can function as TM for a group in several ways. It is a way of encoding and storing complex ideas and relationships in one place. It has a "meta-tag" (the image itself) that is easy to remember and quick to access using computer search capabilities. It also provides a "mirror" for the individuals who create, critique, extend, or apply the metaphor because a metaphor functions as a kind of Rorschach test, casting light on the people who interpret and use it. In this sense, use of metaphors and images reveals to the group much about itself and its members—the group's tacit knowledge, its resourcefulness, and its capacity for collaborative support and constructive critical analysis. It creates, in effect, "a group mind" (Wegner, 1986, p. 185). Metaphor-based dialogue online serves all of the main functions of information management, traditionally defined in terms of encoding, storage, and retrieval of information but also including the transactive functions of communication, negotiation, coordination, exchanges, and creation of meaning through shared experience (Rulke & Rau, 2000, p. 377).

Gareth Morgan makes a powerful case for the use of metaphor, especially in organizational management (Morgan, 1986, 1997; Morgan & Ramirez, 1984). His argument can be summarized on three levels.

First, the *concrete language* of metaphor provides a more stable and workable frame of reference for group dialogue, compared to the slippery meanings of abstract terminology. Morgan uses terms such as "strategic termites" (Morgan, 1997, chap. 7), "psychic prisons" (Morgan, 1986, chap. 7), and "spider plants" (Morgan, 1997, pp. 63-90) to characterize specific models of organizational behavior. The concreteness and specificity of terms such as these provide a much more focused and accessible discussion thread. An unabridged English dictionary contains upward of 500,000 entries (Merriam, 1939), so there are plenty of ways to anchor a metaphor. The value of using metaphor in electronic discussion forums is that one can use a search term such as "termite" and jump directly to the discussion one was looking for. That doesn't work so well for abstraction words such as "behavior" and "change."

Critical dialogue is another advantage. Morgan points out that metaphors invite people to bring their own ideas into a discussion, more than they would in discussion of abstract terms that carry a greater weight of authority and tradition. A metaphor, by its nature, raises questions about how well a particular image or concept applies to any particular situation. The thing depicted is more concrete, yet the subjective basis of its selection is more apparent—a reminder that every idea is based on pooling of subjective judgments. Over the years, Morgan has evolved toward the view that all language, no matter how abstract, is a form of metaphor—the use of words to capture essences of situations. "Ideas . . . are always based on implicit metaphors that persuade us to see, understand, and manage situations in a particular way" (Morgan, 1997, p. xxi). But concrete metaphors are more accessible to critique based on everyday language and experience, so they are better suited to cross-disciplinary discussion and validation in particular contexts (Morgan, 1986, chaps. 10-11; 1997, chaps. 1-2).

In this sense, Morgan argues that use of metaphors is liberating, not just by the creativity involved in what he calls "imagin-iz-ation" but also by bringing to our attention the fact that all knowledge is in some sense "socially constructed." Concepts taught from textbooks have the aura of being somehow objectively "true" because they derive from an authority in the subject matter. Metaphors constructed within a group, however, can convey ideas that are rich in values and meaning to people in their own context. Morgan uses images most often as a way to move us beyond traditional theories of management, reminding us that the term *management* originally stems from putting a horse through its paces (Morgan, 1997, p. 15)—connoting a fixation with command and control as seen in military organizations, bureaucracies, and business organizations built on the metaphor of machines, as in "re-engineering the corporation."

Morgan's third major point refers to *picture power* as a tool for learning and action (Morgan, 1997, chap. 10). Verbally constructed images can be as powerful as literal graphics. Many other writers have made this point, especially in relation to the art and science of management. Some talk about the critical need for alignment around central purposes through "vision" statements anchored in graphic language (Peters, 1987, pp. 482-494). In making this same point, Collins and Porras (1994/1997, chap. 11) emphasize that the more "audacious" the vision, the more power it has to capture people's imaginations and attention.

Metaphor as "Collage" for Group Dialogue in Place of Linear Monologue

Most written expression has a linear structure, moving in a thread from one thought to the next in a planned sequence. In a group, however, expressions come in more random patterns in reaction to a point of departure. The dialogue departs substantially from the ideal of an "Aristotelian, monolinear syllogistic arrangement," instead building on a more discursive, roving, and loosely connected series of observations. It becomes a collage more than a linear argument. The cohesiveness of logical sequence tends to dissolve, so something else needs to take its place. The poets Ernest Fenollosa and Ezra Pound addressed this problem in their exploration of nonlinear forms and together ended up with what they call the "ideogrammic method" based on use of images. Fenollosa came to this approach through the study of Chinese writing, noticing that its hieroglyphic nature provided visual elements lacking in the West, where writing is based on a bead-string of phonetic letters (Fenollosa, 1968; Nogami, 1999). The use of imagery to liberate writing from linear monologue is explored in Fenollosa's (1968) book, *The Chinese*

Written Character as a Medium for Poetry, and is put into effect in Pound's (1954) *Cantos.*

Adult online learning calls for a similar break from rote, using image-based concepts that can be viewed from all sides and responded to from different perspectives. The subject then becomes not so much the initial object as collage-like extrapolations created by the group. This can be a radical departure from most online instruction, perhaps analogous to the departure of cubism from traditional ways of seeing an object only from a single static perspective. Picasso, indeed, discovered collage technique on his way to developing cubism (Nogami, 1999).

The unfolding of a successful metaphor works through confirmation or modification among storytellers and listeners. This same mutualism occurs in improvisational theater (Johnson, 1998), where one tool is the establishment of vivid situations through verbal imagery ("Oh, no, don't make me go back in the icebox, please!"). Imagery as an important vehicle for dialogue is also seen in the ancient tradition of haiku poetry (originally *renga*), where people came together in social clubs, taking turns to add lines of verse to a collaborative product and feeding off of each other's inspiration much like a jazz ensemble (Hass, 1994, pp. 299-307).

"Concrescence": The Power of Loosely Coupled Systems

Metaphors are different from traditional information systems in that they are much less rigidly structured in a predefined hierarchy. They are not contained in particular texts, or compartmentalized according to organizational division, or limited to a particular lesson plan. Traditional information management applies the "correspondence theory of truth," where words correspond to fixed objective realities. Images, on the other hand, draw more on Heraclitus's view of reality—that all is change and emergence (Chia, 1999, pp. 210-211). This view resonates with Whitehead's (1929/1978) concept of "concrescence"—self-creative aggregations leading to novel outcomes, where "being" is constituted by "becoming" (p. 29). Things become meaningful because of their novelty, "snatched out of a static, forgotten background of unchanging sameness" (Chia, 1999, p. 218).

Casti (1994) makes a parallel point about the "creative imprecision" of language, which applies to its use in verbal images. Information consists of surprise, discovery, change, and learning. Language encodes imperfectly, so ideas are not locked together inflexibly like bricks in a mortared wall. Instead, each piece is malleable and interchangeable with certain other pieces, allowing the variability necessary for change and evolution. Christopher Alexander analyzes the importance of "loose coupling" as a basis for well-adapted design for architecture and urban planning in his seminal book, *Notes on the Synthesis of Form* (Alexander, 1964). Weick (1976) discusses the value of loose coupling for educational adaptation to rapid change, uncertainty, and individual initiative taking.

A striking demonstration of loose coupling and creativity comes from Raymond Queneau, a French poet, novelist, and mathematician who in 1961 conceived of a "sonnet machine" capable of producing 100 trillion poems. Queneau's device was very simple—the printing of 10 sonnets on 10 reinforced pages. A sonnet always has 14 lines, and Queneau constructed the book so that any given line of each page could be turned independently. Thus, the 7th line of the 1st sonnet could be flipped over and made part of any of the other 9 sonnets—and so on for all 14 lines and 10 sonnets. The 1st line of the sonnet has 10 possibilities, as does the 2nd (resulting in $10 \times 10 = 10^2 = 100$ possibilities)—and so on through 14 lines. The resulting possibilities then multiply out to $10 \times 10 \times 10 \ldots$ [14 times], yielding a number with 14 zeros ($= 10^{14}$), which equals 100 trillion possibilities—and which is enough to keep someone busy reading for more than a million centuries (Idensen, 2001).

A meaningful result depends on whether random combinations can produce sensible coherence when the line of one poem is substituted for the same line of another. This seems to work out in practice because that poetry—like epic sagas, linguistic syntax, and mental processes in general—tends to follow generalized underlying "scripts" or structures of argument. The scripts lie deep in the history of language evolution but also derive from particular cultural exposures—social class, commercial and political messages, in-group code words, speech habits developed by professions, and so on. In the case of the sonnet machine, it also helps for the poet to have a good feel for the task.

A metaphor is not quite a sonnet machine, but it works somewhat on the same principle. A metaphor has a limited number of parts, related through a basic structure, each part with a slightly different interpretation, depending on how it is applied and how people bring their own language, experience, and issues into the interpretation.

Steven Schatz proposes the concept of "meta-tags" as a way for groups to work in collaboration, especially in problems of design and in training designers (Schatz, 2001). Meta-tags, like metaphors, function as a way to organize loosely related ideas into a discernible whole without imposing rigid structures or boundaries but allowing evolution and mutual adjustment between the parts and the whole. Knowledge usually comes in bits that are constantly being updated from disparate sources and increasingly from the Internet. In past paradigms of training, knowledge was considered linear—packaged with a beginning, a middle, and an end in stand-alone clusters. In the future, the paradigm will shift to more open-ended sources of knowledge, loosely bounded, overlapping, constantly forming, and amalgamating. The computer allows disparate sources of information to be drawn into any given application without freezing the clusters into fixed packages. The bits can be quickly updated, seamlessly integrated, and collaboratively applied in a way that was never possible before computers and the Internet.

On this basis, Schatz (2001) sees a need to shift the focus of training from "knowledge bits" to development of skills in searching, melding, and projecting combinations of bits through the use of "meta-tags," which "allow you and/or your learners to find specific knowledge bits quickly and effectively." Computer search engines play an important part in this, and use of meta-tags has specific implications for software design. But meta-tagging is also a matter of personal skills applied by "self-directed learners." The importance of doing it yourself is that each learning group has its own purposes and concerns, its own view of the ultimate audience, and its own priorities and limitations. The choice of tags needs to be open-ended and honed by trial and error within a particular group setting. Group character co-evolves with the emergence of the tags themselves. Schatz does not address the role of images explicitly, but his functional definition of a meta-tag seems to parallel very closely this whole discussion on the role of metaphors.

The traditional packaging of information into bits, and its abstraction from context and personal meaning, leaves us with ideas that are very thin on context, meaning, tone, and action implications. Wheatley (1999) suggests that this, coupled with the explosion of inert data, has left us with "an epidemic of poor communication" (p. 93). It leaves us suffering from "a fundamental misperception of information: what it is, how it behaves, how to work with it" (p. 93). She elaborates:

> The strong focus on the "thingness" of information has kept us from contemplating its other dimensions: the content character and behavior of information. . . . All life uses information to organize itself into form. A living being is not a stable structure, but a continuous process of organizing information. (pp. 94-95)

The development of appropriate, well-tuned metaphors goes straight to the heart of critical thinking and collaborative learning. They involve a form of visual learning that includes recognition of prototypes and attributes within them, discriminating between primary and secondary features, recognizing conditions that enhance or attenuate their validity, and projecting implications for behavior (Jaikumar & Bohn, 1986). To achieve these ends, ideas need to be expressed in ways that resonate with other people's experiences and perceptions, but in ways that are subtle and in ways that are unconscious, as they do in poetry or professional photography.

All of these approaches share the view of learning as a social and collaborative endeavor. Whereas classrooms operate more as an assembly line, attaching bits of rigidly sequenced knowledge to a parade of individual students, online learning offers a different model. Loose agglomerations of ideas and personal experience are brought into meaningful relationships through concrescence, the objective being not just mastery of facts but also development of learning how to learn as a group. This is the skill of creating a "learning organization" within—and distinct from—the larger context of the "teaching organization."

Role of Image in Learning Organizations

The concept of a "learning organization" (Argyris, 1999) has special relevance to adult learning in the context of globalization, exponential growth of information, and rapid economic and technological transformation. It is also reflected in the postmodern view of reality as something constructed out of social dynamics rather than objective "givens." Boulding (1956) makes the case that organized behavior of all kinds is governed by images describing what organizations do in particular contexts.

These views are finding their way more and more into the language of metaphors. Hamilton (1998) expresses them in the context of "Web-centric" organizations. Handy (1994) describes them in terms of "the doughnut principle." Morgan (1997, chap. 4) discusses the idea of decentralized, self-organized, flexible management systems in the image of "spider plants"—clustered entities that retain connections with the original parent but break away in self-sustaining offshoots, unburdened by traditional hierarchies and lines of communication, to pursue opportunistic forays outside the original base. In a similar metaphor, Chia (1999) talks about "rhizomic" plants, such as bamboo, as a model for adaptive learning organizations. Unlike most plants that grow along a main channel connecting roots with branches, a rhizomic structure has no center and does not follow binary branching: its roots go in every direction, extending indefinitely, connecting with anything, and creating new entities (tubers and bulbs) wherever it wants. It is "restless, subterranean, agglomerating, planless, non-linear" (p. 222). Organizations based on this model don't follow a blueprint or even a goal but spread into fields of possibilities, more like a leakage than a line of development.

Senge (1990, chap. 10) stresses the importance of these mental models for learning organizations, arguing that "deeply held internal images of how the world works" impose powerful constraints on thinking and acting in new ways. New insights are not enough. Change takes a deeper approach, "the discipline of managing mental models—surfacing, testing, and improving our internal pictures," as a promising "major breakthrough for building learning organizations" (p. 174). The same need for attention to image-based models would apply, of course, to adult online learning. Argyris (1999) describes the technique of "action mapping" as a basis for organizational learning. Recent research, he points out, "provides many insights into how people make sense of their worlds in order to act. For example, they organize data into patterns, store these patterns in their heads, and then retrieve them whenever they need them" (p. 415). The use of images is extremely effective as a way of organizing information in meaningful, readily accessible patterns.

Similar points are made by others about the importance of images for organizational effectiveness. Mintzberg and Van der Heyden (1999) stress the role of mental maps for organizational coordination in challenging the use of traditional organizational charts that promote top-down command and control. New forms of leadership call for alternative "pictures" of how organizations perform through more distributed forms of intelligence, expressed not in hierarchical organizational charts but rather in more horizontal arrays of sets, chains, hubs, and webs.

Christopher Alexander has taken the systematic use of images very far through the development of a "pattern language" for use in collaborative architecture and urban planning. Alexander has given a great deal of thought to the way in which spatial and social relationships are depicted in language and concludes that image-based symbols are more exact, more powerful in expression, more convenient, and easier to hold in memory than are verbal expressions. With others, he has devised an entire pattern language for collaborative work in the design of towns, buildings, and landscapes (Alexander, Ishikawa, & Silverstein, 1977).

The concept of a learning organization makes a practical contribution to adult online learning on three levels. First, it helps instructors to make the shift from a "teaching" mentality (knowledge "push") to a "learning" perspective, based on mature students' capacity to "pull" knowledge from each other and from the world beyond formal education. Second, it opens up a whole new source of pedagogical theory and practice, based not on traditional educational theory but rather on emerging insights into organizational behavior. The *Harvard Business Review* and *Journal of Management Inquiry* turn out to be rich sources of "how to teach" because they describe successful innovations in "how organizations learn." They learn by drawing on well-defined group processes and by recognizing that learning breakthroughs happen when organizations let their members break out of hermetically sealed contexts, whether an enterprise or a classroom.

Finally, the organizational learning model helps to shift the educational emphasis from short-term, test-measured objectives to a longer range and broader set of goals more appropriate to adults. These are the goals of "learning how to learn" and the skills of self-organization and resourcefulness. In this larger playing field, adult online education provides more latitude for breaking out of the mold and for using creative imagination as a group process. This brings us back to the important role of images as a medium of self-organized group learning.

Creativity, or ways to build creative thinking into groups, has been linked by many writers to the systematic use of images. Gordon's (1961, chap. 2) method of "synectics" makes use of "symbolic analogy." De Bono's (1968/1971, chap. 4) method of "lateral thinking" makes use of visual exercises to bring other senses into play besides intellectual concepts, which tend to dominate from embedded habits of inflexibility. Edwards (1989) uses techniques for "drawing on the right side of the brain" to engage perceptions and powers of expression that are neglected in normal—especially academic—settings.

Wenger (1999) uses the technique of "image streaming" at the Institute for Visual Thinking in Maryland as a method of problem solving (Lumsdaine & Lumsdaine, 1993, p. 259). This approach is based on use of thought experiments in science (Sorensen, 1992), but Wenger (1999) cites Socrates as an originator of image streaming. Socratic questions were often directed to asking students to examine inner and external perceptions and to describe what they found for comment. The aim was not just to sensitize perception but also to nourish understanding and personal growth as a mark of true education.

All of these writers emphasize the importance of playfulness that can be introduced by use of images—a tone that provides tolerance for individual differences, for new ideas and experimentation, and for errors and mistakes. These elements of creativity apply directly to group collaboration as well—and especially to adult learning online.

Boulding (1956), like Morgan, sees the importance of image as a counter to so-called objective knowledge or accepted theory or assumed meaning of words; images have a more explicit acknowledgment of the subjectivity of it all (p. 6). He talks about the validity of images as a way to depict "structured experience," going beyond pure information and statistical relationships to generate meaningful messages that affect behavior (p. 7). These images can directly capture not only facts but also values, causalities, implications, and even self-image. Images are a mix of public and private knowledge and serve as an "intermediary" for dialogue about group issues. Through dialogue, an image can evolve almost as if through a kind of metabolism (p. 18), taking on a life of its own but subject to influence from the group or any individual. A good teacher, says Boulding, knows and works through every student's "inward teacher," using collaboration built around images. Boulding reaches the conclusion that "a really adequate theory of behavior" needs to call on "the growth of images, both public and private, in individuals, in organizations, [and] in society at large" (p. 18).

Boulding (1956) looks at the science of images in broader, more systematic terms, however, in two ways. First, he analyzes how images work at both conscious and unconscious levels to determine behavior. Second, he describes specific levels of consciousness that determine how well we can locate ourselves with respect to ourselves, organizations, and the larger social and natural environment as ways of effectively managing those relationships. In this sense, he addresses some of the same paths to "getting outside the box" as do Freire (1970) in education and Senge (1990) in organizational learning as well as Argyris (1999) in fourth-order consciousness and Maruyama (1982) in double-loop learning. Specifically, Boulding sees a parallel progression in the levels of organizational learning and the kind of self-image it projects:

- As a *jigsaw*, the organization deals with people and groups as pieces to be "fit into place."
- As a *thermostat*, it makes continual adjustment to a fixed benchmark of homeostatic equilibrium.
- As a *cell*, it addresses deeper levels of metabolism, such as need for nourishment of the parts.
- As a *wolfpack*, it considers the importance of reading the environment, use of subtle signals, coordination among dispersed parts of a team, and a motivated instinct for the hunt.

With increasing sophistication in the use of images, an organization can go still further beyond these stages to become better at managing changes over time, perceiving things beyond the immediate horizon, considering "what if's" beyond the obvious possibilities, and ultimately addressing the question of how individual consciousness can best interplay with organizational consciousness, both in becoming one with the whole and in remaining authentic as an individual, able to think outside that very box of group participation.

But Are Metaphors Rigorous Enough for Scientific Thinking?

With metaphors usually discussed in the context of humanities subjects such as literature and anthropology, one might ask whether they really have any relevance to scientific fields of inquiry, either in the social or natural sciences. In point of fact, metaphors play a strong role in science. Hypotheses are formed (if not tested) by creating mental images about the outcome if we do *this*. Even without formal proof, acceptance of an idea's plausibility is heavily dependent on development of a powerful image. Einstein's theory of special relativity won broad acceptance decades before the first empirical proofs were obtained because he spent a great deal of effort in thought experiments trying to visualize the possibilities. One of his crucial insights came from trying to visualize what it would be like to ride on a photon traveling at the speed of light.

Another example of the power of image in establishing "acceptable" evidence comes from Richard Feynman's role as part of a team investigating the explosion of the space shuttle *Challenger*. Several theories had been tossed around—including the correct one—but none emerged from the group until Feynman took the step of dramatizing at a press conference what he thought was the real cause. The demonstration was carefully staged and timed and was well rehearsed. He submerged in ice water a flexible rubber O-ring like the one used on the *Challenger*. At the moment when cameras swung round to his part of the dais, he pulled out the cooled O-ring and snapped it in two, showing the effect of cold weather on launch day in making the O-ring too brittle to serve as a seal against spillage from the fuel tank in flight. The conceptual explanation had been put forth earlier, but with little effect. It took an image of the thing happening for the reality to strike home (Feynman, 1988).

Despite the potential looseness of metaphoric elements, visualized images play a central role in science on at least three levels. First, in its stringency of proof and parsimony of expression, scientific theory calls for us to define reality only in terms of what we can actually observe. Gravity does this or that when we observe its effects on two bodies. But why or how it acts like that can never be told. So when we talk about the "pull" of gravity, we are using a metaphor (gravity behaving like a strange rubber band that pulls harder the closer we get to its anchor). Science requires a language of similes; this system behaves "as if" it were something known to us in terms of other kinds of experience. Faraday's work on electricity was done in part to refine better images of what was happening, not just as a means but also as an end in itself. Without images—of flows, of magnetic fields, of atomic and electron behavior—there is only limited understanding of how to make sense of it or put it to use.

Second, scientific truths are always partial and incomplete, and in this sense, too, they are no different from metaphors. Even when we can define natural laws that are extremely precise and consistently verifiable, it almost always turns out that those relationships are not exact and need to be qualified by later understandings. Gravity needs to be adjusted for the effects of relativity and quantum effects; sub-particle behavior is subject to the Heisenberg uncertainty principle. And when you look at how atoms behave, and they have a choice of two paths to take, it turns out that atoms choose both at once. "That is the same with all our other laws—they are not exact. There is always an edge of mystery, always a place where we have some fiddling around to do yet" (Feynman, 1965, p. 27). Scientific "fact" is not different from any other metaphor in this respect.

Image also comes into science at the point of discovery. A good deal of scientific thought is simply a matter of "organized reasoning" (Feynman, 1965, p. 35), and images play a large role in this. Einstein remarked that "words . . . do not seem to play any role in my mechanism of thought, [but only] psychical entities . . . , more or less clear images which can be 'voluntarily' reproduced and combined" (quoted in Brann, 1991, p. 320). Thought experiments are one of the most powerful tools of science (Sorensen, 1992), a bridge between what is known and what can be extrapolated, between the intellect and the intuition, between public knowledge and personal insight, between human understanding and the natural world.

All of Feynman's scientific writings carry the theme of looking for clarity in a world that is full of shadows, mysteries, and unknowables. Science requires the discipline of not asserting more than can be verified. Equally important, assertions count as scientific only if they can be tested and proved false if untrue. Metaphors need to be put to the same kind of test—not just thrown out as "plausible," but systematically compared and contrasted against the things they mean to depict. Metaphoric analysis, like science, goes beyond the stage of discovery to the stage of validation, just like any other kind of assertion. It is a group process and calls on critical thinking.

Image as Language and Interpreter of Culture

An important question for the use of metaphors is the scope of their reach in handling complex ideas. Are they able to address only simplistic concepts, or can they serve for critical inquiry about mind-sets deeply buried in culture?

As Einstein pointed out, images play a bigger part than words in solving difficult problems about the way in which things work. Historically, too, images precede language. Insects see and interpret without speech, bats construct images of objects using echo-location, and *Homo sapiens* painted story-images of animals on cave walls thousands of generations before coming up with a written language. Dreams tend to be based on pictured events rather than on verbal exchange. Memories are carried in images more than in sentences. Everyday experience and perception is organized by images based on pre-language infancy. Traffic lights have been around for less than a century but now serve as a powerful global shorthand for managing the intricacies of traffic flow.

Different civilizations, however, have put greater or lesser emphasis on use of images. Islamic doctrine explicitly discourages the use of images, whereas Buddhism has a powerful tradition of visualization (Brann, 1991, p. 11). Plato made significant use of images, both as the means to make a point and as an essence of the point being made. Plato viewed the educator in the role of turning people's heads from the shadowed outline of things seen on cave walls to look at the world directly outside the cave.

Thomas Aquinas pointed out that imagination is necessary to process things received through the senses. To even "see" something, he argued, the intellect has to actively process it, transforming what is received into something else. Thoughts are created couched in images. Teaching is done through concrete examples. To understand something is to translate it, change its shape—"transform" it. Feynman describes his own need to understand science by going back to its roots and re-deriving the axioms and theory from scratch. In that spirit, he invented what has since become known as "Feynman diagrams," a simple but powerful graphical way to visualize subatomic reactions previously difficult to analyze in mathematical terms. Science is not an a priori reality; it is always a creation.

This differs dramatically from earlier views of enlightened empiricism voiced by Hobbes, Locke, Leibnitz, and Berkeley, who dismissed images as imprecise and an interference with reason. For these thinkers, mental images were a form of "decaying sense" made up of faded fictional replicas of sensory truths. It was Kant who led the way out of this, reversing his earlier rationalist phase with his critique of pure reason and his recognition of the powerful role of intuition and the transcendental power of imagination (Brann, 1991, pp. 91-99).

Images are fundamental to understanding. Take the early view of atoms as little planets with electrons spinning around them on a plane like the rings of Saturn. That image has proven inaccurate in several ways, yet it has served as a way to congeal thinking and set a direction for the work to follow. The outdated model continues to serve nonscientists in visualizing things— for example, the combination of an electron (negative charge) and a proton (positive charge) to create a neutron (zero charge) without going into the more accurate but elusive laws of conservation that apply to sub-atomic physics.

A single iconic convention can set in motion a whole branch of science. Mathematics, for example, was cumbersome or nonexistent in the West until the use of zero was imported from India via Middle Eastern trade routes, through Arabic scholars (whence "algebra"), and Moorish Spain, to Renaissance Europe. The convention of using zeros came up against a deep Western bias against the concept of a void, whereas in Eastern thought emptiness is a more central and positive element. Once given a name, a function, and a set of rules, this strange image—a circle enclosing a space—transformed mathematics in the West (Guedj, 1996/1997; Kaplan, 2000; Seife, 2000).

The power of extrapolating from immediate sensory input to a world of shared feelings is not just a matter of literary sentiment. It goes to the foundations of group cohesion and trust and to the entire architecture of social institutions. Adam Smith, although best known for laissez-faire economics, devoted most of his writing to the moral foundations of society. In this, he emphasized the importance of "sympathetic imagination" as expressed in his *Theory of Moral Sentiments* (Smith, 1759). Smith understood sympathy as the foundation of all moral capacity and stressed that sympathy depends entirely on the imagination (Brann, 1991, p. 790). Engell (1981, pp. 149-151) expands on this, arguing that creative imagination is what allows us to know a person in the context of his or her own condition and situation. This imagination is strengthened by a tendency for it to be reciprocated; it can lead to personal transformation, and from there to social transformation. Indeed, Smith's works on this subject were hugely popular and helped to bring about a shift in political and social thought away from the earlier preoccupation with Hobbes's dark view of people driven only by self-interest (Brann, 1991, pp. 91-93; Heilbronner, 1999).

Images, Psychology, and Civilization: Parsing the Serpent

One might think that imagery is mainly a right-brain function, operating through intuition and pattern formation rather than the language and logic of left-brain thinking. But both kinds of thinking are involved. Stonehenge, for example, is both a cultural expression and a logical, sequential left-brain kind of achievement in the alignment of those huge stones with the sun and moon; in their shaping and transportation to the site; and in the underlying sciences of astronomy, mathematics, and engineering that made all of this both possible and compelling (Eisler, 1987, pp. 74-75).

The power of images is not in their static finality but rather in their suggestiveness and open-endedness. Take one of the most familiar and ancient images of Western civilization, which depicts events in the Garden of Eden. In Judeo-Christian sacred texts, the serpent is seen as cunning and dangerous, using feminine wiles to seduce the first man into tasting the fruit of knowledge. But in the earlier civilizations being displaced during the period when the Bible was being written, that same snake had an older and very different character—a symbol of mystic insight and wisdom. The serpent was guardian of the tree of knowledge (groves of sacred trees being integral to many older religions), keeper of the arts of healing (seen today in the caduceus symbol of the physician), and companion of the goddesses who cared for harvests and provision of water—honored roles in the culture of peoples throughout Europe and much of the Near East. In Egypt, the cobra was used as the hieroglyphic sign for *goddess*, whereas the rearing serpent was often depicted on the foreheads of Egyptian royalty. Among the ancient Canaanites, the cobra goddess was the original creatrix of the world.

The Biblical injunctions—to fear the snake, to spurn the tree of knowledge, and to reject the advice of women immortals—makes sense only if one sees those images as dangerous carryovers from an earlier culture being discredited by the new waves of tribes from further east. Beginning their invasions about 4000 BCE, those tribes based their culture not on agriculture and storage of harvests but rather on raising of horses, fabrication of swords, and levying of tribute from conquered neighbors (Eisler, 1987, pp. 18-21, 70, 86-89).

The point I want to make here is not about archeology and religion but rather about the power of an image to endure for literally thousands of years and to continually allow for multiple interpretations that penetrate deeply into our sense of who we are and where we belong. The same application of critical dialogue, focusing on the meaning of images, applies to groups and to individuals in groups. As John Keats pointed out, every man's life is a continual allegory (cited in Dwyer, 2001, p. 6).

There, exactly, is a key issue of living in the jungle. How is one to immerse oneself in the thickness of if, while also being able to carve out a clearing that bestows one's own sense of place? How is one to balance the fear of being lost—the knowledge of being lost, the willingness to have a very incomplete view of things—and yet have a sense of bearing to keep moving in the right direction?

Metaphors? Yes; Graphic Renderings? Maybe

Before concluding, I want to clarify a point about the use of images for online learning. I am primarily talking about verbal and mental constructs as a framework for online dialogue and not about visual graphics. Many people—especially software providers—advocate the use of online software that allows graphic pictures to accompany text, but I am inclined against that for several reasons. First, it compromises the principle of "minimalist" software advocated earlier. Second, a graphic image can be too specific, too static, and too literal to allow ideas to evolve beyond their first representation. A graphic is no longer a metaphor; it is a fixed statement or illustration. Third, the very indefiniteness of words allows people to bring their own meanings to the metaphor, enriching its content, critically challenging applications that don't fit, and comparing and contrasting different interpretations.

In fact, actual graphic images can be disabling because they impose a regimentation of memory with no soft edges that invite the integration of personal perceptions and meanings. Literal graphics can be manipulative, insistent in their focus, context, and expression to the exclusion of other frames of reference. As Wittgenstein has pointed out, "While I am looking at an object I cannot imagine it" (cited in Brann, 1991, p. 776). Metaphoric images can draw on a vast treasury of perceptual memories, dreams, and extrapolations, free to "jump the tracks" to consecutive linear reasoning and explore the power of the possible without immediate negation (p. 785).

Morgan makes a point about separating metaphor from literal depictions with the story of "Weick's map." A hiking group gets lost in the Alps, caught in a blizzard, as night is falling. One of the hikers finds a map in a forgotten corner of a rucksack. Barely legible, it nevertheless sparks them with confidence in the path to follow, and they are saved. Only later do they see that the map was not of their path, or even of the Alps at all, but rather of the Pyrenees. The value of a map is not that it is necessarily accurate because any map, like any metaphor, has much latitude for what it conveys. Its power is as a catalyst for self-organization, for coordinated activity, and for providing a sense of place (Morgan, 1997, p. 16). Its role is to help us see things that we would otherwise ignore, to pick up signals from our own experience, to find resonances and see nuances, and to move toward shared understandings as well as understanding of differences.

The Suspended Image

Having said all that, I wouldn't want to completely rule out well-chosen graphic images as an initial frame of reference for online dialogue and for "locating" discussions through graphic landmarks in a discussion forum.

Joseph Campbell points to the importance of graphic icons in mythology when he observes, "Pictures invite the eye not to rush along but to rest a while and dwell with them in enjoyment of their revelation" (Campbell, 1974, p. xi). Powerful icons can anchor particular discussions in an otherwise undifferentiated landscape of text to create, in Hemingway's (1926/1996) words, "a clean, well-lighted place."

This capacity to take ideas, embody them, and suspend them before the eye is part of discovery and creativity in many fields. Mozart described a good working session of musical composition in similar terms:

> Nor do I hear in my imagination the parts successively, but I hear them, as it were, all at once. What delight this is I cannot tell! . . . The whole piece, though it be long, stands . . . in my mind, so that I can survey it, like a fine picture or a beautiful statue, at a glance. (cited in Brann, 1991, p. 321)

Feynman (1965/1994) uses a somewhat similar metaphor in describing the discovery and validation of scientific knowledge. Scientific laws turn out to be remarkably simple in most cases; laws that apply on earth apply to the entire universe, and the simplicity confers power as well as beauty. "Nature uses only the longest threads to weave her patterns, so each small piece of the fabric reveals the organization of the entire tapestry" (p. 28). Whether as metaphors or graphic pictures, well-constructed images allow time for suspended reflection and critical examination of elements, moving back and forth between specifics (the things one can observe) and larger patterns (the things extrapolated).

The same process can be seen even in the most "literal" kind of graphics in professional photography. Szarkowski (1981) describes the work of Ansel Adams's photographs in terms of the way in which they "translate the anarchy of the natural world into . . . perfectly tuned chords of gray" to produce "a sense of heightened order that is often mistaken by non-photographers for sharpness." Adams's photographs are not sharper but more *clear*—"a matter not of better lenses but of a better understanding of what one means." To achieve this kind of synthesis, says Szarkowski, a photograph "must depend on its opposite: symbol. Large issues must be inferred from trivial data" (p. xi).

For Adams, symbolism cannot be left abstract; it must be incorporated into "physical specifics." He distrusted categories, looking for the image to be its own expression, an invitation and absorption, not a "command performance" to illustrate some larger concept. Ideas can only sound a chord "consonant with our memories of what it was like, or our dreams of what it might be like . . . , or a glimpse of what we also once knew" (Szarkowski, 1981, pp. viii-ix).

Translating this to verbal images as a basis for learning forums, we can see that words are not just an ensemble of letters that Gutenberg showed us how to collect and reproduce on a printing press. Each word is a kind of photographic negative whose substance depends on its transparency to the light of the writer's intention and whose impact is developed in the liquid medium of the listener's own memory. Words can transcend traditional graphic techniques such as lithography and etching that transmit only a simple yes/no signal. Like photography, words allow a broad range of variations that demand not only good craft but also critical interpretation. The photographer's contribution is to say something but also to leave something unsaid, a space for the viewer to enter, drawn into an experience of synthesis, a space of belonging.

Conclusions

The jungle syndrome arises in adult online education for the same reason that it will become more common in the broader context of "postmodern" organizations at large. The center of discussion and sense of place are becoming far more diffused, adding to the disorientation of each person's identity and self-identity in virtual working groups. In the same way, the classroom is shifting from a lecture hall centered on the mastery of texts to become a distributed, many-threaded dialogue constructed as a process of self-organized discovery. The organization is shifting from a hierarchically structured, headquarters-based form of leadership to a flatter, more decentralized "Web-centric" format that is more flexible, faster changing, and more embedded in an ecology of symbiotic partners, with increasing emphasis on learning as opposed to sheer production.

Communication systems are moving in the same direction toward "distributed intelligence" as opposed to routing of messages through a single nexus of interpretation and expertise. Apart from an increase in sheer quantities of data, information is arriving through more forms of technology and with less regard for the users' location. Singly and together, all of these trends pose a rising challenge to students—and working groups everywhere—about how to establish a sense of place for collaborative work in virtual teams.

The first lesson applies to software procurement. The ideal is something powerful in its reach, simple to use, and not prone to rapid obsolescence—something like a compass or a telephone. Powerful tools of navigation are needed for spaces without walls and for information resources that are virtually limitless. On the other hand, there is a need for simplicity—the minimalist principle—both to keep attention on substance rather than process and to keep forums accessible to a diversity of users regardless of hardware, location, budget, and technical know-how.

A second lesson is to be wary of reverting to artificial structures that re-create the more comfortable environment of a familiar past. Today, adult learners can appreciate the value of shedding campus life and classroom practices that were part of our earlier instructional history—grade curves, fraternities and library hours, lectures and exams. But vendors of software for distance learning still seem to be using that as a model—based on the old pedagogy of top-down instruction rather than on the possibilities of self-organized, mutually supportive learning. The differences are profound in terms of software design, forum design, and the underlying model of how to empower learners.

A third lesson applies to forum coordinators, whether faculty, students, administrators, or team leaders in organizations at large. "Clean" and visible structuring of forums in terms of topics, phasing of tasks, encouragement of personal "voice," and explicit subject headings—little things like that can make a big difference.

A fourth lesson is the one most emphasized in this chapter, and it applies to everyone using an online forum. The use of metaphors to capture complex ideas is not terribly critical in everyday speech and in print materials, even though it is helpful as an antidote to the esoteric terminology and abstract language that tend to prevail in academic and business communication. Nevertheless, metaphors and images play a much more important role than people usually appreciate, not just in everyday language but also in scientific explanation, problem solving, cultural understanding, behavior, memory, and efficient thinking.

Images are even more important for virtual groups because so many of the other normal ways to frame a discussion are missing. Facial expressions, body language, and hand gestures are not in play; the presence or absence of people in the group is often uncertain; and the identity and location of people in a particular dialogue can be unclear.

Most important, metaphors have a key role for adult online education, which dissolves the traditionally static frameworks of learning, creating the kind of disorientation described by the jungle syndrome. Even when all members of the group are familiar to each other and known to be "present," the very substance of the dialogue is evolving, breaking out of confined, textbook-based boundaries. The playing field of ideas comes from students themselves. Consequently, image-based metaphors are important landmarks for *concrescence*—Whitehead's (1929/1978) apt term referred to earlier. The function of specific, image-based language or outright metaphors is not to promote a particular model; on the contrary, it is to provide specific points of reference where people can bring to bear multiple interpretations from their own mind-sets and experience.

There is a final lesson to be considered. One can manage the jungle syndrome in various ways, some of them addressed in this chapter, but the jungle is still there. The worst remedy would be to a "clear-cutting" operation that would dispel all of the shadows and uncertainties and leave everything neatly packaged up in predetermined problems and answers in a reversion to traditional pedagogy. Apart from any navigational tools we can provide, we also have to learn to feel comfortable with seeing only part of the picture.

This partial view was always a fact of life but was hidden from consideration by the compartmentalism of knowledge in classrooms and textbooks, the confining of groups in particular spaces and hours, and the command-and-control traditions of leadership and academic expertise. Now, the postmodern view of things calls for a more relaxed grip on things. Nobody can grasp it all. Nobody has all of the answers. There is no final chapter to any text and no exam that can measure what each person brings uniquely to the dialogue. In fact, the best answers might come from a better awareness of the context beyond traditional assumptions, revealed by a collective reconnaissance of views outside the box.

Navigating the jungle is not a matter of particular techniques but rather a meta-learning skill serving the lifelong learning beyond any organized curriculum. Julia Coupal, a graduate student in our program, pointed out the disconcerting mix of emotions that can arise from intense collaborative sessions online, looking back on her feelings of being both "excited and very panicked" with an awareness that most of her cohorts were going through that same process:

> At the time I thought there was something wrong with me. I began to seek out others . . . [until I began to see] that this process is normal—it is normal to be anxious. . . . I discovered that there are good days—so engrossed in the topic, I lost a sense of my surrounding—and bad days of panic, short-lived and powerful. There's no such thing as a standard plan. . . . The experience was wonderful. I liken it to that of having a child. At first you're nervous. "Can I really be a parent? Oops, just got pregnant, I guess I'm in it for the long haul." The ups and downs of pregnancy—excitement and a little nausea. Then you give birth (your idea comes to life), you nurture your child, and then you send [your child] off to the world and suddenly [the child is] out of your control. (Fielding forum posting, May 18, 2000)

Working in the jungle means giving up control of some things to become more deeply engaged in others. In a way, then, online adult learning consists of an "outward bound" or "ropes course" kind of experience, where part of the exercise is to let yourself get lost and get in over your head. But this takes a sense of deeper security, and if the experience is to be rooted in collaborative dialogue, then trust in the group is very important. Faculty can provide some of that, but it is all too easy to provide so many navigation devices that it preempts what students bring to it from their own resourcefulness or what the jungle itself can provide. David Wagoner's poem, "Lost," speaks to this (Wagoner, 1969). Appropriately enough, I learned about it from Augeard, who first used the term *jungle syndrome:*

> *Lost. . . . Stand still.*
> *The trees ahead and bushes beside you are not lost.*
> *Wherever you are is called Here,*
> *And you must treat it as a powerful stranger. . . .*
>
> *The forest breathes. Listen. It answers. . . .*
> *The forest knows*
> *Where you are.*
> *You must let it find you.*

References

Alexander, C. (1964). *Notes on the synthesis of form.* Cambridge, MA: Harvard University Press.

Alexander, C., Ishikawa, S., & Silverstein, M., with Jacobson, M., Fiksdahl-King, I., & Angel, S. (1977). *A pattern language: Town, buildings, construction.* New York: Oxford University Press.

Argyris, C. (1999). *On organizational learning* (2nd ed.). Malden, MA: Blackwell Business.

Boulding, K. E. (1956). *The image: Knowledge in life and society.* Ann Arbor: University of Michigan Press.

Brann, E. T. H. (1991). *The world of the imagination: Sum and substance.* Savage, MD: Rowman & Littlefield.

Campbell, J. (1974). *The mythic image.* Princeton, NJ: Princeton University Press.

Casti, J. L. (1994). *Complexification: Explaining a paradoxical world through the science of surprise.* New York: HarperCollins.

Chia, R. (1999, September). A "rhizomic" model of organizational change and transformation: Perspective from a metaphysics of change. *British Journal of Management, 10,* 209-227.

Collins, J. C., & Porras, J. I. (1997). *Built to last: Successful habits of visionary companies.* New York: HarperBusiness. (Original work published 1994)

Dann, J. (1995). *The memory cathedral: A secret history of Leonardo da Vinci.* New York: Bantam Books.

Dann, J. (2000). *About the "memory cathedral": Publisher's interview with Jack Dann* [Online]. Retrieved October 2, 2000, from: www.harpercollins.com.au/reading_group/memory_cathedral.html

De Bono, E. (1971). *New think* [American title]. New York: Avon Books. (Original work, *The use of lateral thinking* [British title], published 1968)

Dwyer, F. (2001). *A conversation with Alan Alda, Peter Parnell, and Gordon Davidson in the stage play of "QED."* Los Angeles: Center Theatre Group of Los Angeles.

Edwards, B. (1989). *Drawing on the right side of the brain.* New York: Putnam.

Eisler, R. (1987). *The chalice and the blade: Our history, our future.* New York: Harper & Row.

Engell, J. (1981). *The creative imagination.* Cambridge, MA: Harvard University Press.

Fenollosa, E. (1968). *The Chinese written character as a medium for poetry* (E. Pound, Ed.). San Francisco: City Lights Books.

Feynman, R. (1965). *The character of physical law.* London: British Broadcasting Corporation.

Feynman, R. P. (as told to R. Leighton). (1988). *What do you care what other people think?* New York: Norton.

Feynman, R. (1994). *The character of physical law.* New York: Modern Library. (Original work published 1965)

Freire, P. (1970). *Pedagogy of the oppressed* (M. B. Ramos, Trans.). New York: Herder & Herder.

Gordon, W. J. J. (1961). *Synectics: The development of creative capacity.* New York: Collier Books.

Guedj, D. (1997). *Numbers, the universal language* (L. Frankel, Trans.). New York: Harry N. Abrams. (Original work published 1996)

Hamilton, S. (1998). *Economic webs: A "networkcentric" technology diffusion strategy in a turbulent, connected economy.* Unpublished master's thesis, Organizational Design and Effectiveness Program, Fielding Graduate Institute.

Handy, C. (1994). *The age of paradox.* Boston: Harvard Business School Press.

Hass, R. (Ed.). (1994). *The essential Haiku: Versions of Basho, Buson, & Issa.* Hopewell, NJ: Ecco Press.

Heilbronner, R. L. (1999). *The worldly philosophers: The lives, times, and ideas of the great economic thinkers* (7th ed.). New York: Simon & Schuster.

Hemingway, E. (1996). A clean, well-lighted place. In *Short stories of Ernest Hemingway.* New York: Scribner. (Original work published 1926) Full text retrieved April 17, 2001, from http://classiclit.about.com/arts/classiclit/library/bl-etexts/ehemingway/bl-cle-ehem-cleanwell.html

Idensen, H. (2001). *Raymond Queneau's sonnet machine* [Online]. Retrieved April 17, 2001, from: www.hyperdis.de/txt/alte/gb/archi007.html

Jaikumar, R., & Bohn, R. (1986). The development of intelligent systems for industrial use: A conceptual framework. *Research on Technological Innovation Management and Policy, 3,* 169-211.

Johnson, D. (1998). *Blazing with an inner light: The power of not knowing what comes next.* Unpublished master's thesis, Fielding Graduate Institute.

Kaplan, R. (2000). *The nothing that is: A natural history of zero.* New York: Oxford University Press.

Kauffman, S. (1995). *At home in the universe: The search for laws of self-organization and complexity.* New York: Oxford University Press.

Lumsdaine, E., & Lumsdaine, M. (1993). *Creative problem solving: Thinking skills for a changing world* (2nd ed.). New York: McGraw-Hill.

Maruyama, M. (1982). The second cybernetics: Deviation amplifying mutual causal processes. *American Scientist, 51,* 612-619.

Merriam. (1939). *Merriam-Webster's new international dictionary of the English language, unabridged, with reference history* (2nd ed.). Springfield, MA: Author.

Mintzberg, H., & Van der Heyden, L. (1999, September-October). Organographics: Drawing how companies really work. *Harvard Business Review,* pp. 87-94.

Morgan, G. (1986). *Images of organization.* Newbury Park, CA: Sage.

Morgan, G. (1997). *Imagin-i-zation: New mindsets for seeing, organizing, and managing.* Thousand Oaks, CA: Sage.

Morgan, G., & Ramirez, R. (1984). Action learning: A holographic metaphor for guiding social change. *Human Relations, 37*(1), 1-28.

Nogami, H. (1999, March). The Chinese written character and the ideogrammic method. In *Modern to Postmodern 2* [Online]. Retrieved February 6, 2001, from: www.seaple.icc.ne.jp/~nogami/essay2_eng.html

Parkinson, C. N. (1964). *Parkinson's Law, and other studies in administration.* New York: Ballantine. (Original work published 1957)

Peters, T. (1987). *Thriving on chaos: Handbook for management revolution.* New York: Harper & Row.

Pound, E. (1954). *Cantos.* London: Faber & Faber.

Reynolds, M. (1999, June). Grasping the nettle: Possibilities and pitfalls of a critical management pedagogy. *British Journal of Management, 10*(2), 171-184.

Rulke, D. L., & Rau, D. (2000, December). Investigating the encoding process of transactive memory development in group training. *Group & Organizational Management, 25,* 373-396.

Schatz, S. (2001). *Paradigm shifts and challenges for instructional designers: An introduction to meta-tags and knowledge bits.* Unpublished manuscript, Indiana University. Retrieved January 23, 2001, from: www.imsproject.com/feature/kb/knowledgebits.html

Seife, C. (2000). *Zero: The biography of a dangerous idea.* New York: Viking.

Senge, P. M. (1990). *The fifth discipline: The art and practice of the learning organization.* New York: Currency Doubleday.

Slater, R. (1999). *Jack Welch and the GE way.* New York: McGraw-Hill.

Smith, A. (1759). *The theory of moral sentiments.* London: A. Millar.

Sorensen, R. A. (1992). *Thought experiments.* New York: Oxford University Press.

Szarkowski, J. (1981). *The portfolios of Ansel Adams.* Boston: New York Graphic Society.

Thomas, L. (1985). *The youngest science: Notes of a medicine-watcher.* New York: Oxford University Press. (Original work published 1983)

UCLA Center for Communication Policy. (2001). *Surveying the digital future* [Online]. Retrieved February 21, 2001, from: www.ccp.ucla.edu/ucla-internet. pdf

Wagoner, D. (1969). *Lost* [poem]. In D. Wagoner, *Riverbed* (p. 75). Bloomington: Indiana University Press.

Wegner, D. (1986). Transactive memory: A contemporary analysis of the group mind. In G. Mullen & G. Goethals (Eds.), *Theories of group behavior* (pp. 185-208). New York: Springer-Verlag.

Weick, K. (1976). Educational organizations as loosely coupled systems. *Administrative Science Quarterly, 21,* 1-9. Summary retrieved April 15, 2001, www.stanford.edu/~krollag/org_site/org_theory/scott_articles/weick_lcs.html

Wenger, W. (1999). *Image streaming.* Web page ©1999 by Project Renaissance. Retrieved April 18, 2001, from: www.winwenger.com/imstream.htm

Wheatley, M. J. (1999). *Leadership and the new science: Discovering order in a chaotic world* (2nd ed.). San Francisco: Berrett-Koehler.

Whitehead, A. N. (1978). *Process and reality: An essay in cosmology* (Corrected ed., D. R. Griffin & D. W. Sherburne, Eds.). New York: Free Press. (Original work published 1929)

Additional Reading

Arnheim, R. (1969). *Visual thinking.* Berkeley: University of California Press.

Carbonell, J. G. (1982). Metaphor: An inescapable phenomenon in natural language comprehension. In W. C. Lehnert & M. H. Ringle (Eds.), *Strategies for natural language processing* (pp. 415-434). Hillsdale, NJ: Lawrence Erlbaum.

Clarke, B. (1997). *Image and imagination: Encounters with the photography of Dorothea Lange.* San Francisco: Freedom Voices.

Denis, M. (1991). *Image and cognition* (M. Denis & C. Greenbaum, Trans.). New York: Harvester Wheatsheaf.

Downin, D. B., & Bazargan, S. (Eds.). (1991). *Image and ideology in modern/ postmodern discourse.* Albany: State University of New York Press.

Gozzi, R. (1992). *The power of metaphor in the age of electronic media.* Cresskill, NJ: Hampton Press.

Held, R. (Ed.). (1974). *Image, object, and illusion: Readings from* Scientific American. San Francisco: Freeman.

Horowitz, M. J. (1978). *Image formation and cognition* (2nd ed.). New York: Appleton-Century-Crofts.

Hunter, J. (1987). *Image and word: The interaction of twentieth-century photographs and texts.* Cambridge, MA: Harvard University Press.

Hyerle, D. (1996). *Visual tools for constructing knowledge.* Alexandria, VA: Association for Supervision and Curriculum Development.

Kegan, R. (1994). *In over our heads: The mental demands of modern life.* Cambridge, MA: Harvard University Press.

Kosslyn, S. M. (1980). *Image and mind.* Cambridge, MA: Harvard University Press.

Marantz, A., Miyashita, Y., & O'Neil, W. (Eds.). (2000). *Image, language, brain: Papers from the First Mind Articulation Project Symposium* [Tokyo, 1998]. Cambridge: MIT Press.

Moore, T. V. (1919). Image and meaning in memory and perception. Princeton, NJ: Psychological Review.

Parnes, S. J. (1988). *Visioning.* East Aurora, NY: DOK.

Parnes, S. J. (Ed.). (1992). *Sourcebook for creative problem solving: A fifty year digest.* Buffalo, NY: Creative Education Foundation.

Prosser, J. (Ed.). (1998). *Image-based research: A sourcebook for qualitative researchers.* Bristol, PA: Falmer.

Pugh, S. L., Hicks, J. W., & Davis, M. (1992). *Bridging: A teacher's guide to metaphorical thinking.* Urbana, IL: National Council of Teachers of English.

Robin, H. (1992). *The scientific image: From cave to computer.* New York: H. N. Abrams.

Schön, D. (1987). *Educating the reflective practitioner: Toward new design for teaching and learning in the professions.* San Francisco: Jossey-Bass.

Singer, J. (1990). *Seeing through the visible world: Jung, Gnosis, and chaos.* New York: Harper & Row.

Spitz, E. H. (1991). *Image and insight: Essays in psychoanalysis and the arts.* New York: Columbia University Press.

Stambovsky, P. (1988). *The depictive image: Metaphor and literary experience.* Amherst: University of Massachusetts Press.

Thiroux, E. (1999). *The critical edge: Thinking and researching in a virtual society.* Upper Saddle River, NJ: Prentice Hall.

Walther, J. B., Slovackec, C. L., & Tidwell, L. C. (2001). Is a picture worth a thousand words? *Communication Research 28*(1), 105-134.

Chapter 9

Harnessing the Power of Complexity in an Online Learning Environment

Jim Beaubien

Distance education is the wave of the future (Worley, 2000). University and corporate learning are moving online. Some suggest that the demand for cost-effective interactive courses will make online learning the norm in most organizations over the next few years (Mottl, 2000; Schaaf, 1999; Weinstock, 2000). The pace of change is rapid, and online learning is growing exponentially (Ferguson, 2000). One observer suggests that virtual universities are popping up like mushrooms and that distance education offerings in traditional venues are multiplying like rabbits (Dyrud, 2000).

Opinions about online learning vary. Critics are concerned that online learning will cause students to become isolated from family and friends (Hara & Ling, 2000), breed passivity (Kerka, 1996), lead to mild depressive features (Bower, 1998), or simply overwhelm people with the demands of working in an online environment (Miller, 1999). Others worry that it cannot duplicate the community of the classroom (Kerka, 1996), will destroy the teacher-student relationship, and may ultimately change the very nature of education (Hiltz, 1997). Enthusiasts see online learning as good news for smart trainers and learners (Abernathy, 1999), a cost-effective method for delivering training to every desk, and a tool for achieving a competitive edge (Koprowski, 2000).

Although much has been written about the potential upside and down-side of online learning, little has been written about online pedagogical frameworks. The emerging complexity sciences hold much promise in this regard. Taken collectively, they provide new models and new tools for think-ing about and crafting online learning experiences. This chapter describes my attempts to harness the power of the emerging complexity sciences in an online teaching and learning environment. The material grew out of my work as an adjunct faculty appointee at the Fielding Graduate Institute in Santa Barbara, California, and at the University of Alberta in Edmonton, Alberta. As of this writing, I have used the complexity sciences as a frame-work to present 16 graduate courses in a totally online environment and to supplement the presentation of 3 other graduate courses in a traditional academic setting.

Although the work is grounded in the scientific literature, the material in this chapter is ultimately based on my personal experience. The chapter begins with an overview of relevant concepts gleaned from the complexity sciences literature. I then explore the potential application of these concepts in an online environment. Finally, I outline how I actually apply these con-cepts to the process of teaching online.

The Complexity Sciences

We are witnessing a historic shift in our understanding of how the world works. New explanatory models and frameworks are emerging on many dif-ferent fronts. Based on a synthesis of recent discoveries in the natural, physi-cal, and social sciences (Axelrod & Cohen, 1999; Matthews, White, & Long, 1999), these nascent models are collectively referred to as the complexity sci-ences (Matthews et al., 1999). Some refer to complexity science as the "sci-ence of sciences" because of its inherent interdisciplinary nature (Clippinger, 1999). The complexity sciences describe the world in terms of the behavior of complex adaptive systems (CASs).

The dictionary (Reader's Digest Association, 1998) defines *complex* as a whole made up of interrelated parts. Complex implies variation and diver-sity. Adaptation is the ability to change to better suit circumstances or condi-tions or to change conditions to better suit needs (Reader's Digest Associa-tion, 1998). Adaptation implies the ability to learn from experience. A system is defined as a group of interacting items forming a unified whole (Reader's Digest Association, 1998). Taken together, a CAS may be described as a uni-fied whole made up of diverse and interrelated parts with the ability to adapt to meet needs. Diversity, interconnectedness, learning, adaptation, and unity are characteristic features of CASs.

Pedagogical Implications

Because online classes are living systems, CAS theory has the potential to contribute to the development of an online pedagogy. A number of CAS concepts are well enough developed to provide a conceptual framework for thinking about and structuring online teaching and learning activities. I have selected seven that I believe to be of particular relevance: free agents, relationships, feedback loops, self-organization, emergence, identity, and nonlinearity. Each is described in the burgeoning literature on CASs.

1. *Free agents.* Free agents populate CASs. Free agents are goal oriented and purposeful in their behavior. They make choices based on their wants and needs (Axelrod & Cohen, 1999). Free agents can change their behavior, adapt to circumstances, react to the behaviors of other free agents, and take steps to modify their environments to meet their needs. Although choice is always constrained by circumstances, free agents are always free to choose from the array of available alternatives.

In a CAS, free agents are not subject to hierarchical control. Power and control are distributed, and each free agent has the ability to make its own choices in its own interests. The marketplace provides an example of distributed control in a free agent-populated CAS. In the marketplace, free agents act in their own self-interests, make choices, adapt to the choices of others, and change their environments to optimize their gains without direction from above.

2. *Relationships.* Relationships are an essential building block in a CAS. A CAS cannot form or evolve without relationships. When free agents are in relationships, their behaviors become linked and the behavior of one has an impact on the behavior of the other. As free agents form relationships, they develop a web of linked interdependencies and the characteristics of a CAS emerge. These emergent group behavior patterns are distinct from the behaviors of the entities acting on their own (Clippinger, 1999, p.11). The nature of these relationships is not predictable a priori. They emerge as an artifact of individual free agents' adaptations to the behaviors of other free agents and conditions in the system.

3. *Feedback loops.* The dictionary defines *feedback* as "the return to the input of part of the output in a machine, system, or process" (Reader's Digest Association, 1998). Feedback is the primary regulatory mechanism within a CAS. Feedback can be either negative or positive. Negative feedback has a stabilizing effect in that it returns the system to a "targeted or inherent" set point. A thermostat regulates the temperature in a room by providing negative feedback to a heating or cooling system that is programmed to close the

gap between the actual temperature in the room and the temperature set on the thermostat.

Rather than returning a system to a predetermined set point, positive feedback tends to destabilize. It feeds on itself and amplifies deviations, driving the system away from current set points and toward new unpredictable ones. A small fire heats the air around it and creates its own draft. As a result, it grows into a bigger fire, which creates a bigger draft, which creates a bigger fire, and so on until a new and unpredictable point of dynamic balance emerges.

Feedback loops, sometimes referred to as flows (Holland, 1995), are the networks or webs of regulatory interactions that emerge in a CAS (Clippinger, 1999, p. 13). Feedback loops provide free agents with information about the consequences of their behavior in the context of the behavior of the other elements in the system. This information allows the agents in a CAS to adapt their actions to the behaviors of other agents or changes in the environment (Kurtyka, 1999). This iterative, never-ending cycle of free agent interaction and adaptation, and adaptation to these adaptations, drives co-evolutionary change within the system. Feedback loops play a critical role in learning, and the ability to learn is a distinguishing characteristic of all CASs (Pascale, 1999).

4. *Self-organization.* The adaptive interactions of free agents in a feedback-rich environment tend to self-organize into stable and predictable patterns without any outside control. In other words, CASs organize themselves into interconnected wholes through relationships, adaptation, and feedback. A CAS may act as a unit, become interconnected with other CASs, and then self-organize into even larger systems (Wilson, 1999). The tendencies toward emerging order, dynamic stability, and increased complexity are an inherent feature of CASs. Adam Smith's description of the free hand guiding the marketplace metaphorically describes self-organization in a large, dynamic, stable, and highly evolved CAS (Smith, 1981). The marketplace essentially operates as a self-organizing entity without centralized control.

5. *Emergence.* The concept of emergence is captured in the cliché saying that the whole is more than the sum of its parts. Emergent properties are not inherently characteristic of the individual elements in a CAS in isolation. Rather, they emerge out of the ever-evolving relationships among the elements. The hallmark of emergence is much coming from little (Holland, 1998). Although emergence can often be described by simple rules, it is always a function of the system as a whole and never under the control of a central executive function (Holland, 1998).

Emergence is relationship and feedback dependent. Without feedback loops, particularly positive or amplifying feedback loops, emergence does not occur. When positive feedback loops are present, very small changes can have dramatic and rapid effects. Once a tipping point (Gladwell, 2000) is reached, emergent properties can spread throughout the system and completely replace the old order. New fashion trends, epidemics, the evolution of the World Wide Web, changes in crime rates, and the increase in "road rage" are all examples of the emergent phenomena in CASs. Complex adaptive systems continually learn, grow, and evolve (Kurtyka, 1999). It is inherent in their nature.

6. *Identity.* According to the dictionary (Reader's Digest Association, 1998), *identity* literally means to be the same, as in identical. Identity establishes boundaries between the self and the non-self. It is the basis for ascertaining what belongs in a system and what falls out of the system. Identity allows a system to develop immunity. Immunity permits a system to develop and maintain a dynamic sense of integrity over time. Tagging is the mechanism that allows self-recognition to take place, and it is the basis of identity (Holland, 1995). Tags are labels that identify an entity and signal its significance within a CAS. Tags define the boundaries and membership conditions of a system (Clippinger, 1999). Without tags, self-organization is impossible. All CASs evolve around a sense of identity and use tags to separate the self from the non-self.

7. *Nonlinearity.* Nonlinearity is a feature of all CASs (Holland, 1995). In a linear system, the future is predictable and the whole is a function of its parts. In a nonlinear system, inputs and outputs are not linked in a linear relationship. The constant feedback of changes throughout the system suggests that even the smallest change in initial conditions can be amplified over time, making long-term prediction impossible (Wilson, 1999). As a result, small incremental changes in inputs can invoke sudden and unexpected changes in outputs (Clippinger, 1999). Alternatively, large changes may have little effect (Pascale, 1999).

Because they are nonlinear, it follows that CASs cannot be controlled in a mechanistic way. Some inputs may have a disproportionate impact on the system and lead to a tipping point (Gladwell, 2000), driving the emergence of completely new and unanticipated outcomes. They can, however, be influenced or perturbed in the hope that they will adapt to the perturbation and evolve new adaptive patterns.

These seven concepts, drawn from the emerging complexity sciences literature, contain a number of implications for thinking about and structuring online learning activities. Following are some of the key implications.

Implications for Online Learning

An online class is a living system. As such, it functions as a self-organizing, self-sustaining CAS. Online classes are populated with interconnected, purpose-driven free agents who exercise choice, vary their behaviors, and modify their environments to meet their needs. As they exchange information and adapt to circumstances, relationship patterns emerge; feedback loops develop; and the class self-organizes around an iterative cycle of interaction, information exchange, and adaptation. Through tagging, the class develops a sense of identity and establishes a norm-based immune system that defines boundaries and membership conditions. Taken together, these processes drive co-evolutionary changes within the system and lead to the emergence of system properties that enable a class to function as a dynamic interconnected and unified whole.

A pedagogy based on CAS theory has the potential to radically change our roles as instructors. If we are too controlling, or too top-down in our approach, then we will inhibit the possibilities and restrict emergence and self-organization. If we use an instructor-centered approach, then we will inhibit relationship development among class members and once again will inhibit emergence and self-organization. If we focus too heavily on content and do not foster relationships among all participants, then the system will not evolve to higher levels of functioning. This means that the hierarchical structures and top-down models of control associated with traditional teaching and learning environments must be replaced with more decentralized models of control if we are to harness the power of complexity in an online learning environment.

This does not mean that online instructors are powerless; it just means that we have to change. We can still influence outcomes even if we cannot control them. We can establish frameworks, create conditions, and continuously perturb the system so that new and more adaptive forms of order can continuously unfold. We must believe that, given the right conditions, learning is emergent. The key is to find the right balance, or the "sweet spot" (Kauffman, 1993), between too much and too little control as systems evolve and order emerges when components are neither too tightly nor too loosely coupled (Kurtyka, 1999).

Now that we have explored some of the implications of key concepts emerging from the complexity sciences, let's look at how these can be used as a pedagogical framework for online teaching and learning.

Guidelines for Online Education

This section describes how I apply my evolving understanding of the complexity sciences in an online learning environment. The framework is based on the following eight key building blocks: planning, relevance, process management, team charter, fostering relationships, identity, quantity before quality, and dialogue over debate. Each is considered in detail.

1. *Planning.* Although planning is important in any teaching context, it is especially important in an online environment based on a complexity

framework. Strive to create a logical and intuitive course description that clearly describes the course objectives, the material to be covered, and the sequence in which it will be covered. Include descriptions of the students' responsibilities, assignments, resources, and time frames. Make the structure clear and transparent so that it is easy for students to navigate from section to section. Design ample opportunity for student interaction and dialogue. From a CAS perspective, dialogue provides the basic building blocks for feedback loops, relationships, identity, adaptation, emergence, and self-organization. Remember that small changes in initial conditions can have significant impact on subsequent developments in a nonlinear system.

2. *Relevance.* Students come to a course as free agents acting in their own interests. They come by choice, engage by choice, participate by choice, and leave by choice. They determine the quantity and quality of their participation. As free agents, they are more likely to engage in the learning process if they believe that the course will help them to meet their learning needs from both the content and process points of view. Make sure that the course has relevance for them. Incorporate students' wants and needs into the course design. Describe course processes and outcomes in terms of benefits that will accrue to participants. Make the design flexible so that the content and process can continuously evolve to meet participants' unfolding needs.

Most of the students I have dealt with in online classes are in mid-career. Most are seeking knowledge and information with immediate applicability. One can increase relevance by creating opportunities for students to immediately apply what they are learning to real-life issues. This will help them to see the course as more than an academic exercise. They will see it as a source of insights and tools that they can use to solve real-life problems. When students find the course relevant, they tend to engage, increase their participation levels, and provide more feedback to their fellow students. This tends to establish an escalating positive feedback cycle that can lead to new forms of self-organization and emergent learning.

3. *Process management.* I use routine as a structural element in presenting the course. I establish a pattern and repeat it throughout the course, typically on a weekly basis. The repetition creates a predictable and transparent framework that allows students to focus on the content and interaction rather than struggling with the methodology. The design is simple. I divide the course into week-by-week segments and then present each weekly segment using the four-round sequence outlined next. A series of readings provide content for the weekly dialogues.

- In Round 1, a lead person presents a "white paper" (key concept summary) of the materials introduced in the readings for the week. Although everyone is assigned the readings, only one person is responsible for the Round 1 posting. Duties are shared, and the responsibility for the Round 1 posting changes weekly. I often use the metaphor of table setting to describe the Round 1 posting. It is designed to launch the interaction and invite the rest of the students into the dialogue. To expand on the table-setting analogy, a well-written white paper will engage people (appetizer), challenge them to think (something to chew on), and give them food for thought (sustenance). Rather than drawing conclusions, Round 1 postings are intended to stimulate questions and promote dialogue. There is no one right way to do a Round 1 posting. I encourage everyone to be creative and to let his or her personality show through. Most Round 1 postings conclude with three or four key questions for other students to respond to in Round 2.

- Round 2 is the dialogue phase; everyone responds to the Round 1 posting. The process is iterative, and students are asked to respond to each other's responses until the dialogue reaches a natural conclusion. This is where the elements of a CAS come into play, including free agents, feedback loops, relationships, tagging, identity, diversity, and adaptation. Round 2 is a crucible for self-organization and emergence. Although I do not control the process, I can influence it by actively supporting and encouraging engagement. It is critical to establish high levels of interaction among the students. If positive feedback loops can be established, then the interaction tends to feed on itself and participation levels increase dramatically. I have seen a number of students move from an average of posting entries 2 or 3 times a week to posting 30 to 40 times a week. It generally takes about 4 or 5 weeks to fully engage students and cultivate the right conditions for this to occur. As the quantity of interaction increases, most students report a corresponding increase in the quality of their learning experience. The best insights, the ones that students find the most relevant and valuable, tend to come after several iterations. They are emergent.

- Round 3 is the summary phase. Here one of the students summarizes the key points that came out of the Round 1 and Round 2 dialogues for the week. The other students then add any final comments, and after a brief period of dialogue, we move on to the next week's topic. There is no right way of doing a Round 3 posting. The intent is to harvest the best ideas and bring closure to the process. The responsibilities for Round 3 rotate weekly.

- In Round 4, I add my final comments, pull things together, and tie up the loose ends. I establish linkages between the material and the "real world." I invite students to look at the relevance and applicability of the material covered in Rounds 1 and 2. I often pose questions and ask for students' input on how we would use the ideas we have developed to address specific problems in their workplaces. Some weeks, my postings may be quite long. Other weeks, they may be quite brief, depending on the nature of the dialogue and my ability to add value. My Round 4 postings usually initiate another brief round of dialogue.

4. *Team charter.* At the start of a semester, I work with the students to jointly develop a team charter for the course (Fisher & Fisher, 2001). A charter establishes a common purpose, defines mutually supported objectives, sets up clear course deliverables, outlines responsibilities, establishes boundaries, and provides a focal point that brings everyone together as a team sharing a mutually supported set of goals and behavioral standards. It also provides a framework for monitoring progress and evaluating results throughout the course.

I keep the chartering process simple. I ask each student to briefly respond to the following points. I then summarize their answers, develop the charter, and circulate the final document for their approval. Here are the directions I give to students (see Fisher & Fisher, 2001):

- Write a one-sentence description of the team's mission (why we are here).

- Outline the course deliverables (five to seven brief bulleted statements describing what we want to learn).

- Describe our team operating guidelines (five to seven bulleted statements describing the behavior we can expect from one another).

A sample team charter developed by students in a class on virtual team design is presented next.

Purpose
Our purpose is to design, lead, manage, and facilitate virtual teams.

Deliverables
- An understanding of the components of effective virtual team design
- A toolkit of virtual team assessments, instruments, and methodologies
- The ability to leverage available technologies to enhance virtual team effectiveness
- Knowledge of specific design principles that can be used in varying settings
- Knowledge of how to develop a team design that will allow for participation by individuals with diverse backgrounds and needs

Operating Guidelines

- ◆ We will respect all viewpoints and perspectives.
- ◆ We will complete postings on time or let the team know if we are unable to do so.
- ◆ We will respond promptly to one another.
- ◆ We will challenge each other in a spirit of discovery.
- ◆ We will find ways to interject humor and fun into the class.
- ◆ We will encourage one another and demonstrate courteousness.

A well-crafted charter is brief, clear, and focused. A well-designed chartering process is open, transparent, and as democratic as possible (sometimes charter requirements are imposed by the institution). The chartering process engages students and helps them to develop a sense of co-ownership. I want them to feel a shared sense of responsibility for the course processes and outcomes rather than to depend on me as their instructor to make everything work.

5. *Fostering relationships.* I try to establish a warm, friendly, and inviting tone from the start of the course. I want to help people connect with one another on a human scale and develop strong relationships. I want to create an environment where everyone can work together collaboratively in everyone's best interests. To this end, I send each participant an e-mail about a week before the course begins to personally welcome him or her, provide an overview of the content, and invite his or her participation. At the start of the course, all participants (including faculty) are asked to post a brief biographical sketch describing who they are, what they do, their past experiences, their hobbies, and their interests. I ask them to include something about themselves that would not normally appear on a résumé. I do this to build linkages, reduce tension, increase feelings of safety, and foster interaction. The biographical sketches help the participants to develop a sense of their teammates, and they lay a foundation for relationship building. I participate fully in this exercise.

Relationships are a critical factor in harnessing the powers of complexity in an online learning environment. They provide the glue that links the students together and allows a sense of community to develop. Community has been described as caring about people more than you have to (Levine, Locke, Searles, & Weinberger, 2000). Community fosters a safe and engaging holding environment (Heifetz & Laurie, 1997), one that supports students' development and encourages full participation. Community stimulates the development of positive emotional attachments and makes the class a safe place not just for students' minds but for their hearts as well. As relationships form, the class develops a web of linked interdependencies (feedback loops), and conditions are set for the characteristics of a CAS to emerge.

6. *Identity.* I encourage the class to develop a strong sense of identity. Identity is always based on similarities and sameness, in other words, things participants see themselves as holding in common, such as values, interests, work experience, and goals. As students interact, they develop a tagging system to characterize and label the attributes they consider to be significant. These tags become the basis for the class's evolving sense of identity. They give participants a feeling of belonging, a sense of shared membership in a community of interest, and a framework for purposeful action. This sense of identity allows the team to establish boundaries and to distinguish self from non-self. With a strong sense of identity and strong relationships, self-organization and emergence can occur and the whole can become more than the sum of its parts.

A number of factors contribute to the development of a strong identity. Developing a team charter and operating guidelines brings people together with a shared sense of purpose and a set of common behavioral standards. Encouraging relationships and fostering community strengthens these ties and fosters a strong sense of identity. Challenging the team to develop a meaningful team name can become a powerful rallying point for identity. I usually wait until the second week of the class before initiating the team name activity. I ask students to develop a unique name that reflects their group personality, a name that characterizes the essence of their identity. The exercise can have a powerful impact on the class.

One online class rallied around the name "Spandex Deluxe." The name was very symbolic in that the students saw the team as a vehicle that would support their growth, allow them to stretch, adjust to their changing contours, and make them look good. Spandex does all of those things. They added "Deluxe" because of its literal meaning: passing all others in its class. They wanted to be the best. The team rallied around the Spandex Deluxe identity and developed into an engaged, supportive, high-performance learning community.

7. *Quantity before quality.* In my experience with complexity-based approaches to online learning, quantity precedes quality. If you focus on increasing the rate of participation, quality will tend to emerge. There are a number of reasons for this. Increasing the quantity of interaction increases the number of connections and the amount of information exchanged. This sets up a self-reinforcing positive feedback cycle that tends to drive the system to new levels through self-organization and emergence.

Focusing on quantity before quality is one of the most important things I have learned about harnessing the power of complexity in an online teaching environment. Much of my role revolves around encouraging participation and interaction. It is much like building a fire. It starts slowly at first, but as the fire builds, it establishes positive feedback loops and rapidly moves to a new, higher-level stable position. Higher levels of participation metaphorically fan the flames of participation, which in turn "fires up" the class's level of involvement.

    8. *Dialogue over debate.* Classes based on the complexity sciences function much like a marketplace in that marketplaces are primarily vehicles for conversations (Levine et al., 2000). Effective conversations are relational, not just transactional. They involve the simultaneous bidirectional exchange of information. I encourage dialogue as a vehicle for achieving effective conversations. The dictionary (Reader's Digest Association, 1998) defines *dialogue* as an exchange or a give-and-take of information. Dialogue is a collaborative additive process in that it continues to add new ideas to the discussion without forcing previous ideas to be set aside. Debate, on the other hand, is competitive and subtractive in that it attempts to establish the superiority of one idea over another. Dialogue encourages diversity. Debate discourages diversity and encourages convergence. Dialogue creates a fertile environment in which new levels of understanding can develop. Conversations can drive co-evolutionary change within the class and create an information-rich holding environment in which learning experiences are emergent.

    Classes based on the key building blocks of planning, relevance, process management, team charter, fostering relationships, identity, quantity before quality, and dialogue over debate tend to follow the developmental pattern described next.

- ◆ Stage 1 is an orientation stage. Here students find their way to the online site and become familiar with the course content, structure, and technology. They also begin to develop relationships with their fellow students. To move on, it is critical that all students develop a clear sense of where they are going as a class and that they establish a safe, supportive, and inviting holding environment. Students must also overcome any underlying concerns they might have about the technological infrastructure that we are using to support the class and about their ability to handle the course material.
- ◆ Norms and procedures are set for the class in Stage 2. Everyone contributes to the development of a class charter. We establish the responsibilities and time frames for the different posting rounds. We agree on who will do what and when they will do it. I am very active in this stage. I provide a lot of encouragement and try to make sure that no one gets trapped by the technology or lost in the process. I try to make sure that everyone is engaged. I challenge the students to set high expectations for themselves, and I gradually shape higher levels of participation by using abundant praise and encouragement. Students must feel comfortable with the technology, the structure, the process, and one another to move on to the next stage.

- Stage 3 generally develops around the fifth or sixth week of the class. It is self-organizing and emergent. Around the fourth week, I ask students to increase their level of participation. I explain that quantity precedes quality, and I ask them to step up the pace of their interaction. As the interaction increases and a sense of identity develops, an aura of playful productivity often emerges. Students become far more active, and they begin to invest more of their discretionary effort into their studies. This establishes a positive feedback cycle, and if things "catch fire," then postings increase dramatically. Some students will do as many as 50 postings in a week when only 2 or 3 are required. This behavior is self-organizing and self-sustaining. Students are generally amazed by the strength of their emergent learning community and by their productivity levels.

- Stage 4 occurs at the end of the class. It involves reflection and disengagement. In some ways, it is like saying good-bye at the end of summer camp. There are many expressions of appreciation and support. I try to create some ceremonial rite of passage to help with the transition out of the class.

Faculty Role: Making It Work

This section describes some of the things I have learned about the personal factors that contribute to harnessing the power of the complexity sciences in an online learning environment.

1. *Persona.* Students want the faculty leader's personality to come through. Let your values, beliefs, and preferences show through in your postings. Reveal your character, and let students know that you have a real life. Give them a sense of who you are and what is going on in your life. Share relevant examples from your personal and professional experience. Your persona should be more revealed than described. Let it emerge gradually in the things you say and do as the course progresses, and use your persona to help develop a safe and supportive holding environment (Heifetz & Laurie, 1997).

2. *Presence.* Presence is a critical element in online facilitation. Be online regularly and participate fully in the dialogue. I make it a policy to be online every morning and every night. I am not always active, but students always know I am there and interested in their postings. Sometimes I simply thank them for a posting or enter brief comments. Other times I capitalize on teachable moments and respond with fairly lengthy comments. Sometimes I simply ask a question or two of everyone (e.g., "What does everyone think about this point?," "How does this fit with everyone's experience?"). Modeling a high level of presence sets a positive norm for the class and encourages students to

do the same. Students always seem to appreciate the fact that I am accessible and present.

3. *Perturb the system.* Developments within CASs can be neither predicted nor controlled, but they can be perturbed. In other words, you cannot predict the future of the class, but you can influence it. Rather than striving for stability and closure, I constantly perturb the class so that it has to adapt to my perturbing inputs. I perturb the system in a number of ways, including the following:

- Constantly keeping a high volume of work in front of students, requiring constant effort on their part to keep current
- Introducing diverse and contradictory readings to challenge students' paradigms
- Asking challenging questions that require complex analysis and synthesis to answer
- Introducing challenging real-life examples and asking students to suggest action paths
- Describing relevant consulting situations where I have "failed marvelously" and asking students what I could have done differently based on the material we are covering in class
- Asking students to respond to points in other people's postings
- Continuously encouraging higher levels of participation
- Having students work on projects with tight time frames

4. *Positive feedback.* Positive feedback tends to bring out the best in people and motivates them to invest discretionary effort (Braksick, 2000; Daniels, 2000). It is an extremely powerful tool in an online environment. It can energize the whole system and significantly increase the interaction frequency. Just being present online and conveying interest in the students' work is very reinforcing for most students. Simple comments such as "Wow, what a great response!" and "Thanks for taking the time to create such a thoughtful response" can have a significant impact on participation levels.

5. *Playfulness.* Playfulness is a great energizer. Having fun is a self-reinforcing activity that tends to increase levels of participation. It strengthens relationships and helps people to develop a sense of belonging. It lowers stress levels and increases feelings of safety. It fosters creativity and increases energy levels. It strengthens identity and increases team cohesiveness.

Playfulness manifests in a number of ways. Victimless teasing, sharing humorous stories or life events, creating a virtual coffee shop where people can socialize, and winning and moving forward together all can contribute to a group's sense of playfulness. I have found playfulness to be one of the most important things I can do to energize students.

Conclusion

This chapter has described my attempts to harness the power of the emerging complexity sciences in an online teaching and learning environment. Based on my experiences this past semester, I still have a lot to learn. I taught two sections of the same course. Although students were randomly assigned to each section and I used essentially the same framework to teach both classes, the outcomes were very different.

One class caught fire. The students engaged, bonded, interacted, and became highly productive. They had fun and enjoyed the learning experience. They were full of regrets when the class ended. The other class never caught fire. A majority of the students were overwhelmed by unpredicted and unexpected challenges that took their energy away from the course. One had a computer containing all of his coursework stolen, another had a sibling involved in a car accident overseas, another lost her job, and another's spouse confused semester completion dates and surprised the student with non-refundable tickets for a week-long cruise in celebration of their wedding anniversary late in the term. This section never bonded as a team, dialogue was sparse, production rates were low, and the students did not have fun. They were relieved to see the semester come to an end.

These two contiguous, randomly assigned classes demonstrate the challenges inherent in attempting to harness the power of the complexity sciences in an online learning environment. When the fire catches, the experience is exhilarating; when it does not catch, the process can be discouraging. In the final analysis, ultimate outcomes remain unpredictable and uncontrollable. Such is the nature of the complexity sciences.

References

Abernathy, D. J. (1999). WWW online learning. *Training and Development, 53*(9), 36-41.

Axelrod, R., & Cohen, M. (1999). *Harnessing complexity: Organizational implications of a scientific frontier.* New York: Free Press.

Bower, B. (1998). *Social disconnections on-line* [Online]. Available: www.sciencenews.org/sn_arc98/9_12_98/content.htm

Braksick, L. W. (2000). *Unlock behavior, unleash profits.* New York: McGraw-Hill.

Clippinger, J. (Ed.). (1999). *The biology of business: Decoding the natural laws of enterprise.* San Francisco: Jossey-Bass.

Daniels, A. C. (2000). *Bringing out the best in people: How to apply the astonishing power of positive reinforcement* (2nd ed.). New York: McGraw-Hill.

Dyrud, M. A. (2000). The third wave: A position paper. *Business Communication Quarterly, 63*(3), 81-93.

Ferguson, L. (2000, Summer). Effective design and use of Web-based distance learning environments. *Professional Safety,* pp. 28-32.

Fisher, K., & Fisher, M. D. (2001). *The distance manager.* New York: McGraw-Hill.

Gladwell, M. (2000). *The tipping point: How little things can make a big difference.* Boston: Little, Brown.

Hara, N., & Ling, R. (2000, March). *Students' distress with a Web-based distance education course* [Online]. Available: www.slis.indiana.edu/csi/wp00-01.html

Heifetz, R. A., & Laurie, D. A. (1997, January). The work of leadership. *Harvard Business Review,* pp. 124-134.

Hiltz, S. (1997). *Impacts of college-level courses via asynchronous learning networks: Some preliminary results* [Online]. Available: www.aln.org/alnweb/journal/jaln_vol1issue2.htm

Holland, J. H. (1995). *Hidden order: How adaptations build complexity.* Reading, MA: Addison-Wesley.

Holland, J. H. (1998). *Emergence: From chaos to order.* Reading, MA: Addison-Wesley.

Kauffman, S. (1993). *The origin of order: Self-organization and selection in evolution.* New York: Oxford University Press.

Kerka, S. (1996). *Distance learning: The Internet* [Online]. Available: www.ed.gov/databases/eric_digests/ed395214.html

Koprowski, G. (2000, August 28). The competitive edge. *Information Week,* pp. 124-128.

Kurtyka, J. (1999). The science of complexity: A new way to view industry change. *Journal of Retail Banking Services, 21*(2), 51-58.

Levine, R., Locke, C., Searles, D., & Weinberger, D. (2000). *The cluetrain manifesto.* Cambridge, MA: Perseus Books.

Matthews, K. M., White, M. C., & Long, R. G. (1999). Why study the complexity sciences in the social sciences? *Human Relations, 52,* 439-462.

Miller, K. (1999, November). *Teaching computer ethics using the World Wide Web.* Paper presented at the ASEE/IEEE Frontiers in Education Conference, San Juan, Puerto Rico.

Mottl, J. N. (2000, January 3). Learn at a distance. *Information Week,* pp. 75-78.

Pascale, R. T. (1999). Surfing at the edge of chaos. *Sloan Management Review, 40*(3), 83-94.

Reader's Digest Association. (1998). *Merriam-Webster's collegiate dictionary* (Deluxe ed.). Pleasantville, NY: Author.

Schaaf, D. (1999). The view from the middle. *Training, 36*(9), 4-12.

Smith, A. (1981). *An inquiry into the nature and causes of the wealth of nations* (2 vols.; R. Campbell & A. Skinner, Eds.; W. B. Todd, textual ed.). Indianapolis, IN: Liberty Classics.

Weinstock, M. (2000, October). Virtual learning. *Government Executive, 32*(12), 37-44.

Wilson, J. (1999). Winning through chaos: Part 1. *Credit Control, 20*(4), 27-32.

Worley, R. B. (2000, September). The medium is not the message. *Business Communication Quarterly, 63*(3), 93-103.

Chapter 10

Leadership in Online Education

Strategies for Effective Online Administration and Governance

Christi A. Olson

Leading online academic programs is a new experience for most administrators. As with anything new, it is often helpful to step back from the fray, reflect on the structure and dynamics of our challenges and successes, and consider how to move forward with greater insight into our operating assumptions and actions. In the online environment, new questions arise as a result of our collective leadership experiences to date. As leaders, what do we need to focus on in the online environment to achieve our dual objectives of meeting enrollment goals and sustaining high-quality programs? What does leadership look like in an environment where students, faculty, and staff are geographically dispersed? What are the leadership skills, behaviors, and actions required for online leadership, and how are they different from those required for traditional education? What faculty hiring and training practices need to be developed to fit the online adult learning model? How do we do administration and governance online?

Academic and corporate online programs in the United States continue to grow at an accelerated rate. By 2005, 87.1% of all colleges will be offering online distance learning courses, up from 46.6% in 2000 ("Five-Year Forecast," 2001). By 2010, the number of corporate universities is expected to exceed that of traditional universities (Burnside, 2001). Although distance learning institutions have been around for the past 30 years, online education is still in the early stages of its life cycle. Based on the forecasts, we can expect online education to continue to experience high growth as it moves toward mainstream acceptance over the next 5 to 10 years. This growth has created enormous challenges for academic administrators, who are tasked with developing and delivering online programs to keep pace with the market while maintaining a high level of program quality. One of the primary challenges facing administrators is leadership of these online programs. It can be argued that the academic leadership model needs to undergo a fundamental shift if we are to be successful in leading the growth of online education. This chapter describes four core areas of effective online leadership: paying attention to emerging business models, creating a leadership presence online, hiring and training faculty, and attending to governance.

Table 10.1 illustrates the emerging differences between leading in a traditional classroom and leading in an online environment. These differences form the basis of a starting dialogue on leadership in online education and the significant shifts in perspective, behaviors, and actions for administrators and faculty leadership.

Based on my experience in leading online adult graduate and undergraduate programs, I have formulated three principles of online leadership. First, the primary structure of online adult learning is the relationship between and among the faculty and adult learners and their learner colleagues. In traditional education, the classroom has always been the structure that reinforces the expert learner model. In online education, it is dialogue and the relations that form through dialogue that make the online learning model "work" for both faculty and adult learners. Second, the Internet or World Wide Web is an enabling tool and the means to an end. It is not the core value of online learning. The core value (for adult learners) resides in the quality of the learning experience and not in the technology. Third, it is important to remember that change is the primary frame of reference when considering how to lead online programs and, by extension, online organizations. I articulate the application and benefits of these principles as they relate to the four core areas of effective online leadership.

Paying Attention to Emerging Business Models

The transition to the online environment represents a marked departure from the traditional business model and constitutes an enormous difference in development and delivery costs for faculty salaries and online course

TABLE 10.1 Leadership Differences Between Traditional and Online Environments

	Traditional Environment	*Online Environment*
Business model	Higher ratio of full-time faculty Larger course sizes Low training costs and periodic investment Predictability is valued	Higher ratio of adjunct faculty Smaller course sizes Higher training costs and sustained investment Flexibility is valued
Leadership presence	Connecting face-to-face Behaviors are primarily command and control Delegation with some collaboration	Connecting online Behaviors are primarily connection and contribution Collaboration with some delegation
Faculty hiring and training	Training limited to new technologies Hire content experts Standard student and course evaluations with feedback Established benchmark investment for course development and delivery	Training integral aspect of faculty development Hire expertise in online facilitation and mentoring Formal and informal peer-to-peer mentoring Emerging benchmark suggests 1.3 to 1.5 times greater investment for course development and delivery
Governance	Face-to-face meetings augmented by e-mail Decision making and relations driven by tradition Predictable pace and processes that require infrequent intervention	E-mail and online forums augmented by face-to-face meetings Decision making and relations formed by clear roles, responsibilities, and time lines Dynamic pace and processes that require continuous intervention

development. These differences include a generally higher ratio of adjunct faculty, smaller course sizes, higher training costs and sustained investment, and a requirement for greater flexibility in managing salary and development costs. Lorenzo (2001) writes,

> Ongoing issues, such as the time and resources required to develop an online course, the effective use of faculty and support staff once an online course goes live, hidden overhead cost, identification of enrollment break-even points, and more are all important factors to consider when developing cost models for online learning. (p. 1)

As administrators, we are just now beginning to understand the real costs of online learning.

One of the primary levers in any emerging cost model for the development of new online programs and/or the transition from classroom to online courses is the ratio of full-time faculty to adjunct faculty. Many administrators have inherited the traditional academic model that is based on a higher ratio of full-time faculty than adjunct faculty. This has been driven by many factors, including accreditation, the power of faculty senates or other faculty governance structures, historical hiring practices, pedagogical preferences and biases, and increasing (or declining) enrollments due to increased competition. In many online programs, there is a higher ratio of adjunct faculty, a trend that is the reverse of what we find in the classroom model. For example, in the online master's degree programs in organizational management and organization development at the Fielding Graduate Institute in Santa Barbara, California, the current ratio is 2 full-time faculty to 20 to 25 adjunct faculty. At Golden Gate University in San Francisco, the online master's programs in telecommunications management, electronic commerce, and technology management have a similar ratio of 3 full-time faculty to 25 to 35 adjunct faculty.

One implication of this ratio differential is the growing reliance on adjunct faculty for online course development and delivery. This model has its benefits, among them the ability to bring in skilled and known practice professionals or scholar practitioners to teach on an ongoing and ad hoc basis. Although the adjunct faculty salaries for online programs are substantial, they are also perceived as offering more flexibility to administrators. This is because most adjunct faculty are paid on a per course basis, allowing administrators the flexibility to manage course and program enrollments with costs on a per semester or per term basis. This also allows for more flexibility in hiring in terms of both the numbers of adjunct faculty and the diversity of professional practice experience. The other model I have seen in practice is the hiring of core adjunct faculty, who are often considered part-time but are able to take on a substantive teaching load and participate regularly in program and faculty governance. From an administrative perspective, the trade-off to having more adjunct faculty is spending the necessary time and money ensuring that the online facilitation and mentoring skills of adjunct faculty are in line with cultural norms and expectations for the quality of learning. This last issue relates to faculty hiring and training, which is discussed in detail later in this chapter.

In the classroom model, full-time and adjunct faculty develop their own syllabi and have control over both content and delivery. Instructional design expenses in the classroom model are often considered as research and development expenses for new research and teaching technologies. In the online environment, instructional design and course development is an integral cost associated with online program development. Some institutions hire instructional designers to sit with faculty and convert their classroom syllabi and materials into the online, Web-based course format. Other institutions do not hire instructional designers but instead rely on the faculty themselves to develop syllabi. However, these faculty are often assisted in their efforts by consultants and/or staff who provide training on the specifics of online software, course design, and online facilitation and mentoring. Although the evidence is primarily anecdotal, conversations among online educators and faculty suggest that online course development and delivery takes anywhere from 1.3 to 1.5 times more preparation and teaching than does classroom course development. These are important considerations to build into the online business model.

Many administrators are caught in the transition between the traditional classroom business model and the online program business model. One of the ways through this transition is to (a) understand the benefits and constraints of the classroom model (current reality), (b) develop an appropriate business model that fits the mission and goals of an online program (future reality), and (c) be prepared to chart a multiyear path (road map) starting with the future vision of the online environment and working backward toward the current reality over a 1- to 3-year time horizon. One goal of this type of planning activity is to anticipate and manage the mix of classroom and online courses over the longer term so as to offer more online options for students and still manage the fixed costs associated with full-time faculty salaries. For example, in the School of Technology and Industry at Golden Gate, an early analysis of our online course offerings indicated a 25% jump in overall enrollments during the first year that was attributed to offering more courses online. Thereafter, we began to reduce the number of in-person courses offered and increase the number of online course offerings, fine-tuning the ratio of online courses to in-person courses over a 3-year budget cycle. Working back from our future reality, we developed a road map that took into consideration enrollment growth, salaries, and online adjunct faculty training as we worked to achieve the desired mix of online to in-person courses.

For online institutions, the goals are different because these institutions are focused on achieving market growth rather than migrating from the classroom to an online format. One of the challenges in the high growth of online programs is the availability of qualified adjunct faculty and course size or faculty workload. One strategy for managing costs and quality throughout a high-growth phase is to negotiate with adjunct faculty to set up a sliding salary scale based on student enrollments. For example, in our online master's degree programs at Fielding, adjunct faculty receive a standard course stipend for up to 18 students per course. If enrollment for a given course is between 18 and 24 students (we cap all online course enrollments at 24 students per course based on our quality criteria), then adjunct faculty can choose to teach the larger courseload for a higher stipend. This is done to ensure that the course size is manageable for both faculty and adult learners and to accommodate changes in enrollments that can be difficult to predict from semester to semester. In my experience, adjunct faculty more often choose to teach the larger courseload if asked because they feel that they are being compensated and rewarded for their extra efforts.

A primary consideration for administrators is maintaining the balance between program growth and program quality. Defining quality parameters and managing costs in a way that promotes a program's quality goals also enables administrators to develop break-even points that fit the needs of the adult learners and the faculty (Hanna, 2000). Novak (2001) describes the quality measures being instituted at Rutgers University as it builds its distance learning programs. These include standard protocols applied to both classroom and distance learning courses, with academic departments managing the content and teaching quality, a process for course development that takes into consideration compensation, copyright and intellectual ownership, and an organizational reporting structure that combines administrative responsibility under a single office with close ties to the technology infrastructure team. Other institutions prefer to decentralize, placing the responsibility for both curriculum content and delivery under the auspices of the "school" or program department. Both of these models work so long as the institution acknowledges the unique dynamics of online learning and pays appropriate attention to the differences in the quality of online program development, delivery, and evaluation.

Course size is an important factor in program quality and in determining an acceptable break-even point. In the traditional model, enrollments can range from 25 to more than 100 students per course. In an online course, 20 to 25 students is becoming the norm (Olson, 2001). As mentioned previously, in the organizational management program at Fielding, we cap online course enrollments at 24 students because our experience has been that courses with more than 24 students become unmanageable and can negatively affect the quality of learning. Even the amount of online dialogue generated by 24 students quickly becomes overwhelming for both faculty and adult learners. To preserve our commitment to a quality learning experience for both adult learners and faculty, we create two or three sub-teams within each course. Creating sub-teams generates a higher quality learning experience because students have the opportunity for deeper learning (Stevens-Long & Crowell, 2002). As a general rule, adult learners are divided into smaller sub-teams of seven plus or minus two students. This means that a faculty member is actually facilitating up to three different groups within a single course. Having this agreed-on rule for course size greatly enhances the course dialogue and, by definition, the quality of the adult learners' experience, while enabling administrators to manage costs based on the flexibility of two different break-even points.

Having a clear and executable strategy is another factor that shapes the online education business model. The online education industry has seen numerous strategic alliances and partnerships, among them Lucent and

Babson College as well as Motorola Corporate University and Arizona State University (Burnside, 2001; Wendt, 2001). In his discussion of emerging organizational models for traditional universities, Hanna (2000) describes several strategies for growth that can be applied to online program development, among them program diversification and niche programming. Program diversification involves extending classroom courses and program offerings into the online environment. This is a common starting point, especially for larger institutions that want to "test the waters" of the online education market. Niche programming involves identifying a program(s) that "clearly has a comparative advantage over other providers, usually, although not always, on the basis of program quality or the uniqueness of the program and its resources" (Hanna, 2000, p. 102). This strategy is particularly effective for smaller institutions that need to position themselves to compete in an environment where larger partnerships and brokering of online courses through name or brand institutions become more commonplace.

Two other strategic options for online education can be effectively used to achieve program growth. The first is to offer or develop related degree programs, assuming that the related degree programs are within the institution's core competencies. For example, Golden Gate's online master's degree in telecommunications management was a core growth program throughout the 1980s and 1990s, but during the past 3 years the market growth in electronic commerce began to merge with and outpace the market growth in telecommunications. In 2000, Golden Gate offered a second and related online master's degree in electronic commerce. The degree in electronic commerce complemented the existing online degree in telecommunications management and paved the way for the continued growth of both programs. In 1997, Fielding offered an online master's degree in organizational management. Building on its core competencies in organization development at the doctoral level, Fielding offered a second and complementary online master's degree in organization development in 2001.

A second strategic option is to introduce a new program and seek growth in new markets by extending its core competencies into new areas of need. For example, in 1974, Fielding began providing distance education by offering a doctoral degree in clinical psychology. In 1979, the doctoral program in human and organization development was developed and targeted at a different segment of adult learners. What the two programs had in common were Fielding's core competencies in adult learning and the scholar practitioner model. Fielding had successfully leveraged its core competencies into new markets. In 1997, the same model was successfully applied when Fielding introduced its third doctoral program in educational leadership and change.

As a leader, it is important to develop a strategic vision at both the institutional and programmatic levels (Kotter, 1996; Poley, 2000). One of the primary roles of leadership is to create a sensible and appealing picture of the future and a logic for how the vision can be achieved (Kotter, 1996). Asking key questions is a necessary step in developing a robust vision. Articulating a vision and strategy with the adult learner or "customer" at the core ensures that the vision is externally focused rather than internally focused. An externally focused vision is more tightly matched to the needs and fit of a particular adult learner market segment. Consider the following questions in developing a vision:

1. Who is our target audience?
2. What are the primary needs of our adult learners?
3. What are the desired learning outcomes of our adult learners?
4. What are our three to five core competencies?
5. Who are our competitors?
6. What is our uniqueness compared to our competitors?
7. What are our key markets or niche program areas?

Then begin developing the core elements of the strategic vision as a larger executive or leadership team and online as a community. This ensures a measure of input and agreement throughout the process. The next step is to articulate two to three main elements of the strategy and then decide on one or two starting points for how to achieve the vision and strategy. For example, based on the responses and subsequent analysis of the seven questions just listed, an online institution might decide to focus on the graduate education needs of military service members who are stationed overseas. The institution decides to pursue a niche programming strategy because its core competencies are in the area of technology, specifically computer science and software development, competencies that meet the priority learning needs of the military. The initial actions might include contacting key organizations, such as service members opportunity colleges, to pursue partnering opportunities.

As a leader, if the strategy is not clear to you or other members of the executive leadership team, then assume that it is not clear to faculty, students, and staff. It is recommended to review the institutional and programmatic strategies once every 6 months at a minimum. Develop success criteria and feedback processes that alert the organization to both its successes and the necessary course corrections. Pursue alliances and carefully choose partners that fit with your institution's stated strategy and core competencies. Articulate a vision and chart a strategic course of action that everyone in the organization can understand and take appropriate action.

Creating a Leadership Presence Online

It is Monday morning, and you are in your office, reading through e-mail, scanning the online discussion forums, and organizing your day. There are more than 1,200 adult learners residing in four continents across four graduate degree programs who are enrolled in your online institution. Faculty are geographically dispersed throughout North America, Europe, and the Asia Pacific region. The only people in the office besides you are the central staff and some, but not all, members of the leadership team. There is no water cooler, and there are no hallway conversations with students and faculty. There are no face-to-face conversations, visual cues, or immediate real-time feedback with students and faculty. Instead, the community of adult learners and faculty are present in online cafés, discussion forums, courses, and seminars. They are working and learning together asynchronously across time zones, connected to each other through the World Wide Web. Welcome to the world of online leadership!

Creating and establishing a leadership presence online is absolutely critical to institutional and programmatic success. This leadership challenge is enormous because it requires us to reexamine and change the fundamental beliefs and behaviors around leadership that made us successful in the traditional model but do not necessarily translate into effective leadership in the online environment. Effective online leadership implies that the primary work of leadership is connection, specifically developing leadership skills that enable us to connect with others, foster relationships, and get work done by collaborating with others and acknowledging team members' contributions (Olson, 2000). Command, control, and delegation fit the traditional hierarchical models. Connection and collaboration fit the networked non-hierarchical model of online adult learning. Leadership actions that foster stronger connections among employees, customers, and partners are the keys to organizational success where social capital and social connectedness is valued ("2001 HBR List," 2001). This is certainly true for educational institutions. To be effective online leaders, administrators have to give up their command-and-control behaviors and act in ways that enable mutual connection and collaboration and that enhance the value of social capital throughout the organization. This transition can be made easier if we understand and internalize the first principle of online leadership: that the primary structure and behavior of online learning is relational and connective, not hierarchical and controlling.

In 1998, I made the career transition from business and high technology to online graduate education. I was a department chair at Golden Gate for 2 years before moving on to my current role as program director at Fielding. I was 3 months into my leadership role at Fielding when I experienced my first online leadership epiphany. Coming from business and high technology, I had solid leadership experience in both local and virtual teams. When I arrived at Fielding, I was grappling with creating a new vision and making changes in the program's growth strategy and curriculum. At Fielding, the adult learners and faculty are dispersed; there is no local or central team.

So I immediately started connecting online. I began to check in and check out what was going on in the community. What I learned about the community and its members assisted me in ultimately deciding the path the program needed to take to launch our strategic growth initiatives.

The one constant that kept presenting itself to me was the strength of the relationships between the adult learners and faculty. From there, I recognized that the organizing force of the program is actually its relational structure. In essence, the nature of the peer-to-peer learning relationships between the adult learners and faculty are the glue. This insight helped me to come to know that my primary role as a leader is to foster healthy relations among the faculty and adult learners. This realization was reinforced when I read the deeply personal comments made by students and faculty about their professional and personal lives in their online course cafés and followed the online dialogue in their coursework. As a result, I had to change my leadership behaviors and actions to mirror, or at the very least facilitate and support, the relational dialogic dynamics occurring online in the learning community.

Practically, there are many ways to make the shift from command and control to connection and collaboration. Search for ways to establish the online equivalent of MBWA (management by walking around). Be purposeful about the frequency and consistency of communications. Intentionally seek out ways to communicate online. Spend a minimum of 8 hours each week scanning online forums and seeking connection as appropriate. Create a space for students, faculty, and administrators to come together online in conversation. Examples include creating online community or program-specific forums (discussion topics) for informal conversation, such as a director's café or a president's café, to ensure that students and faculty have consistent access and can easily communicate their needs, wants, issues, and challenges. Initiate a collaborative dialogue using community forums or discussion areas when formulating the institution's strategic plan, establishing institutional and/or program priorities, or solving a new or unknown challenge or problem. Periodically conduct focus groups online, and ask for input and feedback on current issues and concerns. Scan the online discussion topics and seminars. Find out what is going on in the learning community and what matters to people. Check in with students, faculty, and staff. Ask how they are and what resources they need to do good work. Let people know you are "around" online and acting as an interested and responsible member of the community. Kouzes and Posner (1996) urge leaders to model the way. In online leadership, modeling the way means facilitating connection-and-contribution over command-and-control behaviors and actions.

Developing trust by communicating consistently with adult learners, faculty, and staff is also critical to effective online leadership. Fisher and Fisher (2001) highlight 11 key skills, or what they call "tips," for developing trust in

virtual or online organizations. The following four tips apply directly to leading online:

1. Communicate openly and frequently, and do not make people at a
   distance guess what you are thinking or feeling. A lack of interaction
   across distance erodes trust. Embed pictures of team members in the
   online technology so that team members can "see" each other and
   you. This also creates a sense of face-to-face familiarity that assists in
   building trust (p. 92).

2. Do what you say you will do, and make your actions visible (p. 93).
   For example, I let people know that I will respond to an issue or a
   question by a certain time and date. I make it known when I do respond and follow up as promised. I also try to communicate openly
   and clearly the assumptions, rationale, and actions taken regarding
   any issue. I respond publicly, online, in the appropriate discussion
   forum or topic area.

3. Set the tone for future interactions (p. 93). In an adult learning environment that has online dialogue as its core, it is especially critical to
   enter into the dialogue in a relational way that is consistent with the
   established communication protocols and practices of the faculty and
   adult learners. Conversely, communicating in a way that is hierarchical and takes advantage of power and title can be ineffective in the
   online environment because it creates distance instead of promoting
   relational growth through trust.

4. Be accessible and responsive (p. 94). I try to encourage adult learners
   and faculty in our online programs to contact me when they need information, have questions, or want to discuss an issue or a problem.
   Although in practice many students and faculty do not contact me on
   a weekly or even a monthly basis, they do tell me that they feel comfortable and secure in knowing that I would be available when a situation presented itself.

A colleague at an online institution recalled an incident in which one of
the academic programs was working through a leadership challenge between
the administration and faculty. Although my colleague was not the direct
leader of the program at the time, she was required to intervene to assist in
resolving the issue. From her perspective, the intervention would have gone
more smoothly if she had taken the time to establish her online presence with
the program's faculty and students. She remarked, "Establishing a sense of
community and connecting in good times is essential so when the bad times
hit, you have a presence." Her story illustrates the importance of remembering to take the time to become known to all members of the community.

Without an established presence online, it can be difficult to generate the mutual trust necessary to resolve conflicts, make program and policy changes, or ask for and receive feedback in a timely and authentic manner.

Hiring and Training Faculty

Faculty are the most precious asset of the institution in online education. They are the people engaged in the online learning dialogue with the adult learners. They have the skills and passion to mentor adult learners online and facilitate the online learning dialogue. The second principle of online learning, that the core value (for the adult learners) resides in the quality of the learning experience and not the technology, applies to the hiring and training of faculty. Because the core value resides in the quality of the learning experience, and the learning experience is defined as mentoring and dialogic learning, the primary criterion for hiring faculty to teach in the online environment is online facilitation and mentoring and not content expertise. This is a radical but necessary departure from the hiring practices of the traditional classroom model.

There are two challenges facing administrators in this area. The first is hiring faculty who have experience in online education yet still require training because they come from the expert learner model rather than the adult learner model. The second is training existing faculty, who are "experts" in the classroom, to be effective in the online environment. In my experience, hiring faculty with strong content expertise can disrupt the quality of the adult learners' experience because the content experts can be perceived as authoritative and insensitive to the desires of the adult learners to be engaged in relational dialogue. Instead of fostering the expert model, the goal is to hire faculty who have experience in teaching both online and in the adult learning model, backed by content and practice expertise that fits with each institution's curriculum and culture. When hiring, each institution needs to consider the balance among previous online experience, the pedagogical model that informs each faculty member's teaching, and a demonstration of professional practice or scholar-practitioner status in her or his academic and professional life.

In the online master's program at Fielding, faculty training is required for each prospective faculty member. Prospective faculty are invited to a 1- or 2-day faculty training, facilitated by experienced online educators. At the training, prospective faculty learn about the cultural norms and expectations of the learning community, become familiar with the online software application, go through a refresher on mentoring and facilitation online, learn the mechanics and processes of online course design, and dialogue with current faculty about best practices. After they complete the training, each prospective faculty member is mentored for one semester by a current faculty member. The prospective faculty shadow their faculty mentors during the semester, observing the facilitation and mentoring techniques of the faculty, understanding the online etiquette or "netiquette" such as giving and receiving feedback, and gaining a sense of pace and rhythm regarding the learner dialogue and coursework.

A prospective faculty member is scheduled to teach her or his first course after completing the initial mentoring process. During the first course, the new faculty member receives a midcourse evaluation from the students, the faculty mentor, and the program director. This feedback is discussed with the prospective faculty member. Both the faculty mentor and program director try to provide "in the moment" feedback to the prospective faculty member so that she or he has the opportunity to make refinements and become proficient as quickly as possible. A final course evaluation is completed, and if that meets the acceptable level of quality, then the prospective faculty member is hired on a contractor basis. The formal and informal peer-to-peer mentoring is one of the keys to success. It encourages faculty to work together in a peer relationship from the start, thus establishing an important cultural norm. Current faculty learn new skills, techniques, and perspectives from new faculty who bring an outside or external perspective to the scholar practitioner community.

With some modifications, this structured training process can be effective when training existing faculty who are classroom experts to be effective mentors and facilitators in the online environment. The larger challenge is shifting the mind-set from content expert to mentor and facilitator. The peer-to-peer mentoring relationship is an extremely important element in a faculty member's ability to make the shift. The administrator also needs to be visible in the training to reinforce training as a priority, set expectations around program quality, establish good relations, and build trust throughout the training process. Most, but not all, faculty are able to make the shift in role and mind-set. If feedback suggests that the existing or prospective faculty member is not able to be effective in the online environment, then it is best to acknowledge this upfront and as early in the process as possible. Not everyone can make the shift at once. Learn to accept this as a potential outcome. Focus energy and resources on those who excel in the online environment and create lower risk opportunities for faculty who need more time to make the transition.

Administrators need to take into account the learning curve when considering how to evaluate and schedule faculty. It usually takes a faculty member at least one to two semesters, or 3 to 6 months, to become as adept at online teaching as she or he is at classroom teaching. When Golden Gate began training faculty to teach online, almost universally, faculty had lower course evaluations in the first semester they taught an online course compared to their classroom course evaluations. This caused much concern and some resistance among the faculty because the course evaluation scores were linked to their portfolio reviews. The faculty eventually won some relaxation in the portfolio review policy so that they were not penalized for the lower course evaluations.

The time investment for online course development and teaching is higher than that for the traditional classroom. Administrators and faculty estimate that it takes from 1.3 to 1.5 times longer for online course development and delivery. I have developed and taught online courses, and the 30% to 50% greater time investment mirrors my experience. Referring back to our earlier discussion on emerging business models, budgeting for new faculty training, new course design, and current faculty retraining for software upgrades or new technologies must be considered a top priority because it is directly linked to the goal of sustaining program quality. Benjamin (2001) encourages administrators to learn the "three R's"—reassurance, respect, and reward—when recruiting and retaining distance learning faculty. Reassurance or encouragement should be given to those faculty who may be suspicious or have a fear of learning new technologies and practices. Respect should be shown for faculty expertise, especially about course content. And rewards, including monetary benefits, should support the challenge that comes from learning something new and being recognized by colleagues and students in the online learning environment. These are good practices for administrators to put into action.

Governance

Leadership in online education is new terrain for many administrators and faculty. As educators and leaders, we are working toward development of a new context for leading and connecting in a relational nonhierarchical structure. We are trying to expand our leadership behaviors and actions by applying them in radically new contexts that require us to unlearn and relearn new rules of leadership. This is now the hard work of leaders in online education. Dialogue is an essential element in the development of a new context (Laurie, 2000). This is certainly true of online governance.

> True dialogue represents a new kind of behavior and way of working for many organizations. Under management as we have known it, leaders emphasize debate followed by consensus. Too often, the consensus was not authentic and the agreement was disingenuous. Dialogue, however, serves to clarify positions or arguments on various sides of the issue. (Laurie, 2000, p. 124)

One strategy for governing online is to revise the rules of traditional governance based on "experts" and "consensus" and to recreate the structure, communication, processes, and technologies so that they are in alignment with the relational adult learning paradigm. As with most deep change work in organizations, this is easier said than done. The second principle of online leadership, that change is the primary frame of reference when considering how to lead online programs and, by extension, online organizations, is a good principle to remember when engaged in online governance.

The primary challenges in online governance that require us to revisit how we govern online are the motivation and commitment of adjunct faculty, decision-making processes, frequency of interaction (both online and in person), and capacity for change throughout the organization, especially among the full-time faculty and existing governance structure. My leadership experience includes working in traditional classroom, distance learning (video), and online education environments with a faculty that is primarily adjunct, anchored by two or three full-time faculty members. Adjunct faculty are hired primarily to develop courses and teach. They are often not asked to be members of the existing governance committee structure and sometimes do not have an influence or a voice in the critical areas of curriculum, academic policies, and research and development. Their influence is more often felt in areas that relate specifically to course design and delivery, such as teaching technologies and technology infrastructure, academic services, research, and grants. Given that many online programs now employ larger numbers of adjuncts, the role of the adjunct faculty member is becoming central to the growth and well-being of the adult learner and faculty member online learning relationship. It is time to consider how to engage adjuncts as contributing members of the academic community.

A common dilemma that administrators face revolves around the issues of participation and compensation. Adjunct faculty contracts do not necessarily include the commitment to participate in the existing governance structure because historically there has not been any service requirement for adjunct faculty. Now that adjunct faculty are becoming integral to the success of online education, the prevailing question is how to be more inclusive of adjunct faculty needs and ask for an expanded and appropriate level of contribution. My own dilemma is rooted in the belief that adjunct faculty need to be compensated in some manner for their service work on committees. I often find it difficult to ask more of adjunct faculty (beyond the teaching role) if I am not able to compensate them due to budget constraints, which is often the case. Like many administrators, I find myself operating in the middle ground, halfway between the current reality (no budget funds and low adjunct faculty involvement in governance) and future vision (budget line item for governance stipends and increasing levels of adjunct faculty involvement in governance). Full-time faculty resistance to adjunct faculty involvement in issues of power, played out in the appointment of committee chairs or in determining who has voting rights and entitlement, exacerbates the issues of participation and compensation. The good news is that this resistance is much less evident at the collegial level, where full-time and adjunct faculty find themselves in agreement on common goals or concerns around research, quality of learning and teaching, and faculty development.

There are some key strategies for increasing adjunct faculty involvement in the governance structure:

1. Restructure adjunct faculty contracts to include service participation, either by time (e.g., the number of hours or days) or on a project basis (e.g., participation in a curriculum revision project). It is important to negotiate a starting and ending date and to delineate major milestones so that there is a shared understanding among the other faculty and administrators regarding the time line and workload.

2. Find out which members of the adjunct faculty want to become more involved in governance. Work with adjunct faculty who possess the desire and motivation to make a service contribution to the community. For example, many adjunct faculty consider themselves free agents and have multiple affiliations with different educational institutions. Their interest and commitment focuses on teaching only. Do not expect everyone to want to become involved in governance. Understand the level and type of contribution that each adjunct faculty member wants to make to the online learning community.

3. Communicate the administrative needs and specify the areas where adjunct faculty can become involved in the governance structure. Have a plan for what work needs to be done and the priorities. If the program needs to conduct a curriculum revision, then ask adjunct faculty to get involved and even lead the effort. Share the workload and consider how each faculty member can make the appropriate contribution. Create opportunities for full-time and adjunct faculty to work together online.

Because faculty are geographically dispersed, an important consideration for administrators is developing a process for decision making and getting work done online. It is important to establish what and how much work gets done online and face-to-face. In the online master's program at Fielding, we conduct most of our work online through a faculty forum using discussion topics. Discussion topics range from budget updates and policy revisions, to development of new courses and curriculum, to development of student guidelines for the master's project completion. When we decided to create a new vision for the master's program, one of the adjunct faculty members hosted online cafés in both the faculty forum and the community hall so that both students and faculty could participate. Much of the early draft work of the curriculum, for example, can be created by the program director or department chair with another administrator or key faculty member. It generally works better for faculty or team members to have a draft document or policy to respond to online. It can be time-consuming and confusing to co-create a full curriculum revision (e.g., through an online committee of 10 people) without some structure or starting point. As noted previously, clearly stating assumptions, goals, desired outcomes, processes, success criteria, and so forth greatly enhances team effectiveness.

The metaphor of a self-directed team is useful in online governance (Fisher, 2000). Virtually any discussion or governance that is conducted in face-to-face meetings can be conducted online. Here are six simple rules for governing online:

1. Be clear about the decision-making process. Ask yourself how decisions get made in the program or school. Do the administrator and full-time faculty have voting power and the adjunct faculty have input only? Are all decisions made by consensus? Does the administrator make the decision herself or himself with faculty input? Openly discussing how decisions are made, as well as determining what type of decision-making process is appropriate for different types of decisions, reduces confusion and respects team members' time and energy. They are more likely to engage online and participate on a consistent basis if the experience is a successful one.

2. Identify the roles, contribution, and responsibilities of each team member. Do this at the beginning of a project or work effort. Have each faculty member describe her or his role and expected contribution. Or if you ask a faculty member to participate, be sure that the faculty member understands what you expect her or his role to be and the contribution that she or he is being asked to make as a team member. Draw on the collective roles and contributions that have been shared, and engage in a team discussion of project or committee responsibilities.

3. Bound the work with specific dates, times, and major milestones or deliverables. Much, if not all, of the work will be conducted asynchronously through threaded discussion. Negotiate enough time for committee members to both post their individual work online and provide feedback on committee team members' work. Create success criteria at the start of each project or work segment. Break project or committee work into phases or chunks so that the team has near-term goals that are achievable given other committee assignments, teaching load, and so forth. Track back to the initial success criteria at the conclusion of each phase to make sure that the team has met its goals. Celebrate successes whenever possible.

4. Augment the online governance work with planned face-to-face conference sessions. Be purposeful about what work can get done online and what work can best be conducted face-to-face. Create the time and place for all faculty to come together face-to-face at least once a year. For example, curriculum revisions can be initiated and segments

of work completed online because responsibilities and workload can be divided up among individual team members. Integrating the curriculum, however, can be challenging because faculty need to establish a shared mental model for how the curriculum is articulated in the online courses or seminars. Coming together to do curriculum integration work is a good activity for a face-to-face conference session.

5. Online governance processes require continuous intervention because they are dynamic and chaotic. Administrators can create what Abrahamson (2000) terms "dynamic stability" by interspersing major change initiatives among paced periods of smaller organic change. Continuous intervention enables administrators to get a sense of the pace of the work. Are teams moving too fast and failing to take enough time for dialogue around key issues? Are teams resisting change and not moving fast enough on key issues? Is the work of the team focused on the top priorities of the institution? These are the areas to consider when deciding whether and how to make interventions.

6. Keep the energy of the dialogue going, and avoid dialogue killers (Charan, 2001). Dialogue killers include dangling dialogue (ending a meeting or discussion without closure), information clogs (failing to get the right information to team members or getting it to them after a decision has been made), piecemeal perspectives (sticking to narrow views and self-interests rather than encouraging many views and perspectives), and free-for-all (failing to direct the flow and allowing negative behaviors to dampen the energy of the group or divide the group). The presence of these patterns or dynamics may also require intervention from a leader if the group members are unable to sort it out themselves.

Governing online represents a major change in how an institution governs itself. It takes time for the organization to transition to effective online governance. Even educational institutions that are exclusively online face challenges because people come into the system with the behaviors and actions learned in the traditional governance model. View the opportunity to establish and sustain online governance structures and processes as a core leadership initiative.

Conclusion

As educators, administrators, and leaders, we have a responsibility to reflect on our own experiences, learn from each other, and collectively generate knowledge that informs, and in some instances reforms, our behaviors and actions as we lead our online institutions into the 21st century. There are clear differences between leadership in traditional and online environments. The challenge of leadership brought forth in this dialogue is simple: Are we up to the task of changing ourselves as we encourage change within our organizations? We know we are doing the real work of online leadership when we value connection and contribution over command and control, honor the contributions of community members, and collaborate in ways that create dynamic stability and challenge our organizations to do good work.

References

Abrahamson, E. (2000, July-August). Change without pain. *Harvard Business Review,* pp. 75-79.

Benjamin, J. (2001, March 1). To recruit and retain distance learning faculty, learn the three R's. *Distance Education Report,* pp. 1-2.

Burnside, R. (2001, May). *Beauty and the beast: Making learning productive.* Paper presented at the College Board Higher Education Conference on Corporate/College Partnerships, Phoenix, AZ.

Charan, R. (2001, April). Conquering a culture of indecision. *Harvard Business Review,* pp. 74-82.

Fisher, K. (2000). *Leading self-directed work teams.* New York: McGraw-Hill.

Fisher, K., & Fisher, M. D. (2001). *The distance manager.* New York: McGraw-Hill.

The five-year forecast. (2001, March 26). *The Industry Standard,* pp. 82-83.

Hanna, D. (2000). Emerging organizational models: The extended traditional university. In D. E. Hanna & Associates (Eds.), *Higher education in an era of digital competition* (pp. 93-116). Madison, WI: Atwood.

Kotter, J. (1996). *Leading change.* Boston: Harvard Business School Press.

Kouzes, J., & Posner, B. (1996). *The leadership challenge* (2nd ed.). San Francisco: Jossey-Bass.

Laurie, D. (2000). *The real work of leaders.* Cambridge, MA: Perseus Books.

Lorenzo, G. (2001, April). How much? Cost models for online education. *Distance Education Report,* p. 1.

Novak, R. (2001, Spring). Quality at the heart of distance learning. *CAEL Forum and News,* pp. 12-14.

Olson, C. (2000). Leadership.com: Leadership practices in the new economy. *Business, Education, and Technology Journal, 2*(2), 46-50.

Olson, C. (2001, April). *Collaborative online learning: Effective technologies for adult learners.* Paper presented at the Spring Syllabus Conference, Cincinnati, OH.

Poley, J. (2000). Leadership in the age of knowledge. In D. E. Hanna & Associates (Eds.), *Higher education in an era of digital competition* (pp. 165-183). Madison, WI: Atwood.

Stevens-Long, J., & Crowell, C. (2002). The design and delivery of interactive online graduate education. In K. Rudestam & J. Schoenholtz-Read (Eds.), *Handbook of online learning: Innovations in higher education and corporate training.* Thousand Oaks, CA: Sage.

The 2001 HBR list: Breakthrough ideas for today's business agenda. (2001, April). *Harvard Business Review,* pp. 123-128.

Wendt, D. (2001, May). *Industry/higher education collaborations: Changing the way the workforce is developed.* Paper presented at the College Board Higher Education Conference on Corporate/College Partnerships, Phoenix, AZ.

Chapter 11

Breaking Through
Zero-Sum Academics

Two Students' Perspectives on Computer-Mediated Learning Environments

Shelley Hamilton
and Joel Zimmerman

The interconnection of hundreds of millions of people via the World Wide Web doesn't represent just another sales channel (e-commerce) or merely another opportunity to do the same work [better, cheaper, or] faster. Rather, it offers the potential to reframe some fundamental questions about business.

—Mieszkowski (2000, p. 46), *Fast Company*

The elements of change that are driving these momentous shifts [in business] are based on the fundamental dimensions of the universe itself: time, space, and mass. Since the economy and your business are part of the universe, time, space, and mass are the fundamental dimensions of them as well. Until recently, this notion was too abstract to be very useful. Now, we are realizing the extraordinary power this insight has for the business world.

—Davis and Meyer (1998), *Blur*

These insights not only pertain to business in the new economy but also offer the potential to reframe some fundamental questions about education.

Unlike traditional educational environments, space, time, and matter do not limit computer-mediated learning (CML) environments. As Davis and Meyer (1998, p. 6) go on to explain in *Blur,* the new economy is fundamentally different because of the compression of time, the shrinking of space, and the dematerialization of goods into services. Whereas in business the focus may be on the compression of time, space, and matter, in education the focus is on the expression of time, space, and what really matters.

Computer-mediated learning environments distort traditional academic parameters. Time, space, and the core processes of learning are organized quite differently in CML environments. Rather than simply speed up the degree-granting process, provide instantaneous global video lectures, and replace paper tests with digital multiple-choice forms, CML environments make possible whole new ways of learning. They create global learning communities of student and professor practitioners. They connect people across cultures, learning styles, and industries, and they enable global conversations about issues and ideas that matter. They have the extraordinary power to stitch together practical experience, academic theory, personal reflection, and deep emotion.

This chapter is based on the experience of two students who completed the Fielding Graduate Institute's online master's program in organizational design and effectiveness, currently called organizational management (OM). For easier communications, we blend our experiences into a single voice in this chapter using a collective first-person narrative (i.e., using the term "I" or "my" to refer to our common program experience and using the term "we" or "our" to refer to the collective experience of Fielding students as a whole).

We apply our experience as students to explain how CML environments can break through the standard zero-sum scarcity mentality of most academic institutions. When time, space, and core learning processes (what matters) are organized differently, unique opportunities and learning strategies emerge. These opportunities and strategies include (a) the influence of the medium on the content of messages, (b) the integration of professional or business knowledge with academic theory, and (c) the collaborative learning relationships that develop a community of distributed intelligence. Ultimately, these unique opportunities and strategies, embedded and enabled by a networked learning environment, break the traditional zero-sum academic experience.

The Fielding Online Experience

School on the Screen

Most people think of an online degree program as an automated correspondence experience, an independent endeavor wrapped in hazy images of lonely late nights staring off into the trance of a blinking cursor. Or if they have some cyberspace experience, they might jazz up the scenario with some chat room or videoconferencing lectures.

My experience, however, was an engaging and unique mix of a familiar classroom format, complete with classmates and a professor, an interactive professional workshop or seminar, and a Ph.D.-level independent study program. The best way I have found to explain my experience is by beginning with a story:

> Imagine that you go to a university where all of the buildings are empty—no desks, tables, or chairs, just big bulletin boards all over each room. Now imagine that you can go to school anytime you want. The campus is constantly filled with students, teachers, and administrators coming and going at all hours of the day and night. Each person, however, is physically invisible to the others. The only way you can interact with each other is by posting your ideas, comments, and responses to other postings on the bulletin boards.
>
> Each classroom has many different-sized bulletin boards and some extra space for other boards to be added by both the professors and the students. Before the start of a course, the professor does two things. She posts a syllabus and puts topic titles on the top of each board, along with a description of how the space is going to be used. This description may take the form of formal assignments, a creative narrative about being in a café in Santa Fe (thereby creating a virtual coffeehouse), a provocative case study to spark discussion, or an open area for process issues.
>
> Then class begins. As in any academic institution, the experience includes deadlines for coursework, a specific group of students connected to a particular professor, performance expectations connected to grades, discussions, formal papers, required and suggested readings, and research.

And that is about where the comparison ends. When class begins, the experience is totally unique.

So imagine that instead of turning in a paper just to your professor, you post it on a bulletin board for the whole class to read. In fact, the whole class is required to read it and to give you feedback. Also imagine that instead of filing away your paper once you have received feedback, or forgetting about a discussion you had in class 2 weeks ago, everything is captured in writing and stays up in full view throughout the course. Everybody "hears" everything and is expected not only to listen but also to respond. Your professor is a consummate practicing professional in her field and a master of facilitation. She participates in discussions, suggests additional sources of information, provides formal feedback on papers, and keeps the course moving at a steady pace with about the same momentum as you would expect in a professional work environment. Now add to this the fact that your classmates are not a random bunch of schoolkids but instead chief executive officers, organizational consultants for major corporations, union organizers, human resource professionals, and high-tech gurus.

At about this point in the story, my listener often makes a comment like this: "Isn't it strange that you've never met these people before?" So I have to back up and explain our orientation and planning session and biannual gatherings.

When I started at Fielding, I went to Santa Fe, New Mexico. For 3 days, students, teachers, and administrators drenched themselves in face-to-face interactions. Our sessions covered everything from computer troubleshooting, to Internet access and communication tools, to course content, to academic administration in an online environment. Because Fielding envisions its students as educational partners with the professors rather than as subordinates to them, our sessions were more a co-creative process than a "how to" lecture series.

Throughout the orientation, we attended to each other with an intense mixture of curiosity and anxiety. We knew that this would be our only in-person contact for half a year or more. We knew that our success depended on creating a community of learners. We struggled to connect faces with names, learn each other's voices (both literally and figuratively), make explicit our individual communication styles and expectations, and forge a group consensus on norms for our later online communication and behavior.

At one point in our orientation session, while discussing interpersonal communication and group norms, our conversation reached a rather tense intersection. Knowing how difficult it is to convey and receive emotional information online, we could not agree on a group protocol for giving and receiving critical feedback. The conversation went something like this:

> **Ann:** "Since we are here to engage in a rigorous academic experience, I would assume that all postings are open to critical feedback."
>
> **Arneau:** "But what about general conversation and dialogue? Isn't that different from formal papers? I don't want to feel like I have to worry about every little thing I put online."
>
> **Martha:** "Yeah, I would prefer to have people wait for me to ask for their opinion."
>
> **Ann:** "But does that mean that if I always want people to give me feedback, I have to go through the trouble of asking for it in every posting?"
>
> **Arneau:** "What if we leave it up to the professor?"
>
> **Barclay** (the professor): "There are certainly elements of the curriculum where you will be expected to respond to everyone's posting with a critical eye, but it's really up to the group for a majority of the time as to how you want to engage with each other."

What we finally agreed on was to be conscious of the fact that we all had different levels of comfort with giving and receiving critical feedback. We could expect one another to continue to be open, honest, and direct about our learning needs and to always assume that the sender of feedback had only the best intentions in mind—in other words, "When in doubt, check it out." Never sit and stew over unclear interpretations in an online environment.

When orientation was over and the online experience began, the effect was overwhelming. It was at the same time impossibly demanding and enormously fulfilling. People in our stage of life, in our types of jobs, never have enough time just for the normal demands of life. "What was I thinking about?" Times were stolen from my normal schedule—early morning, late at night, lunch hours at the office, weekend hours between doing the laundry and honoring our social obligations. Thank goodness the asynchronous aspect of the online environment lent itself to this kind of crazy schedule.

The subject matter was terribly engaging; it related to work I had done years before and issues I was facing right now. Materials in the text alternately amazed me with their insights and relevance or frustrated me with their theoretical abstraction and naïveté. The online community began to build, along with its own set of emotional highs and lows. "What a brilliant paper she posted; how can I possibly write anything like that?" "What a dolt he is; how am I supposed to team with him on this assignment?"

Wisely, the Fielding professors understood and anticipated the potential for isolation and despair in the online environment. Nearly every course included one or more posting areas that appealed to the personal side of the student experience. Immediately, people began posting messages in the virtual coffeehouse—words of personal encouragement; happy birthday greetings; messages about coping with young children, confused spouses, and difficult bosses.

Deadlines came. Somehow the papers were posted, almost on time. I never had time to do the one more draft each paper really needed. I reacted to my classmates. My mind was always racing.

> Need to be thoughtful now; remember that we're online, and all those face-to-face nonverbal communication tools aren't there to help out. Oh my God, here come all their reactions to my posting! Good point. Good grief; did I really say that in my paper? Let me go back and read what I said. No, I didn't say that, but I see now how it could have been misinterpreted. I hope I took enough time digesting her paper before I reacted. Better remember that for my next paper, which is due—yikes—in 3 days!

I suddenly felt the need to vent a short posting to the coffeehouse.

And suddenly the first semester was over. I was amazed at how fast the weeks flew by. I scanned the Felix software and was amazed again—by the literally hundreds of pages of text that our learning community had generated. How in the world did we do that? Some powerful stuff in there, too. Information I was already applying in my workplace. Phew! One semester down and four to go.

A Specific Experience

In February 1998, we had just begun posting our first assignments in a course on conflict, culture, and complexity. We all were prepared for something having to do with conflict resolution, but no one (including the professor, I think) really understood how we were going to coalesce the three "C" words into a single experience that semester. As fate would have it, just as we were starting our course interactions, President Bill Clinton and Iraq's leader, Saddam Hussein, also began a series of tension-filled interactions. Conflict, culture, and complexity were no longer abstract theoretical ideas. They were coming to us in real time via the world's news media.

The subsequent events of that semester are testimony to the pedagogical strengths of Fielding's online learning technique. The unfolding world events folded seamlessly into the already planned course ingredients and enhanced them enormously. The unique nature of our staff and student body led to a learning experience that could not have worked the same way, or as well, in any other medium.

As tensions mounted early in the crisis, the professor opened a new topic area on the online posting environment titled "War in the Middle East." She didn't say anything like "These events are clearly related to the topics of this course—let's tie them together." She didn't need to. Instead, she simply spoke as a concerned citizen of the world with an educated opinion and a personal emotional reaction to what was happening. Here are some excerpts from her posting:

> I just felt the need to say that I am so sad and scared about the possibility of war. . . . I feel like I did in the fifth grade when I was so frightened to get under my desk in the nuclear war drills. I think that while there is enormous complexity to these events, we have to find a better way. . . . Perhaps if we were to ask ourselves, as Westerners, some opening questions, perhaps if the UN [United Nations] could itself function like a reflecting team—I know it sounds silly, but I do so believe that these technologies for evolving meaning would make a difference.

This posting turned out to be the beginning of a 5-week, full-class interaction that supplemented, yet in some ways focused and defined, the course. Some of this could have happened in a traditional classroom, but only through this unique online format could this experience unfold the way it did.

I was the first to respond to the professor's opener with a posting titled "Is an Alternative to War Possible With Saddam?" Although I fancy myself a moderate, I believed that I was like most of the rest of the country in being upset with Iraq's leader. Although my posting was written with even-handed thoughtfulness and care (in my opinion, of course), the underlying attitudes were impossible to miss: "What nerve this man had to flaunt the UN weapons inspectors and question America's leadership position in promoting world peace. Of course, our position in this conflict was the 'right' one."

Typical of Fielding classes, this one had about eight students. One was in France, and the others were scattered around the United States. We all were mid-career adults, professional people, and verbally adroit. We were equipped with real-world experiences from a variety of entrepreneurial, industrial, and governmental backgrounds. Scattered across six or more time zones, and representing a world of different perspectives, we generated a rich collage of opinions, hypotheses, and theories that tied the course directly into the events of the world around us. My thoughtful, careful perspective on Iraq, it turned out, was not the same as everyone else's.

As a student in a traditional college previously, I recall that an interesting class event would happen when the professor occasionally yielded the floor. About 25 students would then engage in discussion in our small classroom nestled away among the halls of ivy. We were homogeneous in background— not only all Americans but also mostly from the same geographic area, economic stratum, and religious sector. A discussion lasted 50 minutes and involved only those students who were assertive and quick-minded enough to grab the floor. The depth of our remarks was limited by the need to analyze and respond immediately to whatever had been said by the previous student. A train of thought was terminated by the end of a classroom period and seldom pursued in subsequent sessions.

As an online distance learner, I found myself explaining an American's perspective on Hussein to a Frenchman and learning much from his perspective on Clinton. All of the students in the course posted thoughtful contributions to the extent they desired, reflecting their unique insights into the academic and real-world topics. Each person's contribution was read by everyone else. Postings met with responses, counterresponses, and new postings taking off on other interesting tangents. With a discussion extending over 5 weeks, and with the course's "real work" simultaneously educating us about various theories on conflict, culture, and complexity, we analyzed an important real-world example of these concepts in great depth, tested new ways of seeing the world's problems, and allowed our comprehension of these ideas to blossom and grow.

The "real life" conversation was unplanned. It was in addition to the prepared syllabus of topics and papers. But it was not atypical of a Fielding course. For me, this was the quintessential Fielding experience. It was simply a cut above anything I had experienced, or could have experienced, in a traditional on-campus setting.

Unique Learning Opportunities and Strategies in a Computer-Mediated Learning Environment

In the formative days of computer automation, people assumed that technology would be used to speed up their existing business procedures. As the technology has moved from mainframes, to desktops, to the Internet, we have made a quantum leap in our understanding of the power of computers. We now know that the real strategic advantage of Internet-based computing is not the ability to do old things faster; it is the ability to do business in new ways that were never before possible.

Our online experience suggests that this lesson can also be applied to pedagogy and academic experiences. A CML environment, such as Fielding's OM program, is not patterned after traditional classroom paradigms or even distance learning programs; rather, it is unique to its medium. Why simply speed up a correspondence degree with e-mail when you can "think different" in an interactive online program? If academic institutions simply apply the Internet to teach traditional courses in traditional ways, then they are not optimizing the strengths of the new medium. The key is to recognize the unique characteristics of the instructional medium and design courses to take maximum advantage of these unique elements.

Likewise, a successful student in a CML environment must also learn how to cope and succeed in the new medium. The student must learn not only the required subject materials but also how to cope skillfully with the novel apparatus of learning. Traditional classroom behavior calls for excellent test-taking skills, memorization, effective and efficient note taking, and a penchant for making persuasive contributions in class discussions. The online student's success, however, depends on an ability to (a) contribute to the sustained evolution of the learning community, (b) provide critical yet supportive feedback to others, (c) demonstrate an understanding of the subject matter, and (d) apply concepts to real-world situations.

Three areas stand out that affect learning strategies in a CML environment. First, the unique medium has a distinct effect on the way students can both learn new ideas and reflect on the way their learning is taking place. Second, students have access to an expanded pool of learning resources that integrate applied professional knowledge with personal real-time experiences. Finally, students engage in a collaborative learning forum in which they and their professors move beyond traditional pedagogical roles to become complementary participants in the creation of a network of distributed intelligence. Knowledge is not simply transferred; it is created and cooperatively transformed.

These unique strategies are enabled by the novel expression of time, space, and what matters (core learning processes) in a CML environment. In the following three sections, we discuss the effects that these fundamental elements play in creating the unique learning opportunities and strategies mentioned heretofore. Finally, we offer some insights in to how these strategies break through the traditional zero-sum mentality of most academic institutions.

Time

Net time, bandwidth, live videoconferencing, chat rooms, streaming audio and video, instant messaging, and JavaScript animation all are terms that focus on the capability of the Internet to push the time envelope closer and closer to "going live" in cyberspace. The goal seems to be replicating the in-person experience via the computer. The reality is that we are not there yet and, in fact, might not want to go there at all. The goal is thoughtful, critical, and sensitive communication on a global scale. Rather than replace face-to-face interaction, the Internet offers a complement to personal encounters—a forum in which to stay virtually connected during the in-between time spaces.

The power of the Internet to connect us on a worldwide scale, therefore, may not be in its real-time bandwidth or super megahertz power; rather, it might be in its ability to create quiet, intimate, reflective space for thoughtful discussion on important and heartfelt issues. The technology creates this space through its ability to present asynchronous, multi-threaded bulletin board areas for people to come and go at their own pace. The medium supports iterative exchanges of information and opinions over an extended time period, so ideas are not merely "hatched" and delivered but rather allowed to evolve and be refined in a manner that makes information more convincing, narrative deliveries richer in detail, and learning more thorough.

These asynchronous regions provide timeless islands of information, knowledge, and experience that eclipse our real-life sense of past and future and, instead, provide us with a continuous present. Traditional time-based communication limitations—trying to remember what someone said a few minutes ago, keeping the thread of the conversation in mind while also listening to the current speaker, taking notes while listening to the ongoing lecture, and competing for speaking time—all disappear in an asynchronous CML environment. This "time-warped" medium directly contributes to several unique learning strategies.

Medium and Message

The asynchronous nature of the medium creates an excellent forum for thoughtful, extended, reflective dialogue. As described in an earlier section, you can literally go back and see what has been said in the past. The medium also requires you to take a thoughtful pause before responding to another person's ideas. It lets you reread, redo, restate, and reevaluate past comments on a continual basis as the conversation continues to evolve. Not only can you reflect on other people's postings before responding, but you can look back at your own words and understand them through the eyes of another person based on his or her responses to you and the group's combined conversation flow. The self-paced, reflective nature of the CML environment elicits academic content that is much more thoughtful, personal, in-depth, and logically constructed. In our experience, the quality of the interaction is greatly enhanced by the asynchronous medium.

The persistent nature of the medium (i.e., the postings remain online throughout the course) and the threaded nature of the bulletin board forums (i.e., new simultaneous topic areas are created by both students and professors as the conversation branches off in different directions) create a unique conversational map. This visual dialogue compass gives students new context information that is almost never found in a traditional classroom setting. The addition of this meta-information gives students in a CML environment the ability to reflect not only on the content of the information exchanged but also on the way it is being learned. Professors can intentionally integrate this meta-learning capacity into the design of the course. So, for example, in our course on conflict, culture, and complexity, we not only learned about conflict resolution theory but also had the tools to reflect on how our in-class conflict had evolved and had the opportunity to then go back and design an intervention strategy using our own conflict experience as a case example. We learned how to learn.

The final product of asynchronous conversation is qualitatively different. In normal conversation, speakers exchange information rapidly and immediately; so spoken discourse tends to be shallow. People cannot do research and analysis as they carry on a conversation. On the other hand, written materials, such as books and articles, tend to be more substantive, but they lack the give-and-take elements of discourse. Using asynchronous communications, you get the best of both; in essence, you get articles talking to articles. The conversations are interactive and responsive. Yet they contain the depths of research, analysis, and logical development previously found only in written monologues.

Professional Academics

The asynchronous nature of the CML environment also creates "any-time" access to the learning community. This enables students to access the "classroom" at any time of day or night and to integrate learning into various elements of their daily schedules—before work, during a lunch break, or after the kids go to bed. Because of this time-based flexibility, a CML environment is more attractive to working professional learners than to traditional full-time students.

In turn, these student-practitioners are able to bring real-time, business-related, case study issues into the academic discussion. This unique opportunity to expand academic resources beyond theory and library research can be, as in the case of the OM program, intentionally designed into the curriculum. Not to do so would completely miss this powerful learning opportunity afforded by the unique CML environment medium.

Ironically, as outlined previously, it is exactly the asynchronous nature of the medium that opens this possibility for real-life, real-time, business-related case studies—creating a just-in-time learning environment. From an organizational perspective, this just-in-time learning environment provides employees attending a CML environment program with access to current and relevant professional issues and solutions from other organizations. Cross-industry and cross-company idea sharing in a safe nondisclosure environment is a valuable business asset opportunity for both the individual professional and his or her company.

Unique Student-Professor Roles

In a class that is not constrained by time, the professor does not need to focus on managing class time and controlling which students get opportunities to share their ideas. Students must still post papers within deadlines and will not be successful if they enter conversations late, after the community has turned its attention to other topics. However, beyond setting a course's broad time line syllabus, the professor usually allows class dialogue to self-evolve. This removes the traditional student-professor hierarchical boundary based on the professor's singular control of a limited resource—time. With this out of the way, the student-professor relationship can be established on the basis of other, more substantive factors, such as the way the professor facilitates the unfolding of the dialogue, the framing of the course content, and the responsiveness and poignancy of interactions.

The timelessness of asynchronous communication also changes the relationships among the students themselves. In a traditional classroom period of 1 hour, every minute that another student speaks is a minute less of opportunity for me. Unlike a traditional classroom, time in the online community is theoretically limitless; it is not a zero-sum game. Therefore, communication is not controlled by dominant and assertive personalities. Once the competition for class time is removed, students also relate to each other based on more substantive factors, such as the quality of the ideas they share, the feedback they give to others, and their ability to combine academically rigorous theory with real-life practicality.

Finally, the "anytime" access of CML environments allows students to read and reply at their own pace. It is, therefore, a medium that is quite sensitive to different learning and communication styles. Even the quietest, most methodical person has enough time to gather his or her ideas and contribute to the discussion. Fast, flamboyant talkers learn to transform hand gestures and tone of voice into descriptive narratives and pithy bullet points.

The lack of a student-professor hierarchy and the removal of class time competition, combined with an environment that allows for diverse communication styles, create a collaborative learning environment. The pace and timing of the online dialogue organically unfolds on the basis of topics, themes, and qualities of postings and replies rather than from control-based hierarchy or fear-based competition.

Space

Global e-commerce, researching the Library of Congress from Los Angeles, working in virtual teams, accessing abstracts from any number of universities around the world, reading the Hong Kong business news from Sweden, and outsourcing on an international scale all point to how the Internet breaks down traditional geographic boundaries. How long it takes to travel someplace in cyberspace depends only on your connection speed and not on mileage.

The power of this distance-free access is not in increasing our productivity through faster information or in lowering business costs by hiring cheap international labor but rather in connecting us on a global scale in ways never thought possible in the past. This is what Davis and Meyer (1998) call "connectivity." From an academic standpoint, space—the distance between a student and the classroom, between two students, or between a student and a research source—ceases to be an obstacle to learning. In fact, new connectivity options provide the CML environment student with several unique learning opportunities.

Students can now interact with other students, professors, and learning resources on a global scale—an impossibility in a traditional classroom setting. This gives concrete experiential relevance to learning about international organizational issues and cross-cultural communication theory. As mentioned earlier, our courses were populated by students and faculty from nearly every continent.

Another important feature of CML environments for businesspeople who travel is that "anywhere" access allows them to "go to school" literally anywhere—from an airport waiting area, to a hotel in Singapore, to a remote partner office in the jungles of Peru. The lack of distance to a seemingly endless supply of up-to-date Internet-based resources also gives the student-practitioner access to current business news and issues.

The element of connectivity creates a unique many-to-many communication network as opposed to the traditional one-to-many (the professor to the students) relationship. The professor is no longer the sole content expert. The role shifts to framing the learning space rather than controlling access to information.

Medium and Message

As mentioned earlier, in the course in conflict, culture, and complexity, we not only looked at how cross-cultural communication issues affect conflict in a global business arena, but we also experienced these issues by communicating with other students from around the world on a heated conflict issue—the war in Iraq. This course was not an exception in the Fielding program; it is normal for these courses to expand their content into worldwide current events: business, social, and political. The online medium was expertly and consciously used to complement the course content addressing global business and cross-cultural issues.

Because the CML environment is location independent, it can incorporate students, professors, and administrators from around the world. The student body's cultural heterogeneity provides a broad-based natural laboratory of empirical global events that students can exchange to contribute to each other's mastery of the academic concepts. An online program that does not intentionally incorporate this learning strategy into the design of the program misses a great opportunity to truly create a global classroom.

Ironically, linking culturally diverse people from around the world to focus on common interests and shared academic goals results in an intimate atmosphere. On traditional campuses, international students tend to cluster with students from their own countries. The binding force is the common culture. In the CML environment, the binding force is not geographically determined but rather conceptually and intellectually determined. An academic community evolves around shared ideas and knowledge. Cultural influences and perspective are still expressed, but rather than being relegated to ad hoc social clusters, they are embraced and brought forward into the intellectual dialogue.

In this regard, the virtual medium's loss of face-to-face factors becomes a strong benefit rather than a disadvantage. When people are together physically, the initial forces that bring them together into cliques and subgroups are appearances (e.g., similar clothing or skin color) and language characteristics. When people interact via the Internet, appearances are irrelevant and the language is common. People form virtual clusters based on similarities in the way they perceive the subject matter, common problems or concerns, preferences for certain theoretical schools of thought, and so forth. The effects of race, sex, and nationality are minimized or eliminated.

In the future, as hardware, software, and networks continue to evolve, the space-spanning aspects of the media will enhance the substance of the messages even further. The mechanism for this is the hyperlink, which is practically without counterpart in the physical world of traditional academics. Within an Internet document, hyperlinks are used to bring multisourced information into the primary text or to give the reader a path to alternative media. In essence, this eliminates the *physical* separation of material messages that are *logically* connected. In addition to text, hyperlinked messages may be pictures, sound files, animations, or video clips. External links can refer students to other information-rich Internet sites, including personal Web pages, specialized bibliographies, and professional specialists.

Professional Academics

Coupled with "anytime" access, "anywhere" connectivity makes CML environments that much more attractive to working professionals. Many students submit papers from hotels during international business trips, from their offices, or from relatives' houses during family vacations. Rather than segregate life into traditional compartments—work, family, and school or theory, business strategy, and practice—CML environments allow students to integrate these elements into a seamless feedback loop between ideas and experience.

Students who present a case scenario at the beginning of a class can periodically post information about how they have applied the concepts and strategies discussed in class to the original scenario. By integrating academic theory with life experiences, both elements are enriched. Students anchor their learning at a deeper level than they do in traditional classroom learning. Organizational decisions and actions are better supported by relevant theoretical models and intellectual analysis from other professionals.

Computer-mediated learning environments, like the Fielding OM program, explicitly integrate online research into academic expectations. This expands a student's research resources beyond geographically bounded access to libraries. Online, a student can find business profiles on company Web sites, university research databases, international periodicals, independent unpublished manuscripts or white papers, and corporate research from organizations such as Xerox PARC and Hewlett-Packard. A student can even contact authors and other practitioners for primary source information or to get expanded discussions on questions and topics of personal relevance. From a professional perspective, this gives students access to the most up-to-date global business information. It develops critical evaluation skills for assessing the validity and reliability of online information sources, and it develops lifelong habits and expertise for research and problem analysis.

One final opportunity afforded to student practitioners by the distance-free quality of a CML environment is the ability to develop applied skills in the area of virtual work teams. Online academic workgroups mirror the global nature of real-life business work teams. Students get practical experience in cross-cultural communications; develop text-based strategies to convey nonverbal information usually present in face-to-face interactions; experiment with organizing conversations into threaded topic and discussion forums; and learn to format messages with headings, subheadings, and subject summaries. These practical communication strategies are directly transferable to professional work with virtual work teams.

Unique Student-Professor Roles

In traditional classroom settings, group interactions are usually limited to special discussion sections. Information is mainly conveyed in a one-to-many format via lectures or in-class student presentations. Feedback is conveyed on a one-to-one basis via the professor's comments on papers and grade-based evaluations. By contrast, a CML environment oozes with connectivity—linking everyone to everyone else regardless of location. This unique many-to-many communication medium creates a feedback-rich network of shared knowledge and information that is literally distributed around the globe. The spatial difference between the two environments is like the difference between a single thread and a spider's web resonating with movement and activity.

In this CML networked environment, both the students and the professor take on new roles. Rather than act as a content expert controlling access to information, the professor becomes the framer of space or the weaver of the conversation. The professor participates in the group's knowledge creation process and plays a unique role but is not a gatekeeper.

Because everyone has the same virtual "front row" classroom seat—actually, it feels more like you are sitting across an intimate coffee table—there is no competition for location-specific "face time" with the professor and no geographically based ad hoc study groups. In reality, everyone is valued according to their ability to contribute to the learning experience, so there is no need to compete for access to the professor or to the smartest study group. All course information, side conversations, in-class discussions, and process comments about paper deadlines or grading systems are available for everyone else to see. They do not take place offline in another location, such as behind the professor's office door or at the snack machine in the hall.

What Matters

Home pages, "dot com" stores with shopping carts, visits to Web sites, the rush of companies to have a presence on the Internet, and e-mail addresses all speak to the paradox of a nonphysical medium that has the ability to convey a strong sense of place in a material world. Not only is Internet vocabulary loaded with physically based descriptions, but the medium itself provides a "place" for people from across the globe to come together.

Yet the medium itself has no material presence, and the traditional ways in which we perceive and interpret a place or thing do not necessarily help us in cyberspace. Sight and sound are still quite limited by bandwidth, and touch, smell, and taste seem nearly impossible to replicate online. Within the limits of technology, then, CML environments will always be restricted to our ability to code information into computer-readable formats. In this sense, then, the technology will always challenge us to be creative and "do things differently" rather than try to replicate the traditional face-to-face classroom experience. In the end, however, the technological limitations help to drive home the most important point—that the medium is truly only a means to an end and that what really matters is the message.

Medium and Message

At the current state of the technology, the Internet experience is based overwhelmingly on text—the written word. Although many students' first instincts in CML environments are to question the seemingly archaic text-only environment in favor of a more sexy audiovisual cyberexperience, the simplicity of focusing on the written word actually creates a richer experience. Rather than deal with the technological distraction of trying to imitate a real-life face-to-face experience, a text-only environment focuses less on matter and more on what matters.

This asynchronous, open-space medium transforms matter at the speed of light into ideas, information, and knowledge. What matters is not the physical experience—what someone looks like, who is sitting where, tone of voice, or classroom setup—but rather the content of the ideas conveyed and the student's written ability to be both descriptive and succinct, both rigorously academic and business-minded, and both theoretical and applied.

The effect of a limited information channel is actually a kind of interpersonal intimacy and unique communication challenge that compels students to hone their writing skills and pay attention to not only what they are saying but also how they say it. Students learn to create descriptive narrative in a business-appropriate voice. Far from being a flat medium, online text-based communication becomes rich and multifaceted. It combines the reflective elements of journal writing with the precision of professional communication and the rigor of academic argument. Student postings have creatively incorporated poetry, jokes, and anecdotes to help communicate complex thoughts and emphasize key concepts. We do not consider our personal journals, the Declaration of Independence, or Shakespeare's plays as "flat" simply because they were delivered in text. In a CML environment, the goal is to emulate the best of the written word to achieve the strongest communications effect.

The mostly text nature of the current methodology will influence the way in which Fielding's instructional processes will evolve in the future. Because of its roots in the "primitive" text-only Internet, the program has a culture that focuses strongly on the message and is not distracted by the medium. As technology develops and allows the medium to expand—graphics, sound, video clips, and so on—the new media elements will support rather than dominate the process. The media extensions that are beginning to appear in the program now, primarily as hyperlinks, are serving to enhance the text-based messaging.

As mentioned earlier, the use of electronic media, permanent storage, and hyperlinks eliminates the production of ideas in specific segments of time and space. The written, computer-coded ideas remain accessible to everyone throughout the course, conceivably remaining accessible in perpetuity as bits of data on digital media. The result is an evolving yet perpetual map of the intellectual territory covered throughout the program, like leaving crumbs on a path. This intellectual map captures key learning moments and gives students the ability to reread and reflect on the group's communication and the ways in which knowledge was created throughout a course. Future students, or students in other programs, can also access the captured knowledge process as research data and build on it yet further foundations for students yet to come.

Professional Academics

In many ways, traditional college courses are more advanced forms of the same pedagogy that begins in kindergarten and extends throughout high school. In most college courses, the materials from the professor's notes make their way into the students' notes without necessarily passing through the cerebral cortex of either party or being tested for their relevance to work and other relevant aspects of adult life. The computer-mediated learning process is truly education for grown-ups. Within the subject boundaries established by the professor, students take responsibility for developing the course material, mastering the concepts, tutoring and evaluating each other, and applying the materials to the critical events in their lives.

The evaluation process has always been a bugaboo in collegiate academics. The most objective tests are based on recall (i.e., memorization of facts). Tests based on informed opinion, subjective choice, and value-based analyses are, by their nature, virtually impossible to grade objectively. Subjective evaluations in the traditional college come from a single source—a professor—whose abilities and relevance to any one student's educational circumstances may be questionable.

Yet we acknowledge that the application of what we learn in school to the world in which we live and work depends little on memorization. We can always look up the facts. Success depends on the ability to apply information to our life choices correctly and quickly and to use information in a way that leverages the resources we and our colleagues control. Life's tests, in short, are highly subjective, person specific, and totally unlike the evaluative processes found in most academic programs. The evaluation process is based not just on "school smarts" but also the student's ability to contribute to the community of learners. Each person's work is presented not just to the professor but to all of the other students in the course and potentially to cohorts of students yet to come.

Everyone's postings are received equally in the eyes of the technology, and the products are judged by the impressions they make on their total audience. Students quickly learn who transmits fluff and who has valuable ideas to share. The length of one's writings is irrelevant; students spend their time responding to postings in which they find value. Those who communicate good information succinctly become hubs for online discussion threads around which the course's content develops. Those who can also combine their academic rigor with thoughtful sensitivity create a safe conversation space for others to join. The medium creates a victory of substance over volume. The degree to which students attract attention, comment, and agreement from others in the community becomes a metric for performance evaluation.

Unique Student-Professor Roles

The traditional relationship between professors and students is bound to change when students are the same age as the professors and often have more practical experience as well as exposure to cutting-edge concepts. Furthermore, in the message-intense environment of cyberspace, students can commandeer as much of their classes' attention as can professors by virtue of compelling content in their postings. With these factors, the identities and roles of professors are bound to change.

In our classes, it is not unusual for the professor to learn from the students. Students quickly realize that their fellow students have as much to offer to their peers as teachers as does the professor. This is not intended to demean the professors; rather, it is intended to recognize the knowledge and experience that every class of students brings to each learning session. The faculty's greatest contribution is to establish the learning opportunity—to define the topic and initialize the boundaries of inquiry. Beyond that, students often fill many of the traditional professor roles, including acting as sources of information, explaining and illustrating critical concepts, and evaluating student reports and presentations.

The professors who really "get it" take fullest advantage of this. They do not attempt to compete with students, and they are not threatened by strong student contributions. Indeed, in its most extreme forms, some professors in the OM program capitalize on this by using, as one criterion for a student's final grade, their impression of how much *they* have learned from the *student*. Understanding this new environment, professors quickly see that they are fellow passengers on a learning journey that they have organized. Everyone takes a turn at being the tour guide; everyone takes a turn at being the tourist.

Professors no longer dominate the community by virtue of their authority. In a world of intellectually coded bits, the community is also not dominated by people who are tall, loud, or dressed in expensive suits. The community learns to respect those who communicate most forcefully what the community values reading. To communicate successfully, a student must respond within deadlines, making relevant points and convincing arguments and providing other students with stimulating ideas to which they will respond. A student cannot succeed by entering the conversation late, after the community has turned its attention to new topics.

Students who are just introduced to this environment might think the learning apparatus is a computer. But good computer skills do not make a successful student. The computer is simply a tool to support the real apparatus, which is a community of learners exchanging communications. To succeed within this environment, students need to comprehend a course's important ideas; need something to say about these ideas that appeals to other people, both theoretically and practically; and need the ability to communicate in a way that engages the community.

The effect lasts beyond any particular course. The interactions between students and professors in the OM program are carried from course to course and flow into the between-semester, face-to-face seminars that are held biannually. Quite used to working together intellectually via the Internet, quite used to applying these shared intellectual analyses to their daily activities, the students continue to work together online even when "school is out." The alumni community is much more than a bunch of people who wear rings with the same emblem. This is truly a community of practitioner scholars who have lived and worked together in a timeless, space-independent virtual world.

Conclusions:
Breaking Through Zero-Sum Academics

Traditional academics take place within constrained boundaries of time and space. They adhere to fundamental laws of physics that only one element of matter can exist in any point in space at any one time. In the normal educational setting, students compete for the professor's time, for natural resources (e.g., reference books, course enrollments, parking spaces), and for attention and recognition. To a large extent, "what I win, you lose." My educational experience and yours intersect like balls colliding on a billiard table. Through the magic of the Internet, the laws of space, time, and matter are altered. Virtual billiard balls lend themselves to games in which collisions are unnecessary and brilliant cue strokes can be stored away, modified, and reproduced at will.

In the virtual classroom, students have no need to compete for resources. The new laws for time, space, and what matters change the learning dynamic from competition to cooperation and community. The dominant characteristic of the environment becomes a self-organizing expansion of knowledge resources rather than a finite, zero-sum scenario. In the world of online information and knowledge, the more you share, the more that is created. The Internet is a world of increasing returns rather than a physical resource-based, diminishing returns environment.

Traditional brick-and-mortar academic institutions are stuck in the physical world's zero-sum mentality. Computer-mediated learning environments break through that mentality to focus on new expressions of *time* (asynchronous, unlimited "anytime" access and just-in-time learning), *space* (globally intimate connectivity, "anywhere" access integration of professional and intellectual life, and decentralized intelligence networks), and what really *matters* (interpersonal connections, competency, knowledge, skills and attitude, and community).

References

Davis, S., & Meyer, C. (1998). *Blur: The speed of change in the connected economy.* Reading, MA: Addison-Wesley.

Mieszkowski, K. (2000, March). Report from the future: Clued in? Sign on! *Fast Company*, p. 46. Available: www.fastcompany.com/online/32/rftf.html

Part II: Implementating Online Learning

B. *Programs/Environments:*
Corporate

Chapter 12

Synthesizing Higher Education and Corporate Learning Strategies

Bruce LaRue

> It may not be too fanciful to anticipate that the acquisition and distribution of formal knowledge will come to occupy the place in the politics of the knowledge society which acquisition and distribution of property and income have occupied in the two or three centuries which we have come to call the Age of Capitalism. (Drucker, 1994, sec. 2)

This chapter is based on doctoral dissertation research conducted by the author (LaRue, 1999) in collaboration with 12 multinational organizations from industries including network technology, forest products, commercial airlines, financial services, surgical products, chemical manufacturing, and high-technology consulting. The chapter also draws on my work with mid-career graduate students from major global organizations conducting the majority of their studies through an online learning environment.[1] The organizations included in this study span various levels of technological complexity and levels of professional competence required of workers. They all share geographical diversity, thus relying increasingly on the use of network technologies to conduct routine business affairs. Each organization faces similar

challenges in addressing the need for increased skill and knowledge requirements of its dispersed workforce. Each is also facing heightened levels of competition and rapid change due in large measure to economic forces impelled
by the burgeoning use of information and communication technologies (ICTs;
see Cleveland, 1997), leading to what has become known as the knowledge
economy.

The term "knowledge work" is deconstructed to determine fundamental
characteristics needed to function in contemporary work environments irrespective of levels of technical sophistication. Specific technical skill requirements are distinguished from what I later term "epistemological competencies" or the general level of cognitive and systems-oriented thought processes
necessary to perform effectively in different work environments. Knowledge
work is predicated on a significantly heightened level of epistemological
development and theoretical reasoning capacity, wherein otherwise tacit systems of inference, inductive, and deductive reasoning schemata are made
explicit as a basis of communication and coordinated action within knowledge-intensive organizational environments. This characterization of the
geographically dispersed knowledge worker forms the basis for a model of
networked learning that explores new types of collaboration among institutions of higher education and modern organizations.

Revisiting the Role of the University

From the standpoint of the knowledge worker, contradictions are surfacing
with alarming rapidity between the reality encountered in the college classroom and the one encountered in the workplace. These contradictions are no
more apparent than when the knowledge worker, motivated by wrenching
changes in the workplace, makes the "pilgrimage" to the university for further education. Here it appears (perhaps deliberately) that little has changed
for hundreds of years, and the harsh reality of the workplace that originally
compelled the journey fades equally into the distance.

Although public policy debates about the crisis in higher education have
been framed largely in terms of the need for increased access, traditional pedagogical principles associated with the university may be ill suited to the
learning needs of an increasingly mobile and sophisticated adult workforce.
It may well be that the needs of today's knowledge worker cannot be adequately addressed by the university as we know it today and that new institutions will emerge to fill the widening vacuum developing between traditional
higher education and the demands of today's knowledge-intensive workplace. Many have been quick to embrace distance learning systems as the
solution to this problem. However, Brown and Duguid (1995, 2000) offer
serious reservations about mainstream approaches to distance learning that
do not preserve and expand on the university's core competencies, especially

those that will provide access to and full engagement in what they call "communities of practice."[2]

Practical considerations such as rising cost, time, and physical proximity pose significant barriers to the future role of the university in the development of knowledge workers. Given the rising prominence of geographically distributed and networked firms, universities need to be able to provide advanced levels of continuing education to a dispersed workforce in a consistent and collaborative manner. It is increasingly problematic for members of geographically distributed organizations to converge regularly for extended periods of time in a central location from their posts abroad. These factors combine to make these types of firms' workers ideal candidates for some form of what Brown and Duguid call an "open learning system." I believe that the learning needs of knowledge workers can be met through integrating ICTs with the core competencies of organizations and universities.

In agreement with Brown and Duguid, I contend that higher education, taken as an entire system, has certain core competencies that must be not only preserved but expanded and improved on if today's knowledge worker is to be adequately served. Equally important are the development of effective feedback systems between the domains of higher education and the arenas of practice in which workers apply their knowledge. The model of "networked learning" explored in this chapter directly addresses these crucial and highly interdependent issues.

The High-Flex Firm and Its Implications for Advanced Education

The integrated use of ICTs has given rise to new organizational forms that appear unrecognizable from their predecessors.[3] Handy (1996a, 1996b, 2000) refers to the basic structure of these new organizational hybrids as the "shamrock" firm, characterized by a small core of essential executives and workers surrounded by outside contractors and part-time help. He suggests that the rise of such firms is a natural consequence of a shift from a manufacturing to a service economy. Unlike products, services cannot be stockpiled during an economic downturn; hence, firms are increasingly flexing their workforces. Information and communication technologies have, in turn, given rise to various forms of networked organizations characterized by highly flexible relationships among organizational subunits; among multiple "core" firms; and between these firms and their suppliers, contractors, and workers. Furthermore, advances in ICTs, together with an efficient global transportation infrastructure, have meant that these new flexible relationships increasingly occur with little reference to constraints of space and time.

The rise of the flexible network firm has startling implications for the education of workers. Handy (1996b) estimates that during the coming decades, 80% of all jobs in the United States will require cerebral rather than manual skills and that 60% to 70% of these jobs will be of a managerial or professional nature. He estimates that, as a consequence, half will require the equivalent of a higher education or professional qualification to be performed adequately (pp. 168-170).

The rise of the flexible firm also carries far-reaching implications for the manner in which we conceive of learning, education, and training. Whereas skills connote specific abilities that can be readily imparted to the individual in preparation for pre-specified organizational needs and objectives, flexibility implies something quite different. Flexibility connotes the embodiment of a quality or characteristic rather than a specific, definable, even codifiable content of knowledge or ability. Formal education and training, although certainly important, might not be well suited to preparing workers for nonroutine, context-dependent occurrences that increasingly characterize today's "high-flex" workplace.

Therefore, the form that this advanced education will take remains in question. According to the Task Force on High-Performance Work and Workers (1995, 1996, 1997) of the Business-Higher Education Forum, a division of the American Council on Education, the different ideological assumptions rigorously defended by business and higher education are so profound that they can be described as a "chasm" to be spanned. According to recent projections of the U.S. Bureau of Labor Statistics' Office of Employment projections through the year 2006 (see Appendix), the shift to a high-flex workplace is placing unprecedented demands on higher education for the continuing development of knowledge workers. Based on this accelerating trend toward increased levels of higher education, we now return to the particular learning requirements of knowledge workers and the extent to which these requirements are being addressed through existing means.

It appears that many of the qualities, characteristics, and responsibilities that increasingly define workers in today's high-flex work environments were previously the carefully guarded domain of a minority of managers and professionals. It is perhaps no accident that the burgeoning "new professional class" shares one important characteristic with Drucker's definition of knowledge workers: the increasing amount of formal schooling they require (Drucker, 1993, 1999). It is the rising prominence of the knowledge worker that poses the greatest challenge to those institutions charged with preparing this new breed of professional for sustained social and economic engagement.

Reconceptualizing the University

As Drucker (1994) points out, for approximately the last 200 years in the West, to be an educated person meant that one shared a common stock of knowledge or what the Germans called Allgemeine Bildung, a term known later by the English and 19th-century Americans as the liberal arts. In the shadow of the positive sciences, this form of knowledge fell into severe disrepute, as both the German and the Anglo-American liberal arts had no utility or practical application whatsoever. By contrast,

> In the knowledge society, knowledge basically exists only in application, and consequently, to be an educated person will increasingly mean that one has mastered learning itself and continues to learn both within and outside of formal schooling. (Drucker, 1994, sec. 2)

Although Drucker has continued to define knowledge workers according to the amount of formal education they require, he sees little role for the traditional university in fulfilling this need:

> In the knowledge society, clearly more and more of knowledge, and especially of advanced knowledge, will be acquired well past the age of formal schooling, and increasingly, perhaps, in and through educational processes which do not center on the traditional school, e.g., systematic continuing education offered at the place of employment. (cited in Lenzner & Johnson, 1997)

One obvious risk in emphasizing alternatives to formal schooling, such as knowledge-in-action, is the debasement of knowledge into immediately applicable forms. Since the time of ancient Greece, the question about what constitutes verifiable knowledge and truth has been at the heart of the Western philosophical tradition and has become the sole pursuit of the branch of philosophy known as epistemology. Plato's Socrates, more than 2,500 years ago, refused to refer to applicable knowledge as knowledge at all but instead referred to it as "techne" or mere skill.

The modern reincarnation of the controversy over what constitutes verifiable truth (or, for our purposes, knowledge) is perhaps best portrayed in the classic debate between the Continental rationalists and the British empiricists represented by René Descartes and John Locke, respectively. Whereas rationalism holds that verifiable knowledge is arrived at through deduction from irreducible axioms, concepts, or laws, empiricism holds that knowledge is arrived at through induction based on sense perception. The present discussion over legitimate forms of knowledge is most often referred to in terms of theory and practice. These two terms, which arguably should be hyphenated, instead appear as an irreconcilable dichotomy of two concepts that seem to be as far removed from one another as the ivory tower is from the shop floor.

Reframing the classic debate about verifiable knowledge, Schön (1983, 1987) sees profoundly negative consequences for professionals brought about by the hallowed distinctions between theory and practice. Professionals, he believes, are typically different from other workers in that they do not learn technical rules that are then unilaterally applied. Instead, they must learn to think like lawyers, architects, or doctors. He suggests that learning takes place under conditions of surprise, anomaly, and nonroutine circumstances that require heightened awareness, experimentation, and determination of the underlying nature of a problem. "The situations of practice are not problems to be solved, but problematic situations characterized by uncertainty, disorder, and indeterminacy" (Schön, 1983, p. 15). Such situations often require critical reflection and careful analysis of taken-for-granted assumptions and beliefs that may underlie one's approach to the problem. This ability to think like a professional is very close to the qualities required of workers in today's high-flex workplace (Allee, 1997; Bailey, 1989; Bailey & Noyelle, 1988; Benton, Bailey, Noyelle, & Stanback, 1991; Berryman & Bailey, 1992; Brown & Duguid, 1995, 2000; Davis & Botkin, 1995; Drucker, 1993, 1994, 1999; Handy, 1996a, 1996b; Neef, Siesfeld, & Cefola, 1998; Reich, 1992, 1993, 2000; Sheckley, Lamdin, & Keeton, 1993; Task Force on High-Performance Work and Workers, 1995, 1996, 1997; Thurow, 1992, 1996, 1999; Zuboff, 1988). However, the development of such qualities appears, in some important respects, incompatible with the preparation that one receives in the modern university.

> In the varied topography of professional practice, there is a high, hard ground overlooking a swamp. On the high ground, manageable problems lend themselves to solution through the application of research-based theory and technique. In the swampy lowland, messy, confusing problems defy technical solution. The irony of this situation is that the problems of the high ground tend to be relatively unimportant to individuals or society at large, however great their technical interest may be, while in the swamp lie the problems of greatest human concern. The practitioner must choose. Shall he remain on the high ground where he can solve relatively unimportant problems according to prevailing standards of rigor, or shall he descend to the swamp of important problems and nonrigorous inquiry? (Schön, 1987, p. 3)

Schön (1987) sees this dilemma of what he terms "rigor versus relevance" arising from two related sources: "first, the prevailing idea of rigorous academic knowledge, based on technical rationality, and second, awareness of indeterminate, swampy zones of practice that lie beyond its canons" (p. 3). Technical rationality, he holds, has its origins in a positivist epistemology that finds its roots in the very foundations of the modern research university. According to this view, a practitioner is ideally an instrumental problem solver, trained in the application of particular techniques "derived from systematic, preferably scientific knowledge" (p. 4).

From another perspective, the university performs essential functions that arguably would not be performed to the same degree in its absence. The intellectual sanctuary afforded by the Massachusetts Institute of Technology, to be sure, played an important function in fostering the development of

Schön's thinking about the shortcomings of the university. The typical modern corporation, with its often nearsighted fixation on the next quarter's earnings, could hardly be considered a candidate for this role. In the words of Brown and Duguid (1995), "While business might congratulate itself on being a force for change, Motorola and McDonald's universities and most industrial training programs don't offer very bright alternative horizons," a view generally shared by Davis and Botkin (1995) and Drucker (1994).

Davis and Botkin (1995) are quick to emphasize, however, that many of the most progressive corporations serve their international customers and employees in ways that deserve close attention from traditional universities. They cite KPMG Peat Marwick's teaching facilities in 60 countries, AT&T's programs for employees and customers in 50 countries, and even McDonald's hardwired simultaneous translation facilities for 18 languages in its main U.S. corporate training headquarters. "Harvard Business School," they point out, "which did not have a single foreign-language newspaper on its library's periodical table until 1992, could learn a thing or two from Hamburger University" (p. 129). Motorola University has also demonstrated strong leadership in its efforts to form alliances with universities, much like it partners with customers and suppliers.

Strategic partnerships between universities and corporations are also on the rise. According to a recent survey conducted by Corporate University X-change, a New York-based consulting group, 40% of large corporate training organizations will form corporate-university partnerships (Ouellette, 1998, sec. 1). The survey also estimated that by the year 2000 more than half of this custom education and training would be conducted online via computer technologies such as the Internet and videoconferencing. For example, German auto and aerospace giant Daimler-Benz recently contracted with the University of Southern California (USC) to train its midlevel and executive management team. According to Wolfgang Braun, Daimler-Benz's vice president for corporate executive development, one reason why USC won the contract is that U.S. schools have better access to telecommunications and Internet technologies to train workers worldwide (Ouellette, 1998, sec. 1).

Developing closer relationships between the university and modern organizations may also have an important historical precedent. That is, although through one lens the university and the modern business organization may hold divergent ideological assumptions, a slightly different lens may reveal a highly complementary relationship enabled through modern technology. Lewis Mumford, in *The City in History,* described the university's original role in the development of society as an exalted form of the craftsman's guild, professional schools for the study of law, medicine, and theology (Mumford, 1961). It was precisely its detachment from the standards of the market that permitted the university to perform its important function.

In the university, the pursuit of knowledge was elevated into an enduring structure which did not depend for its continuance upon any single group of priests, scholars, or texts. The system of knowledge was more important than the thing known. In the university, the functions of cultural storage, dissemination and interchange, and creative addition—perhaps the three most essential functions of the city—were adequately performed. The very independence of the university from the standards of the market and the city fostered the special sort of authority it exercised: the sanction of verifiable truth.

Too often the major contributions to knowledge, from Newton to Einstein, from Gilbert to Faraday, have been made outside the university's walls. Nevertheless, the enlargement and transmission of the intellectual heritage would have been inconceivable, on the scale actually achieved since the thirteenth century, without the agency of the university. (pp. 275-276)

Using Mumford's (1961) description of the university as an institution for the "enlargement and transmission of the intellectual heritage" that admittedly often has its origins outside its walls is a crucial point for our purposes. Looking at theory and practice in simplified terms, the former has generally been viewed (often disparagingly) as the domain of academia, whereas the "swampy zones of practice" are the realm of material life. Perhaps the problem lies in inadequate feedback loops that would allow the function of "enlargement and transmission" to more adequately and immediately inform the realms of practice and vice versa (Eastman & Mallach, 1998).

Core Competencies of the University

Brown and Duguid (1995, 2000) hold that the university must be viewed as a system that is also evolving due to a changing environment. They believe that the university has certain core competencies that must be recognized and preserved as part of any system reform effort. These core competencies arise from the unique relationship that universities create among pedagogy, credentials, and communities of practice. To preserve these core competencies while also expanding access to the university for nontraditional students, they espouse a system called "open learning." This system includes the development of social, institutional, and technological arrangements in support of the following key criteria: access to authentic communities of learning, interpretation, exploration, and knowledge creation; resources to help them work with both distal and local communities; and widely accepted representations for learning and work (Brown & Duguid, 2000, p. 232).

For Brown and Duguid (2000), the central competency of the university is the community of practice. Students learn "what it takes to join a particular community. In so doing, they may progress from learning about to learning to be, from, that is, learning about a group of different communities toward learning to be a member of one" (p. 220).

Without full engagement in communities of practice, a phenomenon not unlike traditional apprenticeships, Brown and Duguid (2000) maintain that the other two core competencies (knowledge and credentials) are rendered dubious at best. With this in mind, they hold suspect any reformulation of the university based on more efficient means of "delivery." This includes many conceptions of distance learning to the degree that these preclude the development of, and active engagement in, communities of practice. The corporate university system, with its proprietary tendencies, does not by its nature encourage active engagement in a community of practice that extends beyond the walls of the corporation. This characteristic renders cross-fertilization among and within industries extremely problematic and limits the scope of learning and, thereby, the market value of its credentials. Also, these corporate institutions are not yet open to the general public and, therefore, cannot be considered candidates for a more general social solution.

A central theme in Brown and Duguid's (1995) conception of open learning is for the university's core competencies of knowledge generation, conferring of credentials, and engagement in communities of practice to be extended to the distal arenas in which learning takes place. In the following section, I outline a model that attempts to integrate the core competencies of the university with the "swampy zones" of practice where workers apply their knowledge.

The 4-Plex Model of Networked Learning

Although the following model finds its theoretical basis in the preceding arguments, the specific components of the model and their interaction emerged as I observed the learning and development practices of professionals operating in geographically dispersed organizations (LaRue, 1999). The model also emerged as a result of my work with graduate students performing their studies in a networked learning environment[4] and applying their knowledge in a wide variety of public and private sector organizations. In addition, while not operating under the auspices of a university system, my colleagues and I continue to use these principles in our consulting practice, which focuses on executive and organization development in a variety of complex organizational settings. The major objectives of the 4-Plex Model of networked learning are as follows:

1. Provide the infrastructure for an expanded community of practice that transcends boundaries of particular organizations and rigid disciplinary domains.
2. Offer ready and timely access to an arena for theoretical discourse based on the mechanisms of cultural storage, dissemination, interchange, and creative addition.

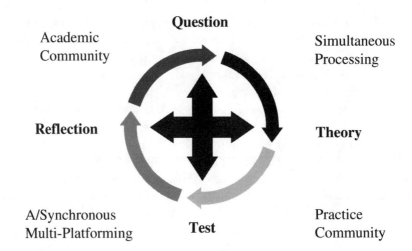

Figure 12.1. The 4-Plex Model of Networked Learning

3. Provide transferable credentials as well as a ready means for keeping these credentials current.
4. Carry out the preceding functions in a manner consonant with the geographic, time, and developmental demands of adult professionals.

To help in understanding this model graphically, I have included a diagram (Figure 12.1).

The four main components of this model—question, theory, test, and reflection—are arranged in a matrix designed to indicate a nonlinear movement among each respective domain. The question and test (or vertical) dimension of the diagram is intended to represent the practice domain, and the reflection and theory (or horizontal) dimension is intended to represent the academic domain. That these two domains are joined by a common axis indicates a "unification" of the two fields, and their distinct quadrants represent their relative autonomy and distinct character. This aspect of the model is intended to directly address the need for the relevance of academic study to the arenas where workers apply their knowledge.

Question and Test Dimension:
The Practice Domain

The vertical axis represents the arena of what Schön (1987) refers to as the "swampy" zones of practice, wherein problematic situations are encountered. In this arena, questions arise, as do processes for evaluating the effectiveness of potential solutions. This dimension is designed to provide grounding for theory and a basis for evaluating the relevance of learning through its direct application in the workplace.

Reflection and Theory: The Academic Dimension

The horizontal dimension offers an arena for informing questions derived in the practice domain with relevant literature and research. It is also a domain of abstracted or "decontextualized" thought and reflection that affords the chance to examine the problem from multiple critical perspectives. Theory also refers to theoretical reasoning and reflection based on the development of cognitive and epistemological competencies required for knowledge work.[5]

Simultaneous Processing

All domains are accessible from all other points in the matrix at all times. Each domain can be used separately or simultaneously in both distal and local arenas. Both academic and practice arenas can be engaged simultaneously through appropriate technologies so that problems encountered at work can be reflected on in the academic environment and vice versa. This dimension of the model is designed to tighten and strengthen feedback loops between academia and complex modern work environments.[6]

A/Synchronous Multi-Platforming

Work at any point (or among points) of the matrix can be accomplished by using any appropriate technological media in both synchronous and asynchronous modes. Such media include various network platforms, phone, fax, and e-mail used wherever and whenever circumstances, time, and geographic proximity warrant. This dimension of the model is designed to address the need for greater mobility and flexibility in workforce learning through the leveraging of appropriate technologies.[7]

Academic Community

This dimension refers to ready access to academic resources such as research libraries, networks, databases, journals, and books. It also includes communities of scholars, practitioners, and researchers engaged through college courses, degree programs, and related support services. This dimension of the model is designed to explicitly conceive of the university as an "infrastructure for expanded communities of practice" that extends beyond traditional practice arenas to encompass various academic disciplines, economic sectors, and social domains. It is expected that the academic community can be engaged either in physical face-to-face settings or at a distance via electronic means as circumstances warrant. This aspect of the model is also intended to address the need for increased mobility and time constraints of knowledge workers.

Quite often, the rapid pace and highly volatile character of many of today's organizational environments do not lend themselves to reflection and to inform actions through relevant theory embodied in academic (and other professional) research. The result is that many organizations inadvertently find themselves in the unenviable position of "reinventing the wheel" as they confront problematic issues that have been the subject of academic inquiry. Students and knowledge workers must be able to obtain the skills for locating and judging the relevance of research as it applies to their particular situations. Students must also become adept at making contributions to existing knowledge.

Practice Community

The practice community refers to colleagues and team members within organizations and also includes professional networks outside of the organization. This dimension of the model is designed to address the workers' need for full engagement in professional networks as an integral component of their learning and developmental process. This dimension also addresses the need for learning accomplished outside the organization to be more relevant to the practice domain.[8]

Example of the 4-Plex Model in Action

The central organizing principle of the model assumes that network technologies are, first and foremost, enablers of simultaneous functioning within all domains represented in the matrix. For example, a student who is also a member of an organization identifies a complex problem (or question) in his or her organization and attempts to generate a solution through dialogue with colleagues (reflection and practice community) through use of the company intranet, phone conferencing, face-to-face meetings, and so on (a/synchronous multi-platforming). Assuming that solutions are not forthcoming, dialogue concerning the problem extends to the Internet discussion groups, a conversation with peers, or a conference hosted by a professional association (professional networks).

As a participant in a university program, the problem can be addressed with peers in a course related to the subject. The student draws from the expertise of faculty and student peers (reflection and academic community) who work in other industries that may have dealt with a similar problem. The individual discovers a body of literature on the subject (theory) that can help him or her to understand the problem in a broader and more systemic context (theoretical reasoning). This process may, in turn, lead to a reframing of the problem as it is informed by relevant literature and further reflection with professional colleagues and peers.

Defining what now appears to be a suitable solution, the learner writes a proposal (submitted for credit in the academic community) for action to his or her company that is now informed by a broad array of resources. The plan is implemented on a pilot basis, and the next iteration of the cycle begins. Existing theory may be insufficient to describe the problematic phenomena, providing the student with an ideal opportunity to add to the body of literature on the subject through further research, theory building, testing, and reflection informed by an expansive array of colleagues and peers.

The central point of this model is that learning, enabled by the use of appropriate technologies, is now capable of occurring in both local and distal arenas simultaneously, with virtually seamless feedback between the domains of academia and practice. Network technologies are not viewed as mechanisms of "delivery"; instead, they are viewed as more or less transparent tools for dialogue and research. The core competencies of academia and business are also preserved, maintaining their respective autonomy while informing one another in a seamless flow of questioning, theorizing, testing, and reflecting, thereby reconceptualizing the relationship among theory, learning, and practice.

Appendix: Higher Education and the New Professional Class

Projected changes in the composition of the labor force during the period from 1996 to 2006 provide further evidence that greater attention must be paid to the continuing education and training of the workforce. Using moderate economic growth assumptions, the U.S. Department of Labor (Bureau of Labor Statistics, 1997) estimated that the total size of the labor force will grow by only 15 million during the period from 1996 to 2006. This represents an increase of only 11% compared to a 14% growth rate during the previous 10-year period from 1986 to 1996. Total employment growth rates will also decrease dramatically over the coming decade, from 19% during the 1986-1996 period down to 14% during the 1996-2006 period (Table 12.A1).

More important than aggregate statistics, however, is how widely employment growth rates will vary within occupations requiring different levels of education and training. Growth rates during the period from 1996 to 2006 will range from 7.4% for jobs requiring postsecondary vocational training to 25.4% for jobs requiring a bachelor's degree. All jobs requiring a minimum of an associate's degree will surpass the 14% average employment growth rate, and all other categories will grow at a lower than average rate, reflecting a general increase in skill and education requirements (Bureau of Labor Statistics, 1997; Table 12.A1).

TABLE 12.A1   Projected Employment Growth Rates, 1996 to 2006,
by Education Category (percentages)

Total	14.0
First professional degree	18.0
Doctoral degree	19.0
Master's degree	15.0
Work experience plus a bachelor's degree or higher	17.8
Bachelor's degree	25.4
Associate's degree	22.2
Postsecondary vocational training	7.4
Work experience in related occupation	12.2
Long-term on-the-job training	9.1
Moderate-term on-the-job training	8.7
Short-term on-the-job training	13.3

SOURCE: Bureau of Labor Statistics (1997).
NOTE: Table assumes moderate economic growth projections.

The average age of workers who will require advanced degrees is also increasing. The number of workers ages 45 to 64 years is expected to grow faster than that of younger workers during the period from 1996 to 2006, reflecting the aging of the baby-boom generation born between 1946 and 1964. Meanwhile, the number of workers ages 25 to 34 years is expected to drop by nearly 3 million during the same period, reflecting the drop in birthrates during the late 1960s and early 1970s (Bureau of Labor Statistics, 1997). In sum, these statistics indicate that to obtain the jobs in the fastest growing, highest wage sectors of the economy during the coming decade, it is imperative that increasingly older, mid-career workers (and hence nontraditional students) have ready access to advanced levels of education and professional training.

It is important to note one apparent inconsistency in these statistics. The Bureau of Labor Statistics (1997) projects the two fastest growing employment sectors, according to education category, as those requiring a bachelor's degree (25.4%) and those requiring an associate's degree (22.2%). However, the fastest growing employment category is that of "professional specialty," which is projected to grow at a rate of 26.6% during the period from 1996 to 2006, followed by "technician and related support" (24.0%) and "executive, administrative, and managerial" (17.2%). The inconsistency relates to whether possessing the bachelor's or associate's degree is sufficient preparation for jobs in the "professional specialty" category, which is the fastest growing employment category for this period.

Notes

1. The graduate program noted here is the master's program in organizational management at the Fielding Graduate Institute. Students meet face-to-face one to two times per year for intensive program orientation and group process exercises. They enter and perform the majority of their graduate studies in one consistent team or "cohort." Work is performed primarily in an asynchronous learning environment using a Web-based groupware system. Dialogue among cohort members and faculty is emphasized rather than didactic or other largely one-way broadcast forms of instruction.

2. For more on the principle of communities of practice, see also Lave (1988), Lave and Wenger (1991), Rogoff and Lave (1999), and Wenger (1998).

3. Such organizational hybrids include the *adhocracy,* the *inverted pyramid,* the *matrix organization,* various forms of the *networked and flat organization,* and the *hypertext organization* (Nonaka & Takeuchi, 1995).

4. My thanks to Charles Handy for his contribution of the "question, theory, test, and reflect" elements of this model arranged in circular clockwise configuration (Handy, 1996a, 2000). The Kolb learning cycle, consisting of reflection, conceptualization, experimentation, and experience, also shares some resemblance to the 4-Plex Model. However, the integration of the four components of network technologies, academic and practice communities, the principle of simultaneous processing, and the addition of nonlinear sequencing among the various components all are unique to the 4-Plex Model.

5. One of the major learning environments considered in this study was based on intense dialogue among course participants and professors. Students were routinely required to analyze problematic organizational issues in light of relevant theory, and vice versa, as an integral part of their formal assignments. These assignments then became the subject of structured course dialogue and feedback, wherein participants would offer supportive yet critical evaluations of one another's assignments under the guidance and facilitation of faculty. The level of theoretical discourse resulted not only from discussion of specific organizational theories presented in course materials but also from demands on students to explicate their otherwise tacit knowledge (Chandon, 2000; Nonaka & Takeuchi, 1995) as a basis of their communicative competence. Theoretical discourse also emerged as a result of students challenging the premises and inferences underlying extant theory in their field of inquiry when such theory failed to provide sufficient explanatory capability. Such discourse based on an examination of the premises and systems of inference underlying theory represents a qualitative shift in the developmental level of students, for example, from Kegan's (1994) third- to fourth-order level of consciousness. This is also a fundamental component of what Zuboff (1988) refers to as "intellective skill" (p. 95).

6. As students engaged in theoretical discourse and dialogue around problematic organizational issues, they would then routinely apply their new and deepened understanding in their work contexts. Often, this would result in changes in these contexts, which in turn became the basis of further reflection within the course forum in a process of multiple iterations (Chandon, 2000). This entire process occurred more or less seamlessly as students engaged in both activities simultaneously through access to the course forum from work, from home, or while traveling abroad.

7. Although the students in the present study were strongly encouraged (and at times required) to keep all of their dialogue contained within the confines of the asynchronous learning environment, in practice (and certainly in their professional lives) multiple communication platforms were used (LaRue, 1999). Students were asked to perform the bulk of their communications within the asynchronous environment to avoid subgrouping and to allow all participants to learn from the collaborative efforts and dialogue of the entire group. This also facilitated the capture of all course forum data in textual form while affording greater time for reflection prior to responses among group members.

8. The importance of this element of the model has already been given substantial attention in this chapter. Adult students engaged in professional endeavors increasingly desire knowledge that is relevant to their professional endeavors. They also tend to make significant and routine use of formal and informal networks of colleagues both within and outside of their current organizations as an integral component of their learning process. Within the networked learning environment examined here, students routinely commented on how invaluable the dialogue with their peers from industries all over the world has been in their learning process (see, e.g., Chandon, 2000, p. 172).

References

Allee, V. (1997). *The knowledge evolution: Expanding organizational intelligence.* Oxford, UK: Butterworth-Heinemann.

Bailey, T. (1989). *Changes in the nature and structure of work: Implications for skill requirements and skill formation* (Technical Paper No. 9). New York: Columbia University, Teachers College, National Center on Education and Employment.

Bailey, T., & Noyelle, T. (1988). *New technology and skill formation: Issues and hypotheses* (Technical Paper No. 1). New York: Columbia University, Teachers College, National Center on Education and Employment.

Benton, L., Bailey, T., Noyelle, T., & Stanback, T. (1991). *Employee training and U.S. competitiveness: Lessons for the 1990s.* Boulder, CO: Westview.

Berryman, S., & Bailey, T. (1992). *The double helix of education and the economy.* New York: Columbia University, Institute of Education and the Economy.

Brown, J. S., & Duguid, P. (1995). *Universities in the digital age.* Palo Alto, CA: Xerox Corporation. Retrieved January 30, 1998, from: www.parc.xerox.com/ops/members/brown/index.html

Brown, J. S., & Duguid, P. (2000). *The social life of information.* Boston: Harvard Business School Press.

Bureau of Labor Statistics. (1997). *BLS releases new 1996-2006 employment projections.* Washington, DC: U.S. Department of Labor. Retrieved October 20, 1998, from: www.bls.gov/news.release/ecopro.nws.htm

Chandon, W. (2000). *Virtual community praxis: Lessons from the swamp.* Unpublished doctoral dissertation, Fielding Graduate Institute.

Cleveland, H. (1997). *Leadership and the information revolution.* Minneapolis, MN: United Nations University, World Academy of Art and Science and International Leadership Academy.

Davis, S., & Botkin, J. (1995). *The monster under the bed: How business is mastering the opportunity of knowledge for profit*. New York: Touchstone Books.

Drucker, P. (1993). *Post-capitalist society*. Oxford, UK: Butterworth-Heinemann.

Drucker, P. (1994). *Knowledge work and knowledge society: The social transformations of this century*. Cambridge, MA: Harvard University, John F. Kennedy School of Government. Retrieved July 15, 1998, from: http://ksgwww.harvard.edu/ksgpress/ksg_news/transcripts/drucklec.htm

Drucker, P. F. (1999). *Management challenges for the 21st century* (1st ed.). New York: HarperBusiness.

Eastman, D., & Mallach, E. (1998, May). *Four modes of organizational network usage: An information modality framework for organizational assessment and choice management*. Paper presented at the International Information Resources Management Association Conference, Boston.

Handy, C. B. (1996a). *Beyond certainty: The changing worlds of organizations*. Boston: Harvard Business School Press.

Handy, C. (1996b). The numbers. In P. Myers (Ed.), *Knowledge management and organizational design* (pp. 167-178). London: Butterworth-Heinemann.

Handy, C. B. (2000). *21 ideas for managers: Practical wisdom for managing your company and yourself* (1st ed.). San Francisco: Jossey-Bass.

Kegan, R. (1994). *In over our heads: The mental demands of modern life*. Cambridge, MA: Harvard University Press.

LaRue, B. (1999). *Toward a unified view of working, living, and learning in the knowledge economy: Implications of the new learning imperative for distributed organizations, higher education, and knowledge workers*. Unpublished doctoral dissertation, Fielding Graduate Institute.

Lave, J. (1988). *Cognition in practice: Mind, mathematics, and culture in everyday life*. New York: Cambridge University Press.

Lave, J., & Wenger, E. (1991). *Situated learning: Legitimate peripheral participation*. Cambridge, UK: Cambridge University Press.

Lenzner, R., & Johnson, S. (1997, March 10). Seeing things as they really are: An interview with Peter Drucker. *Forbes*. Retrieved July 20, 1998, from: www.forbes.com/forbes/97/0310/5905122a.htm

Mumford, L. (1961). *The city in history: Its origins, its transformations, and its prospects*. New York: Harcourt Brace Jovanovich.

Neef, D., Siesfeld, G. A., & Cefola, J. (1998). *The economic impact of knowledge*. Boston: Butterworth-Heinemann.

Nonaka, I., & Takeuchi, H. (1995). *The knowledge creating company: How Japanese companies create the dynamics of innovation*. Oxford, UK: Oxford University Press.

Ouellette, T. (1998, April 13). *Corporate training programs go to college*. Computer World. Retrieved June 26, 1998, from: www.computerworld.com/8525658400720fb8/69747ca2461a6aee852564ea0052c19c/67ca5f57c1414b20852565e50073230a?opendocument

Reich, R. (1992). *The work of nations*. New York: Vintage.

Reich, R. B. (1993). *American competitiveness and American brains*. New York: City University of New York, Baruch College.

Reich, R. B. (2000). *The future of success* (1st ed.). New York: Knopf.

Rogoff, B., & Lave, J. (1999). *Everyday cognition: Development in social context.* New York: toExcel.

Schön, D. (1983). *The reflective practitioner.* New York: Basic Books.

Schön, D. (1987). *Educating the reflective practitioner: Toward a new design for teaching and learning in the professions.* San Francisco: Jossey-Bass.

Sheckley, B., Lamdin, L., & Keeton, M. (1993). *Employability in a high-performance economy.* Chicago: Council for Adult and Experiential Learning.

Task Force on High-Performance Work and Workers. (1995). *Higher education and work readiness: The view from the corporation.* Washington, DC: Business-Higher Education Forum in affiliation with American Council on Education.

Task Force on High-Performance Work and Workers. (1996). *Higher education and work readiness: The view from the campus.* Washington, DC: Business-Higher Education Forum in affiliation with American Council on Education.

Task Force on High-Performance Work and Workers. (1997). *Spanning the chasm: Corporate and academic cooperation to improve work-force preparation.* Washington, DC: Business-Higher Education Forum in affiliation with American Council on Education.

Thurow, L. (1992). *Head to head: The coming economic battle among Japan, Europe, and America.* New York: William Morrow.

Thurow, L. (1996). *The future of capitalism: How today's economic forces shape tomorrow's world.* New York: William Morrow.

Thurow, L. C. (1999). *Building wealth: The new rules for individuals, companies, and nations in a knowledge-based economy* (1st ed.). New York: HarperCollins.

Wenger, E. (1998). *Communities of practice: Learning, meaning, and identity.* Cambridge, UK: Cambridge University Press.

Zuboff, S. (1988). *In the age of the smart machine: The future of work and power.* New York: Basic Books.

Chapter 13

Real-World Learning in the Virtual Classroom

Computer-Mediated Learning in the Corporate World

David Smith

It's April 1996. Hundreds of man-hours have gone into planning the Senior Field Management Symposium. Lester Thurow has been scheduled to provide the keynote speech. Customer executives have agreed to participate in the event to help us understand their business issues. More than 100 people from around the world are scheduled to attend. Several manufacturers of personal computers announce soft quarterly business results and reduce forecasts for the upcoming quarter. Concerns ripple through the electronics industry. The Senior Field Management Symposium is delayed to the start of the next fiscal year in November 1996.

It's June 1996. The field general managers are concerned about the cost and effectiveness of the Senior Field Management Symposium. Some of the general managers already have fiscal year kickoff events scheduled for their regions, and the symposium conflicts with their schedules. The general managers question how much can be accomplished at a 3-day event anyway.

Budgets for the new fiscal year are going to be tight. The Senior Field Management Symposium is cancelled.

It's December 1996. Many in our organization are concerned about the lack of training of our managers. Top management gives the orders to develop a Field Management Forum for a worldwide audience in June 1997. Tentative efforts to define and implement the program begin, with careful attention given to defining the desired business results. Another perturbation occurs in the organization's business performance. The Field Management Forum is cancelled.

It's December 1997. Hundreds of man-hours have gone into planning the Field Management Event scheduled for June 1998. Many meetings have occurred with key stakeholders in the organization. Delicate shuttle diplomacy has been performed by the training program manager between field general managers and product group managers to ensure that the event meets the perceived needs of a wide range of stakeholders. The General Managers Meeting is abuzz about the softening of business performance in Asia and Japan, which are troubled by currency fluctuations. The executive vice president reduces field expense targets by 5%. The Field Management Event is cancelled.

Background

I am the person who planned all of these cancelled events. At that time, I had the responsibility for developing a training program aimed at building the strategic sales competence of my organization worldwide. The use of computer-mediated learning (CML) has extraordinary meaning and relevance to me because it offers a possible solution to the two main frustrations in my work, namely that (a) many key training programs have been cancelled and (b) the programs we do implement are often ineffective. I wrote my master's thesis on this topic. The title of my master's thesis, "The End of Training," was an intentional play on two equally valid meanings of the word "end": demise and objective. On the one hand, I seek the demise of the current way we train. On the other hand, I seek to reach the objective (behavioral change) for which we train people.

During the first 2 years in my job, I had been asked four times to implement a face-to-face training program for a worldwide audience. Each time, my management cancelled the training program after much work had been done. The cancellations of these programs have caused much frustration among those involved in planning the training event, incurred large cancellation charges, and left the business needs unmet. These cancellations also foster a cynical attitude toward training on the part of the sales force.

There are three factors that make large-scale face-to-face programs vulnerable, namely that (a) they take at least 6 months to implement, (b) they are expensive, and (c) they are disruptive to the training participants. Because these programs have long lead times, there is a good chance that at some time in the planning process my company will experience a perturbation in its business performance. My organization's response during these times is to cut costs. Worldwide face-to-face training programs are expensive and very visible. In addition, face-to-face meetings are disruptive for most participants because they have to travel great distances to participate, which extends the time they are away from their jobs. Therefore, cancelling the training program not only minimizes cost but also maximizes productive work in the short term.

Cancelling training programs might seem shortsighted. However, the cancellations may be indicators to reservations that my organization has about training programs, even taking longer range goals into account. The cancellations may reflect neither shortsightedness nor a lack of commitment to workforce development but instead a deeper, intuitive, and unexpressed doubt about the value and cost-effectiveness of traditional training programs. Even when we have implemented training programs, the results have often been disappointing. Other organizations have had similar results (Faerman & Ban, 1993).

Organizations do not want training; they want a focused behavioral change that affects their business results. Perhaps the cancellations reflect an intuitive evaluation with some merit. The cancellations may be a declaration that something else is needed, something that can address more effectively the barriers to effective training. Perhaps the cancellations are a plea for something that can operate more directly on the behavior itself without being tied to traditional models of training. My organization might be reminding me of the end (objective) of training and calling for an end (demise) of training as we have delivered it in the past.

During the late 1990s, I participated in a deeply meaningful learning environment at the Fielding Graduate Institute. Fielding is an accredited graduate school with the mission of meeting the needs of adult learners and mid-career professionals. Students complete coursework using a computer-mediated communication system called the Fielding Education Link and Information eXchange (FELIX). Based on my experience, I believe that a CML environment can be an effective and economical alternative to the cost and disruption of face-to-face training. I also believe that a CML environment can be effective in addressing the barriers to behavioral change that have not been resolved by my organization's traditional face-to-face training approaches. The goal of this chapter is to identify the key barriers to behavioral change and to analyze the effect of a CML environment on those barriers to behavioral change. However, I am not proposing that we merely use CML to do what we have always done in a less expensive and disruptive manner. I am proposing that we focus on the objective of behavioral change and explore using CML in the context of both the objective of behavioral change and the means to the objective. This is a topic that has broad applicability in the organization development community.

Objective

It is a truism in the training field that organizations seldom see the desired behavioral change resulting from their investment in training. In addition, it is expensive and disruptive to bring together a geographically dispersed team for face-to-face training, yet geographically dispersed teams are becoming the norm in today's business environment. This chapter establishes the viability of CML environments in addressing not only the geographical dispersion of the learning community but also barriers to affecting behavioral change in a large multinational corporation.

The Business Case

To facilitate full understanding of the potential business impact of my proposed approach, I provide some background information on my company, which I will call TESTCO. TESTCO is a company with $10 billion in annual sales. TESTCO sells test equipment and consulting services to companies that design, manufacture, and test electronic products. TESTCO is the preeminent supplier in the test marketplace, with a sterling reputation for innovation and product quality. We participate in a broad range of markets, and our stated objective is to be first or second in all of the markets in which we compete. Although the use of electronics is becoming ever more pervasive, many of our customers view testing as a necessary evil that does not add value. Electronics manufacturers are shortening design cycle times by use of computer-aided simulations of product designs, and this reduces the need for prototype testing. The move by companies toward designing for manufacturability and improvement of manufacturing processes also reduces the need for testing. The overall market for the products we sell is relatively flat. However, TESTCO has the stated objective of growing at 15% per year. Because we already have a large percentage of market share, sales growth will be a challenge and will require our sales organization to do new things.

Engineering excellence and technical contribution have always characterized TESTCO. Even internally, engineering is exalted. Well over 90% of our sales force employees have electrical engineering degrees, and we call them field engineers. They have historically done a marvelous job of working with our customers' engineers and first level of management and of understanding and meeting their customers' technical needs. One of the key behavioral changes desired by TESTCO senior management is for sales representatives to better understand our customers' business needs and proactively meet those business needs.

My organization is not merely mandating business growth or expecting 15% more of the same kind of business. We are expanding our capacity to deliver custom solutions and expect that area to account for much of our growth. We are also targeting the telecommunications and semiconductor manufacturing market segments. These are technology-intensive market segments that are experiencing high growth. We have recently introduced some sophisticated expensive new systems solutions in these market segments. We have also restructured our organization to more closely align our sales force with the product divisions that develop and manufacture products for these market segments. However, for these changes to have full effect, our sales organization will have to do new things. We are also restructuring our sales force so that routine add-on orders, as well as orders for less expensive products, are handled by a call center rather than by our outside sales force. It is our expectation that our outside sales force will focus on opportunities for more expensive, more sophisticated products and custom solutions. Again, for these changes to have full effect, our sales organization will have to do new things. We need a behavioral change.

What Is CML?

There are many types of CML environments: (a) chat rooms, (b) pull technologies such as the World Wide Web, (c) push technologies such as e-mail, (d) computer-based tutorials, (e) computer-based simulations, and so on. They span (a) synchronous (users must be online at the same time) and asynchronous (users can log on when it is convenient) communications, (b) interactive and noninteractive environments, and (c) person-person and person-machine interactions. There are significant differences in the efficacy of different types of computer-mediated environments for facilitating the development and reinforcement of behaviors in an individual. When I use the abbreviation *CML* in this chapter, I mean an asynchronous, interactive, person-to-person environment. Computer-mediated learning is an electronic forum, but it is not impersonal. Think of using CML like writing letters that multiple people read and to which they respond. The written medium is different from the spoken word. It amplifies some nuances of communications and attenuates others. In my experience, CML provides a forum for exploring and applying new concepts and developing new skills while getting feedback from an incredibly bright, insightful, and diverse learning community. Computer-mediated learning can be implemented using a variety of available software that supports the multiuser conferencing used to post work that other people can read and reply to. However, the technology is strictly a support system for the interpersonal relationship building and mutual learning that characterizes CML. Computer-mediated learning has some similarities to a chat room in that you see a history of the dialogue that has transpired. However, there are significant differences. Chat rooms are typically synchronous, which means that people engaged in a dialogue are logged on at the same time. Computer-mediated learning is asynchronous, which means that people log on when it is convenient for them, wherever they are in the world. The asynchronous nature of CML leads to a much more thoughtful and considered discourse than is typical in chat rooms. Most of a student's time is spent offline. Students primarily log on only to post their work created offline and to download other people's work for reflection and response. Computer-mediated learning is a very interactive, person-to-person environment. In one formative CML environment in which I participated, the interpersonal rapport among students begins to develop during a 3-day kickoff meeting where students meet face-to-face and work together in small groups. The intimacy of the CML environment sustains interpersonal rapport and even allows it to grow.

Where Are the Instructors?

Instructors do exist in CML, but they do not perform the normal role of pouring knowledge into the open crania of students. Computer-mediated learning is aimed at self-directed adult learners. The instructor (a) establishes the course objectives and content, (b) provides feedback, and (c) facilitates the learning environment. The instructor is an important part of the learning environment. However, what makes CML work is the community of learners taking ownership of their own learning and providing reinforcement and feedback to each other.

Overcoming Barriers to Behavioral Change

The basic thrust of my use of CML is based on the twin premises that you cannot affect complex behavioral change overnight and that, in many cases, peer pressure is more effective than management pressure at affecting behavioral change. As an example of an effective training intervention, I use the Dale Carnegie sales training class. I have experience with the Dale Carnegie sales training class as both a student and a graduate assistant, and I can verify that graduates of the program exhibit new competencies and behave in a different way from how they behaved before the class. There are several distinctive things about the class. The first is that the class addresses one competency at a time, one night a week, over 14 weeks. Each session of the class follows the same format. The instructor lectures on a concept. The instructor role-plays a demonstration of the new behavior with a graduate assistant (models the behavior). The students adapt the concept to their own situations and role-play the behavior of implementing the concept in a way that applies to them. Then the students are given the task of applying the concept in their work during the following week. At the beginning of the next session, the class is broken up into groups, and each individual presents to the breakout group how he or she used the new concept and how the new concept worked for that individual. The members of the breakout group vote on who applied the concept most effectively during the previous week. The ones selected by each breakout group tell their stories in front of the entire class. The entire class then votes on the one individual who best used the concept during the previous week.

This approach to training works, but only if all of the class members can be in the same place at the same time every week. Computer-mediated learning can be used to adapt this training format to geographically dispersed class participants.

CML and the Learning Organization

My manager recently asked me to lead the charge to develop a learning organization culture. I believe that CML can be an integral part of the mix in making that happen. The term *learning organization culture* can mean different things to different people. I begin my definition of learning organization culture by breaking the phrase into two parts and defining each of them separately.

Learning Organizations

Garvin (1993) defines a learning organization as "an organization skilled at creating, acquiring, and transferring knowledge and at modifying its behavior to reflect new knowledge and insights" (p. 80). This definition incorporates three distinct aspects of learning organizations. The first aspect is that organizations learn only through individuals that learn (Senge, 1990). The second aspect is that organizations learn only when knowledge in the organization is managed and transferred throughout the organization. The third aspect is that the behavior of the organization (and of people within the organization) has to change to reflect new knowledge. If an organization lacks any of these three aspects, then it is not a learning organization.

Organizational Culture

The term *culture* can be defined as follows:

> A pattern of shared basic assumptions that the group learned as it solved its problems of external adaptation and internal integration that has worked well enough to be considered valid and, therefore, to be taught to new members as the correct way to perceive, think, and feel in relations to those problems. (Schein, 1992, p. 12)

Integrating these two definitions into the phrase *learning organization culture* has some interesting implications. The definition of learning organization talks about behaviors, which are hard to change. The definition of culture excludes mention of behavior but talks about shared basic assumptions, which are even harder to change. Senge (1990) proposes that creating a learning organization requires creating new shared basic assumptions among the members of the organization. Schein (1992) states that behavioral regularities within a group are often a result of shared learning and, therefore, a manifestation of deeper shared assumptions. Schein states that basic underlying assumptions are the ultimate sources of action, so changing behaviors becomes much easier when basic assumptions are changed.

The Role of CML in Learning Organizations

The following characteristics of learning organizations and organizational culture present as unique strengths and attributes of CML:

- Creating, acquiring, and transferring knowledge
- Modifying behavior to reflect new knowledge and insights
- Solving problems of external adaptation and internal integration

Creating, Acquiring, and Transferring Knowledge

Knowledge is created at both the individual and group levels (Dixon, 2000). Computer-mediated learning can help in knowledge creation by creating an environment where an individual is bathed in new ideas and feedback on his or her own ideas. Moreover, CML facilitates the acquisition of knowledge by individuals and the transfer of knowledge among individuals. As stated previously, CML addresses the problem of too much information at one time by allowing "metered dosage" instruction. It is difficult to implement metered dosage training face-to-face if you have a distributed workforce. There is another aspect of CML that makes it a compelling learning environment: the conversion of tacit knowledge into explicit knowledge. Tacit knowledge is personal knowledge, born of personal experience that is often hard to communicate. Explicit knowledge is knowledge that has been codified in some way so that it can be transmitted in formal systematic language (Polanyi, 1966).

Because CML is a text medium, individuals must articulate what they know to communicate it. Properly facilitated, the interaction among group members forces individuals to articulate tacit knowledge and convert it into explicit knowledge, where it is readily accessible to the group. Anyone who has ever taught a young child to tie his or her shoes has had the experience of converting tacit knowledge into explicit knowledge and realizes how challenging this conversion can be. The conversion of tacit knowledge into explicit knowledge benefits the group by giving its members access to this knowledge. However, this conversion also benefits the individual who possesses the tacit knowledge. Once an individual has made his or her tacit knowledge explicit, the individual can analyze it, refine it, and adapt it to other uses.

Because CML is a text environment, it is self-documenting. This means that all of the new explicit knowledge created and shared in the small CML group can be made readily available to the larger organization.

Modifying Behavior to Reflect New Knowledge and Insights

The conversion of explicit knowledge into tacit knowledge is equally valuable and also facilitated by CML. Explicit knowledge is powerful because it is transferred to another more easily than is tacit knowledge. However, tacit knowledge is more powerful because it enables us to do something more effectively and efficiently. Reading a book about driving a car gives us explicit knowledge, but it is not sufficient to make us good drivers. The only way we become good drivers is by internalizing the knowledge—by driving. The way we acquire tacit knowledge is by *doing*. Acquiring and transferring knowledge, and modifying behavior to reflect new knowledge and insights, is part of a self-reinforcing spiral. By doing, we acquire knowledge and help to convert explicit knowledge into tacit knowledge. Our interaction with the group in CML helps us to convert our tacit knowledge back into explicit knowledge, with the benefits of our own experiences, which contribute to the explicit knowledge available to the group. In addition, our interactions with the group motivate us to try to modify our behavior to reflect new knowledge and then to contribute our own discoveries back to the group.

Solving Problems of External Adaptation and Internal Integration

This aspect of learning organizations comes from Schein's (1992) definition of organizational culture but is also quite relevant to learning organizations. People are most likely to engage in learning when they see that it is relevant (Senge, 1990). Most people do not learn "just in case"; they learn "just in time." People are much more receptive if learning is done in the context of solving problems or achieving some desired future state. Because CML is not as disruptive as face-to-face training, it can be integrated much more readily into the way people are doing their jobs. Computer-mediated learning has a real advantage over face-to-face training because so many work groups are geographically dispersed in today's business environment.

The Three Greatest Barriers to Behavioral Change

In my opinion, the greatest barriers to traditional face-to-face training affecting behavioral change are that (a) we give people too much information to absorb at one time, (b) people do not begin to apply the new knowledge immediately, and (c) the adoption of new behaviors is not properly reinforced.

Too Much Information at One Time

The traditional face-to-face training class in TESTCO is a 3-day class with a fair portion (50% or more) of lecture. Typically, the student gets a lot of information during that time, with insufficient time to absorb the material and practice new skills and behaviors. The Dale Carnegie sales training class works on one major concept at a time and gives the student time to absorb the concept, tailor it to his or her work situation, and practice it before moving on to the next concept.

New Knowledge Not Applied Immediately

When implemented properly, face-to-face classes not only provide information, they also motivate the student to do new things. The knowledge from the class and the motivation to do something new begin to dissipate immediately if the concepts taught in the class are not put into practice and reinforced. The group reporting approach used in the Dale Carnegie sales training class is very effective at getting people to practice a new behavior, for several reasons.

1. Most salespeople are competitive, and they want to win the recognition of their peers.
2. Class members do not want to get up in front of their peers and admit that they did not apply the concept from the previous week.
3. Class members feel left out if they do not have a story to share.
4. Class members find it is very difficult to fabricate a story about how they used the concept if they did not because their peers can see through the fabrication.

Adoption of New Behaviors Not Properly Reinforced

Another factor in the success of the Dale Carnegie training approach is that all of the success stories that students are hearing from other students validate and reinforce the value of the behavioral change as well as add to the students' understanding of the concept. In this way, the Dale Carnegie approach uses a strong peer pressure and peer recognition system to (a) help students to understand the concepts taught in class, (b) facilitate the students in applying the concepts taught in class, and (c) reinforce the desired behavioral change.

CML to the Rescue

The sort of "metered dosage" instruction, immediate application, and peer-group interaction I have described are difficult in TESTCO's work environment. The distributed and mobile nature of our sales force means that face-to-face meetings require travel, which is expensive and disruptive. The CML environment enables extended, focused peer interaction across the boundaries of space and time without travel. In TESTCO's traditional face-to-face training sessions, we get the students together, give them a lot of information, give them (or help them to develop) an action plan to implement the new concepts in their work, and then send them home. There is very little follow-up and reinforcement. The trainer goes on to the next training class. The student goes back to his or her old job with a backlog of urgent matters that have stacked up while the student was in training. The student's manager typically does not do anything different to reinforce the application of the concepts that the student learned in the training class.

With the CML environment, new concepts can be presented in a more leisurely and modular way. Students can apply the new concepts one or two at a time, and this helps them to better understand the concepts and increases the likelihood that they will apply the concepts. Applying the concepts increases the likelihood of real behavioral change and further helps students to understand the concepts. The CML environment is one in which strong peer interactions allow students to learn from one another. In my experience, students often cite peer interaction as a desired, yet unfulfilled, aspect of face-to-face training. The CML environment also uses peer recognition to increase the likelihood that the new concepts are applied and that the application of the new concepts is discussed. This discussion creates a self-reinforcing, upward spiral that builds greater knowledge and familiarity with the new concepts, which further reinforces the desired behavioral change.

Opportunity for CML:
Introduction of Another Traditional Training Class

My experience with CML in the master's program at Fielding made me a believer in the advantages of using CML. As I was finishing my master's program, I saw an opportunity to apply CML in my organization. My organization was in the pilot stage of delivering a new training intervention called the One-to-One Value Proposition Workshop (VPW). I was one of the facilitators of the class. This class was designed as a traditional face-to-face training class. The VPW was a sophisticated synthesis of several concepts that are presented in leading-edge books on sales and marketing. The class was a 1-day conceptual overview of a methodology for the following:

1. Identifying value as determined by different members of a customer's decision-making team
2. Developing a total solution that incorporates only those elements that the customer deems of value
3. Articulating the value of a proposed solution to each individual in the customer's decision-making team in a way that is meaningful to that individual (hence the term "one-to-one")

This new course directly addressed the approach that our sales organization needed to take to grow our strategic selling effectiveness and that was required to meet our business unit's stated objective of 15% annual sales growth. However, implementing the VPW methodology required new behaviors and many competencies that were new or underdeveloped in our sales organization. The VPW touched on these competencies but did not develop them; the workshop described what to do but did not define how to do it. The workshop moved our sales force employees from the "unconscious incompetent" stage, where they were not aware of what they did not know, to the "conscious incompetent" stage, where they realized what they did not know. Once our students realized their ignorance, they became uncomfortable with that state. This introduced an excellent opportunity for a CML intervention.

Applying CML to a Traditional Training Class

The original format for the VPW was an 8-hour lecture with more than 100 presentation slides. I delivered the VPW in its original lecture format to four different audiences. One audience was a group of TESTCO consultants who engage with customers on a for-charge basis. I presented to two different groups of sales representatives and marketing people from throughout Asia. I also delivered the course to a group of sales representatives and their managers from the United States who call on TESTCO's largest customer. From these participants, I collected a rich set of feedback on how to improve the workshop.

Workshop attendees thought that the material in the VPW was good, but they needed help in understanding the concepts and applying the concepts to their opportunities. Many attendees wanted less lecture, yet there was a lot of new information they needed to absorb to move forward and implement the concepts of the VPW. Many attendees also stated that they wanted to apply these concepts to their accounts while in the class. My experience was that they did not have the information entering the class to move all the way through the process. This is understandable given that the occasion of the VPW was the first time that many of the attendees had been exposed to these concepts. Also, the amount of account knowledge varied significantly by salesperson, so some salespeople could move further, and faster, through the exercises. In addition, workshop attendees tended to have varied roles: sales representatives, sales managers, marketing center people, and product marketing people. One course could not fit all people's needs well. I incorporated all of the feedback I received and developed a plan that had a special role for CML.

Training Plan

I developed a three-stage delivery of the VPW that enables a wide range of audiences to get what they need from the course. These three stages build on each other, yet each is a freestanding module with its own deliverable. It is important to note that CML was used only in Stage 3. I view CML as an important and underused tool. However, it is only one of many tools available for education. The training designer must factor in training objectives and contextual issues in selecting the best medium for the training intervention. As I describe each stage of the VPW, I explain why I chose the medium I used for that stage.

Stage 1. The first stage of the course is a self-paced tutorial on the concepts presented in the VPW. I created the tutorial in Adobe Portable Document Format (PDF) so that it had a high degree of portability and could be published and distributed electronically. A sample of implementation concepts, such as the market-focused value proposition (Lanning & Phillips, 1987) and the whole product (Levitt, 1980), were included as well as a proficiency test to ensure that students understood key concepts. Successful completion of this test is a prerequisite for enrolling in Stage 2.

I chose this medium for Stage 1 because it is less expensive and more convenient than face-to-face learning or CML, but it was sufficient to help participants understand the concepts behind the one-to-one value proposition. Trainees did not need an interactive medium to meet my objectives for Stage 1.

Stage 2. This stage is a face-to-face classroom workshop. The class begins with a brief overview of the concepts presented in Stage 1. The majority of the class time is spent in breakout groups of three to five students. The groups work through a case study that tracks the modules in the tutorial and complete worksheets that help them to develop a one-to-one value proposition for the case. In parallel with the case, students spend time filling out the worksheets on one of their own accounts, if applicable. This enables them to identify any gaps in account knowledge that need to be addressed to develop a one-to-one value proposition. The facilitator helps the students to develop an action plan to close their knowledge gaps. The groups present their work on each module to each other, thereby increasing shared learning. After each module, the facilitator presents completed worksheets for each module and leads a group debriefing and discussion on the module. There are multiple answers to the case study modules that have validity, and I was more interested in the students wrestling with applying the concepts than in coming up with any one specific answer. However, the case study is cumulative, and each module depends on the results from the previous module. For me to manage the workshop, the class had to work from the same set of answers to the previous modules.

My organization was quite familiar with classroom training but unfamiliar with CML. To facilitate organizational acceptance of CML, I decided to use CML to augment the traditional training approach rather than replace it. I subtly repositioned the face-to-face class. I used the 1-day VPW to help our students apply the concepts in the course. In addition to working through the case study, I structured the existing class as a 1-day kickoff event and then had ongoing CML related to each module. In the 1-day class, participants worked in teams to begin to apply the concepts of the course to opportunities in their sales territory. As students begin to apply the concepts, they (a) begin to realize which competencies they lack, (b) start to form new bonds and strengthen existing bonds with team members, and (c) begin to form bonds with the course facilitator. The course facilitator begins to form bonds with the students and to understand the students' skill gaps.

Even though the face-to-face medium is expensive and disruptive, I chose face-to-face for Stage 2 for two reasons. First, it is feasible to work through a case study in a well-bounded period of time. This is not true of a real sales opportunity. Second, I felt that the face-to-face medium was needed to meet the objectives for Stage 2. I was particularly intent on the development of interpersonal bonds among the students, and between the students and me, in preparation for Stage 3.

Stage 3. The intent of this stage is to facilitate and reinforce the application of the concepts of the VPW to an actual opportunity. Stage 2 was pretty standard fare for face-to-face training courses. However, in Stage 3, we now introduce the CML environment for follow-up, continued learning, and reinforcement of the desired behavioral change. It is difficult to do this in a classroom because strategic opportunities proceed at their own pace, primarily driven by the customer's business situation, and take place over an extended period of time. Different individuals proceed at different paces. Also, getting people together on a regular basis in a classroom, or even on a conference call, is difficult. Yet there is a real advantage in enabling people to learn from each other's experiences and share their insights and best practices. Stage 3 was implemented through an asynchronous CML environment. We used a tool called Caucus because another group within TESTCO that would give us technical support was using it. The way we structured the course was to work through a series of process steps.

Value Proposition Construction Process Steps

1. Define target opportunity and analyze customer's decision-making unit.
2. Define the core product we will offer.
3. Define the whole product we will offer.
4. Ascertain the cost of the whole product.
5. Gain an understanding of competition.
6. Construct the market-focused value proposition (MFVP) for the target customer.
7. Using the MFVP, construct a one-to-one value proposition for each member of the customer's decision-making unit.
8. Build a sales plan to deliver the one-to-one value propositions.

Stage 3 is structured as a collaborative work group of six learners plus a facilitator and, where possible, the manager of the group. The ideal scenario for the collaborative work group is an intact work group such as a sales district, an account team, or a virtual team focused on a specific project. However, the Stage 3 approach has merit with any group of individuals. The time duration of Stage 3 is open-ended, but participants should expect to participate for at least 3 months, with the expectation to spend 2 to 4 hours a week devoted to this endeavor. The time would be spent documenting their work, responding to other people's work, and reflecting on other people's responses to their work.

Advantages of Using CML for Stage 3

I chose CML for Stage 3 because it has multiple benefits.

1. The asynchronous communication of the Caucus electronic forum enables the training department and sales management to provide instruction, coaching, and reinforcement in a manner that is much less disruptive to the learner than is face-to-face training. Computer-mediated learning also enables training in a manner that is relevant to the student's job requirements, over a longer period of time, and at less cost.
2. Training evolves from an "event" that is soon forgotten to a new way of performing the sales function.
3. The self-documenting nature of the Caucus forum allows us to capture and communicate best practices, which is a key initiative endorsed by senior management.

4. The self-documenting nature of the Caucus forum allows us to capture valuable information for the *check* part of the PDCA (plan-do-check-act) cycle of continuous process improvement.

5. The information in the Caucus forum enables the training department to make behavioral change (Kirkpatrick Level 3) and business results (Kirkpatrick Level 4) measurements on the effectiveness of the VPW training intervention (Kirkpatrick, 1998).

Kirkpatrick's four levels are well-established measures of training effectiveness in the training and development community. Our organization has had difficulty in capturing Level 3 and Level 4 data.

Results of Applying CML to a Traditional Training Class

As a pilot class for the CML-based implementation of the VPW, I selected a group of people called the Field Quality Council. Their function was to work with top management in each of our four worldwide geographic regions to implement quality methodologies in our field sales organizations. The group was composed of members from Japan, Hong Kong, the United Kingdom, and the United States. One of the four field quality managers served as the sponsor for the project, and I served as the facilitator.

The regional field quality managers were a good group to serve as a surrogate for our sales force for a CML implementation of the VPW class. Because they were so geographically dispersed, CML was an approach with a lot of appeal to them. Frequent face-to-face meetings were out of the question, and even teleconferences presented a problem because no matter what time they picked, at least one of the members was calling in the middle of the night. Also, the quality managers were "selling" their concept of quality to the field organization and had to develop and articulate a one-to-one value proposition for different managers in their field operation. The field quality managers felt that they faced a "quality stigma." In some cases, the quality methodology they proposed was viewed as increasing complexity and work, not adding value, being too theoretical, and not being of practical benefit in running a business. The quality managers felt that it would take a period of time to work through the one-to-one value proposition construction process, and they might proceed at different rates, but there was value in working together using CML to do this work. Because of a perceived need to move forward quickly, combined with the difficulty in getting together face-to-face in the short term, the group decided to forgo Stage 2 (the face-to-face case study analysis workshop). We would use only Stage 1 (each member would read the tutorial materials) and Stage 3 (CML forum). I was comfortable with skipping Stage 2 because I already had a high level of rapport with the field quality managers, as they did with each other.

We structured the project into a series of steps, with first-pass time lines for each step. At the end of each step of the project, the sponsor and I would summarize group learnings and formulate next steps.

<u>Process Steps</u>

1. Analyze target decision-making unit—February 15-26 (2 weeks)
2. Define core product for quality—March 1-12 (2 weeks)
3. Define the whole product for quality—March 15-26 (2 weeks)
4. Ascertain cost of the quality product—March 29-April 1 (1 week)
5. Gain an understanding of the competition—April 5-9 (1 week)

*Finalize Steps 1 to 5 using a teleconference, if necessary—April 14

6. Construct the MFVP for quality methodology at TESTCO—April 15-May 7 (3 weeks)
7. Using the MFVP, construct the one-to-one value propositions for target customers' quality—May 10-June 4 (1 month)
   Validate with face-to-face meeting, if necessary—June 8 (London Field Quality Council meeting)
8. Build a sales plan to deliver the one-to-one value propositions for quality—June 14-July 9 (1 month)

Each process step had worksheets requiring specific information that related to developing a one-to-one value proposition for the target opportunity. Filling out the worksheets was not as important as the thought process required to fill out the worksheets. The first-pass attempts at filling out the worksheets were rather shallow, as were the responses from the field quality managers to each other. As the process facilitator, I asked some probing specific questions of each of the field quality managers. The universal response I received from the field quality managers was "Those are tough questions!" The responses to my specific probing questions were much deeper, more reflective, and more tentative.

As the quality managers struggled to answer the questions on the worksheets, they had to face up to some assumptions they had and became aware of some specific gaps in their knowledge. The interactions among the quality managers became much more thoughtful and reflective. They began to point out and challenge assumptions and knowledge gaps among their peers. The discourse was respectful yet challenging. We decided to extend the process step for an additional 2 weeks to enable each of the quality managers to validate some assumptions and try to close knowledge gaps.

The quality managers reported their work in an ongoing manner. It was apparent from the managers' ongoing postings that the conversations they were having with their internal customers were high value and opening up areas of discussion that had previously been unexplored. Easy answers to the questions on the worksheets were still hard to come by, but the overall understanding of each quality manager of the business issues of the managers in his or her geographic region was growing. As the group neared the extended deadline period, we felt comfortable that we had done a sufficient job on the first step. Group enthusiasm was high because of the new insight and direction that the group members had gained.

Working through just one step of the VPW in CML proved to me that the concept was valid and that CML was the right medium for this kind of training. Computer-mediated learning addressed the barriers of giving people too much information to absorb at one time, of people not beginning to apply the new knowledge immediately, and of not properly reinforcing the adoption of new behaviors.

Recommendations for Companies Considering CML

To help those who might like to introduce CML into their organizations, in this section I make explicit my own tacit knowledge gained from the implementation of CML. I draw from my experience with Fielding, my organization, and an online course I took at another postgraduate institution.

Recommendation 1: Do Not Position CML as Training

I overestimated the receptiveness of my organization to the CML implementation of the VPW. Most people were intrigued by the concept but hesitant to move forward, giving some variation of the justification that the time "just wasn't right" to implement this program for their particular group. The problem with getting people to try this new approach was exacerbated by a series of major reorganizations that tended to make people more risk averse. I believe that another unstated factor was also operating: People were confused because what I was proposing did not *look* like training; indeed, it is different from the training they had experienced before. Therefore, I recommend that proponents of CML position it as an alternative to training. Use the fact that CML is different as an advantage. Based on the predisposition of the organization, CML can be positioned as collaboratively building new mental models, collectively solving problems, sharing best practices, facilitating peer review, raising people to a new threshold of consciousness, or some alternate conceptualization that is likely to engender favor in a particular organization. These all can be viewed as valid ways to describe the possible consequences of using CML.

Recommendation 2: Make Sure That the CML Forum Is Used as the Group's Communication Mechanism

After my Fielding experience, I took a course at another postgraduate institution that was supposed to make substantial use of CML. Our class was to meet once a month face-to-face and do the rest of our work collaboratively online. However, most of the work wound up being done with phone calls, through one-to-one e-mails, or in the face-to-face class. I believe that this happened because the other students and the course facilitator were used to a traditional classroom setting, had little experience with CML, and reverted to the approaches they had always used. The result of this breakdown in the process was that there was very little group collaboration and learning from other members in the group. It is important to remember that there are multiple aspects of CML that enhance the learning process, including strong peer interaction and peer recognition systems to (a) help students to understand the concepts taught in class, (b) facilitate the students in applying the concepts taught in class, and (c) reinforce the desired behavioral change. It is also much more difficult for the facilitator to manage group process if there are a lot of back-channel communications among group members, especially if the facilitator is not privy to those communications. Therefore, it is important for the facilitator to ensure that communication among group members takes place in the CML forum. There can be legitimate exceptions, but they should be few and far between.

Recommendation 3: Have a Face-to-Face Kickoff Event

I think that it is imperative to kick off the CML program with a face-to-face event. The objectives for this event should be to begin to develop rapport among group members, establish expectations for group processes and work output, and begin to establish group behavioral norms. These all are things that face-to-face groups must attend to, but virtual groups have added complexities introduced by computer-mediated communication (McGrath & Hollingshead, 1994).

Conclusion

The CML environment has the potential to provide a highly effective and efficient complementary approach or complete alternative to traditional face-to-face training classes. In the face of rising travel costs and the expense of time away from the job, CML is often less expensive than traditional training. Computer-mediated learning can sustain the training class's learning environment well beyond the usual face-to-face meeting time. The self-documenting nature of CML facilitates communication and documentation of corporate best practices and provides a method to analyze training effectiveness. As a new vehicle for corporate training, success does not come easily and requires organizations to (a) position CML as a form of computer-mediated "work" rather than as "training," (b) use the CML environment as the participants' major mechanism for communication to promote group collaboration and learning, and (c) start the CML program with a face-to-face kickoff event to get the group off to a good beginning.

References

Dixon, N. M. (2000). *Common knowledge: How companies thrive by sharing what they know.* Boston: Harvard Business School Press.

Faerman, S. R., & Ban, C. (1993). Trainee satisfaction and training impact: Issues in training evaluation. *Public Productivity & Management Review, 16,* 299-314.

Garvin, D. A. (1993, July-August). Building a learning organization. *Harvard Business Review,* pp. 78-91.

Kirkpatrick, D. L. (1998). *Evaluating training programs: The four levels* (2nd ed.). San Francisco: Berrett-Koehler.

Lanning, M. J., & Phillips, L. W. (1987). [Written materials handed out at seminar titled "Building Market-Focused Organizations"].

Levitt, T. (1980, January-February). Marketing success through differentiation—of anything. *Harvard Business Review,* pp. 2-9.

McGrath, J. E., & Hollingshead, A. B. (1994). *Groups interacting with technology: Ideas, evidence, issues, and an agenda.* Thousand Oaks, CA: Sage.

Polanyi, M. (1966). *The tacit dimension.* Garden City, NY: Doubleday.

Schein, E. H. (1992). *Organizational culture and leadership* (2nd ed.). San Francisco: Jossey-Bass.

Senge, P. M. (1990). *The fifth discipline: The art and practice of the learning organization.* New York: Doubleday/Currency.

Chapter 14

The Executive Master Class

Cyberspace and the New Frontiers of Executive Education

Bruce LaRue
and Mark R. Sobol

We work with many executives who report feeling overwhelmed by the challenges they face and dismayed by the feeling that they always seem to be "behind the curve," never quite grasping the forces that affect all they do. The enhancement of the awareness of leaders may turn out to be a critical element for the evolution of our organizations during this tumultuous time. Too often, individuals lack a keen sense of the system in which they operate and of the powerful internal and external forces that directly and indirectly shape their world. In general, our organizations are missing the facility to provide a perpetual stage for observation and reflection, a sanctuary that shelters us from the tyranny of the urgent.

We asked ourselves whether an executive development process that elicited a heightened sense of awareness, personal accountability, and capacity to initiate personal and organizational change would make a difference. This chapter tells the story of an executive development intervention that accomplished this through a process of online coaching and education.

Introduction

It Began as Face-to-Face Coaching

During the spring of 2000, we were engaged to provide coaching for several executives within the engineering division of a leading telecommunications provider responsible for the design, implementation, and operation of its national cellular network. John, a recently promoted vice president, led the team. He was a longtime veteran of the telecommunications business, an "old hand" whose vast experience and maturity could help to temper the relative youth of his peers. John was at the same time on the glide path to retirement in just 4 years and eagerly looked forward to the day when he could put his career behind him. From his perspective, the pace of change and the complexity of today's business environment seemed better suited to younger leaders.

The prime operating characteristic of the team was that it acted as a collection of "silos," working independently of each other except during their obligatory monthly management meeting, where discourse was generally limited to reports from the six functional areas. Rarely could the team members ever be said to "think together." During a coaching session, we began to explore ways to provide developmental support to the members of John's management team, in keeping with his stated goal of "building the bench strength" of his organization during this time of great change and growth. He set as his measurement of success "the number of managers deemed ready for promotion" by the end of the year. We suggested adopting the combination of an online and face-to-face coaching and education model to meet the challenge.

Evolution to Online Coaching, Education, and Organization Development

We began with a team meeting followed by two rounds of individual interviews for gauging interest and establishing the "What's in it for me?" factor. John made it clear to all, however, that there was no requirement to participate. Together with the team, we determined that there was sufficient interest and desire to move ahead. It was evident that there was no small amount of trepidation about the increased workload, which added several additional hours to an already demanding schedule in a 7-day-a-week, 24-hour-a-day operation. So, with a mixture of curiosity, excitement, and fear, we commenced a 12-week observation and dialogue to explore organizational systems from three interrelated dimensions: the individual, the organization, and society. As our face-to-face and online dialogue progressed, a clear image of the current state of the team began to emerge for all to observe from a variety of different perspectives.

This exploration was meant to enable the participants to discern the assumptions (Drucker, 1999, p. 182) and implicit theories (McMaster, 1996) permeating their organization. It was also designed to surface their espoused theories and "theories-in-use" (Argyris, 1978, 1990, 1992, 1993; Argyris & Schön, 1996) by gaining a deeper appreciation for the gap between these two poles of understanding. When their tacit knowledge became explicit (Nonaka & Takeuchi, 1995) for all to hear, the foundation for preparing the leaders to design and implement their own organization development initiatives was created with minimal reliance on external resources. As we will see, our intention to build *internal capacity* for organizational change in John's director team (rather than perpetuating a traditional form of dependence on external consultants) proved to be a crucial theme of the learning initiative.

What we were unable to predict, however, was that this training would quickly lead to personal and organizational transformation through what came to be known as the Executive Master Class Program. As the participants began to compare and contrast the current state of their team and organization with different theories of operation, a new awareness emerged. The participants reported a heightened sense of consciousness of themselves, their teammates, and their organization. A reflective dialogue was sparked during the 12-week learning process in which the team explored a variety of ways in which to make changes to their personal, team, and organizational behavior.

In the sections that follow, we outline the manner in which we structured the online learning program around the unique needs and challenges that John and his team faced. Along the way, we outline the core principles that serve as the foundation of the Executive Master Class Program together with their broader implications for executive education in the 21st century.

Structuring the Intervention

Connecting With the Team

We first met with John to determine his team's learning and development goals. We wanted to get a sense of his long-term learning objectives while gaining a deeper understanding of the more immediate issues for which he was seeking resolution. Although John had his own goals in mind for his team, the team members were encouraged to determine what was in it for them. The learning opportunity we developed needed to be in alignment with both personal career objectives and the organization's business strategy. Paradoxically, this meant that the learning system we constructed would contribute to making each participant more marketable outside the firm.

Although this approach extends the goals of the learning process beyond those of the current organization, we have found that this is an essential component of an overall retention strategy. Any effective learning system must be sensitive to both the unique learning needs of each individual *and* the organization. We believe that if the learning and development needs of knowledge workers are continually met, they will find little need to venture outside the walls of the firm.

Based on our interviews with John's team members, we knew that we had to construct this learning opportunity in a way that was sensitive to and integrated with their already demanding personal and professional lives. They were familiar with traditional classroom approaches to learning, but they generally found these approaches to be quite disruptive and irrelevant to their personal and work lives. They also found these traditional approaches to lack the kind of stimulating interaction among their peers that they desired. The same held true for many Web-based systems, such as computer-based training, that focus on content delivery rather than peer interaction.

In essence, the aim of this learning initiative was to develop effective communities of practice that were focused on the creation and application of new knowledge rather than to deliver a certain content of knowledge from teacher to student. (For more on the principle of communities of practice, see, e.g., Brown & Duguid, 1991, 2000; Lave, 1988; Lave & Wenger, 1991; Lesser, 2000; Lesser, Fontaine, & Slusher, 2000; Rogoff & Lave, 1999; Wenger, 1998).

We also understood that we were dealing with highly skilled and accomplished specialists in their respective fields of endeavor. Therefore, the aim of this proposed learning system was not to further this area of specialized technical knowledge but rather to develop competencies in and gain a deeper understanding of the areas *of organization development, change,* and *personal mastery.*

By the term *personal mastery,* we refer to the ability of the participants to stand outside of their current situations and their own limited perspectives. This allows the managers or executives to obtain a level of distance from their current challenges and to see them from the broader context of interdependent relationships, political forces, and environmental and market changes and to choose the most suitable approach for moving their organization forward. As we will see, the online learning component of this program played a central role in the development of personal mastery.

The Online System

John's director team happened to be co-located, while many of the sub-organizations reporting to his directors were distributed across the country. Like many modern organizations, his team members needed to build competence in managing distributed work teams. For this reason, and because of their extremely busy and varied schedules, we decided to conduct the program with a mixture of face-to-face and online work. The online system we used was a Web-based asynchronous groupware system, allowing the team members to conduct their work from anywhere in the world and at any time convenient for them within the agreed-on pace and structure of the program. The asynchronous nature of the system allowed the learning experience to occur with a minimum of disruption to the normal work flow of the team members while at the same time capturing and organizing their knowledge in one central location.

Casting the Net

We also learned that John and his directors rarely met to work together aside from monthly strategy meetings, unless an emergency or other contingency compelled them to do so. To stimulate greater interaction among the entire team, we divided the members into groups of approximately three members each. These became known as *lead* teams. Each lead team was assigned a leadership role in consecutive 2-week sections of the 12-week learning module and was responsible for generating a reflective commentary on assigned reading materials. After posting responses to designated areas in the groupware system, the rest of the group provided critical commentary on the work of the lead team with a specific eye toward the development of new applications.

Each of the lead teams was responsible for generating a reflective commentary on assigned reading materials, with an emphasis on the implications of what its members had read for their organizational practice. Following the regular postings to designated areas in the groupware system, the rest of the group provided critical commentary on the work of the lead team, again with a specific eye toward suggesting further areas for application to their workplace.

Combining Face-to-Face
Meetings With Web-Based Learning

The 1-Day Orientation Retreat

We began the program with a 1-day orientation retreat in which we provided participants with a highly focused orientation to the Executive Master Class Program, the online groupware system, and basic norms of online collaborative learning. On the surface, norms of online discourse might seem self-evident. They are essential to creating a safe and productive learning environment. Because the online environment lacks many of the normal physical cues present in face-to-face dialogue, it is essential to make one's emotional intent clear through writing. We also emphasized the importance of timely interaction so as to keep pace with the agreed-on structure and timing of the course. Because participants are required to provide feedback to one another's work, we stressed the importance of (a) being timely, (b) being constructive, (c) paraphrasing and asking clarifying questions rather than assuming the intent of the writer, (d) differentiating between critical commentary and criticism, and (e) offering suggestions rather than merely pointing out problems. We suggested these basic norms, and participants modified them and developed others based on personal and group preferences.

Monthly Face-to-Face Meetings

We met together off-site once a month, where we spent approximately 6 hours with John and his team members. The time was used to engage in further dialogue about pressing concerns facing their organization *in light of what they had learned*. As we will see in later sections of this chapter, through the structured use of online dialogue, we were able to continue uninterrupted our exploration of the critical issues begun in these meetings. In this way, we were able to build and sustain a level of momentum and exploration not possible in face-to-face meetings alone. We now provide a sample of the kind of dialogue we engaged in to raise the level of awareness of John's team, followed by a discussion of the critical role of online discourse in this process.

Blending Theory and Practice

We took John's team members through various group exercises designed to surface conflicting organizational theories operating in their organization (see the subsection titled "The Role of Implicit Theory" later) and to develop ideas for resolving conflicts. We wove the discussion into the theoretical themes explored in the course by providing a bridge between the normally obtuse realm of theory and the thorny problems of daily work. We drew connections between their tacit understanding of work and how their assumptions live through their actions. For example, we queried the following: "Are organizations machines and the people within them mindless cogs in need of strict control, or are they interdependent elements of a highly intelligent organism in need of inspiration and challenge in order to move them into higher levels of achievement and personal mastery?" "Do the assumptions living in your organization have anything at all to do with the precipitous decline in morale you are witnessing and to your ability to attract and retain top talent?" "How are declines in morale and loss of talent affecting your bottom line, especially when this talent often leaves only to enrich the coffers of your competition?"

The history of the industrial age, we suggested, appeared to be strongly associated with the systematic elimination of the human factor from the production equation. This is the legacy of Frederick Taylor and his many re-incarnations through total quality management and various forms of statistical process control, lean manufacturing, just-in-time manufacturing, reengineering, and nine-tenths of the management fads of the month. Mechanical and information-based automation seemed to support the acceleration toward de-skilled work while, paradoxically, emerging forces in the economy were demanding increased levels of knowledge and competence from workers. "If your workers were truly valued as assets and legitimate stakeholders in your company, then why are they still relegated to the cost side of your accounting ledger?" "How is Taylor's legacy affecting your management decisions to this day," we asked, "and how does this behavior stand up in light of Drucker's (1999) assertion that today's knowledge workers must be treated like volunteers—their commitment earned, not assumed?" The room would often fall silent.

During our frequent breaks, the halls hummed with cell phone conversations and the click of laptop keyboards as directors clambered to return scores of messages accumulated during the previous hour. We heard mutterings of Taylor, Drucker, HBR, Xerox PARC, and Nonaka. But would this buzz of dialogue evaporate as we emerged from this elegant boardroom? To the contrary, our questions stimulated discussion that would flourish in the halls of our virtual learning environment over the coming weeks.

Many readers of this chapter have undoubtedly experienced countless weekend conferences and workshops where condensed exercises in workplace enlightenment are explored, only to find newfound enthusiasm and understanding evaporate in the glaring light of the Monday morning grind. Some readers might even have naively imagined themselves sharing their insights with eager colleagues, only to find that the colleagues' eagerness to meet with them had more to do with project deadlines they had overlooked or new crises that had emerged in their absence. Normalcy soon sets in, relegating the insights of the previous weekend to that of a quaint, but now largely irrelevant, respite from real life. If anything, the weekend foray generates jealousy rather than interest back at work.

Meanwhile, Back at the Web Site . . .

. . . Insights Emerge

In the Executive Master Class program, dialogue generated during our monthly meetings moved seamlessly into the online environment. We continually reinforced the integration between relevant literature and the issues that John's team faced. Critical problems were engaged not in the heat of the moment but rather through the thoughtful lenses of all participants, each contributing his or her insights. Unlike phone or e-mail conversations, the participants' thinking is preserved, organized, and easily retrieved.

One example of a critical issue that arose involved new product rollouts. Serious problems routinely surfaced as the deadline for implementation of these new services rapidly approached. Customers were anxiously awaiting the new service based on heavy pre-release marketing initiatives, making delays a matter of serious company-wide concern. As the division of the company responsible for operation and maintenance of the national cellular network, John's team felt an inordinate share of the responsibility for ensuring the reliability of the new service. Yet it was also the last division in the functional food chain to engage in the process of developing and implementing the new initiative. The team had little input into the timing of its release or in the development of the engineering infrastructure for its operation. These crucial responsibilities were the domains of marketing and engineering, two separate and distinct functional silos concerned almost exclusively with their respective roles—often to the detriment of the broader process.

As one might imagine, no small amount of heated finger-pointing and blame ensued as deadlines neared, with John's team feeling most of the heat. From the perspective of each functional division, the blame for problems with the new service offering lay elsewhere. If problems were identified at the functional level, then solutions were expeditiously sought and remedies were put in place, only to see similar problems emerge with the next new product rollout. In some respects, it appeared that, as each division became more efficient, problems between divisions intensified. The result was often a less-than-desirable customer experience, loss of market share, and rapidly declining morale across the organization.

Why, after intensely focusing precious time, resources, and talent, were these problems seeming to intensify rather than go away? Would more of the same management methods achieve a different result, or was an entirely new tack necessary? If the latter, then what would this new approach look like? Should we create a task force, convene a committee, or hire a team of consultants to "fix" the problem? Or perhaps yet another reorganization was in order. His colleagues wholeheartedly affirmed him when Richard, one of John's directors, wrote in our virtual dialogue forum that it might be time to reconsider this approach as well:

> It seems like "reorganization" has become commonplace in our vocabulary. Some of the reading material suggests that we need to throw away the standard solutions and responses we've always used in the past to deal with change. Is our problem that we're still trying to find the right organizational structure or fit to deal with the competitive challenges we face? Are we in the mode of using reorganization as our standard answer when we discover something isn't working or we're not meeting stated goals? Is it possible that some groups still haven't caught up with the last reorganization and are now even further out of sync with the rest of the organization?

It is relevant for the purposes of this chapter to point out that Richard was a very thoughtful yet reserved individual. In regular face-to-face staff meetings, many of which we attended, Richard was usually the last to speak, and when he did so, his reserved demeanor often left his valuable contributions vulnerable to being overshadowed by more vocal members of John's team. In fact, John had confided in me that although Richard was an extremely talented engineer and trusted manager, this issue had contributed to his being overlooked for promotions in the past.

In the online learning environment, Richard came alive. His thoughtful and articulate reflections and responses to the work of his colleagues were on display. Unlike in staff meetings, where others might unwittingly overshadow his voice in the urgency of the moment, Richard's words echo to this day within the virtual walls of our course forum. In the world of online learning, Richard's weakness had suddenly become his strength.

The online learning environment provided a crucial opportunity of pause, continuity, and structured reflection among participants. Although meetings, workshops, task forces, and committees were the order of the day, the online learning environment offered a bridge that allowed the thinking and work of the group, begun in face-to-face meetings, to continue in an organized and coherent manner, largely irrespective of space and time. Participants could compose and reflect on their own thinking in the privacy of their homes, or in airports or hotels, and share it with their colleagues, who would reflect on it yet further. No one interrupts another person; no one has to rearrange his or her schedule; everyone is heard; and new knowledge is created, organized, and stored for future use.

. . . Insights Lead to Organizational Interventions

As we progressed toward the final third of the learning module, we asked participants to generate specific organizational interventions based on the integration of their learnings from previous weeks and to focus on a pressing need they faced in and among their respective functional areas. Generating initiatives in coordination with their bosses and peers also made the acceptance and implementation of these initiatives far smoother than previous attempts at change that tended to come down from the top of the organization.

At this point, the power and creativity of the team members was unleashed. The dialogue and learning that they had experienced during the previous weeks provided them with an entirely new perspective and lexicon. Their interactions had given all of them a new level of awareness about themselves, their teammates, and the interrelationships among their organizational units. They no longer perceived their problems in isolation but instead had gained a new sense of perspective as to how the issues with which they struggled were related to the other functional areas of their vast organization. As two directors wrote,

> I have greater awareness of the bigger picture and of the organization. I am beginning to give everything more thought and reflection. I feel a greater personal ownership and optimism. I have come to know this team better.

> A lot has changed for me. I previously had a fairly broad view of things but not very deep. I have expanded my view in both ways. I see myself focused on things I had not been focused on before. I feel more aware. I am refreshed by the differences and perspectives on our team—what we all bring to the table. I have a new appreciation and feeling for all and am feeling connected and more compelled to speak out to influence and make a difference. Now I want to learn how to reach out to other teams.

Based on their heightened sense of awareness and the shared language they had developed together, John's team members engaged in the creation of cross-functional organizational initiatives of which they could share the pride of authorship. Two initiatives were aimed at resolving conflicting organizational theories, and two others were focused on knowledge management and the development of the attributes of a learning organization.

One director, Nick, wrote a proposal that, in his words, was designed to

> arouse desire to understand what jewels of learning are already imbedded in daily work experience that lead to the power of technical know-how. And then, how to put into practice a few key actions which will further enhance the learning process and the accumulation of technical knowledge.

As we can see from his own comments, Nick had come to realize that his technical organization relied far less on the tangible explicit forms of knowledge embodied in procedure manuals and formal training. Instead, he had come to more fully appreciate the need to capitalize on the informal know-how and improvisation that routinely arise as "these maps and guides fail." Because Nick's proposal was developed in collaboration with his peers and boss, it was immediately accepted and funded. In addition, another director, Richard, integrated many of the learning and knowledge requirements outlined in Nick's proposal in his own initiative focusing on the specifications of an enterprise-wide knowledge management system. Both sets of recommendations, together with those of the entire group, are now being used in the development and deployment of this system overseen by another vice president.

In yet another combined effort, three other directors teamed up with John to create a "learning history" (based on Kleiner & Roth, 1998) designed to document in detail the problems and successes associated with their most recent product rollout. Using this simple yet highly systematic approach, they were able to demonstrate clearly the recurring problems associated with the introduction of new products and services. (Conclusions drawn from their observations can be found in the previous subsection titled ". . . Insights

Emerge.") Based on this learning history, John in turn was able to express very eloquently one of the most fundamental systemic problems facing their organization as a whole: that there were at least three implicit conflicting theories operating in their organization. As a result, the work of John and his director team was brought to the attention of the leader of the entire company, which in turn has brought about fundamental changes in the manner in which new products are brought to market.

In the sections that follow, we demonstrate how the online component of this learning experience played a pivotal role in surfacing the insights that led to this heightened internal capacity to generate organizational change.

Forging a New Developmental Perspective

A Higher Order of Consciousness

Throughout this entire learning process, program facilitators continually reinforced a sense of the importance of shared responsibility, cross-functional collaboration, and a systems-level perspective among participants. Whereas blame and finger-pointing had been the order of the day as an unrelenting barrage of problems in the organization emerged, John's team had now gained a new sense of shared accountability and responsibility for identifying and correcting the issues underlying these problems. As one director remarked, "If we are not going to make these changes, who is?"

They had indeed begun to turn the corner from what Robert Kegan refers to as the "third order" of consciousness into the "fourth order" (Kegan, 1994; see also Kegan & Lahey, 2001). Characterized by a sense of dependency and the feeling that the power for change lies outside of oneself, Kegan likens the third order of consciousness to the rebelliousness and dependency of the adolescent. This ambivalent, at times even contemptuous, stance toward authority is mirrored in the traditional relationship between the employer and the subordinates. By contrast, this learning intervention helped to foster a sense of self-authorship and perspective akin to becoming a mature adult. For example, "I remembered the way I think. This experience is allowing me to feel like an adult in the organization again. This has made life less stressful, I have gained perspective."

Although many employers have gone to great lengths to promote empowerment, self-direction, and personal accountability in their managers and employees, these initiatives may unwittingly strengthen what we see as a silo mentality along the lines of functional and departmental specializations. In turn, these lead to higher levels of fragmentation as organizational units work at cross-purposes rather than with a shared and more systemic view of the whole organization. This silo mentality, and its dysfunctional

TABLE 14.1   The Mental Demands of Modern Work

- Be the inventor or owner of our work (rather than see it as owned and created by the employer); distinguish our work from our job
- Be self-initiating, self-correcting, and self-evaluating (rather than dependent on others to frame the problems, initiate adjustments, or determine whether things are going acceptably well)
- Be guided by our own visions at work (rather than be without a vision or captive of the authority's agenda)
- Take responsibility for what happens to us at work externally and internally (rather than see our present internal circumstances and future external possibilities as caused by someone else)
- Be accomplished masters of our particular work roles, jobs, or careers (rather than have an apprenticing or imitating relationship to what we do)
- Conceive of the organization from the "outside in," as a whole; see our relation to the whole; see the relation of the parts to the whole (rather than see the rest of the organization and its parts only from the perspective of our own part from the "inside out")

SOURCE: Adapted from Kegan (1994, p. 302).

consequences, could often be traced to deeply held tacit assumptions that were uncovered during this learning process. As one director wrote,

> I have learned that this process has helped me to reevaluate myself and the world around me. I need to find ways to keep doing this. I am more awake. I am excited by the opportunity of challenging myself and working with others. As I have gotten to know the members of this team better, I realize there is so much more there—who people are and their depth of knowledge is eye-opening.

The ability to function as an individual based on an understanding of the system or systems within which one is operating (seeing oneself and the organization from the "outside in") is what Kegan (1994) terms the evolution from an inherently dependent mode of functioning, the third order, to a higher level, the fourth order of consciousness. With specific regard to what he calls "the hidden curriculum" of the modern workplace, Kegan offers a summary of the implicit demands placed on today's worker in Table 14.1.

Through intense cross-functional dialogue that judiciously combined face-to-face meetings with online discourse, the level of awareness and accountability in John's team had risen markedly. The typical "silver bullet" solution through dependence on external consultants had been replaced with a heightened sense of personal responsibility through facilitated online dialogue.

Lessons Learned

Praxis: The Hidden Dimension of Executive Development

On the surface, although the Executive Master Class Program is structured much like a traditional 12-week course of study combining face-to-face learning with online learning, many of the similarities to traditional forms of teaching and learning end here. Every course requirement is based on relevant literature in the field of organization development and change and is tightly coupled with application in practice. The gap between theory and its application to resolve pressing organizational issues often appears as a chasm to be spanned. Because this distinction appears to be maintained with a fervor akin to the separation of church and state in many traditional academic settings, a central role of the facilitator is to act as a bridge between these two realms.

Bridging the realms of theory and practice is met with resistance from both sides of the divide. As the late Donald Schön pointed out, academics spend much of their lives being socialized to maintain the pristine character of theory, unsoiled by the often swampy and chaotic world of reality (Schön, 1983, 1987). On the other side of the divide, today's high-tech world epitomizes the impatient culture. The very idea of theory conjures visions of irrelevance and memories of late-adolescent struggles to stay awake in class. Students have little (if any) patience for the rigor of theoretical knowledge. What they want instead is a solution for the myriad problems they face to be solved yesterday.

Praxis is the term we have chosen to describe the bridging of the divide between theory and practice. From an ancient Greek term meaning *doing* and *action*—as well as *custom*, *habit*, and *manner*—the word is ideally suited to describe the relationship between our beliefs and behaviors. The term, as we use it here, connotes a need to critically examine, and when necessary to modify, the assumptions, customs, and beliefs that inform our practice. Praxis can thus be thought of as a dance between theory and practice, each realm informing and modifying the other in a seamless movement, thereby creating novel avenues for effective action. Viewed in this manner, neither theory nor practice is sufficient in and of itself; both realms must enlighten, enhance, and modify each other.

How Theory and Action Inform One Another in the Online Learning Environment

Two kinds of theory play a crucial role in the online learning process, leading to more effective individual and organizational performance. The first, *explicit* or *canonical* theory, is the one most familiar to academics. It is the theory embodied in books, journal articles, models, and methodologies. McMaster (1996) provides a lucid "operational definition" of the explicit form of theory as "a group of statements, taken as a related whole, that is used as our basis for design, judgment, and guidance of action" (p. 19). This definition of theory, as it is applied to organizational life, is probably quite recognizable to practitioners in the empirical sciences. It is explicit, open to scrutiny, constantly tested against results it can provide, and open to modification.

The second kind is what may be termed *tacit* or *implicit* theory. This form is embodied in our unconscious assumptions, silently but powerfully shaping our perspectives and actions. It is so all-pervasive that it becomes illusive and, as such, is highly resistant to change.

The Role of Explicit Theory

In the Executive Master Class Program, participants were exposed to a wide range of explicit theoretical knowledge and were required to evaluate *explicit theories* and test the relevance of what they read through direct application. Participants developed workshops, seminars, and pilot programs in their respective departments to address specific organizational issues. It was the direct application of explicit theory that led to tangible changes in their organization. However, we would argue that it was an awareness of the role of *tacit* or *implicit theory* in individual and organizational life that had the greatest impact on participants in this program.

The Role of Implicit Theory

In his further discussion of the role of theory in organizational life, McMaster (1996) writes, "In corporations, people are unconscious of theory because it is obscured by explicit systems, by control mechanisms, and by accepted management platitudes" (p. 19). He states further that this definition of theory "extends beyond specifics and includes many loosely and tentatively formulated statements as well as any assumptions that underlie the theory—often beyond awareness" (p. 20). Thus, the realm of *implicit theory* is tremendously powerful in that it exists, in whole or in part, just below the threshold of our conscious awareness and, as such, is highly resistant to traditional methods of organizational change. John demonstrated his newfound appreciation for the role of implicit theory when he wrote the following in our electronic dialogue forum:

> This last year, our company launched three major new services that are part of the strategic plan to create revenue and sustain market share. Two of the three projects were delayed beyond their desired launch dates, and all three experienced adverse customer service reaction.
>
> When I was in the U.S. Air Force, I was required to drive a 5-ton truck with a transmission that required "double clutching" to shift without clashing or "grinding" the gears. Until that skill was acquired, the gears would grind, the truck lost momentum, and I was left with very few good choices on how to keep going without damaging the vehicle. I see some parallels here with our product/service launches this last year.
>
> The struggle to enhance our service offerings is not due to lack of skill, dedication, or willingness to work with others. That is demonstrated in the supreme efforts—albeit frantic ones—to launch and support the products/ services by members of all company departments. While follow-up meetings have been held to determine what worked and what didn't, we still seem to struggle. It appears there is something more basic and overarching at work here—something so pervasive that it undermines tremendous effort to succeed.
>
> All parts of the organization that are engaged in launching and supporting products/services seem to be motivated by different objectives or theories.... The three organizational entities that produce and sustain our products/ services . . . should ideally be linked in theory to the timely, cost-effective, and reliable deployment of what we sell. Yet past results seem to show a single-mindedness of each entity towards mostly one part: Product Development is motivated by "time to market," i.e., being the first to market in order to maintain pre-eminence among the competition. Engineering seems to focus on supporting the Product Development drive for timeliness but with strong focus on cost of development. Network Operations seems engaged in implementing and maintaining the service with most attention to reliability, i.e., the end customer experience. All three motivations are valid, yet the heavy emphasis by each team often sets up conflicting actions that, in the end, result in diminished project success.

Conclusion: Five Key Outcomes

At a time when many leaders report feeling overwhelmed by the complexity of their world, the results of the Executive Master Class Program intervention suggest that there is a way through the maze. In facilitated online learning, which can be seen as a form of action research, learning occurs when individuals and groups discover and narrow or eliminate gaps between intentions and results, between thoughts and actions, and between theories and practices. As we look back on our experience in this learning initiative, we can identify five key outcomes.

1. *Enhanced awareness of self.* Working in an online learning environment requires that participants articulate their thoughts, feelings, and perceptions in written form rather than reacting based on a sense of urgency and unconscious impulses. This environment enhances individual knowledge when participants become aware of, understand, and are able to explain the bases of their thoughts and actions.

2. *Enhanced awareness of others.* Because the work of all participants is viewed and commented on by the entire group, participants often learn from one another as much as they do from the program facilitator. In the earlier example, John drew extensively from the work of his directors in generating his own insights and intervention. Each participant also provided substantive feedback on others' initiatives. Thus, the thoughts and ideas of each participant are viewed from multiple perspectives rather than from the relatively narrow view of the facilitator or teacher. In very concrete terms, participants learn that although their perspective may make perfect sense in terms of the operations of their respective organizational unit, it might not always make sense from the vantage point of the actions of several organizational units. As one director commented,

> This has been eye-opening for me, being able to view other teams and people, understand their theories and how they operate. I see great opportunities to more easily and freely make course corrections as I become more aware of the company's operating theories. It has been nice to get to know the others on this team.

The last sentence in this director's comment is especially illuminating given that this was a team whose members had worked together closely for several years. Further testimony to the power of collaborative online learning to raise the level of awareness of self and others appears in the following commentaries:

> I'm still hesitant about sharing myself personally, but I feel myself becoming less shy. I'm learning new things to try as a manager and am gaining a greater appreciation of this team—our insights and knowledge.

> I am learning that the core of who I am is the foundation for how I act and react to the world around me. The ripple effect is phenomenal. I am struck by how open everyone is becoming and how free our self-expression is. I have gained a greater appreciation for everyone.

3. *Enhanced capacity for reflection.* Unlike purely verbal communication, the asynchronous learning environment also permits added time for reflection before response, giving the dialogue a level of depth that is uncommon in other communication media. This capacity of the learning system thus enables participants to become aware of, more fully understand, and appreciate the thinking of others.

4. *New perspectives and knowledge.* The ability to weave multiple viewpoints together creates new knowledge and a broader perspective, thereby increasing *internal* coherence and *capacity* to initiate more effective and coordinated change initiatives.

5. *Enhanced capacity to initiate and sustain change.* Emerging out of the team's heightened awareness and new perspective, members were able to propose several new initiatives that have had a significant impact on the culture and operation of their organization. In addition, because those who would be affected by the change generated these initiatives in a structured and highly collaborative manner from their inception, resistance to implementation was greatly diminished.

We had the privilege of witnessing an awakening of spirit and seeing a growing sense of optimism emerge from an atmosphere previously blamed for extinguishing the vitality of those living within it. Hopelessness and helplessness faded as leaders once again were restored to a sense of confidence and capability. Most important, the intervention appeared to stimulate the ability of individual team members to collaborate on the design and implementation of organizational change initiatives as well as to lead those initiatives. We met with John several months after the conclusion of his team's Executive Master Class Program. The conversation covered a variety of issues related to our ongoing work together. In reflecting on the intervention and his heightened sense of awareness, John noted that the journey he was on was just beginning. His words have remained with us: "Once you've seen what we have had the chance to see, you can never go back."

References

Argyris, C. (1978, September-October). Double loop learning in organizations. *Harvard Business Review,* pp. 115-125.

Argyris, C. (1990). *Overcoming organizational defenses: Facilitating organizational learning.* Boston: Allyn & Bacon.

Argyris, C. (1992). *On organization learning.* Cambridge, UK: Blackwell.

Argyris, C. (1993). *Knowledge for action: A guide to overcoming barriers to organizational change* (1st ed.). San Francisco: Jossey-Bass.

Argyris, C., & Schön, D. (1996). *Organization learning II: Theory, method, and practice*. Reading, MA: Addison-Wesley.

Brown, J. S., & Duguid, P. (1991). Organization learning and communities of practice: Towards a unified view of working, learning, and innovation. *Organization Science, 2*(1), 40-55.

Brown, J. S., & Duguid, P. (2000). *The social life of information*. Boston: Harvard Business School Press.

Drucker, P. F. (1999). *Management challenges for the 21st century* (1st ed.). New York: HarperBusiness.

Kegan, R. (1994). *In over our heads: The mental demands of modern life*. Cambridge, MA: Harvard University Press.

Kegan, R., & Lahey, L. L. (2001). *How the way we talk can change the way we work: Seven languages for transformation* (1st ed.). San Francisco: Jossey-Bass.

Kleiner, A., & Roth, G. (1998). How to make experience your company's best teacher. In *Harvard Business Review on knowledge management* (pp. 137-152). Boston: Harvard Business School Press.

Lave, J. (1988). *Cognition in practice: Mind, mathematics, and culture in everyday life*. Cambridge, UK: Cambridge University Press.

Lave, J., & Wenger, E. (1991). *Situated learning: Legitimate peripheral participation*. Cambridge, UK: Cambridge University Press.

Lesser, E. L. (2000). *Knowledge and social capital: Foundations and applications*. Boston: Butterworth-Heinemann.

Lesser, E. L., Fontaine, M. A., & Slusher, J. A. (2000). *Knowledge and communities*. Boston: Butterworth-Heinemann.

McMaster, M. (1996). *The intelligence advantage: Organizing for complexity*. London: Butterworth-Heinemann.

Nonaka, I., & Takeuchi, H. (1995). *The knowledge creating company: How Japanese companies create the dynamics of innovation*. Oxford, UK: Oxford University Press.

Rogoff, B., & Lave, J. (1999). *Everyday cognition: Development in social context*. New York: toExcel.

Schön, D. (1983). *The reflective practitioner*. New York: Basic Books.

Schön, D. (1987). *Educating the reflective practitioner: Toward a new design for teaching and learning in the professions*. San Francisco: Jossey-Bass.

Wenger, E. (1998). *Communities of practice: Learning, meaning, and identity*. Cambridge, UK: Cambridge University Press.

Online Knowledge Communities and Their Role in Organizational Learning

Mark D. Neff

For many, the quest to form a learning organization is as elusive as finding the Holy Grail. However, some managers are developing learning environments that encourage their employees to participate in online knowledge communities. The establishment of an environment to support online knowledge communities forms the basis of their knowledge management activities.

Online knowledge communities are also known as online social networks or communities of practice. They are essentially groups of people in an organization who extend their natural workspace by working in a common area online with the intent of improving their ability to deliver services or products for clients. With a place to play, work, and co-create, employees establish common ground on platforms that enable them to communicate their needs and wants in both real time (synchronous) and delayed time (asynchronous).

The Work Revolution

Picture a future where networked organizations are all interconnected. The employees, subcontractors, and partners are able to interact through various online knowledge communities. These knowledge communities have tools and links that allow virtual teams to form quickly around various topics. When a client identifies a need, the online knowledge communities are able to unite to form a virtual organization. The virtual organization works with clients to assess their strategy and then allocates appropriate resources to move directly into the development of specific products and services necessary to operationalize the strategy.

Once the client's requirements are identified, the online community establishes a set of criteria and publishes them online for others to review. This results in the formation of several new online communities such as online research teams. The online research team is aided by "bots" (automated electronic agents), which review the client's requirements and scan member profiles to identify team members with matching expertise and interests. An online integration team brings together research and problem-solving efforts to create a system that meets the client's requirements. Other teams examine the application's fit into the client's existing framework and generate reports of the potential impact of the new application to the appropriate people. Those reports may trigger additional knowledge communities to help integrate the new application into the current framework while limiting any disruption to the client's current services. Their goal may be to minimize the number of modifications required in current systems. If that minimum is exceeded, then an online architecture team will assemble in another knowledge community to identify architectures that will help to accelerate integration. That team will make its decisions on what is best for both short-term and long-term maintenance.

The client identifies decision criteria for the team, one of which may be to use an architecture that presents the lowest total cost. Then the complete proposal goes online to a finance committee for approval. All interactions and documents occur online, and each knowledge community has access to a common virtual space to do this work. The finance department has been involved in the process since the beginning with the initial review team and has made suggestions to minimize costs and maximize previous investments. Because the finance department has been involved in the process, its members more readily agree with the proposed solution. Because the people, the software, and the hardware are connected, the new system can come together quickly, and the client is able to see a "real" prototype of the final solution in a brief period of time.

Learning Communities

A learning community is a group of people who take the time to reflect on what they are doing and improve on it so that the next time they do something, they incorporate the benefits of their learning. Their learning can come either from personal experience or through the knowledge transfer that has taken place from working with others. Following are some examples.

1. The U.S. Army (Pascale, Milleman, & Gioja, 1997) uses "after action reviews" to capture lessons learned. The army is moving away from a strict hierarchical flow of knowledge that facilitates decision making and is moving toward a "distributed mind" where an individual is empowered to make appropriate decisions based on the available information.

2. British Petroleum reaches out to others using an engagement strategy called a "peer assist." In a peer assist, employees can call others throughout the organization to support a particular decision. Instances where this has been particularly effective include the evaluation of new drilling sites. At a cost of about $200 per minute (Dixon, 2000), the advice regarding available information and its interpretation from colleagues throughout the world is very valuable.

3. Buckman Labs established a system that allows its employees to pose questions and receive answers from people all over the world. Its network of professionals considers it a responsibility to answer questions or redirect them to others. Over the course of a day or two (Dixon, 2000), the person who posed the question will receive a number of suggestions on how to proceed. The returned information ranges from useful summaries of what has been done in similar situations to complete proposals submitted to previous clients. This type of information is invaluable and provides the immediate answer or leads the person who has the question to people who have related experience.

4. General Electric created a "workout" initiative that encourages every employee to look for ways to improve the way they work and their organization (Tichy & Sherman, 1993). Board members ask what has been done in response to a specific problem. They stimulate the behaviors necessary to institutionalize the sharing of information. When someone comes up with an idea, leaders make it paramount to pass on the idea to someone else. When an employee brings an idea to his or her boss, the first thing the boss asks is where the employee obtained the idea. If the employee did not first hear of the idea from someone else, then the next question the boss asks is who else knows about the idea. General Electric is sharing ideas and reinforcing their importance so that others can leverage them. This, in turn, leads to additional practices that further reinforce what needs to be done to develop a successful knowledge management strategy.

How to Establish a Learning Community

Consider the following key factors in developing a learning community (http://realcommunities.com/products/12principles.htm):

1. *Purpose:* What is the community in place to do?
2. *Identity:* Who are the members—individually and collectively?

3. *Reputation:* What reputation do the community members have, and what do they hope to achieve or develop?

4. *Governance:* What rules will the community live by? What roles and responsibilities will members have?

5. *Communication:* How will the members interact with each other?

6. *Groups:* How will the members segment themselves to address specific interests and tasks?

7. *Environment:* What infrastructure is in place to support the community activities?

8. *Boundaries:* What or who is inside and outside the community?

9. *Trust:* What activities build trust between members? How can facilitators increase group efficiency and enable problem resolution?

10. *Exchange:* How does the community recognize and value different forms of exchange, including values, knowledge, and experience?

11. *Expression:* What will the community do to develop a "soul"? Is the community given the freedom to express itself?

12. *History:* What does the community do to provide new members with an understanding of what has happened in the community before they were members? How does the community help new members acclimate and learn how the community conducts itself?

To establish a learning community, it is typically easiest to leverage specific initiatives that are already in place within the organization. Many organizations already have knowledge management initiatives under way. Communities can be used to leverage knowledge management work.

What is knowledge management work? How can knowledge be transferred? For Davenport and Prusak (1998), the transfer of knowledge operates somewhat like a marketplace. The people that make the products to sell are knowledge engineers. The people hawking their wares are knowledge brokers. The grand overseer of the bazaar is the chief knowledge officer. The bazaar needs to follow the rules established by the town in the same way that a knowledge team needs to follow the rules of the company. Several knowledge management principles emerge from the metaphor.

1. Knowledge must be created and applied for it to have value. For someone to apply knowledge, he or she must see the value in its application. In a bazaar, a purchase will not be made until both parties come to an agreement on an object's value. Then, and only then, they shake hands on the deal.

2. Making "shared meaning" in a bazaar is not important; however, reciprocity is very important. Both the buyer and the seller need to agree on the value of the product or service. Both parties are looking for the best deal. Each

person tries to outmaneuver the other. If the buyer is not a skilled negotiator, then he or she might pay more than the product or service is worth.

3. In a typical knowledge exchange, the ideal buyer and the ideal seller might never meet. As a result, some buyer will purchase something at a price that is less than the object may be worth, but likewise, it will not be used in a way that can bring the most value or return to the buyer. With technological support, it should be easier to connect the right knowledge buyers with the right knowledge sellers.

It is the efficiency of a market that will determine the turnover of knowledge. Some people think that knowledge is something they should keep and not share with others. They see it as a source of power. This restricts the flow of goods and artificially drives up the value of that knowledge. Others will tend to act in kind. As they restrict the flow of their knowledge, the knowledge transfer between people continues to drop. This downward spiral will continue until someone takes the first step to reverse the trend.

Improving Market Efficiency

To improve market efficiency, an organization (a) identifies and prioritizes its needs, (b) profiles its people's expertise and interests, and (c) devises a mechanism to pair up needs and people. The needs can be determined by the market or internal factors that help to spur innovation. There are several tools with which to develop people's profiles. The organization establishes an environment that rewards the exchange of ideas. To improve knowledge exchanges, the organization asks its people to develop personal profiles and builds knowledge communities. The profiles and knowledge communities allow people to locate other people who share work experiences or have common interests and can begin to transfer knowledge.

Patterns for Knowledge Transfer Systems

Dixon (2000) explores five patterns of knowledge transfer to examine the best way to transfer knowledge in a particular engagement. If the knowledge pattern is identified and matched with the best system for transferring that knowledge, then an organization can optimize the knowledge transfer process. The different knowledge transfer patterns are as follows:

1. *Serial transfer.* This is used when a team is doing something now and will do the same thing again a year from now. For example, the U.S. Army uses after-action reviews to capture necessary information.
2. *Near transfer.* Groups are spread out around the world and need to transfer information from one location and group to another. This is

good for the capture and transfer of explicit knowledge. Ford uses this approach with its 37 plants located around the world.

3. *Far transfer.* In this case, the information is in people's heads. British Petroleum has figured out a good way to tap into this information using peer assists. Using a peer assist, people are flown in from around the world to help support analysis of a drill site before drilling begins.

4. *Strategic transfer.* This method involves the entire organization. An example is in establishing strategic alliances with other companies. This requires combining the first three methods, but it usually has a very narrow focus timewise, perhaps 2 or 3 years maximum, and it almost always involves a different team.

5. *Expert transfer.* This involves the ability to reach out and tap an expert network somewhere in the world.

Each of the transfer patterns exists in an organization at different times, depending on its specific goals. The system needed to transfer knowledge varies with the different transfer patterns. In one case, the situation could require a person to physically fly to the other side of the world for a personal consult. In another case, when time is of the essence, the situation could require the creation of a virtual simulation of what is happening physically. Knowledge management and various systems are used to help establish learning behaviors and transfer knowledge from one person to another or to connect people with other people who can help them in specific situations. This forms the basis for the development of learning communities.

Engaging a Learning Organization: Strategy and Sponsorship

To encourage people to work in online knowledge communities, an organization needs to create an environment in which its employees feel safe and needs to provide the tools they require to do their work. Once the organization decides to pursue a strategy of bringing its employees or members together in a learning community, the entire landscape changes. In the past, it was sufficient to give people a task to do, and they did it year in and year out. Today, it is not only insufficient but even negligent to disregard the "distributed intelligence" available in an organization. People need to engage in dialogue. Relying on one-way communication no longer makes things happen or change as quickly as needed for an organization to remain competitive (Pascale et al., 1997). An organization must foster an environment of trust. Teams with higher levels of trust coalesce more easily, organize their work more quickly, and manage themselves better (Lipnack & Stamps, 1997).

Creating a "There . . . There": Developing the Knowledge Base and Maintenance Activities

In creating a "there . . . there," an organization needs to grow beyond the model of "build it and they will come." In a typical organization, the building of content or technology is only one third or less of the work that is needed to create a thriving community. A community tends to develop when an organization meets and discusses needs freely. Knowledge communities are closely aligned with what some have called "communities of practice." Communities of practice are composed of three dimensions: mutual engagement, a joint enterprise, and a shared repertoire of practices (Wenger, 1998). Mutual engagement refers to reciprocity of action. A joint enterprise indicates that the people are collectively focused on a common purpose. A shared repertoire of practices refers to a collective set of activities that are common among the members of the community and to the work they do on a daily basis. These elements all can be seen in online knowledge communities as well. Some other elements of an online knowledge community are listed here:

1. *Community size.* Communities come in all shapes and sizes. If a community is too large, then it may stifle participation. If a community is too small, then it may never reach critical mass and become self-sustaining.

2. *Previous socialization.* Several sources indicate that face time is critical to establishing trust levels within a community (Duarte & Snyder, 1999; Lipnack & Stamps, 1997; Smith & Berg, 1997; Sproull & Kiesler, 1998). In today's environment, many communities will work without the benefits of socialization. Each community will need to look at different strategies to simulate face-to-face meetings or look for ways to have at least some of the community members come together as a core group to help establish and maintain community momentum.

3. *Moderator proficiency.* Some moderators are better than others. Over time, a community's maturity will overcome any differences in moderator proficiency.

4. *Community latency.* Longer standing communities may already have worked through the basic issues of how to stimulate participation and establish relevance. However, this might not always be the case.

5. *Cultural issues.* Participating in a community requires close interactions between members. Sometimes the cultural issues that interfere with collaboration in face-to-face interactions surface in a community. It is important to look at the different types of work that will be done in the community. When it is apparent that cultural issues will

surface that may distract rather than enhance the community's performance, the moderator needs to make sure that the cultural issues are raised and discussed in a proper forum.

6. *Support.* This is a critical component to establish and maintain communities. Communities need to be encouraged to form and be given tools to do community work. They need to understand organizational needs. This allows them to form and address components of the organization's vision without strict accountability. They should not be required to provide direct line delivery responsibility. This would discourage them from continuing to evolve their best practices and spreading knowledge across the organization.

Three Critical Questions

In each organization, three critical questions need to be answered before starting online knowledge communities:

1. What business objectives need attention?
2. Am I willing to sponsor communities to address business needs?
3. Am I willing to establish an infrastructure to support the communities as they emerge to meet evolving business needs?

Once these questions are answered in the affirmative, communities can be established. One of the key factors in building successful communities is to pay attention to leadership. Although standards and guidelines can be put into place, the important work can be addressed quickly only if a trained moderator is allowed to facilitate the community.

The Role of the Moderator

Online knowledge moderators stimulate participation in an online knowledge community. They are aware of different knowledge transfer patterns and differing needs of people. Their primary goal is to attract and retain knowledge workers in online knowledge communities. They work with the members of a community and help them to establish mechanisms to increase knowledge transfer within and across communities. Moderators frequently demonstrate by example the behaviors that they are trying to elicit from their community members. Their goal is to help a community become self-sufficient. At that point, the community should be able to sustain itself with minimal participation by moderators.

Characteristics of a Good Online Knowledge Moderator

Moderators help an online knowledge community to achieve its objectives. They are results-focused and take into consideration the community's social needs. They help to establish overall goals for the community and then stimulate action necessary to reach those goals. They know that the paths that different communities take to accomplish their objectives will be different. An excellent source of suggestions for hosting a community as an online facilitator can be found in Howard Rheingold's primer, *The Art of Hosting Good Conversations Online* (www.rheingold.com/texts/artonlinehost.html).

Online knowledge moderators have to be very good "listeners." They need to read all online postings carefully and seek clarification when necessary. Moderators look for patterns of behavior and posting rhythms. They start conversations and then back out when enough other people are keeping the conversation going on their own. They look for ideas that should be shared across all communities. They stay in touch with other moderators and share best practices to continue to improve the practice of online knowledge community moderation. In time, this establishes the foundation for community learning that can lead to overall organizational learning.

Moderators seed conversations or ask others to seed them to provide focus and balance. The process of seeding includes making posts, or asking others to post information that is relevant to the community topics, and asking questions that encourage members to clarify their questions or reflect on them. On the other hand, moderators need to be careful not to overwhelm their communities with questions and information that members are not ready to absorb. In time, members will respond to the communication rhythms in their communities and adjust their actions accordingly.

The greatest opportunity for growth occurs at the "touch points" between different knowledge communities. These are the places where communities have overlapping areas of interest, where the members of one community reach out to exchange ideas with the next community. Good moderators keep in contact with other moderators. They help members to expand their knowledge and to leverage that knowledge in different environments.

Establishing Norms of Behavior and Support Mechanisms

Once an online knowledge community is established, what can be done to energize the members? One of the easiest ways is to encourage them to talk about themselves online. This, however, can pose a significant challenge because people disclose only as much as they feel safe in disclosing. A moderator can begin by acknowledging the first time that new members make posts and by making them feel welcome by asking questions. The moderator can reference other Web sites where new members might find additional information to support their views. Every so often, a good moderator will take the time to summarize conversational themes. The summaries are a useful way for new members to access the history of a community without having to read through all of the posts that may go back for several months or years.

Once a community has been established, it needs to generate new knowledge. "Knowledge practices" include discussion techniques to stimulate new knowledge (see Denham Grey's Web site at www.voght.com/cgi-bin/pywiki?knowledgepractices).

Moderator Tactics

To stimulate participation in online knowledge communities, try some of the following:

1. Post an initial hello and request that other members do likewise.
2. Establish a directory (some people call these yellow pages) where people with similar interests can find each other.
3. Post a couple of questions that you would like to see the group address.
4. Offer examples of your work and ask for feedback.
5. Describe a problem that you are trying to solve. Inquire whether others have had to address a similar problem and how they addressed it.
6. Benchmark processes against other organizations. This can help members to improve the way they do their work.
7. Identify people with whom you can network. Future work will be completed in online social networks, and it is critical to start building them as soon as possible.
8. Play games to help people establish bonds. The more you can help members to establish relationships, the more likely they will want to work together.
9. Develop a newsletter to let people know what is happening on a regular basis within the community.
10. Answer requests for assistance. If you do not know the answer to a question, then pass the question on to someone who might. The more relationships you help form, the more learning you enable.
11. Establish or identify a compelling event or reason for people to participate in online communities. This is more art than science. Coax; do not exert pressure. In time, people will respond.
12. Invest in support mechanisms. Develop a help desk. Develop a set of frequently asked questions. Develop a local knowledge base and a network of people who can answer questions.

13. Invest in training. Give the users an orientation to the tools that they will be using. Make sure that the community leaders know how to serve as virtual leaders. Although they may be good task leaders, online community building requires constant attention and cannot be delegated. When the community coalesces, additional leaders will surface. In time, the community will begin to run itself.

14. Be patient. The bottom line is that online knowledge community building takes time. It takes work and constant nurturing.

Last Words: Why Stimulate Participation?

Stimulating participation in knowledge communities helps them to build learning capabilities. Aggregating learning capabilities serves as a stepping-stone toward the goal of becoming learning organizations. There are several theories on how communities should form. Some people believe that they should be allowed to emerge by themselves. Others believe that for communities to be effective, they should be treated as virtual teams with designated leaders and then given very specific charters and deliverables for which they are responsible. The introduction of trained online knowledge moderators is a middle-of-the-road approach that will lend a little more structure to online knowledge communities while still respecting their emergent nature.

Is your organization prepared for the changes that communities will bring about? What level of support are you willing to give these communities? As they develop, are you willing to keep your hands off them and allow them to continue to develop while providing them with the necessary tools to do their job? Do you document your organizational goals? Do you align them with the members' personal goals? When a community misses its mark, do you allow it to self-correct or do you step in quickly to change the direction? The answers to these questions will help to indicate the maturity of your organization and the work that needs to be done prior to implementing online knowledge communities as part of your knowledge management strategy.

Appendix: Online Knowledge Community Moderator Aids

Following are several aids to explore for your own use. An online knowledge community moderator can use a strategic visioning process (Aid 1) to help identify community purposes and gain consensus on community directions. The moderator can use the online knowledge community life cycle (Aid 2) to help determine a community's level of development and how to be helpful at each level. The online knowledge community kit (Aid 3) is an ongoing collection of online resources that the moderator can use as a reference.

Aid 1: Strategic Visioning Process

One of the tasks that the online knowledge community moderator needs to do is to help an online knowledge community establish its goals. The strategic visioning process is one way for the knowledge community moderator to help an online knowledge community. For additional resources that support this process, refer to Grove Consulting's Web site (www. groveconsulting.com).

1. *Establish a current state.* The community members identify their viewpoint, allies, and resources. This can be done by taking people through a "history walk" as described on Grove Consulting's Web site.

2. *Establish a desired end state.* This includes the community members identifying a target, objectives, and observable behaviors. Developing an article or a press release set in the future can do this.

3. *Identify obstacles to overcome.* In this exercise, community members look at things to overcome as if they have already achieved the desired state and are looking backward in time from the future. This act of balancing reflection and inquiry is very powerful.

4. *Identify enablers.* Identify the resources or initiatives that will help the community to move toward its goals. Leveraging enablers makes it easier to move a community in the desired direction.

5. *Plan actions.* Identify the sequence of steps and allocate the appropriate resources necessary to move the community toward its desired end state. Develop milestones to check progress and establish goals that will help determine progress along the desired path. Sometimes it is necessary to re-plan. This is required whenever new obstacles or enablers are identified that need to be addressed or leveraged.

As an online knowledge community develops, these steps can be performed one at a time to help the community members become used to working together in an online environment. If an online knowledge community has already done some work in these areas, then the moderator can take the community through the remaining steps. Also, these steps can be performed iteratively and should be revisited if any of the basic assumptions or norms of the community have changed or been altered.

Aid 2: Online Knowledge Community Life Cycle

An online knowledge community moderator needs to conduct a periodic assessment of a knowledge community to determine its maturity. The community's maturity level and stage of life determine the type and frequency of moderator interaction. Some questions to help an online knowledge community moderator to assess a community's maturity level and stage of life are the following:

1. How long has the community been in existence?
2. How many people are in the community? Of that number, how many people are posting on a regular basis?
3. How many posts have been made in the past month? By how many unique posters?
4. What kinds of posts are there (e.g., introductions, questions, offers of assistance, work products, review comments, book and Web reviews, suggested activities, action items, meeting minutes)?
5. What is the general tone of the posts (e.g., friendly, adversarial, academic, experience based)?

■ Online Knowledge Community Stages of Life and
Suggested Areas of Concentration for the Online Moderator

1. *Start-up.* During start-up, the significant elements to consider include building relationships and establishing trust among the charter members. Look at sponsorship issues and make sure that the knowledge community has developed an appropriate business case for the specific work environment. Work with the initial group to recruit new members. Look for people who are enthusiastic and willing to work online. Advocates and champions are key to making online knowledge communities successful. Help the community members to develop a useful "What's in it for me?" case and look at ways to market and communicate the idea. Establish an initial charter. Establish a set of group norms. Determine what the community will do. Identify the content and activities of value to the membership. Seed the online discussion forums and monitor them frequently.

2. *Growth.* New members are joining regularly. Ensure that new members are welcomed and escorted virtually until they are comfortable in the online environment. Focus on stimulating conversation and engaging in deep dialogue. Establish events that draw the membership into sharing forums. Develop a set of frequently asked questions to support the community. Start looking at questions such as the following. Can the group adapt to increased membership? How do you stimulate the new members without forgetting the old ones? What can you do to integrate new members into the group quickly?

3. *Production.* Move past the building phase to working as a community. Look at ways to move discussions from theory to practice. Continue to scout available resources for new material that might be of value to a growing and maturing community. Adapt materials so that they apply to your specific

context. Start establishing measures of value to the community so that members can monitor their own health. Collect individual and collective success stories. Build the network. Continue to reach out beyond the borders to bring in additional people. Deliver services and products to clients, and recycle materials back into the community. Continue to invigorate and refresh the membership.

4. *Stagnation.* Signs of the "beginning of the end" include losing members, waning interest, and the business case being not quite right anymore. Continue to serve the membership. Clean shop. Archive out-of-date material. Determine whether renewal is possible, or prepare for the end-of-life stage for the community.

5. *Renewal.* This is a new beginning. After determining that there is value in continuing the online knowledge community, revise its charter to reflect more accurately how it brings value to the organization. Go back to the start-up stage again. Determine whether the members who left would be interested in the new charter, or look for new members outside of the original community. Revisit the work products and references for the community to see whether they are still applicable. Go through the stages of the community life cycle again, but recognize that you may be in the middle of a short growth stage before entering the end-of-life stage.

6. *End of life.* It is time for members of the community to move on. Provide a ceremony for proper closure. Transition planning is critical here so that people feel appreciated for what they contributed and know what is needed to go forward. Thank the members for their contributions. Ask them to keep whatever they want before moving all materials to an archive. Archive the community space so that it can be searched or retrieved at a later time.

Aid 3: Online Knowledge Community Kit

This aid provides a collection of resources that are available to the online knowledge moderator for starting an online knowledge community and nurturing its members through their life cycle. As you use these resources or come across new ones, please add them to the Web site list maintained at www.voght.com/cgi-bin/pywiki?knowledgecommunitykit.

- ■ A. Community Design (from www.naima.com/community/intro)

    1. Define and articulate your *purpose.*
    2. Build flexible, extensible gathering *places.*
    3. Create meaningful and evolving member *profiles.*

4. Design for a range of *roles*.
5. Develop a strong *leadership* program.
6. Encourage appropriate *etiquette*.
7. Promote cyclic *events*.
8. Integrate the *rituals* of community life.
9. Facilitate member-run *subgroups*.

■ B. Community Goals

When you first begin, you need to work with the community members to identify a purpose. What is the community trying to do, or what would it like to do? Add or delete goals as appropriate.

- Enhance team morale.
- Establish virtual team-building capabilities.
- Develop boundary-spanning competencies.
- Increase appreciation for the multicultural elements of the organization.
- Enhance understanding of the advantages of online communication.
- Increase competitive advantage.
- Reduce cycle time for delivering quality products and services to clients.
- Improve communications.
- Increase organizational learning.
- Enhance the process for developing and sharing ideas.
- Improve the ability to develop virtual teams.
- Increase individual willingness to explore and develop ideas with one another.
- Urge and support community members to build trust relationships with each other.

■ C. Community Deliverables

Determine the extent to which your knowledge community wants to conduct itself as a project team or virtual team instead of as a support network or user group. In either case, think about the deliverables that you want your community to be known for or would like to work toward producing.

- Knowledge environment (infrastructure)
- Knowledge processes

- Knowledge sub-communities (e.g., assigned task forces that are focused on specific activities that will benefit the whole community)
- Specific knowledge reports or work products that pertain to your knowledge domain
- Knowledge ontology pertinent to your knowledge domain
- Member profiles and related expertise for tapping across the organization
- Strategy and positioning white papers
- List of useful references (relating to community topics of interest and work activities)

■ D. Community Outcomes

It is useful for the community members to determine what they hope to derive from working together as an online knowledge community. This changes over time, but some reflection here can help community members to determine whether they really want to be in this community or another that is more closely aligned with what they are doing or where they want to go.

- An understanding of what is required to equip virtual team members
- Reduction of business costs
- Composite profiles of staff competencies
- Improved training and development
- Suggested methods for implementing additional knowledge processes
- Interesting conversations
- Creation of new knowledge that pushes the boundaries of known best practices
- A better global understanding of what is happening in your area

■ E. Community Norms

Each online knowledge community will evolve norms. This will occur either formally or informally. It is valuable to document the community norms and revisit them occasionally to see whether they still apply. New community members may have suggestions for what can be done differently to make the community more efficient. One question is this: Does the community want to be efficient, or does it prefer more frequent and longer periods of time for reflection?

Here are possible norms for community adoption:

1. Everyone needs to take responsibility to jump in and comment when appropriate.

2. Each community will start with a designated leader and a moderator. It is anticipated that each team will become self-directed over time, with distributed leadership based on the contributions of the members.

3. Once the knowledge community is under way, everyone needs to take personal responsibility. This allows the community processes to emerge as different people take on different roles. Everyone needs to take responsibility to make unique contributions.

4. Everyone should strive to be as clear and direct as possible in all communications. We are all here to assist one another.

5. Each person needs to take responsibility to document problems as they occur. This documentation should, wherever possible, convert problem statements to specific requests to the group. Or even better, develop a proposal for a solution to the problem.

6. All group members need to feel heard and comfortable in establishing their presence in the group. Ask how others are doing. Let them know that it is okay to ask for help.

■ F. Community Competencies

Although it is incumbent on each online knowledge community to determine its own objectives, the collection of knowledge communities is expected to help achieve the goal of becoming a learning organization. Included here is a list of boundary-spanning skills as defined by Dori Digenti on her Web site (www.collaborative-learning.org/boundary.html). Each organization needs to define which of these are required for its growth by performing an internal gap analysis.

- ◆ Skill 1: Double-loop learning
- ◆ Skill 2: Communications (listening and dialogue)
- ◆ Skill 3: Mediation
- ◆ Skill 4: Peer learning
- ◆ Skill 5: Systems thinking
- ◆ Skill 6: Intercultural relations
- ◆ Additional information from: www.collaborative-learning.org/ systemsthinker.pdf

■ G. Additional Resources

- ◆ www.voght.com/cgi-bin/pywiki?knowledgecommunity (a set of community links from Denham Grey)

- ◆ www.fullcirc.com/commresources.htm (a set of suggested guidelines on how to set up a community, a list of resources for setting up a community, and a list of community support from Nancy White)
- ◆ www.fullcirc.com/community/communitymanual.htm (a list of tools that are related to community building from Nancy White)
- ◆ http://thinkofit.com/webconf/ (a list of conferencing software from David Woolley)

References

Davenport, T., & Prusak, L. (1998). *Working knowledge: How organizations manage what they know.* Boston: Harvard Business School Press.

Dixon, N. (2000). *Common knowledge: How companies thrive by sharing what they know.* Boston: Harvard Business School Press.

Duarte, D., & Snyder, N. (1999). *Mastering virtual teams: Strategies, tools, and techniques that succeed.* San Francisco: Jossey-Bass.

Lipnack, J., & Stamps, J. (1997). *Virtual teams: Reaching across space, time, and organizations with technology.* New York: John Wiley.

Pascale, R., Milleman, M., & Gioja, L. (1997, November-December). Changing the way we change: How leaders at Sears, Shell, and the U.S. Army transformed attitudes and behavior—and made the changes stick. *Harvard Business Review,* pp. 126-139. (HBR Reprint 97609)

Smith, K., & Berg, D. (1997). *Paradoxes of group life.* San Francisco: New Lexington Press.

Sproull, L., & Kiesler, S. (1998). *Connections: New ways of working in the networked organization.* Cambridge: MIT Press.

Tichy, N., & Sherman, S. (1993). *Control your destiny or someone else will.* Garden City, NY: Currency Doubleday.

Wenger, E. (1998). *Communities of practice: Learning, meaning, and identity.* Cambridge, UK: Cambridge University Press.

Part II

Part II: Implementating Online Learning

C. Courses

Chapter 16

Designing and Using a Course in Organization Design to Facilitate Corporate Learning in the Online Environment

Tracy C. Gibbons
and Randi S. Brenowitz

In today's computer-mediated economy, distance learning provides more than just an opportunity to unite students from different locations in a common educational goal. It serves as a bridge from the often theoretical basis of academic studies to the real-world practices necessary for success outside university walls. With workers in both traditional and technology-based companies using computers and the Internet to accomplish their tasks, developing technological skills through learning by doing becomes increasingly important. In addition, people must learn how to engage one another on a personal level and develop mutual respect in an environment where face-to-face interactions are absent or scarce.

More and more organizations, particularly those with satellite offices across the country and around the globe, seek alternatives to flying participants to a common meeting site. Leveraging the unique talents of diverse employees and applying them toward a singular project or goal requires a collaborative process that may be new to some. An increasingly common solution to this problem is the creation of virtual teams (VTs) or geographically dispersed teams (GDTs). These are groups of people who share responsibility and accountability for a product or other output, are interdependent for the purposes of its development or creation, and are not physically co-located. Students accustomed to researching and writing on their own, and employees performing certain tasks that were previously done in relative isolation (e.g., writing, programming), often find collaboration to be a challenge above and beyond the project itself. Groupware applications are one way to accelerate projects whose contributors are geographically dispersed, adding to shared information and messages through the Internet and e-mail. Online education allows students to gain practical experience using technology to accomplish tasks and develop interpersonal relationships, which increases their value as future employees.

Addressing how distance learning prepares students for the business, social, and collaborative realities in the Internet economy, this chapter provides a summary of our experiences and discoveries in teaching an online, experience-based seminar in organization design at the Fielding Graduate Institute. For the coursework, a group of geographically dispersed students—often working in different time zones—collaborated to create a redesign of an organization they selected from among their real-world cases. This chapter reviews the factors that are essential to the success of online collaboration in general and examines the insights we gained from our specific experiences working in a distance learning environment.

Organization Design in the Online Environment

Among the offerings at Fielding, our organization design seminar presented unique challenges and opportunities for online learning. Organization design is the process of developing or modifying the major elements of an organization so that they are in alignment with the overarching purpose, mission, and goals of the organization as well as with each other. A complex undertaking, organization design requires the ability to work in real time with often competing organizational needs and variables. The very nature of organization design demands a comprehensive understanding of the varying dynamics of a company or an institution. To do this, an individual might need to step outside his or her functional role to view the circumstances from another perspective.

Increasingly, teams that represent segments or cross sections of the organizations that are being designed or redesigned do organization design work. By collaborating with a group composed of diverse individuals with different job titles and roles, each person not only contributes a unique perspective but also sees other viewpoints that might be new to him or her. A successful collaborative team will incorporate all of these perspectives to find the solution that best meets the organization's needs. And performance is measured by the outcome—the common product of the collaborative team.

We developed an online course through which the students learned by creating their own organization design: examining a case study from a variety of perspectives and then merging their findings into a cohesive relevant design. The students defined and developed their project by working as an interdependent GDT where the success of each student depended on the success of the team. To work collaboratively in an online environment, the group needed to first develop its own method of organizing the task at hand. This provided the students with an unusual level of "meta-learning," that is, doing what they were learning (organization design). All the while, the group members were also learning to use computers and a groupware application to accomplish their tasks. This experienced-based approach gave students practical skills in using technology to transcend barriers of time and space, collaborating with a multicultural and multifunctional group, and building an organization design model informed by a variety of perspectives.

We found that for this learning and working model to be effective, the size of the team was a critical variable, ranging from 6 to 10 individuals. The minimum number was a function of the workload vis-à-vis time constraints of the course; fewer people could not have completed the assignments in a semester. The maximum was a function of the complexity of the interactions and group dynamics in an asynchronous online environment; with more students, it would have been impossible to manage.

Team-Building Factors That Affect Online Education

Although online learning has become a standard mode of education at many institutions, including Fielding, a unique factor of our organization design seminar was the collaborative process, the interdependency of all team members, and the resulting evaluative structure in which the work of the team was more important than any particular individual's contribution. For such a course to be successful, we needed to consider not only online learning standards but also those standards relevant to the effectiveness of a GDT.

Many elements of successful VTs mirror those of successful face-to-face teams. Communication and collaboration are two of the most important factors in any team's success. Although agreements about goals, policies, and procedures are necessary within any group working collaboratively, they need to be even more explicitly discussed and clearly defined by a team working solely in a technologically mediated environment. In their book, *Mastering Virtual Teams,* Duarte and Snyder (1999) outline critical success factors for VTs. Standard organizational and team processes, organizational culture, and leadership are among those most relevant to designing an online course.

Standard Organizational and Team Processes

Although initially requiring a certain time commitment that could be seen by some as outside the project goals, setting standards at the beginning stages of a team's formation can actually reduce start-up time. By getting each team member's input and buy-in on goals, methodology, and processes—as well as on what to do in the event of conflict or failure to adhere to the agreements—a collaborative team avoids having to negotiate these issues as they arise, which is distracting to the task at hand.

Organizational Culture

Developing comprehension of and mutual respect for differences of culture (whether national, organizational, or functional) helps to mitigate misunderstandings and disagreements based on style, expectations, values, and assumptions. In one of our classes, for example, we had students from several countries (including a variety of English-speaking countries). It had already been established that English would be the language of the course. Because many students would be working on pieces of the final paper, one student suggested that all writing (even initial drafts) be created in "American English." An Australian student took offense at this because she found that having to edit her thoughts in real time would significantly reduce her creativity. Quite a debate ensued and tempers flared. Eventually, the team decided that any English would do for drafts and that those for whom English was not their native tongue should not worry too much about grammar and spelling. In the end, one person would be assigned the task of making the final paper read "in one voice."

For VTs, cultural respect must be explicitly stated and transgressions must be immediately addressed. Although the anonymity of cyberspace erases certain biases of gender, race, age, and social strata, it also eliminates key indicators of intent, such as body language, facial expression, tone of voice, and intonation. In a text-only environment, a tongue-in-cheek comment can be easily misinterpreted, and the lag time between a posting and a response can cause emotions to simmer and resentment to build. Differences in language can also cause misunderstandings, not just among different nationalities but also among diverse functional roles. Terms may have narrower meanings among certain groups than among others. Common definitions must be discussed and agreed on for a diverse collaborative team to function effectively.

Leadership

Lipnack and Stamps (1997) emphasize the fact that VTs require stronger leadership than do conventional teams. Co-located teams can sit in a conference room and circle around an issue until they come to consensus. With electronic communication, a discussion might never close when keeping it open is as simple as clicking on the "reply" or "next" button on the computer. Leaders must manage the process of bringing the team to closure and consensus. They should ensure full participation of team members and help to keep the multiple dialogues straight and on task, creating structure and defining boundaries. This is not meant to control the members or restrain initiative or creativity; rather, it is to keep teams from becoming immobilized by the ambiguity of working in cyberspace.

Leadership roles must be defined and supported by the group. Whether leadership is practiced by one team member for the entire project or divided by task, leaders must fully support collaboration and VTs as a way of doing business. They must take advantage of the diversity of the team to develop and use each team member's expertise to the fullest potential, set and uphold realistic expectations, allocate the appropriate time (and, in real-world situations, the money) needed to accomplish the project, and (most important) model the collaborative behavior that will contribute to the success of the team.

Duarte and Snyder (1999) also list essential skills for both leaders and team members to develop. Of these competencies, two are crucial to online education: building and maintaining trust and using interpersonal awareness. As we explore our own course experience, we highlight the tools we used to develop these skills among the group members. In addition, we address particular situations that challenged us as facilitators and the students as a collaborative team, further illustrating the importance of trust and awareness in the distance learning environment.

Fielding Course in Organization Design

Course Design

To use technological and other media to their greatest advantage for an online, team-based learning experience, the facilitator (instructor) must clearly articulate the design criteria for the course. As co-facilitators for the organization design seminar, our goals were to provide an opportunity for learners to (a) learn the basic concepts of and models for organization design, (b) work collaboratively as a team in an online environment, (c) experience doing organization design for a real organization, and (d) have a learner-centered learning experience in the Fielding tradition that requires learners to take responsibility for their learning and the course environment.

The facilitator—who, even in a self-learning model, is acting in a leadership role—must have direct knowledge of and experience with the dynamics of work teams, how to create a collaborative work environment, and online facilitation. For our organization design seminar, we drew on our extensive experience with both co-located and VTs to design an online environment that supported the learning goals we had set. Taking advantage of the structure of Fielding's computer-mediated communication (CMC) application (known as FELIX), we divided the course into seven distinct and interrelated phases: (a) reading assignments, (b) team start-up and development, (c) case writing and selection, (d) development of a work plan, (e) project work, (f) documentation, and (g) evaluation. For each phase, learners posted messages and responses relevant to the topic at hand. FELIX tracked in an outline and topic-based format the discussion that occurred asynchronously. This enabled learners to keep multiple dialogues going at the same time while maintaining a logically threaded discussion. It also allowed the next phase to begin while learners were still grappling with a previous phase, without interrupting the dialogue flow.

Another essential element in course design is to consider the time available (usually a semester or trimester in the academic environment) and to limit the coursework accordingly. Those experienced with virtual teamwork understand that GDTs typically require more time than do co-located teams to perform similar tasks. Grappling with anomalies such as time differences, without the benefit of immediate answers to questions, team members can easily feel overloaded and get frustrated. We focused our course on the essential elements of organization design to allow only the most relevant work within the limited period of time.

One of the greatest challenges for collaborative distance learning, or for any GDT, is defining the boundaries in which the work of the team will occur. In cyberspace, we are less bounded or constrained by the conventions that govern work done by groups. Thus, we must set concise, clearly defined goals, procedures, and boundaries to create a framework and context within which the team can feel secure.

As a kickoff to the course, we posted an initial greeting (including contact information for both of us) along with a detailed syllabus containing an overview of the course, a description of the methodology, rules for postings and frequency of participation, an outline for each assignment, the grading system, our role as facilitators, and the reading list. Regarding rules for postings and participation, we devised a new time standard: Fielding Standard Time (FST), designated as midnight on any calendar day in Santa Barbara, California (Pacific Time). This was necessary to ensure that learners in different time zones were meeting the required deadlines. Because of the interdependent nature of the coursework, we asked learners to check in three or more times per week and not to save all of their work for the weekends. We strongly encouraged them to bring a laptop computer when travel took them away from their home bases for more than a few days. We also directed learners to use the title field of their posts to reflect the content of their messages as an aid for tracking the flow of an interactive dialogue among multiple participants.

Reading assignments. To provide learners with the conceptual underpinnings of organization design, we gave the group lists of required and suggested readings. The required readings included materials that offered an overview of organization design concepts and variables, specific models of organization design, and the history and evolution of the field. Learners were encouraged to augment the required reading with sources that were relevant to the specific cases they worked on and with materials and learnings from other courses they had taken. We expected learners to read the materials and to explore and apply them to the content or tasks as they progressed through the course. Our reading list consisted of 3 required books and 5 required articles. In addition, we recommended 18 other relevant resources.

Team start-up and development. The initial team start-up and development was the most crucial phase of the course. During this phase, the team set standards relevant to goals, created processes, and developed agreements for reaching consensus in the online environment while also building the trust and interpersonal awareness that are so critical to successful VTs. The first assignment in the online space involved expanded introductions, where we asked learners to post what attracted them to the course; their learning goals; their fears, concerns, or reservations; their experience in the Fielding program thus far; their roles in their jobs and how they found these roles useful to the coursework; what they felt they could contribute to the team; and some information about themselves personally (e.g., where they live; what it is like there; their family, hobbies, and interests). We also asked each participant to respond by commenting on similarities and differences among the team members. This enabled learners to get to know one another on a social and professional level before diving into the coursework itself. It brought up common interests, topics for side conversations, and differences in writing style that helped learners to become familiar with each other's ways of communicating.

Whereas this kind of communication usually happens in the hallways or before the bell in a classroom situation, in an online environment the facilitator must promote this interaction through a specified assignment and time allocation. In fact, the facilitator must be a model for interpersonal awareness and trust building. Early on, we addressed the participants' concerns and fears, reassuring them, for example, that they would not be penalized for technological failures; even the best applications and Internet service providers limit access at times. We encouraged casual conversation, even seemingly irrelevant musings, and we responded to each learner individually to make sure that everyone felt heard. Humor, too, provides fertile soil for trust and human interaction. To ensure that comic moments were read as such, we modeled the use of electronic "emoticons"—symbols or words to express emotion, humor, or irony, such as ;-) and (smile!). Getting used to text-only communication can be difficult for some, and it was crucial that we permit enough time and nonthreatening content to allow the more reticent technology users to feel confident. Although this was neither their first distance learning course nor their first experience in using Fielding's CMC application, we were asking our students to use—and stretch—the technology in a different way from what they were accustomed to. In situations with new users, we believe that this start-up time would require even more time, attention, and training.

After the "getting to know each other" topic was completed, we gave the team the task of reaching consensus in three areas: team goals, team agreements, and—as part of the meta-learning process—how to reach consensus. Mastery of this process is critical to the team members' ability to work together successfully during their life together as a team. During this phase, team members posted their ideas about team learning goals and working agreements (or norms) about topics such as decision making, online participation, collaboration and interdependence, what to do if deadlines could not be met, how to allocate/manage the leadership role during the various phases of the project, and how to handle an unexplained extended absence of a team member from the group. Respect for each person's opinion motivated the discussion that followed everyone's postings, which further developed the trust that the agreements were designed to foster. Then one person took on the role of the synthesizer or "weaver," taking the different strands of discussion and weaving them into a tapestry that reflected what seemed to be the consensus. The team members then discussed and fine-tuned the consensus before polling to indicate their agreement.

As facilitators, we stepped in to support good progress and express concerns related to, for example, limiting goals to what is reasonable and addressing what to do if someone falls short on an agreement. Some learners naturally gravitated toward the leadership roles during this process (e.g., sending up the "trial balloons" to define consensus, encouraging stragglers to weigh in with their opinions). We found that these were often the same people who took social leadership roles as well, supporting others, interjecting humor, and inquiring about team members who lapsed into "radio silence" (not posting any messages for one reason or another).

Case writing and selection. During the case selection phase, the team developed the content on which it would focus its collective wisdom and energies. We asked each member to write an organization design case study, including the current organization design, its appropriateness for the course, and the owner's (team member's) familiarity with or access to information needed to complete and test the design activity. Using a model outlined in one of the assigned readings, we also specified definitions for certain key terms—such as *purpose, mission, objectives,* and *tasks*—that would be used in the assignment so that everyone would have the same understanding of these terms. Explicitly defining a common language is more important in text-only virtual environments than in face-to-face situations where language can be immediately clarified through queries or accentuated with nonverbal cues.

When all of the cases were posted, the team members developed selection criteria by which they would choose a single case to work on together as a "consulting" team for the duration of the class. This was the team members' first opportunity to make a major decision, thereby testing the agreements that they had put into place during the previous phase of the class. It required that someone step forward as a leader to mediate the discussion and build the model for consensus. We suggested factors that the team might take into consideration, including how the case fit the team's goals; the scope of the project (making sure that it was manageable during the limited time period in which the team would be working); how much access the owner had to critical information; the availability of the owner (e.g., travel schedule, outside commitments such as family or job); the extent to which the information present in the case was clear, complete, and usable; and how well the case permitted the examination of all aspects of the model chosen from the required reading.

To assist in the analysis process—which, if left unaided, could easily become unwieldy—we assigned each team member a review of two other cases, ensuring that each case would be reviewed by two people and that no one would review his or her own case. However, the actual criteria for selection and the process by which team members would make the decision were left up to the team. Because this was the first real test of the agreements the team had formulated, it was often the first time that these agreements were challenged. In one case, some team members posted reviews in a timely manner while others lagged behind. This left some cases with two reviews and others with one or, in the worst case, no review, which posed a serious problem for informed selection. The person who had stepped forward as leader was charged with suggesting procedures and decisions to allow the project to move forward despite the fact that the input was incomplete. In one case, the leader asked other members of the team to do additional reviews. In another, he proposed modifications to the formal review process, based on the content of the unreviewed cases that had been read by all participants. The participating team members agreed, and the challenge was met without unduly slowing down the process.

Development of a work plan. The team planning activities, which occurred simultaneously with case development, asked learners to determine a plan for how they would best use the resources available to them to decide how they would choose and analyze the case, prepare and document recommendations for the redesign of the subject organization, and justify the solutions based on the resources they discovered and used. In the plan, the team developed a schedule for its work, determined roles and responsibilities, and addressed the leadership needs of the project.

As facilitators, we found that a certain amount of structure was needed during this phase to keep the team on track and to assist the team in dividing up the tasks. We suggested the following macro-level tasks that needed to be accomplished: analysis of the existing organization; understanding the contextual dynamics of the organization; understanding/researching issues, concerns, and opportunities mentioned by the "client"; redesigning each of the elements using the model from the required reading; testing the redesign and adjusting for overall fit and balance; and writing the final report. We asked the team to decide how best to divide up this work; to use the technology, FELIX, to produce the work; and to determine a timetable for delivering the work.

Typically, one person took the leadership role, developing an outline for the elements of the work plan and posing the essential questions that generated the discussion needed to flesh out the plan. The ensuing dialogue refined the outline, and individual team members volunteered to be the point persons on particular tasks. The leader frequently updated the team on the status of the plan, which informed everyone regarding who had volunteered for what and which tasks still required leadership. We checked in to support the progress and offer our assistance when concerns arose regarding participation of all the team members.

Project work. The team's analysis of the current organization design in the selected case and the proposed redesign using the assigned conceptual model formed the heart of the course and the bulk of the work performed by the team. To provide a framework for the final report, we posted a description of the tasks/sections to be addressed with pertinent questions the team should consider when working on that task. We also stated our expectations for the final report in terms of format, style, professionalism, consistency, accuracy, and attention to detail. In addition, we posted key questions that the team should answer while developing the different elements of the organizational model we had asked the team to follow, which included strategy, structure, people, processes, and reward systems (see Appendix). By specifically guiding team members' thinking for each of the tasks and elements, we reduced the chances that they would be led off track by the potentially overwhelming challenges of the project. The guidelines and boundaries set for a VT's work determine its ability to succeed in the project. A project that is too expansive will certainly lead team members astray, as will sidetracking into irrelevant material.

However, it is critical that a certain kind of sidetracking be encouraged to promote social interaction and provide relaxation from the stress of performing in an online environment. During one of our courses, after posting the material relevant to the topic, we would lapse into discussions of basketball and friendly rivalries over whose team had the better coach or more talented players. Not only did these conversations lighten the tone of the serious work we were engaged in, but they also served to strengthen the bonds among the team members that are so crucial to building and maintaining trust.

One issue that became apparent during this stage of the course was the fear of being misunderstood. Although the loss of certain traditional communication barriers, such as anxiety when speaking in front of groups and lack of confidence in verbal skills, empowered some students to express themselves more freely than they would in a traditional learning environment, others found the lack of verbal and nonverbal response cues to be intimidating. Misunderstanding, either as a result or a cause of conflict, is common in both intellectual content and interpersonal face-to-face exchanges. Moreover, misunderstanding and its subsequent resolution can contribute to group formation, synergy, and creativity. But when it occurs in a VT, learners are frequently at a loss for how to deal with it, and the problem becomes an obstacle. In an online learning environment, the fear of one's written message being taken the wrong way often surfaces as a long unwieldy preamble to the main point of the posting in an attempt to predict and counter every possible interpretation of the text being written. Sometimes participants disengage from an activity or avoid dealing with situations that could contribute to conflict. The practical effect of this fear is reduced willingness to take risks, and this can lead to gridlock in the group.

Conquering the fear of being misunderstood involves trust—accepting that team members will not judge one another negatively through their own misinterpretations. The acceptance of all viewpoints and voices, however deftly or awkwardly expressed, reduces misunderstandings that can stymie the group. Facilitators can mitigate these situations by modeling and encouraging clarification. When team members reflect back what they interpret from another's posting before making assumptions about the intended meaning, they give the originator a chance to further clarify his or her intent.

Documentation: The final report. The capstone of the group members' work together was a final report that summarized the particulars of the case they had selected, their analysis, the proposed design solution and rationale, and other recommendations for the client organization. Unlike most other courses—both online and classroom—learners did not write and submit individual work. Instead, consistent with the other elements of this course, the team was required to produce the final document jointly and interactively. This turned out to be the most difficult aspect of the course for several reasons. Common among all groups was the end-of-trimester time crunch. Underestimating the complexity of some of the earlier assignments, and of the dynamics of the team and the medium, team members began to fall behind and were unable to reprioritize or make up for the slippages. Because the class had a definite end point, team members had less time than originally allowed to produce the paper. Those teams that had a member with strong writing skills who drafted the document, as well as a clear process for how others would participate in shaping and editing it, produced the best papers. This typically occurred when a strong leader emerged who was willing to drive and manage the process to conclusion in a fairly directive manner—and others were willing to allow this while contributing fully and within the time constraints. In one case, the group allowed a team member to volunteer to draft and coordinate the editing of the report when, if fact, this person was not well suited to this task—and even though, as it turned out, others on the team were aware of this. In another case, the writer was well qualified but, by the end of the class, did not have the personal bandwidth to complete the task. In neither case was the team able to manage itself to a more satisfactory outcome. The result was that the papers did not adequately reflect the content or quality of the work that preceded them, and many team members were disappointed by this anticlimactic end to their experience together.

Evaluation. In keeping with the learning goals of the course and the interdependence of the team, we created a process for evaluation that assessed both team performance and individual contributions. We outlined our system for grading in the syllabus so that there would be no surprises when evaluations were solicited and received. We based our grades on a system of 100 points: 25 for the quality of the team's plan, product, and process (everyone on the team received the same number of points for this component); 25 for a team member's self-evaluation based on how well he or she met personal and team learning goals; 25 for the evaluations each team member received from the other team members related to his or her participation in and contributions to the team; and 25 for the facilitators' evaluation of each team member's individual participation, contributions, intellectual and practical curiosity, and command of the subject.

What was unique about this system was that it reflected the interdependence of the team members, not only for the accomplishment of the project but also for the evaluation of performance. We felt that it more closely mirrored a real-world work scenario where the outcome of the joint project determines the success of the individuals involved. A collaborative project is only as good as its weakest element, and part of the team's work was to determine how best to use the resources and talents it had at its disposal.

Several issues arose as a result of our interdependent evaluation model. Some team members had difficulty in evaluating their peers or had fears about what others would say about their own contributions. Others expressed concern that their grades would be tied to the work of others, the quality of which they could not control. For the evaluative process to function correctly, we needed each team member to complete the evaluation assignment, which was the final task for the course and the one most likely to be neglected. Not all students gave the assignment the same level of attention: some contributed very high-quality evaluations, whereas others provided only cursory responses.

This kind of group evaluation process proved to be quite time-consuming for us as facilitators. We had to merge all of the comments while maintaining the anonymity of the contributors. For each student, we prepared a large packet with both quantitative (points) and qualitative (narrative) evaluations. Despite the great amount of work that the evaluations represented for both the students and the facilitators, students indicated that these complex evaluations were much more valuable than merely receiving a letter grade and an assessment based only on the instructors' perceptions.

Resolving and Accepting Contrasting Elements

One of the most surprising things that we discovered in our organization design seminar was how certain contrasting elements inherent to education in general presented unique problems to be solved or to be accepted as irreconcilable in the online environment. The traditional differentiation between faculty and students tended to blur in the online environment, where there was no podium to stand behind or board to write on. All of the postings, whether from facilitators or from learners, were equivalent; each was given a number by FELIX and merged with all of the other postings. Apart from our initial syllabus and assignment postings, our commentary as facilitators resided alongside the discussion of the learners, thereby eliminating the hierarchy usually associated with the teacher-student relationship.

The synchronous versus asynchronous nature of work could not be resolved within the context of our course because nearly all of the discussion was asynchronous and each individual participated at a time that best suited his or her schedule and local time zone. The same was true for face-to-face versus virtual interaction. We had to accept that there would be no face-to-face meetings and that interpersonal relationships were mediated by technology. The loss of face-to-face contact, both formal and casual, carries a great impact. Studies show that in face-to-face discussions, a message is conveyed 55% by body language, 38% by tone of voice, and only 7% by actual words. In telephone conversations, a message is conveyed 87% by tone of voice and 13% by actual words (Mehrabian & Ferris, 1967). In our course, students grappled with the limitation of communicating solely through written words. However, when severe problems arose, we used the telephone to have real-time discussions so that we could find appropriate solutions. But the standard practice was to use the technological medium to bring up issues, gather input, consider options, and make decisions on how to proceed.

As an example, one of the most consistent problems that teams face when using this medium as their primary means of interaction is radio silence, that is, when a team member goes for an extended period of time without participating (i.e., posting a message to the team space). ("Extended" here is relative to the team's norms/agreements and the requirements for collaboration specific to the task or project.) It creates at least two obstacles for the team. First, effective teams typically have agreements or expectations about how frequently each member will participate; a project schedule with deadlines, interdependencies, and so on; and/or specific individual assignments or action items. The nonparticipation of even one member can quickly bring the team to a standstill. This then forces the team to take time to decide what to do about both the person and the project so as to keep working and progressing. Second, once relationships are formed (implying some level of trust and concern for each other), team members begin to worry about the absent member, particularly because in a GDT no one else on the team will run into that person in another setting, either to inquire about his or her absence or to verify a "sighting." In our course, we intentionally constrained the use of other media so as to test the limits of CMC as a tool for GDTs. However, in situations like the one described, we used other means to contact an "MIA" (missing-in-action team member) and to resolve the situation. The resolution typically was highly individual and ranged from one learner getting new equipment to another learner withdrawing from the course due to not being able to keep up with the workload.

We resolved the issue of theory versus practice by focusing our online learning model on practice. The theoretical base for our course came largely from the readings, and there was no formal review or discussion of these theories. Instead, learners were expected to apply what they had read to the practice of organization design, which formed the core of the course. This practice occurred on two levels: the actual coursework in redesigning the case study they chose and the meta-level of organizing themselves to perform the task.

One of the challenges in the practical learning model is how best to use the skills and experience of the group. For example, someone might volunteer for a task for which he or she is not well suited. This may occur at a time when others, including the faculty, are still unfamiliar with the participants' various strengths and limitations. When possible, it is up to the leader to diplomatically suggest that the talents of this person might be better used elsewhere and to gain support for this deferral from the rest of the group. The person in question is much less likely to be offended by the suggestion if the rest of the team offers rousing support for applying that person's skills to another task.

Despite the attempts of the faculty to compensate, the relative lack of structure, the absence of face-to-face contact, and the reduction of familiar social cues can create considerable ambiguity in the group. As a result, a balance between autonomy and accountability must be struck by and among team members. This requires participants to find ways to make individual and original contributions to the work and learning of the team while also respecting the norms and agreements set by the team. Without the willingness of at least a few members to experiment with a range of behavior, the team may remain under-differentiated. At the same time, if even a couple of members are unwilling to adhere to the agreed-on standards and conventions, an almost unmanageable situation for the others can develop. A constant distraction from the main purpose of the team, behavior outside the "norms" requires extra attention to team dynamics and challenges others to confront the disruptive team members. Failure to face and resolve these issues can lead to anarchy in the group. Although these dynamics also occur in face-to-face groups, they are more easily managed by factors such as the authority of the faculty/leader; nonverbal cues and other reinforcers of group norms; and informal, person-to-person interaction and feedback. For example, failure by one member to meet agreed-on deadlines for submitting work on which others are dependent creates a situation that snowballs through the semester. It may cause the team to do rework when that member's posting eventually appears, and it can also result in the team running out of time on the final project or documentation.

Another issue that generated a certain amount of fear at the beginning of the course was structure versus flexibility. As we have discussed, structure is essential to successful online teamwork as well as to distance learning in general. Tasks such as organizing or coordinating subtasks and integrating outputs of individual work almost always require more leadership in a GDT than in a co-located team. Although team members may recognize the need for such structure and manage themselves well under more conventional circumstances, their lack of familiarity with raising issues in a technologically supported forum may dictate the need for a leader to manage these tasks. If the leader creates the required structure, which includes identifying the need, recruiting/naming a person who will be responsible for managing the task or process, providing the necessary support and coaching, and holding both the task manager and the other team members accountable for engaging and reaching closure, then team members are less likely to experience frustration and gridlock.

On the other hand, this increased structure needs to be balanced with a degree of flexibility, which is not to say that learners can disregard deadlines or offer one of the wealth of excuses with which most teachers are quite familiar (e.g., "The dog ate my homework," "My computer crashed"). Back-up systems, composing messages offline, and alternative means of communication (e.g., e-mailing a posting to the helpdesk at Fielding if access to FELIX is denied) provided the kind of flexibility necessary to keep the course moving in the event of technological failure.

The unique design requirements of this course relative to others in the program curriculum, as well as to other more traditional courses, posed other dilemmas. Some learners found the workload, requirements for regular and frequent online participation, and demands of collaboration in an ambiguous medium to be more difficult than anticipated. It was not possible to succeed as an individual in this course, and there was no online version of cramming or pulling an all-nighter at the end of the semester. A manageable number of learners fell behind, and over the space of several offerings of the course, a couple dropped out for various reasons. If too many had done either, then the dynamics of the course would have been at risk, and with it the overall integrity of the learning experience. This was not, however, a situation that we had to confront.

Advantages and Disadvantages of the Online Environment

Alongside these contrasting elements are sets of advantages and their corollary disadvantages that we discovered in our experience with interdependent distance learning. One advantage is that working with GDTs allows an international experience without traveling. But the disadvantage of the same is that there are sometimes surprising cultural and language barriers, even when one is diligent about trying to avoid them. We witnessed a certain amount of conflict during the editing of a written project where the contributors spoke different national styles of English (e.g., Australian vs. American). Even though we had specifically stated that both forms were acceptable, when it came to merging the two together, bad feelings arose among team members. This is an example of where immediate conflict resolution was necessary to prevent wounds from festering and to prevent one or more participants from feeling disenfranchised.

One particularly agreeable advantage of the online environment is that age, gender, and race get neutralized, particularly for women and people of color who are often discounted in teams where they are a minority. This can, however, lead to loss of identity for some who base their view of themselves on those very things.

Another advantage and academic leveler is that people who are not quick on their feet can participate equally because they have time to think before they post. The disadvantage is that there is lag time before getting feedback, and this can lead to feelings of not being heard. And, as we have already mentioned, when conflict arises, it might not be immediately addressed, and the delay can increase frustration and hurt feelings.

The Internet allows worldwide communication and access from almost anywhere, which is a great advantage in today's global market and mobile workforce. However, Internet service providers outside the United States can be unreliable, and this puts some learners, particularly those in developing nations, at a severe disadvantage. Nevertheless, we successfully conducted the course with students living as close as Los Angeles and as far away as South Africa.

Conclusion

We discovered that a course design based on collaboration and assigned projects that require interdependence and teamwork can be successful in the online environment. A collaborative team can achieve high-quality results without face-to-face interaction. However, a team working in a virtual environment requires more structure than do traditional teams, including agreeing on norms and procedures, setting realistic expectations and boundaries, and providing the leadership to keep the team on track and moving toward each goal.

In an online environment, there is a strong social component through which participants form close bonds and true affection in their relationships. But it does not happen in the casual way that student-to-student relationships develop in the traditional teaching environment. Social interaction must be modeled and encouraged by the instructor/facilitator, and significant time and space should be dedicated to this task from the outset. And where students whispering in the back of the real-life classroom would be a distraction to the instruction taking place, side conversations and chitchat on seemingly irrelevant topics are constructive toward building trust and interpersonal awareness in an online environment.

Finally, our experience with this course further emphasized that the online collaborative work product has real-world applications as the modern workforce becomes more geographically dispersed. By working together in a technologically mediated environment, learners developed a set of skills that are imperative in today's global marketplace. And by engaging in a double level of learning—learning to organize themselves so as to learn to organize another company or institution—members of collaborative teams gain twice the practice of learning by doing, the kind of active engagement that proves to be more successful in adult education experiences.

Appendix: Guidelines for Final Project

Assignment #5: Organization Design Project

The purpose of this assignment is for you to work as a consulting team on the redesign of the organization described in the case you have selected.

The outcome of this assignment is the completion of your case analysis and redesign recommendations and presentation of them to the other team.

The deadline for this assignment is December 1 FST.

Part I: A description of the organization being redesigned. Much of this can come from the original posting of the case. Bear in mind that the other team has not read all of the cases and will need some context and introduction to the organization. In addition to a summary of the organization, please ensure that you consider the following questions:

- What are the *desired outcomes* of the design effort for the business, the organization, and the people? (These can also be called "design criteria.")
- What's the core work of the organization? What's the input → transformation → output that the organization must execute to deliver its products/services?

- What are the primary *interdependencies within* the organization's boundaries?

Part II: A description of other contextual dynamics of the organization (e.g., culture, political forces, variables that affect the target organization that are outside the direct control of the management team) that need to be considered in a design solution. In addition to others you will think of, please consider the following questions:

- What are the primary *interfaces* with other organizations and entities **outside** this organization's boundaries?
- What are the design constraints being imposed from outside?
- What are the political realities/constraints?
- Who, in addition to the client and the management team, must buy into or approve the proposed design? How easy or difficult is it likely to be to get such approvals? Why?

Part III: An in-depth analysis of the existing organization design using Galbraith as your principal frame, supplemented with the theories and principles from other authors or sources, including each of the components of the model; the overall fit among the components; and the extent to which the current arrangement enables the organization's purpose, mission, guiding principles, objectives, and strategy. You will need to delve into the initial analysis provided by the "owner" in his or her case.

Part IV: A recommended redesign of each of the components of the organization that corresponds to the Galbraith model, ensuring an overall fit of all the components with each other and with the strategy and guiding principles of the organization.

What follows is a set of questions to consider when evaluating the "fit" of an organization design. Please note that this is NOT an exhaustive list. It is meant to be a guideline for your team. You should add to and modify this list depending on the uniqueness of your particular case.

Structure

- How do the various components of the organization as you have designed it relate to each other?
- Why did you choose to differentiate the functions in this way, and what mechanisms/processes have you designed for integrating them where interdependence is required?
- What are the mechanisms/processes for managing interfaces outside the target organization?

- Is the structure adequate to meet the demands of the required work/tasks?
- How is power distributed in this structure?
- What are the implications for interdependencies within this structure?
- Does the structure enable the desired communication patterns?

Work/Task

- Are there implications for work/job redesign?
- To what extent do the tasks (i.e., the way the work is organized and designed into "jobs") provide opportunities for individuals to meet their needs and obtain the desired rewards?
- Do you have enough individuals on board with the skills and abilities to meet the task demands? If not, where or how will you get them (see "People" section next)?
- Do you have enough management talent to fill all of the management needs? Do you have enough "technical" talent to fill all of the "technical" needs? If not, what plans do you have to hire or grow this talent?
- Will the tasks and work/job design specified meet both individual and organizational goals?

People

- What implications does the design have for selection criteria for hiring?
- What implications does the design have for recruiting and retaining people?
- To what extent does the design facilitate the training and development of people? To what extent is it required for the new design to work?
- To what extent does the design allow for promotion and transfers?
- What implications does the design have for leadership and management styles?

Decision Making and Other Processes

- What information systems need to be in place?
- What communication patterns and forums need to be established?
- What planning systems need to be in place?
- How will decision making, opportunities for initiative, and power be distributed in the organization?
- How and by whom will decisions get made and communicated?

<u>Reward Systems</u>

- What implications does this design have for job classification and compensation systems?
- How will people be rewarded in this system?
- How will people be recognized in this system?
- How will the reward system encourage or facilitate the desired outcomes and behaviors throughout the organization?
- What obstacles are you likely to encounter in redesigning or modifying the formal and informal reward systems?

Part V: Implementation and communication plan. Assume that your proposed redesign has been approved. What is your plan for implementing this new design and communicating it throughout the organization?

We have created a topic titled "Final Presentation." Please post your final report there, and we will ensure that it gets posted to the other team. We have not created any other topics for this assignment. We encourage you to do so in line with your work plan and the needs that will emerge as you continue to work on this project.

If your work plan provides for tasks to be delegated to individuals and/or subgroups, please make sure that their work is available online (as a clearly identified topic) to other members of the team for observation and input.

Please consider your final report to be a scholarly as well as a professional piece of work. You may choose to write as if your document were a report to the "client." In this case, however, it should also show attention to such things as style, format, organization, citations within the text, and a complete list of references. Spelling, grammar, punctuation, logical organization, and so on "count" and are important in the discipline of being a scholar-practitioner.

Please remember that you are to work as a team and keep your team agreements. Try to keep your perspective and have some fun while working on this assignment. We will be logging on regularly and will help if we see you getting stuck. Please feel free to contact us if you need any further clarification/help.

References

Duarte, D. L., & Snyder, N. T. (1999). *Mastering virtual teams: Strategies, tools, and techniques that succeed.* San Francisco: Jossey-Bass.

Lipnack, J., & Stamps, J. (1997). *Virtual teams: Reaching across space, time, and organizations with technology.* New York: John Wiley.

Mehrabian, A., & Ferris, S. R. (1967). Inference of attitudes from nonverbal communication in two channels. *Journal of Consulting Psychology, 31,* 248-252.

Chapter 17

Teaching Virtual Leadership

Using the Case Method Online

Barbara Mahone Brown

Competent leaders must master the management of attention, meaning, trust, and themselves (Bennis, 1993). Imagine how daunting this challenge becomes when one is leading from afar. Yet today leaders of global corporations are often required to manage geographically dispersed projects and teams—perhaps even several teams of individuals and multiple projects on different continents all at once. For business executives, the usual challenges of leadership are compounded by the absence of frequent face-to-face interactions with direct reports, with supportive friends or peers, and even with their own bosses. What is lost in the absence of such direct human contact? What new skills must be mastered to surmount the difficulties as well as to harness the unique opportunities afforded leaders in the networked organizations of the information age?

This is the subject matter of a course titled "Virtual Leadership" that I created and have taught for the past several years. The course is offered as an elective to graduate students who are mid-career professionals in a variety of industries on four continents, via the Internet, and regionally to Northern and Southern California transportation managers, via interactive video-conference technology. The virtual leadership course emphasizes the case method and includes as a central feature the students' research and construction of leadership cases based on their own professional experiences. This chapter describes the course objectives, teaching methods, environmental conditions, and outcomes that foster graduate teaching and learning about virtual leadership with the case method in online networked classrooms at a distance.

Background and Need

Intellectual Capital and Virtual Leadership

Knowledge is increasingly the commodity that determines economic success and failure in the business world. According to a recent U.S. Department of Education study, college graduates who participated in additional training from the beginning of their employment earned an average of 30% more per week, compared with those who did not (Baker, 1999). Global businesses struggle to retain competitive workforces. The demand for superior leadership and technical knowledge grows steadily, spurring new government proposals for education and training as well as private flows of capital into information-creating and information-disseminating enterprises.

Managing the changes that come with the information age and advances in networking capabilities requires a redefinition of the skill sets that leaders and managers need to be effective. The organizational- and system-level changes of reinventing and restructuring, redefining core competencies, and reinvigorating relations with customers all require individuals who are capable of change. These individuals and the teams they lead will be expected to master new processes of knowledge creation, interpretation, and diffusion (Davenport & Pearlson, 1998). Such practices will be managed often from a distance with the aid of computer information networks and communications software. Managers will be forced into roles of virtual leaders. Their personalities, strategic visions, and ability to motivate others will continue to be key determinants of success. However, successful achievement in the network—a complex web of continually shifting priorities and burgeoning information—means having mastered the traditional skills associated with organizational learning and change (Senge, Kleiner, Roberts, Ross, & Smith, 1994, 1999). Moreover, leaders will need to define and test new competencies, to solve new types of problems, and to maximize opportunities in global information enterprises (Stewart, 1997). Managers in technology businesses, financial services industries, business consulting, and others competing in global markets will have special incentives to acquire the competencies of virtual leadership.

Understanding Virtual Leadership

The course in virtual leadership focuses on the ways in which a virtual medium can foster and constrain human leadership, using the case method in conjunction with independent readings and research. The course was originally developed for the Fielding Graduate Institute's master's program in organizational management. Conceived as an elective emphasizing just-in-time concepts, this course is one of the "event-based" seminar series, designed to capture new knowledge derived from recent events and firsthand professional experiences. This course has also been taught (with significant modifications for interactive videoconferencing) to students in the master's in transportation management program at San Jose State University. Students are given an opportunity to develop their own case studies based on critical issues in their work environments and in their professional lives. Each student is responsible for the presentation of at least one case and assumes leadership of the discussion session for that topic.

There are important distinctions between virtual work and virtual leadership as well as between leadership in general and virtual leadership in particular. Leadership in virtual media has special characteristics, some of which are unique to environments where human face-to-face interaction is limited or entirely absent. This deficit changes both the nature of work and the leader's role in forging organizational values in significant ways. Both new technical skills and new people skills are required in addition to many of the same skills that leaders typically have been identified as needing.

For example, recently the range of media to aid in communicating an organization's vision and values has expanded dramatically, even as direct "face time" has been reduced. Virtual options include conventional telephoning, conference calling, videoconferencing, e-mail, voice mail, faxes, cellular phones, digital handheld devices, and so on. Which media should leaders use under what circumstances? What should be said to whom, and how should the message be framed for different media? What about timing? How often must one resort to face-to-face interaction to sustain interpersonal influence? Or suppose that a transitional team must continue to work and function day to day while undergoing dramatic technological change. This requires strategic thought and planning. Clearly, new skills in "digital literacy" (Gilster, 1997) are needed. A leader's skill level is ideally higher than that of other virtual workers or community members. The virtual leader needs to adopt a personal communication style or persona in the aural, written, and visual texts of electronic messages; to develop the ability to feel comfortable with various media; and to manage shared databases to supplement Web site communications. A leader also benefits from setting target response times to e-mails and from committing to regular periodic face time with subgroups of virtual workers.

Course Objectives

The primary objective of the course in virtual leadership is (a) to allow students to explicate a leading-edge concept called *virtual leadership* through their case studies. Other course objectives are (b) to develop student competency in using the case method online, (c) to foster an environment for student learning and creativity, (d) to facilitate new research and development efforts, and (e) to build student leadership skills in navigating virtual media.

At the beginning of the first week of the course, students are offered suggested study topics by the professor as options, and they are encouraged to select one that best fits their work situation. If none of the topics seems to fit, or if they prefer to suggest another perspective, they are permitted to do so. The following topics have been suggested: (a) communicating a vision (exploring how leaders get their messages across in networked environments), (b) virtual workspaces (leading groups that are fragmented by alternate work styles, time, and distance), (c) digital literacy (identifying the personal, technical, and critical thinking skills needed by virtual leaders), (d) organizational chaos (learning from turbulence, instability, and environmental change), (e) e-commerce (competing for leadership in the electronic marketplace), (f) community building (examining how consensus is forged in electronic networks), (g) virtual laughter and tele-friendships (dealing with issues of identity, stamina, emotional stress, and spiritual well-being), and (h) inventing the future (creating new directions for virtual leaders). Other topics have been considered from time to time.

Students are guided in the process of researching their selected topics. Resources online, in conventional libraries, and in management information systems are used in case preparation. Early in the term, the professor models the case research, development, and presentation process for the students. The teacher also posts the first case online for students so that they can practice and gain familiarity with the electronic environment. In my class, this is a sample case for initial experiential learning purposes. The case analysis is not graded; only subsequent student cases and responses are evaluated.

Initial required reading for the course is the best-selling classic *Being Digital* (Negroponte, 1995), which still resonates with meaning for our technological age, even some years after its initial publication. Students are encouraged but not required to read a variety of other monographs, most of them published within the past decade. Suggested titles are shared with the instructor and with students in the course. In the past, these have included works by Gilster (1997), Wheatley (1994), Shenk (1997), Turkle (1995), Sproull and Kiesler (1995), and Dertouzos (1997). Students have been wonderfully resourceful in supplying additional titles from their own research and readings. As noted earlier, the just-in-time, event-based content supports the knowledge base under creation in this course.

Methodology

The Case Method

Interest in the case study method has increased dramatically during recent years, in part as a reaction to higher education's traditional dependence on lecturing. Case discussion classes help to achieve core educational objectives (Christensen, 1987), including core leadership qualities, qualities of the mind (e.g., curiosity, judgment, wisdom), personal qualities (e.g., integrity, responsibility, sensitivity), and the ability to apply specific knowledge and general concepts to particular situations. The case method has proven to be a highly effective pedagogical approach to accomplishing these objectives. I believe that it is true for virtual classrooms as well.

The case method provides a useful model for exploring the corporate and organizational culture and for modeling individual and group behaviors within that context. This method works well in event-based seminars, in just-in-time elective courses designed around real problems and opportunities, and with student-generated topics as "living" case studies. Cases may take a variety of forms, but most are narratives of real-life situations that students explore critically. For example, a case might present a manager's or leader's dilemma in a particular work situation. One of my favorite student-generated cases has to do with a semiconductor manufacturer's decision to develop a major new product with a design team in India and software engineers in California's Silicon Valley working together on the project.

The case focuses on the project manager's challenges as she confronts multiple pressures from technical experts in the home office and overseas, her boss, disrupted timetables, and the potential threat of competitive activities. The manager wishes to bring the project in on time and on budget because this would represent a major coup for the firm as well as a feather in her cap personally in terms of her own career development. The challenges of the case center on the project manager's ability to lead the geographically dispersed team effectively. To solve this situation, the manager will have to (a) communicate well to align the visions of the two groups of employees on different continents, (b) ensure effective work routines with the necessary oversight of multiple aspects of the project, and (c) command the personal respect and credibility needed to guide and motivate direct reports.

The writer of this case captures the realism of interpersonal pressures, organizational norms, executive judgment, intuition, technical guidelines, financial formulas, and rules of thumb. The presentation is a rich psychological narrative text that is also embedded with numbers and algorithms. There is a nice mix of quantitative and qualitative concepts. Not all cases have this mix, nor is it necessary in most cases.

The student posts the case narrative online as a written document. The case submission is concluded with discussion questions that focus student analysis. The case writer then leads an extended discussion session—a threaded conversation of postings and replies to postings. At the end of the allotted time (usually 1 week per case), the case writer synthesizes all of the discussion in summary and concluding remarks. The instructor may be a participant or an observer during the week's discussion. I tend to wait until the conclusion of student interactions before offering the instructor's comments unless someone solicits input from me directly. The group receives the instructor's summary evaluation (posted online) of the team interaction. The case writer/discussion leader receives in-depth feedback and a detailed critical evaluation at the end of the term. The students also critique each other's cases at the end of the term during wrap-up sessions.

In addition to the narrative, cases may include charts, graphs, and pictures that are relevant to the situation. Case studies vary in length from a few paragraphs to book-chapter length. (The North American Case Research Association guidelines recommend no more than 30 pages.) Cases come with and without appendixes. Some include discussion questions at the end to focus the reader's attention on certain issues. Others do not include questions, and part of the challenge is to define the real issues of the case. Sample cases may be found in casebooks; as sections of textbooks; with publisher's services; or adapted from newspaper and magazine articles, created as fiction, or based on real-life experiences.

Critical Thinking Skills

Bloom's (1956) taxonomy of critical thinking skills fits well with the case method. Bloom suggests that critical thinking ranges from relatively low levels of comprehension; to higher levels of application, analysis, and synthesis; to the highest level of evaluation. In reality, most of us move back and forth among these various levels—often intuitively—in our thinking. The case method challenges students to consciously and formally (a) describe what they have understood and absorbed from the case, (b) apply whatever decision rules seem relevant, (c) analyze the facts, (d) synthesize what has been learned, and (e) evaluate the data for qualitative and quantitative implications with recommendations for action and implementation. This is the general approach to critical thinking using case study materials.

This approach is also an apt description of knowledge creation, as distinct from merely providing raw information. Leaders especially are capable of doing this well. In fact, much (but not all) of the leadership talent involved lies in a leader's capacity for astute critical thinking under pressure. In my virtual leadership classroom, students are asked to write their own cases and to discuss one another's cases. They are expected to read and reread each case carefully and critically. They must also consider the discussion questions to focus their efforts. They should ask "What information is here?" and "What is missing or needs to be prepared?" In event-based seminars, if just-in-time learning is the norm, then students reflect on what they know from personal experience or recent exposure to similar situations on the job or elsewhere.

The electronic group software provided to the classroom forum most often leads to lively discussion among peers. The special challenge for the writer-researcher is to facilitate this discussion well. As noted earlier, because of the case study format I adopted, students are expected to research and write their own cases. Each student chooses a content area related to virtual work groups and one week of the term for posting his or her case as the topic of the week. The other students analyze the problems and opportunities posed by the case. Then they develop case solutions that are posted as replies under the weekly study topic.

A sample of case titles from my classes includes *Lone Eagles* (establishing a virtual chamber of commerce), *Digital Literacy* (a consulting start-up game), *Online Persona* (focusing on human communication), *Wellsound Labs* (a collaborative effort presented jointly by two students working virtually), and *Monster.com* (online corporate recruiting). The students take turns moderating the discussions, and the appointed moderator assumes primary responsibility for synthesizing the key points in a final summary posting for that week. Minimum levels of participation are established for all students, but an exciting topic generates much more discussion. There are also deadlines for student postings to the forum, and broad-based participation is the norm. Obviously, this is a lot to keep track of, and fortunately, there are software utilities to assist with monitoring the flow of messages. The instructor's role is to facilitate discussion, to provide feedback and closure, and to insert supplemental and transitional material where needed.

The Sample

The data obtained in developing this chapter come from a variety of contacts with master's students. For three terms (1997-1999), I taught this course at an accredited graduate institute along with a second leadership course using a different method. There were 24 adult learners in the subject group, all of whom enrolled in the computer-mediated seminar titled "Virtual Leadership." In addition, 18 students, all mid-career transportation engineering professionals, were taught in a modified, two-way interactive videoconference course in leadership. These experiences are forms of distance learning. In some instances, students were geographically spread across the United States, Canada, Europe, and Asia. Approximately half of the students had prior experience in leading virtual work groups, and the other half did not. All expressed a desire to develop expertise in this area.

Findings and Implications

Flattening the Playing Field

Although students come with varying backgrounds and skills, the Internet serves as an equalizer. The Internet is sometimes referred to as a "flat" medium, which suggests a certain superficiality. In reality, it supplies real depth and texture to the virtual classroom experience. The idea of a flat medium has been misconstrued to mean something other than what the term was originally intended to denote—that is, *"a kind of organizational flattening . . . that did not necessarily follow hierarchical lines of management"* (Stefik, 1996, p. 125, italics in original). The decentralized control, or so-called "cyber-democracy" originally touted as characteristic of the online virtual community, is a notion that is now challenged by critics (Brook & Boal, 1995; Porter, 1996) but finds perhaps its best expression in a networked educational environment such as the virtual classroom.

Faculty Issues in Virtual Teaching

There are many tacit assumptions and myths associated with learning in a virtual classroom (Brown, 1998). There are also issues of educational process that challenge traditional modes of classroom instruction. For example, the Internet has been variously characterized—not only as a "flat" medium for widely distributed control and decision making but also as an "efficient" means of communication (Sproull & Kiesler, 1995) and, yet still, as an "impersonal" environment for distance education (Kubala, 1998). Several largely unproven assumptions underlie these somewhat iconoclastic descriptions. For that reason, computer-mediated work and learning merit further investigation and research.

For example, much has been written about technological efficiency and the potential of the Internet as an educational medium to save time and money or to increase productivity. My experience inspires a healthy skepticism in this regard. After teaching students in conventional classrooms for more than 20 years, I experienced the virtual classroom as a more time-consuming place to teach, at least initially. This is true from the standpoint of both the upfront course design and preparation and, later, the painstaking, labor-intensive hours online—creating messages for the classroom forum, reading and downloading from the screen, posting new material, providing feedback, checking community bulletin boards, e-mailing student comments and grade reports, and so forth.

Workload issues should not be underestimated. On the Internet, there are times when I feel torn between my real life and my virtual life on-screen, in an identity-challenging sort of way (Turkle, 1995), simply because there do not seem to exist enough hours in the day to do justice to both. This is the case even in an asynchronous environment where I have the flexibility to conduct electronic office hours in my bathrobe over morning coffee or to post feedback in the dead of night.

Moreover, absent face-to-face contact and ordinary nonverbal cues, even very mature students on the Internet demand more frequent interaction and reassurance in dialogue with their professors, an observation confirmed in student course evaluations. Students demand more feedback, and the more feedback they receive, the more interaction they want. There are at least two possible explanations for this phenomenon. One explanation is that it reflects the way students are compensating for the lack of face-to-face interaction. The other is that this medium disinhibits student communication, thereby stimulating the message exchange process. As the intellectual excitement of online conversations grows, so does the amount of interactivity in the virtual community (Rafaeli & Sudweeks, 1998). Both of these hypotheses deserve further investigation.

Regarding workload, one estimate is that this mode of instruction requires roughly 40% to 50% more work on the teacher's part in comparison with conventional classroom delivery (Brown, 1998). Whereas I might put approximately 36 hours of work per week routinely into a regular courseload with a total of 120 or more students in four traditional class sections at a large public university, online instruction at the graduate institute has required 40 hours or more per week—with only 24 students in just three sections of my virtual classes. Perhaps this was the result of being low on the learning curve in a new teaching medium, but it is not, in my opinion, an efficient means of course delivery to a large number of students.

The videoconference version of my course also requires extensive advance preparation, more so than with a conventional class. Here design and control issues are compounded by the highly structured and perishable nature of television transmission time, meaning that everything needs to be more precisely planned and orchestrated. Teaching via a two-way interactive television (ITV) system effectively requires a systematic approach to course design, material design and development, equipment, delivery, remote site origination, computer interaction with ITV, and computer-delivered presentations. I found developing Web site materials and PowerPoint presentations for each class session to be especially useful. It is also desirable to have faculty able to understand the legal, administrative, and ethical issues related to teaching in this way (Thomas, 1999).

Teaching online is far more intense and absorbing from my point of view and, therefore, is simultaneously more exhilarating and more exhausting mentally. It also takes longer for faculty and administrators to reach consensus in electronic group meetings. The amount of mental effort expended can be tremendous. As a result, the economic efficiency of this mode of instruction is clearly contingent on institutional models and assumptions. The economics is fundamentally different when the educational product is a premium one, delivered by a private institute to a select group of adult professionals, many of whom receive corporate reimbursement for their tuition. As others have observed (Baer, 1998; Ives & Jarvenpaa, 1996; Swope, 1994), the new educational paradigm shifts the old definition of productivity as cost per hour of instruction per student to a new definition of productivity as cost per unit of learning per student. This paradigm shift does not directly address the issue of the market value of the university professor's productive labor as a knowledge worker in new media. I predict that the issue of the valuation of faculty expertise online will grow in importance in the future.

Impersonality in the Virtual Classroom: Student-Faculty Relationships

Another assertion that one frequently encounters about computer-mediated instruction is that it is so impersonal. People assume that in the absence of face-to-face interaction, relations automatically become more distant and impersonal. Traditional distance learning formats are said to be plagued with this problem (Kubala, 1998). This is not so in my experience with the interactive virtual classroom. There is a type of intimacy achievable between teachers and students in this medium that is quite extraordinary, reminiscent of what Sproull and Kiesler (1995) refer to as "second-level" social effects of the technology. I believe that this intimacy derives from a sense of shared control and responsibility, commitment to collaboration and dialogue, and increased willingness to take risks in communications with others online. The verbal- and writing-intensive nature of a course like mine in a text-based forum network also forces participants to make their thoughts very explicit; there is little room for subtlety. No matter how tentative, people's ideas and mental models are to be shared. As one administrator put it, "In an online environment, words matter. . . . Words are everything."

It also takes longer for groups to reach consensus in brainstorming and problem-solving situations online. People's feelings can be hurt easily, so more time and effort are put into explaining meanings and supplying detailed contextual background to enhance mutual understanding. Thus, writers get to know one another intimately over time while computer-mediated conversations (both formal and informal) are unfolding. Neither e-mail nor chat, the forum classroom environment calls for and inspires thoughtful, composed (after reading and reflection), asynchronous networked interactions without sacrificing human warmth.

At this stage in the evolution of virtual educational networks, we all are learners. There is also a sense that we are innovators and early adopters who "crossed over" early in the technology diffusion process (Moore, 1995). The attention given to group process (face-to-face and online) and the thoughtful nature of master's-level conversations establish an intimacy within the group, belying any expectations of impersonality.

The Medium Is the Course: Some Lessons

Studying virtual leadership in a virtual medium means that, meta-analytically, the medium is the course. On a higher plane, content and process coalesce; professors and graduate students assume responsibility not only for their own learning but also for the learning of others in the group. Although we may be far-flung in a geographical sense, the bonds of shared learning and the progressive experience of new frontiers means that the course becomes a leadership opportunity for all involved. As both leaders and followers together, we come to appreciate the unbounded nature of our undertaking.

Several important lessons taken away from these experiences in virtual classrooms revolve around the challenge to the traditional classroom. The lessons of the new online graduate programs include remembering that the critical function is to design the technology to fit the desired learning outcomes and not vice versa. Too often, institutions buy into an infrastructure of hardware and software that constrains, rather than enhances, the learning experience. In the case of the organizational management program, the two different technologies seem well matched.

Another valuable lesson for any type of technological start-up operation is to expect turbulence and to create an organizational culture that will embrace uncertainty. This is a risk-taking enterprise, and one should expect the unexpected. Glitches in the technology and technical problems of one sort or another are a periodic frustration for both teachers and students using computer networks. One must not panic. In the online education culture, embracing chaos and change is almost emblematic. Turbulence becomes a metaphor symbolizing organizational learning and change in progress.

Moore's Model: A Diffusion Lesson

There are also lessons about the sorts of people best suited to this undertaking. There is a technology adoption curve that permits innovators and early adopters to "cross the chasm" sooner than other, more conservative or reluctant educators and students. Moore's (1995) model of the technology product adoption life cycle has several important implications for this new learning.

New adopters have different orientations toward the technology and risk. The model asserts that the very first adopter group is the technophiles, who will build their own peripherals, write their own software, and generally find a way to make it work. The second adopter group is the visionaries, who will adopt the new technology in the form of trial products, create projects requiring customization, and often turn the organization on its head. The third adopter group is the pragmatists, who want the "whole product" to be available, want to see a real benefit (productivity improvement?) of the technology, and want to see a minimum of trauma in adopting the new technology. A fourth adopter group is the conservatives, who will keep the old technology until forced to adopt the new one and who want very practical, easy-to-use, and cheap technology. The last group is the laggards, who will resist adopting the new technology and try getting by without ever adopting, if possible.

The implications of this model are important. There is a natural discontinuity between each adopting group. The "chasm" occurs between the visionaries and the pragmatists. This chasm stems from the pragmatists' desires for a "whole product," which represents a quantum jump from the customized product sold to visionaries. Pragmatists need a credible referral before they will adopt; they do not see visionaries as credible due to the trauma that visionaries cause. To cross the chasm, educational leaders must find a beachhead of pragmatists who badly need the whole product and will serve as an easy reference for other closely related opportunities.

Conclusion: The Most Likely to Succeed

Virtual leaders are innovators and visionaries first. But the true test of their powers lies in their ability to guide and influence others—in other words, to manage the attention, trust, and meaning of others as well as to manage themselves in this process. Educational leaders who are most likely to succeed in this medium are able to teach well while they enjoy working in technology-driven virtual networks. They are serious lifelong learners. These teachers tend to favor experimental and collaborative styles. They enjoy upfront conceptual work and are skilled group process facilitators. Educational leaders in this domain make their expectations explicit to their students and use clear evaluation and assessment methods. They also provide detailed developmental feedback at frequent intervals, as desired by their students.

Students who are most likely to succeed can be described as independent active learners. They are folks who enjoy working independently, and when they are alone, they structure and manage their time well. These are often accomplished busy professionals. They are often mid-career businesspeople with superior verbal and analytical skills. They are also risk takers who are good problem solvers. Their strong interpersonal skills are reflected in their commitment to peers and to the group process. Finally, they learn (as their teachers must also learn) how to be comfortable with asynchronous rhythms. This type of virtual work is both energizing and fascinating.

References

Baer, W. S. (1998). Will the Internet transform higher education? In *The emerging Internet: Annual review of the Institute for Information Studies* (Vol. 9, pp. 81-108). Queenstown, MD: Aspen Institute.

Baker, R. (1999). The education of Mike Milken: From junk-bond king to the knowledge universe. *The Nation, 268*(16), 11-18.

Bennis, W. (1993). *An invented life: Reflections on leadership and change.* Reading, MA: Addison-Wesley.

Bloom, B. (1956). *Taxonomy of educational objectives.* New York: David McKay.

Brook, J., & Boal, I. (1995). *Resisting the virtual life: The culture and politics of information.* San Francisco: City Lights.

Brown, B. M. (1998). Digital classrooms: Some myths about developing new educational programs using the Internet. *T.H.E. Journal, 25*(12), 56-59.

Christensen, C. R. (1987). *Teaching and the case method.* Boston: Harvard Business School Press.

Davenport, T., & Pearlson, K. (1998). Two cheers for the virtual office. *Sloan Management Review, 39*(4), 51-66.

Dertouzos, M. (1997). *What will be: How the new world of information will change our lives.* New York: HarperEdge.

Gilster, P. (1997). *Digital literacy.* New York: John Wiley.

Ives, B., & Jarvenpaa, S. (1996). Will the Internet revolutionize business education and research? *Sloan Management Review, 37*(3), 33-40.

Kubala, T. (1998). Addressing student needs: Teaching on the Internet. *T.H.E. Journal, 25*(8), 71-74.

Moore, G. (1995). *Crossing the chasm: Marketing and selling technology products to mainstream customers.* San Francisco: HarperBusiness.

Negroponte, N. (1995). *Being digital.* New York: Vintage.

Porter, D. (Ed.). (1996). *Internet culture.* New York: Routledge.

Rafaeli, S., & Sudweeks, F. (1998). Interactivity in the nets. In F. Sudweeks, M. McLaughlin, & S. Rafaeli (Eds.), *Networks and Net play: Virtual groups on the Internet* (pp. 173-189). Menlo Park, CA: AAAI Press.

Senge, P., Kleiner, A., Roberts, C., Ross, R. B., & Smith, B. J. (1994). *The fifth discipline fieldbook.* Garden City, NY: Doubleday.

Senge, P., Kleiner, A., Roberts, C., Ross, R. B., & Smith, B. J. (1999). *The dance of change.* Garden City, NY: Doubleday.

Shenk, D. (1997). *Data smog: Surviving the information glut.* New York: Harper Edge.

Sproull, L., & Kiesler, S. (1995). *Connections: New ways of working in the networked organization.* Cambridge: MIT Press.

Stefik, M. (1996). *Internet dreams: Archetypes, myths, and metaphors.* Cambridge: MIT Press.

Stewart, T. (1997). *Intellectual capital: The new wealth of organizations.* Garden City, NY: Doubleday.

Swope, S. (1994, Summer). The approaching value-added education. *Educational Record,* pp. 17-18.

Thomas, K. (1999). Teaching via ITV: Taking instructional design to the next level. *T.H.E. Journal, 26*(4), 60-66.

Turkle, S. (1995). *Life on the screen: Identity in the age of the Internet.* New York: Simon & Schuster.

Wheatley, M. (1994). *Leadership and the new science.* San Francisco: Berrett-Koehler.

Chapter 18

Teaching Statistics Online

Pat Hodges and Lynne Saba

Having taught several online courses, including six advanced statistics courses, over the past 10 years, we have found many advantages in the online format. This chapter focuses on the mechanics of teaching statistics online and presents course content and examples of how to make the course a lively interactive experience.

Learning statistics is a source of anxiety for many graduate students. Feedback from students confirms that our use of live chat, visual aids, music, and humor, in combination with traditional materials such as a textbook, homework, and quizzes, has been an effective way to reduce anxiety and increase learning. An Internet live chat format tends to promote more interaction and dialogue than does the traditional classroom lecture format. The synchronous live chat stimulates questions and curiosity, and the immediate faculty feedback aids student mastery and understanding and also reduces concern and self-doubt.

Rowntree's (1986) suggestions for course development are very useful to the design of an online statistics environment:

1. Develop your own style of communicating so that you and the students feel comfortable. The online course lacks the nonverbal cues that let students know when a remark is important or humorous. We

call attention to statements with color or underlined text, and we comment on the humor with a smiley face (unless voice chat is used).

2. Be precise, use familiar wording, and eliminate superfluous words. (With "math phobic" students, this has been a challenge.)

3. Use active verbs.

4. Use the vocabulary of the specialty with care, and explain the terms again and again.

Overview of Course Design and Implementation

To keep the statistics course interactive and lively, we use synchronous voice chat, asynchronous e-mail, and a forum where documents can be uploaded and downloaded and where discussions can occur. The statistics course is divided into 11 sections from basic algebra to an overview of more advanced techniques such as multidimensional scaling and structural equation modeling. For each of the sections, lecture and animated slides that illustrate statistical procedures are placed on a forum for the students to download. Every other week, we hold a 3-hour chat that covers the 11 content areas. By meeting every other week, students are given adequate time to complete the homework and quizzes. Two online textbooks are required. Students receive the Web sites or URLs for the texts prior to the start of the course. Chapters in online texts are assigned for each chat. A reference list of hard copy textbooks is also provided so that students can supplement their reading on weekly topics.

Technology Requirements

Students need to have current models of computers, up-to-date software, and sufficient computer skills to prevent distracting preoccupation with technological problems. We send an e-mail list that specifies hardware and software requirements. Hardware requirements include an IBM-compatible computer less than 3 years old, a sound card that allows a microphone and speakers, and a dial-up service or broadband service that is available on an unlimited basis. Current software requirements include SPSS 10.1, Word 97 or above, PowerPoint 97 or above, and an operating system of Microsoft Windows 98 or above to support newer versions of SPSS. Students are required to purchase the student version of Statistical Program for the Social Sciences (SPSS) and to perform the SPSS tutorial before the class starts. Computer skills include the ability to attach and send and receive a document from an e-mail, to download and upload word processor files or programs from the Internet, and to access Web sites or URLs. Only students who meet these prerequisites are permitted to enroll in the course.

Technology Orientation

We establish specific times for students to attend a "technology chat" orientation. Usually, Yahoo Internet Messenger voice chat is used due to its universal reliability and capacity for up to nine individuals in the chat room. Recently, we have started using PalTalk voice chat, which also has a large chat room capacity. Other instant messengers, such as AOL Instant Messenger and MSN Instant Messenger, can be used, but they restrict the number of individuals who can participate in a private conference chat—usually five or fewer. Some of the proprietary chats do not offer VOIP (voice over Internet protocol), and one must rely on a phone conferencing system that adds to costs. We have chosen not to use phone conferencing because the availability of a free service stimulates the students to hold additional private chat conferences among themselves.

During the orientation chat, we work with all students to ensure that they have the ability to use their microphones and speakers, type in text chat, access the Web, download materials, and discuss statistical assignments for the class. We also establish some online courtesy rules for communicating and ask the students to do their socializing after the formal class chat. We show them how to use the chat facility to contact and talk to one another just as students would "sit around" in a coffeehouse. We encourage collaboration among the students and discussions about course content when the instructors are not present. Often, students will form and use peer relationships from across North America to solve statistical and technological problems.

Course Content

The following outline describes the content of one of our typical online statistics courses:

Week 1:   Introduction and descriptive statistics
Week 2:   Inferential statistics and sampling
Week 3:   Nonparametric tests (e.g., chi-square)
Week 4:   Parametric tests (e.g., t tests, analysis of variance [ANOVA])
Week 5:   Factorial ANOVA, midterm, and article review
Week 6:   Correlation and regression
Week 7:   Regression
Week 8:   Multiple regression
Week 9:   Factor analysis
Week 10: Advanced statistics overview: Logistic regression, discriminant function analysis, canonical correlation, multidimensional scaling, and structural equation modeling
Week 11: Final examination

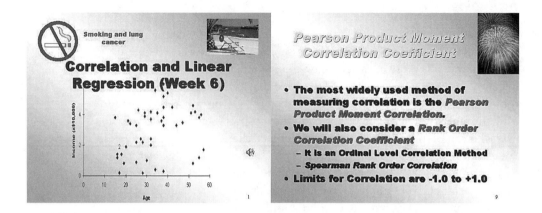

Figure 18.1. Sample Weekly Slide Presentation Discussing Correlation Procedures

Lectures and slides with animated illustrations are posted to a forum prior to each week's live chat (Figure 18.1). Chapters from online texts are assigned for each chat. Every other week, we deliver a 2- to 4-hour live voice chat that covers the lecture materials and allows the students to ask questions if they are confused, miss a point, need clarification, or want additional information.

Students are able to download the log of questions and answers from the typed chat. All brands of instant messengers have a "save" command within their programs, and students are taught to save their typed notes. The class interactions can be reviewed by students and provide more detailed notes than in a traditional classroom. During the lecture, students bring up their statistical analysis program (we are using SPSS, but another program could be used if the instructor wished to do so) and work with a small data set online. This allows faculty to determine whether students understand correctly how to enter data, select the appropriate statistical techniques, prepare the data prior to each analysis, and interpret data output. We answer any statistical questions students may have as they encounter them when using the data analysis program or interpreting the results. In addition, we offer online "office hours" (posted) to respond to additional questions.

Content of the Chat

The following is a list and description of the main components of the synchronous chat portion of the statistics course.

1. *Socialization period.* Students tell us a little about themselves, including their geographic locations and their experience with graduate and undergraduate statistics. During Weeks 2 through 11, we encourage informal

socializing and questions about the previous week's assignment and the current week's lecture. Personal events such as birthdays, marriages, births, travel, and accomplishments are also addressed briefly, adding to the sense of community.

2. *Lectures.* Each week's lectures are posted on a statistics forum so that the students can download and read them offline (or online if they have a fast Internet connection). The lectures are a complete lecture script, not just an outline; the students can read the lectures before the class discusses them. We discuss the salient issues related to the weekly lecture and explain common misconceptions. We can also copy and paste additional information directly into Yahoo Messenger or discuss the lecture document using application-sharing software. When the lecture is presented in application-sharing software, the faculty can clarify a point with annotations or add typed comments while the class is online. Students routinely ask a great many questions about statistical topics and statistical definitions.

Statistical examples can be visually presented using real-world situations. For example, on January 28, 1986, the space shuttle *Challenger* exploded because two rubber O-rings were damaged during takeoff due to the low air temperature at the time of the launch. The link between O-ring damage and ambient temperature had been established prior to the flight. No clear link between temperature and O-ring damage had been visually presented by the engineers who had recommended that the launch be delayed. Unfortunately, the launch proceeded with disastrous consequences. A simple scatterplot showing the link between O-ring damage and temperature from previous launches might have predicted serious problems and, consequently, might have changed the decision about launching (Tufte, 1997; Figure 18.2).

3. *Slides.* Slides are provided as an asynchronous (available offline) tool to enhance the lecture materials. The content is discussed in the same manner as the lecture material (Figure 18.1). The slides are in color with animation and sound. Microsoft PowerPoint slides are used to demonstrate statistical concepts and to give visual and pictorial representations of the statistical test. Feedback from the students has indicated that the time-consuming effort of preparing the slides is worthwhile. For example, an ANOVA table is presented in lecture and slides, and students are asked how they can use the information from the table to answer questions such as "How many participants are included in the study?" and "How many levels of treatment are used in the study?" To teach different ways of interpreting an ANOVA summary table, the principle of repetition is used and we present the same material many times. In addition, the use of humor and entertaining visual material effectively decreases the anxiety level of the math phobic participants.

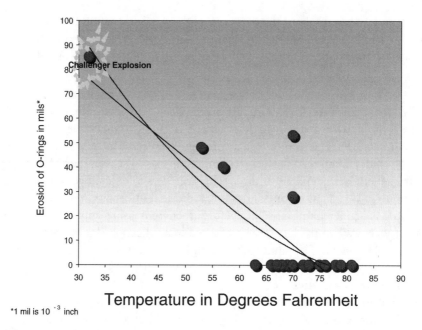

*1 mil is 10^{-3} inch

Figure 18.2. Scatterplot of Correlation Between Ambient Temperature and O-Ring Erosion Showing Previous O-Ring Erosion Patterns, Regression Trend Lines, and a Hypothetical Value From the *Challenger* Disaster Data
Adapted from Tufte (1997), *Visual Explanations*.

4. *Data analysis.* During the class sessions, data sets are sent to students via file transfer (located within the instant messenger). Files are also available on the statistics forum or in the posted PowerPoint slides. Students learn how to enter and define variables. An example of a data set is found in Table 18.1. In each session, we focus on a particular statistical technique and walk the students though the data analysis process. We help them to understand the choice points for each analysis and teach them how to use the special features of SPSS such as the statistics coach, the results coach, and the definition and help box. By the end of the course, the students are familiar with common statistical techniques, including multiple regression, principal component analysis, factor analysis, and discriminant analysis. They have had an overview of multidimensional scaling, logistic regression, and structural equation modeling.

5. *Demonstrations of data analysis.* Analyses of data using SPSS are accomplished online and offline. Online, application-sharing software such as Webex, Microsoft NetMeeting, or Raindance Collaboration (formerly Evoke) allows the instructor to launch SPSS, demonstrate each mouse movement, and explain the purpose and logic for each step of the analysis. Offline, a recording of an application program (Webex or Raindance) can be replayed to reinforce learning (Figure 18.3). Again, we find that repetition contributes to student retention and the ability to use statistical software.

TABLE 18.1   Example of a *t* Test Statistics Quiz With a Small Data Set

1. A psychologist hypothesizes that education is a critical feature in the MMPI-2 mean scores of the Latino workforce. The psychologist collects a small sample of Latinos, both educated and un-educated. Please conduct *t* tests to ascertain which group has a more elevated MMPI-2 than the established cutoff score (T = 65) and how the groups compare to each other.		
Uneducated Latinos	Educated Latinos	
62	59	
76	62	
65	53	
68	58	
57	42	
65	58	
61	49	
66	60	
50	55	
56	48	
2. The psychologist's research assistant, who actually obtained the above data, informs the psychologist that the data were gathered from 10 Latino students entering a community college program and that a follow-up test then was given 2 years later. What are the findings and how do they compare?		
3. Please include your rationale (brief), procedures for performing any *t* test above, and interpretation of findings. Include your output from SPSS. Please also discuss (briefly) if any of the assumptions for *t* tests we talked about in the chat were violated.		

6. *Assignments.* As we near the midpoint of the course, we assign articles for students to read and critique. The articles are selected to encourage students' critical thinking skills and to introduce them to controversies in the area of statistical reasoning. For example, we use Hagen's (1997) article, "In Praise of the Null Hypothesis Statistical Test," to illustrate the issues raised by the concept of the null hypothesis. At the end of the lecture, students are given a quiz and homework to complete offline before the next chat (Table 18.1). The homework and quiz responses are sent to us as e-mail attachments so that we can review each student's progress. Students are expected to respond to quizzes and homework in a timely manner. If they are late in responding to

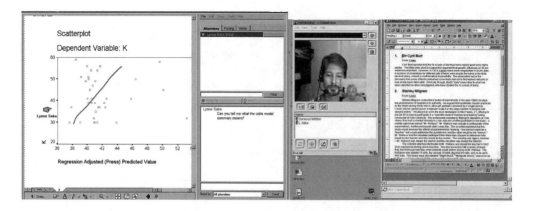

Figure 18.3. Application Sharing With Webex and Microsoft NetMeeting

quizzes, then we send an e-mail to follow up on their progress and offer help. Rarely do students miss a class, and if they do, they can review the statistical analysis application recording, their fellow classmates' notes, and the lectures and slides. Assigned "office hours" can be used to augment missed classes. It has been uncommon for students to miss classes. This might be due to the novelty of taking classes "online."

7. *Examinations.* At the end of 5 weeks, we have an online, open-book midterm examination. Progression to the second half of the course requires passing the midterm at a 70% level or better. Much to our delight, the pass rate has been close to 90%. We also give each student individualized feedback via e-mail. At the end of the course, there is an online final examination consisting of multiple-choice questions and an SPSS problem that requires the students to complete an analysis of a stepwise and hierarchical regression. Throughout the procedure, we expect students to give a meaningful explanation for each of their statistical analyses.

8. *Feedback.* We have been particularly sensitive in how we give feedback. A constructive critical comment that can be stated in a warm and supportive tone face-to-face might not convey the same supportive and caring qualities over the Internet. We send our feedback individually, not to the group. In the chat, we amplify our comments and ask for elaboration from the students. Students are encouraged to reflect on their experiences and learning, and we directly ask the quieter ones for comments. It is necessary to be alert to creative responses from students and to encourage their initiative. We have also established an anonymous bulletin board where students can offer suggestions, criticism, and comments. The suggestions that students have made have helped us to improve the course. In addition, they have been

helpful in alerting us to common misunderstandings and problems that may occur. We continue to follow this process throughout the 11 weeks of the term.

9. *Assignment management.* One of the major problems in teaching online is the management of individual student files. Keeping track of each student's progress can be difficult. It is necessary to attend to all student messages as they are received. Some e-mail programs have electronic file systems that make record keeping easier. It is always possible to print the student responses and keep student records as hard copy. Another option is to create a grid with a list of student names and class activities to monitor student progress. Records can also be kept in an uploaded interactive Excel spreadsheet. Sending individual student comments to a discussion forum, when appropriate, helps to decrease the number of e-mails that faculty must process.

10. *Participation.* We require participation in the chat. A portion of the grade is allocated for participating in chat and asynchronous discussions. We tell the students that they must post a specific number of items each week for each topic and that they must send back attached e-mail quizzes. The posts engage students and improve the quality of their work. We have observed that students are reluctant to have their peers perceive them as slackers or inadequate. Online interaction helps to develop a group bond and makes each student motivated to do his or her share. Students acquire team spirit, which in turn provides them with a powerful incentive to become more engaged in the online seminar activity.

11. *Student collaboration.* A major pleasure in teaching online has been the collaboration between faculty and students. We do not assume that incoming students know how to collaborate; rather, we create situations that require cooperation among students. The use of chat and an asynchronous forum allows for cooperative learning; students can easily communicate with one another. For example, one of our students posted a list of Web sites that gave interesting and humorous information to help remember statistical information. We have found natural "leaders" in each of our groups and have encouraged them to help others develop online communication skills.

Advantages of the Online Statistics Course

The general advantages of any online course fall into three major categories: (a) advantages for the instructor, (b) advantages for the student, and (c) advantages for the institution.

For the instructor, the online "classroom" is open and public; others can easily review the materials, the evaluation process is observable, and instructors can rapidly respond to individual student questions and comments. The interactive chat format allows the instructor to develop a personal relationship with each student.

The delivery of online courses can be varied to use synchronous chat, voice chat, and streaming video. Slide presentations and movie clips can easily be incorporated into the lectures and discussions. These can also be provided in an asynchronous format. Prepared lectures and articles can be downloaded by students. As with any traditional class, a syllabus is prepared and can be placed on a forum so that students have a preview of what is required for the course. Additional Web sites or URLs can be linked to the lecture and reading materials. The instructor can adapt the course to the technological sophistication of the target audience and select technology that is broadly available. As Sherry (1996) states, "The most important factor is a caring, concerned teacher who is confident, experienced, at ease with the equipment, uses media creatively, and maintains a high level of interacting with the students" (p. 355).

The particular advantages for students that we have found in teaching statistics with a synchronous component are many:

1. The course is interactive.
2. The course is collaborative.
3. The course is multimodal.
4. Students learn how to use a statistical software program.
5. Students become familiar with Web technology and online environments.
6. Students become critical consumers of the research literature.
7. The course reduces anxiety and fear of mathematics through the use of sound, music, art, and humor.

The interactive milieu encourages students to take an active part in their learning, and they respond with enthusiasm. Students are encouraged to collaborate in a voice chat platform as well as through e-mail and the statistical forum. Students form buddy relationships over large geographic distances, and those who want to interact will post messages with the times that they are available and ask other students to chat with them. The relationships have led to visits and ongoing friendships.

For the students, the primary advantage is clear: The work and study can be done at home, and there is considerable flexibility in timing. Students save commuting time and can schedule responses to homework and quizzes at their convenience. Use of the lecture and discussion logs allows students to review material in its original form (including clarifications to questions and answers) as often as necessary. For many students, the online learning process is preferable to the traditional classroom.

The easy access to course materials from their own homes makes the online form of instruction advantageous for students with disabilities. They are able to adjust the timing and pace of coursework in ways that are not possible in a traditional campus setting. There are specialized software programs available that can be added to help deaf or visually impaired students as well. For deaf students, accessibility captions can be added, and for visually impaired students, voice-activated programs make communication easier (www.microsoft.com/enable/microsoft/technology.htm).

For the institution, online courses can serve as community outreach and help to develop new academic markets. Archived classes and discussions provide a resource for other instructors and students. Faculty interested in developing new curricula can readily determine which areas have been of interest to students. By reading student comments, faculty can evaluate the effectiveness of different online teaching modalities and use the feedback to improve their own courses. We have listened attentively to our students as we frequently reshape our combination of synchronous and asynchronous modalities in the online learning process. We are convinced that a multimodal approach serves our students best and are comforted by recent research that supports the effectiveness of this strategy (Arbaugh, 2000; Guzdial et al., 1997).

The Process of Moderating an Online Course

For newcomers to the world of online education, the skills required to moderate an Internet course may seem highly specialized and complex. On the contrary, these are skills that a dedicated instructor can easily learn. The traditional statistics classroom instructor's skills are transferable to the online environment. For example, in a traditional classroom, a statistics instructor uses a blackboard; most chat environments have a whiteboard. In a traditional classroom, a lecture is presented; online, a "copy and paste" lecture text can be posted. Most educational settings that use conferencing as a teaching medium prepare guidelines for effective moderating, and several research articles have been published on the subject (Kerr, 1990; Maki, Maki, Patterson, & Whittaker, 1999; McGiven, 1994; Poole, 2000).

Guidelines for Faculty Moderators

The guidelines for developing computer conferencing skills for the instructor/moderator fall into three general categories: organizational, social, and intellectual. These are discussed next.

Organizational role. One of the first sets of duties of an online instructor is to create an agenda for the chat, objectives of the forum discussion, timetable, procedural rules, and decision-making norms. It is imperative to post these on a Web page or in a downloadable document prior to the beginning of the course. Managing student interactions with strong leadership and direction is a primary ingredient of a successful chat. When there are technical and/or logistical problems with network providers, it is necessary to deal with the class members' frustration tolerance. For example, during one of our chats, there was a hacker attack on Yahoo. The attack overloaded many well-known servers and blocked our communication. By having a backup (redundancy) system that used another chat program and having prepared students with that information, we were able to continue the chat. Even established technology systems, such as television programs and phone service, may be interrupted at times. We remind the students of this possibility and direct them to alternative tools to reduce their frustration.

Many student comments are directed at changes in the context, norms, or agenda of the conference forum due to their own lack of problem-solving skills, failure to complete assignments, and information overload. Just as in traditional courses, the online instructor needs to let students know what to expect in terms of course requirements, activities, and time lines. We inform the students that courses will be conducted as graduate-level courses and that they will be expected to function at this level throughout the term.

Social role. Creating a friendly social environment for learning is also seen as an essential moderator skill. Sending welcoming messages at the beginning of each session and encouraging participation throughout the course are specific examples. Providing feedback to students and using a friendly personal tone are considered equally important. Positive feedback and encouragement are especially helpful early in the course. The instructor must be sensitive to the needs of participants and create a context conducive to critical thought, creativity, and self-esteem. Rewarding positive contributions is the essence of community building, which is an essential aspect of online conferencing.

In responding to questions during the chat and office hours, one recommendation is paramount: Exercise patience. Students are usually frustrated and anxious by the time they have contacted the instructor during office hours. Patience, gentleness, and affirmation are reassuring.

Intellectual role. The most important role of the faculty moderator is to be an educational facilitator. As in any kind of teaching, the moderator should focus discussions on crucial points, ask questions, and probe responses to encourage critical thinking. Some students can remain passive during both asynchronous (noninteractive) and synchronous interactions, and it is important to make them aware that participation and collaboration with other students is an expected part of the seminar. We sometimes prompt the quieter students with private online messages, and we make a point to appreciate their comments and participation.

There are many ways in which an intellectual online community can be established. These are usually similar for synchronous and asynchronous courses. We integrate and weave the discussions by synthesizing points raised by students, develop and build on themes that emerge, and link the themes to the scholarly literature. Weaving together the disparate concepts is truly a challenge of computer conferencing. Typing, posting, or verbally presenting a "weaving" comment online suggests an important faculty relationship to student discourse. Weaving comments allow online groups to achieve a sense of accomplishment and direction. They supply the group with a code for framing its history and establish a common connection among past, present, and future courses.

The faculty moderator must model scholarship and direct the discussion to this goal. We have discovered that when students participate in some of the moderator's functions, discussions become more absorbing and successful and contribute significantly to students' educational development. The initiative taken by adult students in sharing some of the intellectual functions with the faculty leader is a hallmark of highly effective, self-directed learners (Mason & Kaye, 1989).

The organizational structure that faculty moderators use during online chats can, paradoxically, create problems. For example, online conferencing assumes its own direction and is often difficult to control. It is something like Alice's (in Wonderland) effort to play croquet with live flamingos—they kept moving! Although the instructor wishes to have the dialogue be lively, he or she must deftly guide its direction.

Misunderstandings are common in learning statistics online (and elsewhere). Students tend to overgeneralize from one concept to another. For example, we have had students who tried to equate the beta error of hypothesis testing with the beta of regression. Not surprisingly, they are puzzled when they do not find a relationship. On the other hand, our online interactions have developed much more enthusiastically and satisfyingly than we had anticipated because students often make large conceptual leaps that positively affect their progress in the program. For example, many of the students who have taken our course have moved into leadership positions and report an ability to function more easily in other courses and to handle the frustrations that sometimes occur in graduate education with greater equanimity.

Each course has its own evolutionary process despite the strong leadership and agenda provided by the faculty moderator. This organizational dynamic is similar to the development of a jazz ensemble. Participants do not know in advance what roles they will play in relation to the others. They begin the ensemble in pursuit of a theme, but how that pursuit will progress, how individual members will contribute, and how it is to be satisfactorily resolved at the conclusion remain to be discovered. It is the moderator who organizes and leads each participant to create the ensemble.

Creating a Social Environment for Learning

Being friendly and welcoming, personal, and responsive to participants is deceptively easy. In the hands of an expert facilitator, these mundane actions become powerful educational tools. We have learned that it is the leader's enthusiasm and passion for the material that accounts for the success of the online seminar. Participants will forgive a long-winded discussion and pages of detailed comments from an instructor who is passionately interested in the topic.

An effective online learning environment is participatory. Students learn when they are participating, not when they are passive listeners. Lurking, as opposed to participating, is not a learning style that leads to success in graduate education. We have found that students learn from themselves and from each other as much as they do from us as instructors. Our students have appreciated that we were thoroughly involved in the class and that they could count on our presence in each session. Even though many of our students enroll in the course doubtful that they will ever enjoy statistics, they generally leave valuing what they have learned as well as the process of learning.

In any given course, students can differ enormously in terms of academic backgrounds, skills, and life experiences. Some students lack the confidence to assert themselves in public. Some do not like to write. Some are afraid that they will embarrass themselves with postings that are not clever, erudite, or interesting to others. One of the goals of online teaching is to help students overcome these concerns.

Future Technological Innovations

In addition to newer technologies of streaming media and voice chat, the year 2001 has brought interactive application sharing that is particularly relevant to the teaching of statistics. In this new technology, the faculty instructor can demonstrate the exact steps to perform a statistical analysis and then ask students to reproduce the demonstrated model. Vendors such as Webex, Raindance, and Microsoft NetMeeting allow application sharing, and Webex and Raindance allow recording of a visual demonstration. For students, these functions can be superior to a face-to-face presentation of how to use statistical software. Multipoint video presentations now allow up to 12 videos to be viewed at once and to be combined with voice chats. CUseeMe (Figure 18.4) has recently introduced multipoint software, and there are plans by other companies to have multimedia with multipoint video and audio available. Many of these applications are in their infancy stage, but in spite of current

Figure 18.4. Group Videoconferencing With CUseeMe®

technological limitations, synchronous interaction seems to offer a viable vehicle for learning statistics online.

Conclusion

It is our belief that the adoption of a combination of asynchronous and synchronous computer-mediated methods constitutes an effective approach to teaching statistics. During synchronous chats, both with and without voice, students have time to organize the data and learn the material with the help of other students. When all is said and done, it is the faculty moderator who controls the quality of the seminar. When the instructor is a true participant in the course and provides extensive feedback (both critical and encouraging), students will be more involved and the quality of their work will improve.

We encourage the reader to develop an online course. Although time-consuming and periodically frustrating, the rewards of producing an interactive seminar are long-lasting and help to propel students, faculty, and institutions into 21st-century learning communities.

References

Arbaugh, J. B. (2000, December). How classroom environment and student engagement affect learning in Internet-based MBA courses. *Business Communication Quarterly, 63*(4), 9-27.

Guzdial, M., Hmelo, C., Hubscher, R., Nagel, K., Newstetter, W., Puntembakar, S., Shabo, A., Turns, J., & Koloder, J. (1997). Integrating and guiding collaboration: Lessons learned in computer supported collaborative learning research at Georgia Tech. *Computer Support for Collaborative Learning* [Online]. Available: http://guzdial.cc.gatech.edu/papers/lessons

Hagen, R. L. (1997). In praise of the null hypothesis statistical test. *American Psychologist, 52*(1), 15-24.

Kerr, S. T. (1990). Wayfinding in an electronic database: The relative importance of navigational cues versus mental models. *Information Processing and Management, 26,* 511-523.

Maki, R. H., Maki, W. S., Patterson, M., & Whittaker, P. D. (1999). Evaluation of a Web-based introductory psychology course: I. Learning and satisfaction in online versus lecture courses. *Behavior Research Methods, Instruments, and Computers, 32,* 230-239.

Mason, R., & Kaye, A. (Eds.). (1989). *Mindweave: Communication, computers, and distance education.* New York: Pergamon.

McGiven, J. (1994). Designing the learning environment to meet the needs of distant students. *Journal of Technology and Learning, 27*(2), 52-57.

Poole, D. M. (2000). Student participation in a discussion-oriented online course: A case study. *Journal of Research on Computing in Education, 33*(2), 162-177.

Rowntree, D. (1986). *Teaching through self-instruction: A practical handbook for course developers.* New York: Nichols.

Sherry, L. (1996). Issues in distance learning. *International Journal of Distance Education, 1,* 337-365.

Tufte, E. R. (1997). *Visual explanations.* Chelshire, CT: Graphics Press.

Chapter 19

Health Care Meets Technology

Web-Based Professional Training, Consultation, and Collaboration

Dean S. Janoff

The revolution in distance learning and electronic collaboration has extended beyond academic degree programs to professional training, consultation, and support services provided over the Internet (Brown & Duguid, 1996; Figallo, 1998; Nickelson, 1997). This chapter focuses on three examples of professional training and consultation for health care professionals who live and work at distances yet are able to continue their collaboration online in the comfort of their own places and time.

1. A postgraduate group psychotherapy training program is described that applies computer technology to complement face-to-face training when students and faculty are located at a distance. The combined approach integrates intensive face-to-face meetings with online case discussion and consultation.

2. An extension of the group psychotherapy training project is applied to a combined face-to-face and online postgraduate training program for mental health professionals in the treatment of anxiety disorders.

3. An example of cardiac rehabilitation follows in which health care providers (a cardiologist, physical and exercise therapists, a psychologist, a nutritionist, yoga and meditation trainers, and an administrative person) develop a "virtual" patient record and collaborate via asynchronous Web forums to provide ongoing case supervision, consultation, and program planning.

Online training offers added value to traditional face-to-face professional training and collaboration efforts. However, advantages in technology do not come without a price. Proper preparation, oversight, and management of the online environment are crucial to the success of Web-based training and collaboration (Lipnack & Stamps, 1997; McGrath & Hollingshead, 1994). The chapter concludes with a discussion of the specific training, clinical, and ethical concerns inherent in combining face-to-face and online training and collaboration. The guidelines presented will help educators and health care professionals to better prepare for the design and development of future online communities that meet the needs of ongoing professional training and collaboration.

Applications of Web-Based Collaboration to Professional Training in Health Care

As professional educators and trainers, we are challenged to provide our services to students located far from training sites. Many mental health professionals are limited in time and resources; they have family and work commitments and are unable to travel or disrupt their daily activities to access needed continuing education, supervision, and training. We are also challenged by the costs of bringing talented faculty, particularly "master teachers," to one location when they might not be living near a training site. In response to these conditions, new forms of distance learning environments have developed that are relevant to the training of health care professionals (Nickelson, 1997).

In 1995, the Fielding Graduate Institute applied its experience in adult and distance learning to group psychotherapy training and developed a 2-year training program for licensed professionals and graduate students in mental health. Each training cluster was located in a different part of the United States and was led by a highly experienced certified group psychotherapist. The model that evolved illustrates how face-to-face training can be integrated with online clinical training and consultation activities. Although this work is fully described elsewhere (Janoff & Schoenholtz-Read, 1999), the program and our conclusions are summarized here to illustrate how our model of online team collaboration in health care training evolved.

The core components of the group training program were theory presentations on group psychotherapy methods, experiential work on group leadership facilitation, and ongoing clinical case consultation. The format included 16 on-site meetings over 2 years, 7 hours per day. The meetings were scheduled about 6 weeks apart and on the weekends. Between the face-to-face meetings, the group maintained contact through e-mail and use of the Fielding Web site, which allowed users to post documents and respond to threaded conversations. The program trainees were licensed mental health professionals at the master's or doctoral level or were students in a graduate program that led to professional licensure. Ages ranged from the late 30s through 60 years.

Table 19.1 illustrates the program components for both the face-to-face group cluster meetings and the online training and case consultation. The activities were repeated in each cluster meeting: reentry with other group trainees, formal case presentations, discussion of theory, experiential exercises, and attention placed on the individual's and the group's ongoing process. The integration of the clinical training and consultation flowed from face-to-face cluster meetings to at-a-distance learning activities, which took place via the Web site.

Face-to-Face Cluster Meetings

The main goal of the on-site cluster meetings was to provide trainees with a forum to discuss relevant theoretical material and to discuss clinical considerations about their real-life group leadership experiences. Trainees were asked to provide the cluster with a formal description of their therapy group: group composition, presenting problems, and examples of group member interactions with one another and the leader. As trainees responded to the clinical case material, faculty attention was placed on presenting relevant theory as well as on discussing each trainee's development and the overall training group's development throughout the 2-year period.

Online Group Training Activities

The goals and format for online case discussion and consultation were formalized at the beginning of training. Trainees had specific weekly deadlines for posting a clinical case or dilemma; an applied theory question; or a professional, ethical, or legal question. A time line for replies was also posted. Although a main benefit of asynchronous communication is the ability to respond when it is convenient for the user, inclusion of a specific "post by . . ." date greatly improved the use, quality, and pacing of both trainee and faculty online work. Furthermore, it was emphasized that posted questions and/or

TABLE 19.1   Fielding Model of Face-to-Face and Online Group Psychotherapy
Training

---

1.   Face-to-face training group meetings

  Component 1:   Reentry
  - Trainees provide a personal and professional update since their last face-to-face contact

  Component 2:   Formal case presentation in group
  - Each trainee presents a group case
  - Faculty supervisor introduces relevant group psychotherapy theory
  - Trainees and faculty respond to each other's case material

  Component 3:   Experiential application of group theory to practice
  - Trainees use role-play and other exercises to practice the application of different theoretical approaches with their groups

  Component 4:   Process group time
  - Trainees work on transferential and countertransferential issues raised in earlier components

  Component 5:   Closure—Integration of theory and practice
  - Trainees and faculty review the day's learning
  - Faculty give online assignments

2.   Online, Web-based training group activities
  - Faculty post theory questions or new ideas
  - Group members post ongoing case dilemmas
  - Group members and faculty circulate information and resources
  - Group announcements are posted
  - Important documents are posted
  - Consultations are requested
  - Weekly activities are scheduled with specific dates to post and reply

---

SOURCE: Adapted from Janoff and Schoenholtz-Read (1999).

clinical case dilemmas, and their replies, needed to be written clearly and concisely to maximize the use, relevancy, and effectiveness of the collaborative efforts of the group.

Trainees stated that the ability to continue active clinical case discussions between cluster meetings, and at a distance, added an important dimension to the group training process. It appeared that the most successful type of online case consultation occurred when trainees continued in the Web forum a conversation that had begun in the face-to-face training meetings. The felt sense of the group was maintained as the training group cluster continued its support and learning online. The training process continued online with the important clinical and personal themes that began during the face-to-face case presentations. Interactive Web technology provided faculty and trainees with the opportunity to include important references as active Internet links. These links to important Internet addresses were then placed in a much larger database as a "virtual library" for group psychotherapy resources and references.

We learned a number of important lessons from our experience in this early attempt to implement an online, Web-based training model for mental health professionals. Trainees and faculty enjoyed the combined face-to-face and computer-mediated training process. Trainees appreciated the opportunity and ease of continuing the training and collaboration process online. Trainees and faculty noted that there was more equal participation among the participants in the clinical case discussions online than in the face-to-face meetings, where participation was more varied. Trainees also noticed that online communication required more concise and precise clinical thinking and writing. Everyone appreciated the ease and immediacy in using Internet links, embedded in the text of posted entries, to reach additional important Web sites.

However, a significant amount of time was also spent responding to trainee complaints regarding hardware problems, initial apprehension and difficulty in learning and becoming proficient in using the Web site interactive software, and delays in access to timely support and troubleshooting (which often was desired immediately). The faculty supervisor noted the amount of time involved in the preparation, training, and review of a significant volume of online written communication as main concerns. The training group also noted the need for significant backup support from Fielding's Webmaster and support personnel for various Web site and software questions and difficulties. Finally, trainees and faculty acknowledged the need for proper training regarding the appropriate norms, etiquette, and limitations of online work.

A number of clinical training issues became clear as we progressed in our online group training. The interactive Web environment became a central gateway to clinical resources for the group psychotherapy trainees. Trainees had to become proficient in the use of the program's interactive Web site and the Internet to collaborate and conduct online research. Faculty had to be knowledgeable and able to offer online demonstrations and lead discussions about topics such as Internet browsers, online service providers, interactive collaborative software, and online group process.

Closely tied to the technological and training issues were a variety of important ethical concerns that emerged in our training of mental health professionals online. Issues of consent and confidentiality need to be handled sensitively when clinical case material is discussed in face-to-face training groups. There is an even greater threat to privacy when confidential material is further discussed over the electronic network of e-mail and the Internet. We required that certain guidelines be followed that were developed by a colleague at Fielding (W. Kouw, personal communication, 1998) and later supported by initiatives such as the eHealth Code of Ethics (Internet Healthcare Coalition, 2000). First, use of the names of patients, clinical settings, or other identifying information was not permitted in electronic case presentations. Second, all e-mail material and Web site posts and replies were deleted after a 6-month period and, therefore, were not used for any other purpose. Third, safety measures such as private access codes and appropriate administrative oversight ensured that only correctly identified individuals were able to participate in the private online conversations.

The issues of group boundaries and online group norms emerged as further ethical and clinical training concerns. At the end of one face-to-face meeting, two group trainees began to argue. The group members, including the two who were still disagreeing, felt that the conflict was unresolved by the end of the training day. As a result, the group members decided to continue their discussion online. Online, the faculty supervisor asked the trainees to describe their leftover feelings from the face-to-face meeting. After some discussion, several trainees posted replies that stated how uncomfortable they felt about discussing the matter "virtually." The faculty supervisor decided to terminate the online discussion as the level of interpersonal risk became palpable. At the next face-to-face meeting, the trainees expressed the need for explicit guidelines about the proper use of face-to-face and online communications for conflict resolution. Issues concerning trust, safety, privacy, and the need for proper containment while negotiating conflicts were paramount for the trainees. This example highlights the important ethical and professional training issues surrounding the use of online communication when conflict emerges in a group. Furthermore, professionals and their trainees must be vigilant in their ongoing review of ethical dilemmas and clinical training issues as they emerge in the areas of online group dynamics, conflict resolution, problem solving, and decision making in Web-based health care training programs (Janoff, 1998).

Web-Based Training for Mental Health Professionals in the Anxiety Disorders

Since completing this initial exploration into online training and consultation, our interest in promoting better collaboration and teamwork among health care professionals led to the development of a similar postgraduate training program for clinicians in the treatment of anxiety disorders. This training also included face-to-face training modules combined with online theory presentations, case consultation, and online team support. Because our efforts were an extension of the combined program just described, only a brief summary of the training approach is presented here.

Participants were practicing mental health professionals who desired continuing education and training in the treatment of anxiety disorders.

Face-to-face meetings focused on the presentation of theoretical material covering the diagnosis, case formulation, and clinical assessment of the anxiety disorders. Specific treatment approaches and clinical protocols were also a main focus of the training. Seven participants met as a group, face-to-face, at approximately 6-week intervals over a 10-month period. A highly interactive Web environment supported the trainees' online collaborative efforts (see Groove Networks at www.groove.net). This online collaborative software supported ongoing case consultation discussions as well as the development, storage, and easy retrieval of important assessment and psychoeducational materials. The trainees were able to download the information and use it immediately with their anxiety disordered patients.

Based on our experience in the combined face-to-face and online training of group psychotherapists, trainees were provided with extensive training and preparation in the use of the interactive software and appropriate group norms and communication strategies that accompany effective online teamwork. Table 19.2 lists the strategies for fostering collaborative learning that we stressed in our online training environment. (The specific guidelines listed were developed by Fielding faculty [Shapiro & Hughes, 1997] for their distance learning programs and have been modified here for our training purposes.)

The guidelines or online "netiquette" were considered quite helpful for trainees as they learned about asynchronous collaboration and online group dynamics. Trainees stressed that the ease of assembling, storing, and retrieving work products from a central (virtual) place on the Internet was vastly superior to mailing/faxing papers or using individual e-mail to collaborate. However, the predominant feedback from trainees was on the significant advantages and benefits from working together online. First, the shared space used collectively by the group closed the gap of "distance" (geographical and professional) that existed for the group of trainees, even though half of them were from the same small city. Congruent with the research on asynchronous collaboration (Sproull & Kiesler, 1991; Weisband, 1995), and similar to our online training experience, trainees emphasized more equal participation and increased shared leadership in their online collaboration versus their face-to-face interaction. As they discussed these differences both online and face-to-face, trainees noted a spillover effect in which their overall interactions were significantly improved by working together in the two different modes. Third, trainees noted that the discussions were more oriented toward the faculty leader in their face-to-face training sessions than in their online collaboration. Online, group members participated more freely, and this had the impact of generating more cohesion among the team of trainees. Thus, the trainees indicated that the mutual support and collaboration of the group was a significant benefit over and above the resources and learning materials provided by the faculty.

TABLE 19.2   Strategies for Fostering Collaborative Learning in an Asynchronous
Web Forum

We have learned that consciously addressing several strategies for promoting effective online dialogue and collaboration before our trainees begin working at-a-distance makes a big difference. Here are some issues and strategies to consider.

1. *Be responsive.* Interaction and feedback are critical. If a trainee posts a lengthy response to a case or reading, then he or she is looking for some response and feedback to the posting. Responsiveness is far more than saying "good job" or "thanks for the posting."

2. *Use active approaches to learning.* Online electronic learning requires an active learning strategy rather than a passive one. The trainee/student who is content to sit and take notes in a classroom setting will find this medium to be much more challenging.

3. *Never forget that the person on the other side is a human being.* Assume the honesty and good intentions of the sender. Remember that you are building community.

4. *Be brief and to the point.* Keep your intended audience in mind. Stay on topic. Post messages in the appropriate topic area. By reading previous messages before sending one yourself, you will be able to get a sense of the ongoing conversation and inherent themes.

5. *Your messages reflect on* you; *be proud of them.* Without the visual cues of face-to-face interaction, we focus on the words only. Words can be impacting, informative, engaging, motivating, infuriating, and so on. Think about the impact you desire and how the others may experience your communications. Take time to make sure that your messages are easily read and understood.

6. *Use descriptive subject headings in your messages.* Use the subject line to tell people what your message is about. If you are giving feedback or responding to a message from Laura, then note in the subject line "Reply to Laura" rather than simply "Reply."

7. *Be careful with emotion, humor, and sarcasm.* Without voice inflection, facial expression, body language, and so on, it is easy for communication to be misinterpreted. If expressing emotion, then do so clearly; state your feelings as your own (not someone else's); and avoid use of inappropriate humor, irony, sarcasm, and subtlety to express yourself.

8. *Summarize what you are following up.* Brief quotes from the previous message are sometimes helpful in clarifying what you are following up on specifically.

9. *Give back to the community.* Make your collaboration with others meaningful, value added, and relational. Try not to repeat what has already been said. Assess what you have to add to a conversation, give proactively, and receive fully. Maintain the values and culture of a supportive and collaborative community.

10. *Cite references where and when appropriate.* If you are using facts to support a cause, then state where they came from.

11. *Assume that any messages you send are permanent (until the closure of your group).* Inappropriate dialogue may affect the entire community. Think about what you mean to say, and say what you mean. Conversations in this environment are public in that they are part of an evolving community of important people.

Web-Based Collaboration in Cardiac Rehabilitation

We have extended our online clinical training and consultation work with professional teams in health care to the field of cardiac rehabilitation. In this health care project, the cardiac rehabilitation team consisted of a cardiologist, physical and exercise therapists, a nutritionist, a psychologist, meditation and yoga trainers, and an administrative person. The cardiac rehabilitation specialists all were independent practitioners, working in separate offices and involved in numerous other services and programs. The group members met face-to-face over a period of 6 months to (a) plan the new cardiac rehabilitation program and (b) develop their team identity and effective group working relationship. Although all of the professionals worked within a 5-mile radius, getting together was time-consuming and stressful because it meant time away from their respective practices. Setting up face-to-face meetings was difficult, so contact was accomplished through phone calls and the use of e-mail.

After the initial 6-month planning process, the team began working together online over the Internet (see TeamWave software at www.teamwave. com). The use of e-mail for teamwork was discontinued in favor of an interactive Web site where programmatic materials were centrally located and easily accessed. First, team members began posting work documents on the Web site, including materials such as program brochures, treatment outlines, educational handouts, and other administrative documents that the staff had developed. The team agreed that the development of written materials and all subsequent revisions were to take place online. Dates for review and revision of program materials, by specified team members, were scheduled at regular intervals. Next, the rehabilitation team developed a virtual patient record in which referral and important intake information were cataloged for each program participant. This information included patient demographics, relevant medical history, past cardiac procedures, current medical and psychosocial needs, a specific treatment plan, and an ongoing care regimen. Furthermore, the team members initiated several discussion forums (asynchronous collaboration) for their ongoing conversations about the patient groups and the overall program.

The cardiac rehabilitation program began with a 3-day retreat intensive, followed by 8 weeks of 3-hour meetings, twice a week. Most of the program staff were present for at least part of the 3-day intensive and were scheduled only as needed during the weekly meetings. Thereafter, continued face-to-face staff meetings or conference calls, where same time and place collaboration was involved, were considered an "extra." As a result, the rehabilitation team's working Web environment began to expand into a more complete collaborative space for the entire scope of work projects and work relationships. The team members began to experience their "electronic office" as a great host for their professional community, including the building of improved relationships among the clinicians.

As work progressed, the rehabilitation team continued to meet quarterly, face-to-face, to discuss (a) overall program goals, (b) progress and development of the team's asynchronous working relationship and work products, and (c) quality of the team's face-to-face working relationship as dedicated health care professionals. Over time, the face-to-face meetings became more of a time for socializing and mutual support. That is, most of the programmatic work took place online and through an occasional phone call to clarify or finalize a decision.

It should be noted, however, that there were a number of difficult issues or disagreements that required resolution between two or more team members. Examples included last-minute scheduling changes that required flexibility in everyone's busy schedule. Also, there were numerous discussions about on-site training activities where team members disagreed or wanted changes in how material was presented to the program participants. The team decided that these issues were to be discussed over the phone or in person between the appropriate parties. The results of these discussions were posted on the Web site so that the team members could be aware of changes and know that the issues had been resolved. It became clear that such disagreements or exchanges were handled more quickly in direct conversations (phone or in person) than by conversing in writing over the Internet. This observation was consistent with our previous experience of online asynchronous working relationships. It is our opinion that complex interactions (e.g., conflict resolution) are more easily resolved when the more subtle aspects of human communication, such as voice tone and facial expressions, are present. As for these program difficulties and/or interpersonal struggles, all that can be said is that computers have not lessened the need for big hearts, open minds, and good communication skills.

Conclusions and Recommendations

The demands of managed care settings, public health clinics, hospital in-patient units, and private practice settings influence the supervision, training, and collaboration needs of today's health care professionals. Increasingly, active professionals want training delivery systems that fit into their busy schedules and that minimize travel and time away from work and family. This chapter has described several training and professional collaboration projects that combine face-to-face meetings with continued training and consultation online, at-a-distance.

Our experience with the training programs outlined in this chapter highlight many of the advantages and limitations for supervisors and trainers who want to integrate online collaboration into the training process. The advantages include the following:

1. Ongoing access to the trainer and other group members' input and expertise can take place in between face-to-face meetings.

2. The dynamics of the group online allows new aspects of members' personalities and skills to emerge and be observed. The necessity for brief and precise communication, and the leveling of participation among group members, adds a new dimension for teamwork.

3. Health care professionals have access to team members and collaborative work in between face-to-face meetings. Therefore, individuals can post new ideas or introduce needed materials in a way that is practical and directly connected to on-site experiences.

4. The training group can continue online as a virtual support group with continuous connection and interaction in between face-to-face meetings.

At the same time, there are limitations that need to be addressed. First, online communication might not bring about an immediate response. Professionals need to know when to meet face-to-face or use the telephone and not to rely on the computer alone. Some situations demand an immediate response and might not be perceived as urgent through a telecommunicated message. Second, there can be misunderstandings and hurt feelings that arise when the usual person-to-person cues are not available. Third, individuals may omit critical information that might more easily be explored if the professionals or team members were meeting face-to-face. Fourth, ethical considerations are serious and need to address the limits of confidentiality when personal information is disclosed over the Internet. Without clearly defined guidelines on how to safeguard information and conversations, there is the serious risk of ethical breaches. Fifth, professionals need the financial resources to invest in computer equipment and basic training. Although we have not found this to be a major inhibition (most professionals today have found it necessary to be somewhat computer and Internet savvy), it is a factor that everyone needs to cost into the start-up phase of the training or professional collaborative process. Sixth, the training institution or professional team needs to support the use of technology through access to a Webmaster and other resources, such as a technical expert or help desk. Seventh, the professional team or group of trainees must possess the requisite technological skills or have the energy, time, and commitment to develop these essential skills, including a thorough understanding of effective online communication, group dynamics, and limitations of this new medium for professional training and collaboration.

Based on our experiences with this type of integrated face-to-face and online teamwork, we propose a number of recommendations for supervisors and trainers who seek to adopt computer-mediated methods for the training of health care professionals (Janoff & Schoenholtz-Read, 1999). Each training group or professional team needs to develop clearly articulated norms about when to use or not use computer communication. The size of the group or team should be limited to 8 to 10 professionals. As with face-to-face groups, the small group size permits adequate time and space for everyone to participate and for intimacy to develop. Individuals must also remember to check in continuously (we recommend two or three times per week) to see new work posted or requests for additional collaboration. In our experience, if participation is varied or infrequent, then teamwork deteriorates quickly. Finally, face-to-face team meetings are still seen as necessary and desirable as a means of conflict resolution, complex decision making, and peer support.

From the examples described here, extensive online collaboration can evolve into an electronic community of interacting professionals and virtual work. The notion of developing online communities in cyberspace has received extensive attention as the proliferation of public Web sites, with their forums and chat rooms, has dominated the Internet (Figallo, 1998; Kim, 2000). Although some of these interactions and communities appear aimless at best or destructive at worst (which also can be true of face-to-face groups that have little or no focus), we believe that our efforts have demonstrated the increased efficacy and utility for health care teams that have a clear purpose, identity, and need for Web-based professional training and collaboration.

References

Brown, J. S., & Duguid, P. (1996). Universities in the digital age. *Change, 28*(4), 10-19.

Figallo, C. (1998). *Internet world: Hosting Web communities.* New York: John Wiley.

Internet Healthcare Coalition. (2000). *eHealth Code of Ethics* [Online]. Available: www.ihealthcoalition.org/ethics/ethics.html

Janoff, D. S. (1998, May). *Demonstrating the future: Internet psychosocial rehabilitation services, clinical supervision, and training.* Paper presented at the Sixth Congress of the World Association for Psychosocial Rehabilitation, Hamburg, Germany.

Janoff, D. S., & Schoenholtz-Read, J. (1999). Group supervision meets technology: A model for computer-mediated group training at a distance. *International Journal of Group Therapy, 49,* 255-272.

Kim, A. J. (2000). *Community building on the Web.* Berkeley, CA: Peachpit Press.

Lipnack, J., & Stamps, J. (1997). *Virtual teams: Reaching across space, time, and organizations with technology.* New York: John Wiley.

McGrath, J. E., & Hollingshead, A. B. (1994). *Groups interacting with technology.* Thousand Oaks, CA: Sage.

Nickelson, D. (1997). Telehealth poses opportunities and challenges for psychology. *Practitioner Focus, 10*(2), 12. (American Psychological Association, Washington, DC)

Shapiro, J., & Hughes, S. (1997). *Getting started in the community of scholars: Tips and suggestions.* Unpublished manuscript, Fielding Graduate Institute.

Sproull, L., & Kiesler, S. (1991). *Connections: New ways of working in the networked organization.* Cambridge: MIT Press.

Weisband, S. P. (1995). Group discussion and first advocacy effects in computer-mediated and face-to-face decision making groups. *Organizational Behavior and Human Decision Processes, 53,* 352-380.

Chapter 20

A Virtual Knowledge Café

Bo Gyllenpalm

> A well designed forum of people of average intelligence and consciousness can pro-
> duce exceptionally intelligent, even wise results. . . . Contrast a poorly designed
> forum of the very same people that produces nothing but chaos, or some lowest-
> common-denominator compromise. . . . Note that the individual intelligence of the
> participants has no correlation with the collective intelligence of the group. . . . The
> only difference between the collective intelligence of the first group and the sec-
> ond—made up of the very same people—is the process design.
>
> —Tom Atlee, founder, Co-Intelligence Institute

When asked to design an online course on organization development
(OD) concepts and methods for the organizational management (OM) program at the Fielding Graduate Institute, I wanted to try a new way of designing
the curriculum and running the course. I sincerely believe that online learning
by adult students is very different from classroom teaching. In my consulting
practice, I have been working with a new approach to learning and creating
knowledge called the "world café method." This is a face-to-face method for
catalyzing collaborative learning and collective intelligence. It has been developed by a friend and colleague from the Society for Organizational Learning,
Juanita Brown, who is also a co-facilitator with Peter Senge for the Executive
Champion Seminars. Brown has done extensive research about the café methodology in face-to-face settings, and together we have participated and run
cafés and seminars about the café learning approach.

In her study, Brown (2000) finds that the world café is both an innovative *methodology* for collaborative dialogic learning and an evocative *metaphor* enabling us to notice the generative power of conversation in human systems at increasing levels of scale. The world café illuminates the ways in which dynamic networks of conversation and social learning enable us to discover shared meaning, access collective intelligence, and bring forth desired futures. It describes underlying principles that allow leaders to engage and focus these living networks in the service of institutional and societal change and renewal. The study's findings articulate four simple operating principles that, when used in combination, support a human system's capacity to engage authentic conversation, collaborative learning, collective intelligence, coherent community, and committed action at increasing levels of scale. Seeing organizations as dynamic networks of conversation and meaning making provides the opportunity to re-conceive organizational learning, strategy innovation, technology design, and leadership development based on the ways in which human systems co-evolve the systemic intelligence they need to learn, adapt, and thrive.

These are the four basic operating principles that underlies the café approach to collaborative learning:

1. Creating hospitable space
2. Exploring questions that matter
3. Connecting diverse people and ideas
4. Listening together for patterns, insights, and deeper questions (Brown, 2000, p. 97)

However, when I first started to test the café method online, I did not know what to expect and what principles could be transferred to this new environment. I had been experimenting with a couple of different approaches but have now found a design that seems to work very well with adult learners. The following description about a "virtual knowledge café" is based on Brown's research and my own experiments. I am indebted to her for allowing me to incorporate many of her findings and references.

Creating Hospitable Space

The spirit is to create a physical space that enables you to move in that space and create a social space that encourages you to swap and share and help each other. If you can design the physical space, the social space, and the information space all together to enhance collaborative learning, then that whole milieu turns into a learning technology and people just love working there and they start learning with and from each other.

> How do you actually construct a space that brings people casually together so that they start listening to each other . . . and find that they can contribute something?
>
> —John Seely Brown, chief scientist, Xerox Palo Alto Research Center
> (quoted in Creelman, 2000)

The first challenge I encountered when transferring the principles of a face-to-face café to the virtual environment was how to create a hospitable space. In the face-to-face cafés, we have found how important it is to create a room that evokes intimacy, warmth, and collaborative conversation. This is done by creating a café environment, including small round coffee tables with red-checked tablecloths and fresh flowers on each table. We also add white paper sheets over the tablecloths, just like in many cafés, along with small containers of colored markers to use for doodling.

To use the café principles in an online environment, the participants must feel safe and comfortable. Many of my participants have never seen each other face-to-face, although they have had some experience with the software we use because this course is offered toward the end of their educational program. In the literature, there are numerous references to the importance of creating a "hospitable space" for fostering authentic conversations. For example, Howard Rheingold, a pioneer in computer-mediated communication and the online world, talks in his book, *The Virtual Community* (Rheingold, 1993), about the powerful way in which the Internet has come to fulfill the role of a "third place," a comfortable informal environment for people to gather for conversation, community, and connection—to each other and to things they care about. The "third place" in human communities is a term coined by sociologist Ray Oldenburg in his research focused on the importance of feeling "at home" for the evolution of democratic practices and informal public life throughout history. Oldenburg (1989) emphasizes the way in which a third place offers the opportunity to feel "at home." He describes a third place as an intangible "feeling of being at ease" or the "freedom to be" (p. 41). John Seely Brown and Paul Duguid's *The Social Life of Information* reaffirms Rheingold's assertion that even in computer-mediated environments, creating informal social contexts where people can talk together, share ideas, and contribute to each other's learning is critical to effective work (Brown & Duguid, 2000).

During the first week of my course, I introduce an assignment aimed at initiating the creation of this third place or hospitable space. I ask the *participants* (I don't call them *students*) to introduce themselves, give their backgrounds and interests, and explain why they have chosen this course. I also ask them to tell all of us what they want to get out of the course—their goals and expectations. I encourage them to suggest some common norms for how to use this space and how to carry on a dialogue rather than have discussions. I tell them that the word *discussion* comes from the Latin root words *dis*, meaning *apart*, and *cutere*, meaning *to cut*. During discussions, we usually cut apart each other's statements and argue who is right and who is wrong. The root word for *dialogue* comes from the Greek words *dia* and *logos*, which translate to *meaning flowing through*. I encourage the participants to have dialogues and to respectfully listen to each other and learn from each other instead of having discussions or trying to win arguments and show off. I encourage them to speak from their hearts and to use the first-person form in their online postings. Similar to the personal introductions in a face-to-face café, this initial check-in helps to establish mutual trust and a willingness to be open. I also participate in this first assignment to set the tone and communication style.

During the second week, I ask the participants to read and write a book review to establish a common ground of the different concepts and methods used in OD work. The first dialogue consists of commenting on each other's reviews, with a focus on the new insights they have experienced. This activity is designed to help the participants to feel comfortable in giving positive feedback and to realize that there is no right or wrong way, but rather many different ways, to view a topic. In this course, they can choose one of two books to review. One is more academic, and one is more applied. The intent is to demonstrate that there are multiple ways of approaching a topic. I also tell them that I am not going to "teach" them; rather, I am going to participate in their learning as a peer. As the facilitator, however, I need to create a climate and atmosphere that is welcoming and inclusive, but at the same time, must establish clear expectations of acceptable online behavior.

Exploring Questions That Matter

Asking the proper question is the central act of transformation. (Estes, 1992, p. 52)

A vital question, a creative question, rivets our attention. All the creative power of our mind is focused on the question. Knowledge emerges in response to these compelling questions. They open us to new worlds. . . . The quality of those worlds depends on the quality of our questions. (Allee, 1997, p. 230)

After the first 2 weeks of check-in and getting comfortable, we set up the virtual knowledge cafés. There are usually three café rounds of 3 weeks each, followed by a final week of mutual reflection on the café process as a whole, including personal and collective learnings. In each 3-week café round, there are two or three areas of inquiry or topics going on simultaneously in different cafés. Every participant serves as a café host for at least one topic during the 12-week course. The café question/topic might be connected to a project that the participant is involved in at work or a concept that he or she wants to learn more about.

During the first week of each café round, the hosts post "think papers" with information about the topics, their own reflections, and why these topics matter to them. They include references to a variety of additional resources, including books, articles, and Web sites, where the café visitors can find more information. The hosts also frame the questions that will serve as the "attractors" for the café dialogue during the periods when they serve as the hosts.

One of the most important discoveries in the café methodology is the pivotal importance of discovering, shaping, and exploring "questions that matter." Café hosts around the world have found that disciplined attention to discovering and exploring powerful questions (in contrast to identifying issues or problems) is one of the distinguishing characteristics of the café approach to dialogue and collaborative learning (Brown, 2000).

David Cooperrider, the founder of the appreciative inquiry (AI) movement, assessed the results of more than a decade of research and practice in the area of AI by stating unequivocally that "the most important insight we have learned with AI to date is that *human systems grow toward what they persistently ask questions about*" (Cooperrider & Whitney, 2000, p. 70, italics in original). C. West Churchman, an operations researcher and pioneer in systems thinking at the University of California, Berkeley, notes in *The Design of Inquiring Systems* that, in spite of the fact that an individual might

> never come to feel the act of discovery as part of his own natural life . . . , it would be foolish to say that most people are indifferent to inquiry. They are curious about all the important things of their life . . . , but their style of inquiry is not that of a scientific discipline. . . . An inquirer is not a special kind of person; rather, every person is a special kind of inquirer. (Churchman, 1971, p. 268)

Churchman adds, "There are no experts in inquiry" (p. 269). He encourages designers of inquiring systems to create opportunities where the inquiry can happen within people and not be an activity that they merely observe being conducted by outside experts (p. 271). Rather than creating a focus on "teaching," Churchman's insights encourage a focus on learning together in which the facilitator chooses a less directive role.

In one of my courses, AI was a café topic. The host, after her presentation of a think paper, asked the following questions:

- How does AI relate to some of the other subjects we have discussed in class?

- What are some of the wider implications of AI? Is it a way of living or just a methodology or intervention to analyze issues?

◆ How could you apply AI in your own organization, personal life, or community?

In the cafés, there are ongoing dialogues, with questions posed by the hosts and questions posed by the participants or café visitors. As a facilitator of the process, my role is to make sure that questions that matter are raised. At times I raise a question or point to an area that could be of interest to the participants. I also give them hints and tips regarding where they can find interesting information to gain new insights and learning. Examples of this in the café on AI include the following contributions from me:

◆ What constructive criticism do you have of AI?

◆ Is there anything in the philosophy behind AI that you struggle with? How do the underlying principles fit with your own views on the nature of reality and social systems?

◆ One good Web site that you might check is www.bus.sfu.ca/homes/ gervase. This section of the site for Simon Fraser University contains a list of articles by Gervase Bushe.

◆ Another good Web site is www.geminitiative.org/global.html. This is the site for the Global Social Innovations initiative, which is sponsored by Case Western Reserve University. This link takes you to the *GEM Journal,* where many AI articles are available.

Fran Peavey, a community organizer and pioneer in the area of large-scale social change (particularly in developing countries), has written a monograph titled *Strategic Questioning: An Experiment in Communication of the Second Kind* (Peavey, 1992). A version of this monograph (published later) illuminates the evolution of Peavey's (1994, 2000) thinking about strategic questioning as a vehicle for transformative change. She describes strategic questions as ones that create a "resonant field . . . into which your own thinking is magnified, clarified, and new motion can be created" (Peavey, 1992, p. 4). According to Brown (2000), one of the key assumptions underlying the café learning approach and how it can help to access collective intelligence is

> the assumption that the stakeholders in any system already have within them the wisdom and creativity to confront the most difficult challenges. Given the appropriate context and support, including the introduction of catalytic questions, it is possible for members to access their own collective deeper knowledge about underlying causes and leverage points for change. (p. 141)

It is interesting to see in the online knowledge café that those who first believed they had no experience in OD work found that they had considerable knowledge when they were able to ask and participate in exploring questions that really mattered to them. In café conversations with their peers, they discovered that they had more ideas and creative options than they did in traditional teaching settings.

Connecting Diverse People and Ideas

Intelligence emerges as the system connects to itself in diverse and creative ways.
—Margaret Wheatley, Berkana Institute

Brown's (2000) research findings suggest that one unique contribution of the world café lies in its capacity to support dialogic learning in very large group settings—to connect the intimate authenticity of small group conversational inquiry with very large group collaborative learning. World café conversations have been conducted successfully with groups of from 12 to 1,200 people.

I had participated in several dialogue groups on the Internet, and my experience was that too many participants made the dialogue hard to follow. In my virtual café work, I have discovered that the number of participants is very important. The best number seems to be between six and nine participants. If there are fewer than six, the dialogue becomes less dynamic; there are not enough postings to keep the dialogue alive. If there are more than nine participants, the exchange of ideas is extremely hard to follow. Because the virtual café uses threaded dialogues, it is important to follow the dialogue continuously. If there are more than nine participants, the threads can be incredibly long and complicated and it is easy to get lost and end up in chaos. With larger classes, I usually divide the students into two or more groups, each consisting of six to nine participants.

Mitchell Waldrop, author of *Complexity: The Emerging Science at the Edge of Order and Chaos* (which describes the early days of the Santa Fe Institute, where multidisciplinary scientists did groundbreaking work in the field of complex adaptive systems), discusses Stuart Kauffman's discoveries about autocatalytic sets, the emergence of new collective properties in a web of transformations among molecules. Waldrop (1992) cites Kauffman's discovery from working with genetic networks: "If the connections were too sparse, the networks would basically just freeze up and sit there. And if the connections were too dense, the networks would churn around in total chaos" (p. 293). What Kauffman finds resonates with my own discovery of optimal membership size for virtual knowledge cafés.

John Holland, another Santa Fe Institute pioneer in Waldrop's intellectual adventure story, focuses his research on fundamental processes of learning and adaptation from cells to social systems. Holland emphasizes that optimal learning and development occur in systems where there is a rich web of interactions among multiple agents along with an environment of novelty where new opportunities and spaces of possibilities can be explored

(Waldrop, 1992). Holland's discoveries are complemented by Doyne Farmer's theory that the emergence of surprising new possibilities in any system lies not in the individual parts or nodes of the network but rather in what emerges from the connections among them (Waldrop, 1992). Humberto Maturana, an evolutionary biologist, and Francisco Varela, a noted cognitive scientist, add a key insight to this exploration by hypothesizing that we bring forth the world we experience through "the social coupling through language in the network of conversations" in which we participate (Maturana & Varela, 1992, p. 232).

The preceding principles from the new sciences also underlie the café work. I have found that when the participants move from café to café, carrying seed ideas from one café conversation to another, they continually exchange thoughts, ideas, and questions. This rich "coupling" brings forth the world that the members experience, as Maturana and Varela suggest (Capra, 1996, p. 267). Participants also bring additional references into the evolving online café conversations. Because each café round spans a period of 3 weeks, there are many opportunities for concepts to combine and recombine, forming a rich web of interconnections and interactions between the participants.

In a café on cafés, held with a group representing nine different countries at the 1999 Systems Thinking Conference, the members commented on the phenomenon of café conversations in the following ways:

- Having multiple conversations keeps people unstuck.
- People feel responsible for carrying their own as well as other people's ideas with them as they move, so more connections are happening all the time.
- It's like improvisational jazz. One person starts a riff, others pick up the beat, then everyone in the room gets up and starts to dance. Everyone's doing a unique dance, but there's a new rhythm that wasn't there before.
- It's like discovering a collective intuition.
- It's like a reverberation of thought.
- [It's] like harmonizing meaning rather than freezing it—more like a work in progress.
- A café is like creating a painting in common versus making a collage where the different individual pieces are stuck onto the canvas. (Brown, 2000, p. 184)

These findings seem to apply equally to virtual knowledge cafés. I encourage the hosts of cafés to visit other cafés that are going on at the same time. This allows them to link with other cafés and build on and make connections to the ideas being developed at their "home cafés." The participants who are not hosting in this café round are also weaving ideas among other café conversations in which they have engaged. This moving around and cross-fertilizing of ideas and experiences between cafés creates a highly collaborative learning experience between participants and faculty.

Here is a quote from one of the participants about the process:

> I really liked the café process of hosts creating initial "thought papers" followed by an extended conversation in the cafés. While I will admit I did not fully understand the expectations in the beginning, it was obvious that the entire group developed new skills, particularly the skill of layering a deep conversation on later topics. This last learning about conversation and how it deepens was pretty amazing! Each person brought [his or her] own perspective and style to the discussions so that the learning had a web design rather than being focused on Bo's perspective. I also think that the opportunity for students to facilitate the café dialogues was a real bonus.

As a faculty member, I facilitate simply by participating in the different cafés, making new connections, or encouraging a direction of inquiry that might not have occurred to the participants. I also host a café that is ongoing the whole semester called "Bo's Special Café," a social space where people can drop in at any time for a chat with me or others regarding non-topic-related interests and concerns. This is one of the cafés where the most authentic personal dialogue occurs around key issues in people's lives and work.

Because the participants all are working in different fields and coming from different backgrounds and cultural settings, the diversity of the group contributes to the mutual learning in a very powerful way. I have found that it is important not to structure the virtual knowledge café syllabus too rigidly so that this diversity may find expression. I usually encourage the students to suggest improvements to the process and find their own ways of participating and contributing to the whole. Too little structure elicits chaos; too much structure stifles creativity, especially for adults with many life experiences.

Capra and Flatau (1998) point out that the "spontaneous emergence of new forms of order, which is manifest in the phenomena of development, learning, and evolution, is one of the hallmarks of life" (p. 4). They discuss two different and generally mutually exclusive ways in which new structures and order evolve in human systems. The first, which they term "embodiment through design" (p. 7), results in static structures such as those created by the designers of machines or formal organizational policies. The second, which they term "embodiment through emergence" (p. 7), reflects more informal processes that create structure and order through adaptation and evolution rather than through design. Capra and Flatau observe that "there is a tension between designed and emergent structures. . . . The challenge is to find a creative balance between the structures embodied by design and those embodied through emergence" (pp. 4, 11). Brown (2000) asks, "Could the use of questions as 'attractors' coupled with fostering a rich and diverse web of connections among people and ideas in café conversations be one way of encouraging both informal emergence and purposeful coherence at the same time?" (p. 189). I think that this is possible. These ideas underlie the design of a virtual knowledge café.

Listening Together for Patterns, Insights, and Deeper Questions

> Jam . . . to take a theme, a question, a notion, a whim, an idea, pass it around, break it up, put it together, turn it over, run it backward, fly with it as far as possible, out of sight, never retreating . . . but yes, here it comes, homing in, changed, new, the essence, like nothing ever before. (Kao, 1996)

In the world café work, we encourage the participants to suspend interpersonal judgment or blame while listening to the reflections of other members. Brown (2000) states, "In café learning, the group is invited to engage in *shared* listening—'listening *with*' each other collectively for insights that are *beyond* the individual, even though they may be experienced *through* the individual" (p. 207, italics in original). This "listening with" is an aspect that is strengthened in the asynchronous environment. Here is what one participant in a virtual café said:

> Every member contributed a high level of intelligence, brought wonderful and relevant personal experience forward, and exhibited engagement and participation that created a supportive and creative learning environment. I was impressed [both with] the academic level as well as with the caring and desire for each of us to have a good time while learning important material in the cafés. (quoted in Brown, 2000, p. 171)

The participants in online knowledge cafés are encouraged to look beyond their own ideas and reactions. As Brown (2000) puts it, "They are invited to notice emerging patterns and themes of meaning as they co-evolve through several rounds of conversation where people and ideas are, literally, traveling around the room, cross-pollinating, linking, and connecting" (p. 208).

Christopher Langton, another key player in the Santa Fe Institute, believes that biological, intellectual, and cultural evolution embody complementary aspects of the same dynamic processes of emergence that seem to characterize many café conversations. In human systems, with the capacity for conscious awareness, Langton believes that social co-evolution occurs through the process of concepts combining and recombining, leaping from mind to mind, all the while being recorded in the basic DNA of cultures and language (Waldrop, 1992).

I ask the participants to focus on what is evolving, not only in one of the cafés but across the different cafés. According to Brown (2000), "This enables a different relationship between the individual and the collective at a larger scale than is possible in many dialogic situations" (p. 210). Often in group settings, there is a tendency for individuals to maintain their positions and judgments. This can lead to fragmentation, incoherence, and excessive individualism in the group. Because the participants are not in competition with each other for grades, the café dialogues create a pattern of relationship to the larger whole that is different from what seems to be the case in many other settings.

Here is a comment from one participant:

> I certainly perceive my knowledge level very differently now. I found the café topics complementary. I could see themes woven throughout and saw a glimpse of the bigger picture for the first time. This course was far-and-away the richest learning experience that I have had yet. I loved the open "adult" learning method using the café. It forced us (the learners) to find and share resources and knowledge. It seemed as though [we] were engaged with serious learners who were speaking from their passions as well as their intellect. This café idea reinforces the need for me to be in community with others and to hear what they know, think, suspect, experience, and discover.

During the first week of the subsequent 3-week café sequence, new hosts frame their topics and prepare their think papers. During this time, the hosts of the previous 3-week café conversations synthesize the patterns and discoveries that have emerged in their cafés. Simultaneously, during the first week of each new café round, all participants can go back into the café conversations from the previous round, as every dialogue is in written form and accessible to them, to reflect on their own personal learning and insights and to review resource material.

The participants have commented that by having the different cafés running simultaneously as well as consecutively, they notice common threads weaving from one café to another. Members often become what Brown calls "theme weavers" as they contribute their insights. The virtual knowledge café emphasizes the role of contribution. The café hosts post their think papers as "gifts." The method of the café is not to criticize but rather to give and contribute something. Participants are asked to contribute their own experience, their thoughts, and their ideas or references to different resources. By doing this, they experience how knowledge is alive and growing as different themes, threads, and patterns begin to emerge. New questions are asked, and these start new dialogues and new threads.

During the final week of the semester, all members develop reflection papers about what they have learned from the overall café process and share how they can use this new knowledge in their lives and work. These synthesis papers are then posted in a special "reflection café." This enables all members to end up with a fuller sense of the whole by seeing the patterns made by everyone's diverse contributions and the different learnings that the participants have gained.

Discoveries About Café Learning in a Virtual Setting

> The real voyage of discovery lies not in seeking new landscapes, but in having new eyes.
>
> —Marcel Proust

Although participants in a virtual knowledge café are at first a bit hesitant about how the course will work, they soon realize that the quality of their learning and knowledge creation can be much higher than in a normal face-to-face classroom setting where the instructors put themselves in the role of experts. In the virtual café, everyone is the expert. Everyone's knowledge is part of an egalitarian whole.

To my surprise, I have found that virtual knowledge cafés have the capacity to create collaborative learning as powerful as that which occurs in face-to-face cafés. First, in the virtual café setting, members have more time for reflection than they do in a face-to-face classroom setting, before they make their contributions. Second, they can see everyone's contribution in writing, which often helps people to think more clearly. They can identify patterns and weave ideas together more easily when they can read through and see what everyone has said before them. Third, they have time to find relevant resources and make a deeper contribution to each café topic.

Here are some comments from the participants:

> The reflection time we had while each new café was gearing up was key to my learning. It gave me the opportunity to really digest the previous conversations instead of waiting until the end of the whole thing.

> Every member contributed a high level of intelligence, brought wonderful and relevant personal experience forward, and exhibited engagement and participation that created a supportive and creative learning environment. I was impressed with both the academic level as well as with the caring and desire for each of us to have a good time while learning important material in the cafés.

I cannot say enough about the level of learning this approach has afforded me. The give-and-take interaction in the group was very powerful. My expectations for the class were to learn about team dynamics. I came away with much, much more.

Finally, and perhaps most important, a diverse multicultural group of global leaders gets the opportunity to connect their thinking and ideas across a variety of online conversations before they begin to synthesize their own personal learnings. Through moving ideas and experiences around from café to café, both within and between café rounds, the participants learn from each other's experiences and questions in a deep and coherent way. It is like weaving a knowledge web across many different dimensions and perspectives, creating a powerful collaborative experience from the matrix of conversations.

Here is one student's comment: "This was not only a program of content, it was a program of experience. We experienced cultural differences, new group processes, formal and informal leadership, empowerment, and new ways of working with technology in the cafés."

There are many "cafés" on the Internet. Most of them are more like chat rooms. Chat rooms are fine, but they are not really virtual knowledge cafés based on the face-to-face café principles. My experience shows that café learning using these principles can be done online. If structured well, café dialogues can yield excellent results for knowledge sharing and new knowledge creation. This suggests that café principles do not depend on the setting, whether a collaborative conversation is face-to-face or online. Perhaps the cafe is a vehicle that can enable humans to be in real dialogue and think together in ways that create new knowledge, wherever they are.

Appendix: OD Concepts and Methods
With Bo Gyllenpalm (bgyllenpalm@fielding.edu)

Syllabus: An Excursion and Dialogue in the World of Organization Development

■ Introduction to the Seminar

I imagine this course to be an excursion into the OD world. We will search together and find information about the concepts and methods of this world and have a dialogue about their use. I will give you some basic reading material to start us off, and I also want you to find and recommend other interesting articles, books, and Web sites that give us more material about which to have a dialogue. You will build a personal library of useful concepts and methods and will discover the pros and cons of using these methods.

Areas of interest might be benchmarking, empowerment, open space, future search, reengineering, learning organizations, learning communities, strategic conversations, and so on. You are all welcome to come up with suggestions and ideas and to choose one concept or method of special interest.

■ Format

There are two groups in this seminar. You belong to Section I, and this group consists of Deb, Mark, Amy, Stan, Beth, Margaret, Mary, John, and Fred.

With this posting, I would like to give you more information about the process. I will use Topic 1 as a forum for process information, questions, comments, suggestions, and other things you want to bring up that do not fit under an assignment topic. I would like you to use the reply button, and in the appropriate field, to write a very short title to describe the posting and sign it with a "from . . ." at the end. This will make it easier to scan the topics and follow the discussions. If you are answering or commenting on someone else's reply, then reply to that reply with a title and your name. Follow the same procedure for the café topics. If you have any questions or suggestions, I also invite you to contact me via e-mail. I want everyone to check in at least twice every week to follow what is happening and offer some input.

Topic 2, called Bo's Special Café, is a virtual café for chatting and commenting on anything you like. It is a place to go to relax and have some fun. If, for some reason, you won't be able to check in for some time due to travel or other reasons, please notify us in advance at this location.

You will each host a personal café topic during a 3-week period. This means that there will be three parallel topics running during each period. The host of each café will present a short "think paper" about the concept or method that he or she has chosen, including personal reflections, thoughts, and questions that the host would like to propose for a dialogue at the start of a period. The rest of us then post our ideas and thoughts and make comments to the host and to each other. We might also post new questions to move deeper into the topic. We all act as consultants to the topic host and provide input in different forms, including references to articles, books, or Web sites where more information can be found. This means that the rest of us should search for interesting materials and also share personal experiences with the host and one another. After each topic period, the host should make a summary of his or her learnings and post it the following week.

This seminar is divided into six periods. Deadlines are always 12 midnight Pacific Time.

■ Period 1 (September 21 to September 24), Assignment 1,
Due Sunday, September 24

Under Topic 3

1. Write a short autobiography about yourself, including your interests in this seminar.
2. Include in the posting what you want to get out of this course—your goals and expectations—and state whether there are certain norms you would like us to follow to make you comfortable.

■ Period 2 (September 25 to October 1), Assignment 2,
Due Sunday, October 1

Under Topic 4

Read one of the two books, *Management Masterclass* (Glass, 1998) or *Organization Development* (French & Bell, 1998), and write a reflective paper about your thoughts and ideas about the book. Start with a very short overview and then focus on the concepts that interest you the most. Also respond to the different postings with your comments and reactions.

■ Period 3 (October 2 to October 22), Assignment 3

First Week

I will set up special topic cafés for each of you where the hosts post their input ("think papers" with descriptions of the topics and some initial thoughts, references, and questions) at the beginning of this period under Topics 5, 6, and 7. The rest of us will visit the cafés and read and post our thoughts, ideas, questions, and suggestions as replies to the hosts and others who have visited the café and, thus, carry on a dialogue. The hosts will also visit the other two cafés and participate in those dialogues.

Topics 5, 6, and 7 café think papers from hosts are due October 8.

Second Week

Team members respond to café Topics 5, 6, and 7, due October 15.

Third Week

Continue responses and dialogue on café Topics 5, 6, and 7,
due October 22.

■ Period 4 (October 23 to November 12), Assignment 4

First Week

Here we will have three new hosts under café Topics 8, 9, and 10. We will follow the same process as during Period 3. The hosts from café Topics 5, 6, and 7 will post their summaries of learnings in their cafés as a conclusion to their café topics. The other participants will have a chance to reflect on their learnings as well.

Topics 8, 9, and 10 café think papers are due October 29.

Second Week

Team members respond to café Topics 8, 9, and 10, due November 5.

Third Week

Continue responses and dialogue on Topics 8, 9, and 10, due November 12.

■ Period 5 (November 13 to December 3), Assignment 5

First Week

We will have three new hosts under café Topics 11, 12, and 13. We will follow the same process as during Periods 3 and 4.

The hosts from café Topics 8, 9, and 10 will post their summaries of learnings, due November 19.

Topics 11, 12, and 13 café think papers are due November 19.

Second Week

Team members respond to café Topics 11, 12, and 13, due November 26.

Third Week

Continue responses and dialogue on café Topics 11, 12, and 13, due December 3.

■ Period 6 (December 4 to December 10), Assignment 6

The hosts from café Topics 11, 12, and 13 will post their summaries of learnings, due December 10.

The last assignment for all is to reflect on what you have learned and how the process worked.

I would also like you to give each other some feedback about how you have perceived your own and the other members' participation in this process, due December 10. Post this under Topic 14.

■ Grades and Feedback

The grading scheme for the seminar is based on a possible 100 points. You are not individually in competition with each other for points. You may receive up to:

5 points for the first period/assignment

10 points for the second period/assignment

25 points each for the third, fourth, and fifth period/assignment

10 points for the final period/assignment

As prescribed by the OM program, each of you will receive individual feedback from me. I will give you preliminary feedback after Period 3 about how you are doing. I will also participate during the different periods as a consultant and facilitator.

References

Allee, V. (1997). *The knowledge evolution: Expanding organizational intelligence.* Boston: Butterworth-Heinemann.

Brown, J. (2000). *The World Café: Catalyzing collaborative learning and collective intelligence.* Unpublished manuscript, Human and Organization Development Program, Fielding Graduate Institute.

Brown, J. S., & Duguid, P. (2000). *The social life of information.* Boston: Harvard Business School Press.

Capra, F. (1996). *The web of life.* Garden City, NY: Anchor/Doubleday.

Capra, F., & Flatau, M. (1998). *Emergence and design in human organizations: Creative tension "at the edge of chaos."* Unpublished manuscript, Elmwood Institute.

Churchman, C. W. (1971). *The design of inquiring systems.* New York: Basic Books.

Cooperrider, D., & Whitney, D. (2000). Exploring appreciative inquiry. *Perspectives: A Journal of the World Business Academy, 14,* 69-74.

Creelman, D. (2000). Interview with John Seely Brown and Paul Duguid based on their book, *The Social Life of Information* [Online]. Retrieved June 10, 2001, from: www.hr.com/index.cfm/weeklymag.html

Estes, C. P. (1992). *Women who run with the wolves: Myths and stories of the wild woman archetypes.* New York: Ballantine.

French, W. L., & Bell, C. H. (1998). *Organization development: Behavior science interventions for organization improvement.* Englewood Cliffs, NJ: Prentice Hall.

Glass, N. (1998). *Management masterclass: A practical guide to the new realities of business.* London: Nicholas Brealey.

Kao, J. (1996). *Jamming: The art and discipline of business creativity.* New York: HarperBusiness.

Maturana, H. R., & Varela, F. J. (1992). *The tree of knowledge: The biological roots of human understanding.* Boston: Shambhala.

Oldenburg, R. (1989). *The great good place: Cafes, coffee shops, community centers, beauty parlors, general stores, bars, hangouts, and how they get you through the day.* New York: Paragon House.

Peavey, F. (1992). *Strategic questioning: An experiment in communication of the second kind.* Unpublished manuscript, Crabgrass.

Peavey, F. (1994). Strategic questioning: An approach to creating personal and social change. In *By life's grace: Musings on the essence of social change* (pp. 86-111). Philadelphia: New Society.

Peavey, F. (2000). *Strategic questioning: A Web resource* [Online]. Retrieved June 10, 2001, from: www.jobsletter.org.nz/vivian/stratq97.html

Rheingold, H. (1993). *The virtual community: Homesteading on the electronic frontier.* Reading, MA: Addison-Wesley.

Waldrop, M. M. (1992). *Complexity: The emerging science at the edge of order and chaos.* New York: Touchstone.

Author Index

Subject Index

About the Contributors

Dorothy Agger-Gupta is Associate Dean for Research in the Ph.D. Program in Human and Organization Development at the Fielding Graduate Institute. She received her Ph.D. from the School of Management at the University of Massachusetts, Amherst. Her research interests include theory and methods of online research, information management in networked organizations, virtual teams, and Web-based community development. She has more than 30 years of professional experience as a systems developer and is co-founder of ShareWorks, a consulting group that helps organizations to design, build, and sustain Web sites for collaboration and knowledge sharing.

Jim Beaubien holds adjunct faculty positions in the Master's Program in Organizational Management at the Fielding Graduate Institute and in the M.B.A. program at the University of Alberta. He received his Ph.D. in educational psychology from the University of Alberta. He is the co-founder of and a principal in HOPE Learning Systems. He has more than 30 years of experience as an educator, consultant, speaker, and facilitator. He specializes in helping organizations to improve performance and achieve results. He works primarily as a senior consultant to executives in business and health care organizations.

Randi S. Brenowitz is Principal of Brenowitz Consulting, an organization development (OD) consulting firm that specializes in building collaborative work environments. Her focus is on improving clients' productivity through teamwork and collaboration. She holds an M.B.A. from Babson College, specializing in organizational behavior, and is a member of the OD Network, American Society of Training and Development, and Northern California Human Resources Association. A human resources (HR)/OD practitioner for more than 20 years, she works in partnership with internal HR and OD colleagues to develop teams, team leaders, and team members and to create team-friendly environments. In addition, she sits on the board of directors of an international philanthropy, where she is heavily involved in building collaboration across national and cultural boundaries.

Barbara Mahone Brown is a founding faculty member of the Master's Program in Organizational Management at the Fielding Graduate Institute. She also serves as president of her own communications firm, Elbow Room Consulting, in Santa Cruz, California. She earned her M.B.A. from the University of Chicago and her Ph.D. from Stanford University. For many years, she taught communications, marketing, and leadership courses at San Jose State University, the University of Texas at Austin, and Stanford University.

Charles Crowell is Chairperson of the graduate Organizational Management Program and Associate Professor of Management at the School for International Training. He has an extensive background in the public and private sectors, serving in key advisory roles in government as a financial economist and holding executive positions in finance and management in industry. He has studied management at both the Union Graduate School and Fielding Graduate Institute, where he played an important role in the development of the Master's Program in Organizational Management, and he is currently enrolled to complete his doctorate in knowledge management at the University of Lancaster. He is also the director of the Institute for Virtual Inquiry (www.virtualinquiry. org), a research, education, and consulting organization.

Gary Fontaine is Professor in the School of Communications at the University of Hawaii and an adjunct faculty member of the Master's Program in Organizational Management at the Fielding Graduate Institute. He obtained his Ph.D. in social psychology from the University of Western Australia in 1972. His professional focus is on persons, groups, and organizations as they encounter the challenges of novel and rapidly changing ecologies characterized by new people, places, and technologies. He has applied this focus to contexts such as international assignments in business and government, diverse and rapidly changing workplaces at home, and geographically dispersed teams.

Tracy C. Gibbons is President, Coastwise Consulting, Inc., an organization development (OD) consulting firm that creates competitive advantage for its clients by leveraging the power of organization design, strategic alignment, and collaboration. She holds an M.S. in counseling psychology and a Ph.D. from the Fielding Graduate Institute, where she studied and researched the developmental attributes and processes of transformational leaders. An OD practitioner for 25 years, she partners with senior executives and their staffs at Fortune 500 and other companies to create solutions to problems and strategic opportunities for which no previously known solution existed. She is a member of the NTL Institute for Applied Behavioral Science and of the OD Network, and she is a founding member of the Fielding Alumni/ae Network.   .

Bo Gyllenpalm is the president of Situational Services, a Swedish consulting company, and works as a speaking partner to chief executive officers and senior executives in international organizations. He is the coordinator and a board member of the Swedish fractal of the Society for Organizational Learning. He is also an adjunct faculty member and member of the board of trustees of the Fielding Graduate Institute. He is also a senior international research fellow at the Center for Leaderhip Studies. He has an M.B.A. from INSEAD in France and a Ph.D. in human and organization development from Fielding.

Shelley Hamilton is the founder and principal of NetCentric Designs, a business strategy, team facilitation, and organization design firm. She is also an affiliate researcher with the Institute for the Future, where she focuses on the long-term horizon (10-20 years) of new organizational structures, practices, and leadership strategies. She applies a variety of systems-based disciplines to her research and consulting projects through her background in living systems and complexity sciences, information technology, and anthropology. She has an M.A. in organization design and effectiveness from the Fielding Graduate Institute and has lived and traveled throughout Asia, Europe, Russia, Alaska, and South America.

Pat Hodges has been a full-time faculty member in the Psychology Program at the Fielding Graduate Institute for many years. Prior to that, she was the chair and a professor in the Department of Psychology at California State University. She received her Ph.D. in psychology from the Claremont Graduate School. She has a diplomate in administrative psychology and is a founding fellow of the American Academy of Clinical Sexology. She is the author of several published articles. She has been teaching online for more than 10 years and has taught synchronous voice chat classes for more than 3 years.

Barclay Hudson has been a founding faculty member of several innovative programs, including the Graduate Program in Urban Planning at the University of California, Los Angeles; the Center for Regenerative Studies at Cal Poly Pomona; and the Master's Program in Organizational Management at the Fielding Graduate Institute. He received his Ed.D. from Harvard University and has worked with the Harvard Center for Education and Development, the Harvard Office of Programmed Instruction, and the Harvard Economic Research Project, where he participated in forecasting studies under Nobel laureate Wassily Leontief. His overseas consulting on educational and economic development has included Chile, Costa Rica, Bangladesh, and Tunisia, mainly with the Ford Foundation, Harvard, and the United Nations. During a 7-year departure from academics, he worked full-time as project manager, economist, and industrial process analyst with FSEC, a Los Angeles engineering firm, specializing in assessment and commercialization of technologies adapted from aerospace.

Shelley K. Hughes has been Director of the Fielding Graduate Institute's online academic environment since 1997. She oversees academic Web page development, configuration and use of the institute's discussion forum software, and orientation of new students and faculty to the online environment. She is coauthor, with Jeremy Shapiro, of a journal article, "Information Literacy as a Liberal Art" (*EDUCOM Review,* 1996). Her background in counseling psychology informs her work with adults around the use of technology. Current interests include the intersection of social behavior with technology, information management, and navigation.

Dean S. Janoff is a practicing psychologist, author, consultant, and faculty member of the Master's Program in Organizational Management at the Fielding Graduate Institute. His consulting, writing, and teaching exist around the integration of electronic-networked teams in "brick-and-mortar" business and health care environments. He holds a Ph.D. in counseling psychology from the University of California, Santa Barbara.

Bruce LaRue is a partner with Leadership Strategies International, a Seattle, Washington-based consultancy specializing in executive and organization development. He is an adjunct faculty member at the Fielding Graduate Institute and the University of Washington, Tacoma. He received his Ph.D. in human and organization development at Fielding. As a consultant and professor, he has worked with managers and executives from numerous industries such as telecommunications, aerospace, petrochemicals, financial services, pharmaceuticals, and nonprofit sectors.

Mark D. Neff is a knowledge communities architect for Computer Sciences Corporation (CSC). He has been working on community activities for the past 2 years with CSC and for several years before that with others on the Internet. After obtaining his M.A. from the Fielding Graduate Institute, he transferred from his position with human resources and development to the corporate knowledge program within CSC. His current interests include defining different community strategies and supporting the development of a business architecture that supports the development and maintenance of communities within a business setting.

Christi A. Olson is Director of the Master's Program in Organizational Management and the Master's Program in Organization Development at the Fielding Graduate Institute, where she received her Ph.D. in human and organization development. She is a managing partner in The Olson Group, a consulting firm specializing in evolving leadership practices. She leads workshops and consults in the areas of leadership, business and market strategy, and organizational change for clients in industry, public agencies, government, education, and not-for-profits. Her research interests focus on leadership in distance learning organizations and on adult learning in the online environment.

Rena M. Palloff is a member of the faculty of the Fielding Graduate Institute, teaching in its Master's Program in Organizational Management. She has worked extensively in health care, academic settings, and addiction treatment for more than 20 years. She holds other academic positions at Capella University, Thomas Edison State College, John F. Kennedy University, and California State University, Hayward. She holds a master's degree in organization development and a Ph.D. in human and organizational systems from Fielding. She and Keith Pratt are the managing partners of Crossroads Consulting Group and the authors of the Frandson Award-winning book, *Building Learning Communities in Cyberspace.* Their second book, *Lessons From the Cyberspace Classroom,* was released in March 2001.

Keith Pratt is a project manager for Datatel, overseeing software installations at community colleges around the United States, and also teaches in the Master's Program in Organizational Management at the Fielding Graduate Institute, in the online teaching and training specialization at Capella University, and at Thomas Edison State College. He began his government career as a computer systems technician with the U.S. Air Force in 1967. He was most recently an assistant professor in the International Studies Program and chair of the Management Information Systems Program for Ottawa University in Ottawa, Kansas. He has a master's degree in human resource management from

Chapman University. He holds a master's degree in organization development and a Ph.D. in human and organizational systems from Fielding and an honorary doctorate from Moscow State University.

Kjell Erik Rudestam is Associate Dean in the School of Psychology and a founding faculty member of the Master's Program in Organizational Management at the Fielding Graduate Institute. Prior to that, he was a Professor of psychology at York University in Toronto. He holds a Ph.D. in psychology (clinical) from the University of Oregon and an honorary doctorate from the Professional School of Psychology. He is the author of six books, including two recent Sage publications (*Surviving Your Dissertation* [2nd ed.] and *Your Statistical Consultant,* both with Rae Newton), and numerous published articles in the areas of clinical psychology (psychotherapy and change processes and suicide), research methodology, and online pedagogy. He is a fellow of the American Psychological Association (Division 12) and a diplomate of the American Board of Examiners in Professional Psychology (clinical).

Lynne Saba is an adjunct faculty member of the Psychology Program and Program Director for WEBCAST CE, a completely online program for continuing education for mental health professionals, at the Fielding Graduate Institute. She received her Ph.D. in clinical psychology from Fielding. She has taught statistics, research methods, test construction, and faculty development courses online. She is a licensed clinical psychologist in California and Hawaii, and she conducts multicultural research.

Judith Schoenholtz-Read is Associate Dean for Clinical Training in the School of Psychology at the Fielding Graduate Institute. She received her Ed.D. from the Department of Counselling Psychology at the University of British Columbia (UBC) and served as a coordinator of a treatment center at the UBC University Sciences Hospital. She has been studying retention in distance learning and online environments for the past 7 years. She has written about clinical training online (with Dean Janoff) and has published articles on topics related to gender and psychotherapy. She was recently secretary of Division 49 of the American Psychological Association (group psychology and psychotherapy). She is a fellow of the American Group Psychotherapy Association and of the Canadian Group Psychotherapy Association.

Jeremy J. Shapiro is a faculty member in the Ph.D. Program in Human and Organization Development and Senior Consultant on Academic Information Projects at the Fielding Graduate Institute as well as Co-director of the Citizen Computing Institute. His Ph.D., in the history of ideas, is from Brandeis

University. With a background in critical social theory and computer science, and with experience as an information systems professional, his current research interests are in computer simulation as a social and historical phenomenon and in nonhierarchical classification systems for information and knowledge. He is a co-author of *Mindful Inquiry in Social Research* (Sage, 1998) and of *Computers for Social Change and Community Organizing* (Hayworth Press, 1991).

David Smith is currently the field development manager for Agilent Technologies. In this position, he is responsible for skill development of the sales and support organization of Agilent Technologies' largest product group. He has been with Hewlett-Packard and Agilent Technologies for 24 years in a variety of sales, marketing, and management roles. He has a master's degree in organization design and effectiveness from the Fielding Graduate Institute and is currently doing doctoral work in organization development.

Mark R. Sobol is president and one of the founding principals of Leadership Strategies International, a management consultancy based in Seattle, Washington. His experience spans more than 20 years of consulting with companies in a wide range of industries throughout North and South America, Great Britain, Europe, and Asia, with an emphasis on high-level corporate advisory services, especially within highly technical environments. He holds a master's in organizational management from the Fielding Graduate Institute. He is a co-author of *The Visionary Leader* and its latest edition, *The Mission-Driven Organization*. With his co-authors, Bruce LaRue and Kerry Larson, he is currently at work on his next book, *The Fourth Order*, which examines emerging strategies for organizational change and leadership.

Judith Stevens-Long is an associate dean of the Ph.D. Program in Human and Organization Development at the Fielding Graduate Institute. She was co-director and founder of the Organization Design and Effectiveness Program at Fielding. She received her Ph.D. in developmental psychology from the University of California, Los Angeles. She has written several textbooks on human development, including four editions of *Adult Life: Developmental Processes*, and numerous articles on personality development, theories and paradigms in adult development, group process, and the role of empathy in human development.

Joel Zimmerman is an information systems director for the Royal & Sun Alliance insurance company in Charlotte, North Carolina. His work team maintains Royal's corporate financial systems. He has worked in the information systems (IS) industry since 1982, first as a programming consultant and then as an IS manager. He has managed systems development teams at Fleet Mortgage Group, First Union National Bank, and the Financial Information Services division of Moody's Investors Service. He has a Ph.D. from Northwestern University, an M.S. from Purdue University, and an M.A. from the Fielding Graduate Institute. He taught as an adjunct faculty for George Washington University in Hampton, Virginia.